Women Warriors in Early Modern Spain

THE EARLY MODERN EXCHANGE

Series Editors
Gary Ferguson, University of Virginia; Meredith K. Ray, University of Delaware

Series Editorial Board
Frederick A. de Armas, University of Chicago; Valeria Finucci, Duke University; Barbara Fuchs, UCLA; Nicholas Hammond, University of Cambridge; Kathleen P. Long, Cornell University; Elissa B. Weaver, Emerita, University of Chicago

The Early Modern Exchange publishes studies of European literature and culture (c. 1450–1700) exploring connections across intellectual, geographical, social, and cultural boundaries: transnational, transregional engagements; networks and processes for the development and dissemination of knowledges and practices; gendered and sexual roles and hierarchies and the effects of their transgression; relations between different ethnic or religious groups; travel and migration; textual circulation/s. The series welcomes critical approaches to multiple disciplines (e.g., literature and law, philosophy, science, medicine, music, etc.) and objects (e.g., print and material culture, the visual arts, architecture), the reexamination of historiographical categories (such as medieval, early modern, modern), and the investigation of resonances across broad temporal spans.

Titles in the Series

Involuntary Confessions of the Flesh in Early Modern France, Nora Martin Peterson

The Enemy in Italian Renaissance Epic: Images of Hostility from Dante to Tasso, Andrea Moudarres

Retelling the Siege of Jerusalem in Early Modern England, Vanita Neelakanta

Advertising the Self in Renaissance France: Lemaire, Marot, and Rabelais, Scott Francis

Women Warriors in Early Modern Spain: A Tribute to Bárbara Mujica, edited by Susan L. Fischer and Frederick A. de Armas

Women Warriors in Early Modern Spain

A Tribute to Bárbara Mujica

Edited by Susan L. Fischer and Frederick A. de Armas

UNIVERSITY OF DELAWARE PRESS
Newark
Distributed by the University of Virginia Press

University of Delaware Press
© 2019 by Susan L. Fischer and Frederick A. de Armas
All rights reserved
Printed in the United States of America on acid-free paper

First published 2019

ISBN 978-1-64453-015-3 (cloth)
ISBN 978-1-64453-016-0 (paper)
ISBN 978-1-64453-017-7 (e-book)

1 3 5 7 9 8 6 4 2

Library of Congress Cataloging-in-Publication Data is available for this title.

Cover art: Herbert G. Schmalz, Britain, 1856–1935, *Zenobia's Last Look on Palmyra*, 1888, London, oil on canvas, 183.4 × 153.6 cm. (South Australian Government Grant 1890, Art Gallery of South Australia, Adelaide)

Contents

Introduction: Rethinking the Early Modern Spanish Woman, from Victim to Warrior ... 1
SUSAN L. FISCHER AND FREDERICK A. DE ARMAS

Part I. Women as Dramatic Subjects

Self-Fashion Show: Women in the Plays of Cervantes and Significant Others ... 33
EDWARD H. FRIEDMAN

Chained by Her Words: Calderón's *La gran Cenobia* and the Perils of the Sublime ... 50
FREDERICK A. DE ARMAS

Folklore as Queer: Vélez de Guevara's *La serrana de la Vera* ... 66
EMILIE L. BERGMANN

Mujer vestida de hombre to the Extreme: Catalina de Erauso in Montalbán's *La monja alférez* ... 89
TERESA SCOTT SOUFAS

Part II. Women *in* the Theater: Actors, Producers, Constructed Subjectivity

Career-Oriented Women in the Theater: María Álvarez, Bárbara Coronel, Fabiana Laura ... 105
ELIZABETH CRUZ PETERSEN

Women in Charge: *Autoras* and Actresses in the Reign of Felipe V ... 119
SUSAN PAUN DE GARCÍA

Lope de Vega's "Warring" Female Characters   140
ISAAC BENABU

Part III. Women in Literature and Culture: Poets, Readers, Holy Subjects

"Entre las Otras Sois Vos": The *Cancionero de Herberay* and Women's Cultural Production   159
EMILY C. FRANCOMANO

Sense(s) and Sensibility in Two Sonnets of Catalina Clara Rodríguez de Guzmán   172
CHARLES VICTOR GANELIN

Women's Vision, Women's Truth: Teresa of Ávila's Defense of Women's Access to God   186
GILLIAN T. W. AHLGREN

Teresa of Ávila and Jeanne Guyon Read the *Song of Songs*   203
SHARON D. VOROS

Part IV. Teresa of Ávila Refashioned on the Stage and on the Page

Vision, Vulnerability, and the Provocative "Higas" in Lope de Vega's *Santa Teresa de Jesús*   221
SHERRY VELASCO

Teresa of Ávila, Spiritual Warrior Secularized: Going for the Subjective in Bárbara Mujica's Biographical Fiction   241
SUSAN L. FISCHER

Revisionism, Prolepsis, and Anachronism: Two Contemporary Spanish Novels about Teresa of Ávila   261
ALISON WEBER

Part V. Epilogue: Call to Battle

Bárbara, la alquimista de palabras   281
MARJORIE AGOSÍN

Contributors   287
Index   293

Women Warriors in Early Modern Spain

SUSAN L. FISCHER AND FREDERICK A. DE ARMAS

Introduction
Rethinking the Early Modern Spanish Woman, from Victim to Warrior

SINCE THE LAST DECADES of the twentieth century, provocative new research has led to a reconsideration of women's roles in society and dispelled many commonly held notions about the lives of women throughout history. It now seems clear that despite societal restrictions, many early modern women exercised considerable agency over aspects of their lives, and some even became entrepreneurs, theater managers, writers, religious leaders, and political figures. In recent years, the focus in women's studies has shifted subtlety, although with considerable overlap, toward emphasis on women's engagement on behalf of their communities, their families, and themselves. Thus, the title of this introduction refers not to an evolution in women's lives from victims to warriors, but to a shift in critical focus. Women's studies scholars are now delving into archives, libraries, and personal collections, unearthing heretofore unexamined primary sources and reevaluating long-held notions about women's behavior. The first part of this introduction focuses on earlier scholarship, which, influenced by postmodernism, often portrayed women as the losers in an eternal power struggle. The second part highlights newer scholarship, which emphasizes women's creativity and agency.

Research on early modern women has burgeoned in the last forty years thanks in part to the increased accessibility of new editions of key documents of the period. One far-reaching publication project that has benefited scholars enormously is The University of Chicago Press's series The Other Voice in Early Modern Europe, founded in 1993 by Margaret King and Albert Rabil.

Additional publishers have followed suit, among them the University of Nebraska with its Women and Gender series, and the Amsterdam University Press with its series Gendering the Late Medieval and Early Modern World. Other resources include the Arizona Center for Medieval and Renaissance Studies and Iter: Gateway to the Middle Ages and Renaissance. These projects have inspired not only valuable inquiry, but also a plethora of new editions of period works by and about women.

Women as Victims

Early modern Europe was much concerned with the "woman question," or *querelle des femmes*, a term referring to the literary debate on the nature of women and their role in society. Moralists had begun considering these issues as early as the eleventh century, when Marbod of Rennes (c. 1035–1123) depicted women as one of the traps for men laid by the devil. During the following century, Walter Map (1140–1209), Andreas Capellanes (dates unknown), and a host of other writers launched similar attacks. The first major defense of women, *La Cité des Dames*, by Christine de Pizan (1364–1430), is often considered the initiator of the *querelle des femmes* debate, which continued beyond the end of the Renaissance.

The focus of Renaissance humanists on social institutions led to a codification of the behavior of different categories of people (for example, princes, clergy, artisans, actors), among them, women. The revival of Neoplatonism in the fifteenth century led theologians and moralists to a reconsideration of the nature of women and the role of marriage. Building on courtly traditions, Renaissance Neoplatonism at first preserved the notion of the lady on the pedestal—an unreachable ideal to which the lover could aspire, and in so doing, purify his heart and spirit. However, theologians and moralists objected to this image, arguing that it elevated women to the level of gods to be worshipped. Thinkers gradually revised this image, transforming women into a conduit to the divine. Neoplatonism saw human beauty as a reflection of celestial beauty. By loving and serving a beautiful woman, a man elevated and purified himself, coming closer to God, as reflected in the idealized female person. Gradually, the lady on the pedestal was replaced with the lady by the hearth, as the ideal woman became the angelical wife, whose presence in the household brought harmony and order. In Northern Europe, Luther's insistence on the unhealthiness of celibacy and the benefits of marriage boosted the prestige of the institution, but even in Spain, marriage, once considered an inferior state, rose in esteem.

Yet the "woman question" was not resolved. Pro-woman moralists defended a positive image of women, while anti-woman thinkers continued to see them as debased creatures. Of course, the questions that concern today's feminists, such as social, political, educational, and economic equality, were inexistent in early modern Europe. Thus, early modern "feminists," almost all of whom were men, held views quite different from those of feminists today. These defenders of women first had to establish the very humanness of female persons (Jordan 8). The anti-feminists, on the other hand, based their arguments on natural law to establish that women are not entirely human, but rather incomplete versions of men. Some went so far as to allege that women lack a soul. Pro-women thinkers countered not only that women have a soul, but also that the soul is androgynous. Thus, a biologically female person could demonstrate characteristics usually considered masculine, such as intelligence, aggressiveness and perseverance, just as a male person could demonstrate characteristics usually associated with women, such as patience, resignation, and tenderness. Elizabeth I of England's ascension to the throne ignited debates throughout Europe over a woman's capacity to govern. John Knox argued that the very notion of a female head of state was a desecration of divine law, while John Aylmer countered that the fact that Elizabeth had inherited the throne was proof that God wanted her to rule (Jordan 137). Although even pro-woman thinkers accepted that the female sex was prone to irrationality, they believed that for women with strong masculine characteristics, it was possible to suppress their natural impulses and behave judiciously.

One of the most significant of the early pro-woman texts was *Declamation on the Preeminence and Nobility of the Female Sex*, by Henricus Cornelius Agrippa (1486–1535), originally published in 1529. Agrippa argues that women are as capable as men in many areas, including government, because men and women have identical souls (43). While earlier defenders of women had simply provided lists of outstanding heroines, Agrippa argued that women had been excluded from public spheres of activity due to social conditioning, lack of education, and prejudice. If women are not recognized for their superiority, it is because "the excessive tyranny of men prevails over divine right and natural laws" (94). Consequently, "the freedom that was once accorded to women is in our day obstructed" (94). In spite of his fervent defense of women, Agrippa did not advocate radical changes in the social structure. He believed that women were capable of performing duties normally discharged by men when circumstance demanded, but he did not call for more occupational opportunities for women. Like other pro-women writers, he was content to accept the status quo, while challenging notions of the intrinsic inferiority of women.

One reason so many early studies of Renaissance women focused on victimhood was the proliferation of prescriptive literature from the sixteenth century and beyond. During this period, Europe, including Spain, saw an explosion of conduct manuals by pro-woman authors who lauded the positive qualities of women, while providing them with instructions on how to behave. Georgina Dopico Black notes that "the sheer number of conduct manuals" written during this period is "staggering," and lists scores of them (17). Certainly, conduct manuals do not provide an accurate portrayal of how women actually behaved. Travelers to Spain sometimes remarked on the cheekiness of Spanish women and Inquisitional records provide ample evidence that many women simply did not follow the rules. Yet, the manuals do provide a glimpse into the expectations of moralists—portraits, so to speak, of the ideal woman.

One of the most influential was *De institutione feminae Christianae* [On the Education of a Christian Woman] (1524), by Juan Luis Vives (1492/3–1540), a key document in the redefinition of woman as a crucial component of the family, and thus, of the social structure. Praised enthusiastically by Erasmus and Thomas More, *De institutione*, a manual for female education from childhood through widowhood, was one of the most pro-woman books of its time. Vives favored instructing girls in reading and household management. Although he was considered extremely forward-thinking in the sixteenth century, his highly proscriptive agenda for female education is likely to strike the modern reader as misogynistic.

Vives's primary focus is female sexuality: "A woman's only care is chastity," he writes (47). The purpose of educating girls and women, in his view, is to enable them to preserve their virtue. They should read to keep their minds occupied, but only devotional literature, not imaginative fiction that could spark impure thoughts. Girls should learn to run a household from a tender age. Rather than with dolls, which he associates with idolatry, they should play with miniature pots and pans to prepare themselves for their future roles as homemakers. They should also learn to spin to keep their hands and minds busy. Girls should not attend dances or banquets, argues Vives, where they might be exposed to "elegantly dressed boys with their hair curled," for such activities might stimulate lust (55, 57, 199). A properly educated girl, in Vives's view, will become an excellent wife, who brings her husband satisfaction and delight.

Although Vives stresses companionship rather than procreation in marriage (he himself was married, although childless), he believed that the wife must be subject to her husband's will. It was her duty to obey him, and his duty to discipline her, using physical punishment if necessary. If she suffers or considers the chastisement unjust, explains Vives, she should remain silent and remember how Christ suffered for humanity on the Cross. Because females were viewed as flighty and easily led astray, once married, a woman was to be constantly supervised, for a man's primary concern was his wife's purity. If a woman was literate, she was to read to her children spiritually illuminating works that would instruct them in Christian values, not frivolous stories (175, 180, 251).

Vives's views on widows reflect conventional biases against unsupervised women. He considers widows a threat to society because they have already experienced the pleasures of the flesh and therefore are anxious to corrupt young virgins through devious methods. He does not urge widows to remarry, but to retire from the world and devote themselves to Christ. However, in spite of moralists' recommendation that widows lead secluded, serene lives, Stephanie Fink De Backer's study of widowhood in early modern Spain shows that many widows did not become recluses, but rather were actively engaged in family life and in a variety of businesses.

Charles Fantazzi, translator of *De institutione feminae Christianae*, suggests that Catherine of Aragon may not have been pleased with Vives's manual, as she requested another from Erasmus of Rotterdam (1466–1536), who published *Christiani matrimonii institutio* [The Institution of Christian Marriage] in 1526. Rather than pre-marital chastity, Erasmus focuses on partnership and mutual understanding. Unlike Vives, who envisions marriage as a kind of paternalistic despotism, Erasmus advocates intellectual exchange between spouses. He recognizes that men as well as women make mistakes, and that both spouses must be willing to forgive. However, he shares many of the misogynistic biases of his time, arguing that girls and women must be kept busy with chores so that their minds will not turn to evil, and that a husband must never surrender his authority in a marriage. Despite these concessions to convention, all of Erasmus's works—which reached great popularity in Spain—were placed on the 1559 Index of Forbidden Books. Although some were later cleared, the *Institution of Christian Marriage* was not.

The most influential of the pro-woman moralists of the time in Spain was Fray Luis de León (c. 1527–1591), author of *La perfecta casada* [*The Perfect Wife*] (1583). The book was revered by Spaniards throughout the early modern period and was often given as a wedding gift to Spanish brides well into the twentieth century. An immediate success, it was reprinted five times in five years. Like nearly all Catholic moralists of the time, Fray Luis considered marriage inferior to celibacy, yet defends it as "a noble and holy state, highly regarded by God" (León 244). He saw women as imperfect beings to be molded and formed by their husbands, but believed a good wife was a treasure that would greatly enhance a man's life. In Fray Luis's view, it was the husband's duty to instruct his wife, not through violence, but through kindness and good example. Like Vives, Fray Luis argued that women should learn to read, but limit themselves to inspirational books and never indulge in romances that might plant impure thoughts in their minds. Although *La perfecta casada* was considered revolutionary in its pro-woman stance, Luis agreed with Vives that wives must obey particular rules of conduct and submit to their husbands' authority. They must excel at household management, childrearing, and the supervision of servants. They must be frugal, industrious, and pious, but should avoid spending too much time in church because garrulous priests and local gossips, who often congregate in houses of worship, can lead married women astray. Fray Luis is as prescriptive as Vives was, yet insists more than Vives did on women's capacity for integrity and goodness, and far less on their propensity for wickedness.

Histories of Spain from the mid-1900s hardly mention women and, when they do, they reinforce the image fostered by the conduct manuals of early modern women as passive, cosseted domestic ornaments. Women were "nearly invisible in traditional disciplines," argue Allyson Poska, Jane Couchman, and Katherine McIver (1). In *Imperial Spain: 1469–1716*, written in 1963, J. H. Elliott stressed the lasting influence of Moorish customs after the Battle of Granada, noting that, "The Spanish upper classes had inherited the Moorish custom of keeping their women secluded . . . . But the strongest reminder of the Moorish past was to be found in the extreme inequality between the sexes . . . [T]he position of the upper-class Spanish woman seems to have altered far less between the Middle Ages and the seventeenth century than that of her foreign counterparts" (305). Similarly, Marcelin Defourneaux writes that, although foreign travelers sometimes commented on the brazenness of the Spanish women who frequented public squares and promenades, "They knew nothing about the women who stayed at home and became models of the 'perfect wife,' as portrayed by Fray Luis de León." Spanish women were kept confined, he avers, as the result of centuries of Arabic influence: "They seldom left their homes, and then only to perform their religious duties" (146). Although there is certainly truth to this view—civil and ecclesiastical laws, mores, and social demands did exert stifling pressure on Spanish women— recent research shows that the situation was far more complex.

Conduct manuals and the dearth of information on women's lives naturally led the first early modern feminist scholarship to emphasize the constraints placed on women. In 1977, Joan Kelly-Gadol published a watershed article,

"Did Women Have a Renaissance?," in which she argued that the period we associate with the cultural flowering of the West and the expansion of Europe's intellectual and artistic horizons actually entailed serious setbacks for women. Kelly-Gadol pointed out that developments such as increased regulation of female sexuality, declining economic and political roles for women, and new restrictions on access to education resulted in diminished power and creative production for women. The article provoked a maelstrom of responses, some supporting Kelly-Gadol's position, others challenging it.

Writing at the end of the 1980s, Ruth El Saffar carried the ideological focus into the seventeenth century. By then, argues El Saffar, the "feminist" stance that characterizes much of the moral writing of the sixteenth century ceded to new attitudes that were less favorable toward women. She further argues that the individualistic, self-made man epitomized by Don Quixote could no longer relate to women as flesh-and-blood beings but instead preferred the idealized woman exemplified by Dulcinea ("Literary Reflections"). El Saffar later opined that women were unable to achieve individuation and wholeness because Spanish culture suppressed the female psyche (*Rapture Encaged*).

Early feminist scholars tended to focus on the idealization or victimization of women in literature, seeing the voiceless lady of the Renaissance sonnet as an example of men's projections of their own erotic illusions, and the murdered wives of Spain's honor plays as expressions of the misogyny entrenched in Western culture. Studies such as those of El Saffar expose the ways in which age-old attitudes and fears permeated law, ethics, marital relationships, and social mores. "By the end of the [sixteenth] century," writes Bárbara Mujica, "the notion of marriage as a partnership, albeit with one superior partner, had given way to a new era in which women were increasingly marginalized" (*Sophia's Daughters* xxxix). The new sense of self-determination that found expression in works such as Miguel de Cervantes's *Don Quixote*, Calderón de la Barca's *Life Is a Dream*, and Francisco de Quevedo's *El Buscón* led to an individualism that left men convinced of their own agency, while largely ignoring women. Mujica adds: "The rupture between culture and nature, and the new cerebralism that will culminate in the Cartesian revolution, create an environment in which man sees himself in control of his universe—a universe dominated by mental and physical prowess—in which woman is little more than a pawn" (xl). Representative of this trend is Juan Huarte de San Juan's *Examen de ingenios para las ciencias* (1575) [Examination of Wits], in which the author (1529–1588) clearly describes women as intellectually inferior and urges couples to have male children. Many critics have noted that portrayals of women in early modern literature reflect these patriarchal, misogynistic attitudes. Yet, as Anita K. Stoll and Dawn L. Smith stress in *Gender, Identity, and Representation in Spain's Golden Age*, the realities are complex: early modern literature raises a plethora of gender-related issues and provides countless examples of both men and women who function outside of prescribed norms.

Groundbreaking studies such as Paul Julian Smith's *The Body Hispanic: Gender and Sexuality in Spanish and Spanish-American Literature* (1989) and *Representing the Other: "Race," Text, and Gender in Spanish and Spanish-American Narrative* (1992) focus attention on the status of women as a marginalized group in a male-dominated culture and the possibility of female resistance. Basing his arguments on a variety of theorists from Freud and Marx to Foucault and Kristeva, and drawing examples from Spain and Latin America, Smith considers early modern women within the broader context of "others," or non-mainstream groups, such as racial minorities and gays. Smith's studies were among the first to explore how issues of sexuality and gender influenced women's lives and societal attitudes toward women.

Much of the research on early modern women during the 1990s and early 2000s had to do with corporeal alterity. Black argues in *Perfect Wives, Other Women* that, during the early modern period, women's bodies became a growing source of male anxiety due to their illegibility—that is, the lack of visible signs of transgression—which left men unable to know for sure the paternity (and ethnicity) of their offspring. She sees a correlation between the proliferation of conduct manuals, whose objective was to control women's behavior, and adultery-honor plays, in which women suspected of transgressive conduct are murdered by their husbands. Lisa Vollendorf shows in *The Lives of Women: A New History of Inquisitional Spain* that biological sex, not gender identity, served as a justification to limit women's activity. She cites the example of Eleno/a de Cépedes, a Morisca slave girl who grew a penis-like appendage and identified as a man. She married a woman and became a surgeon highly praised for her skill until the Inquisition forbade her/him from living as a man and practicing medicine. Vollendorf writes that "although Cépedes's lived experience led him to enact and defend flexible notions about physiology and gender," the authorities determined that biological sex was "clear-cut and indisputable" (21). They sentenced him to ten years unpaid labor in a hospital using "the knowledge and skills he had acquired as a man, but only as an unpaid woman" (29). Their aim, she concludes, was to stigmatize the non-normative body and set an example for others who might want to cross the gender line. Vollendorf cites several other notable examples of women prevented from practicing masculine professions or receiving credit for their work solely because of their sex—among them Oliva Sabuco, the humanist scientist whose treatises were published under her father's name. Elizabeth Rhodes further elucidates these misogynistic currents, analyzing violence against women in literature, religious tradition, and reality in *Dressed to Kill*.

Women as Warriors

Constraints on women's intellectual activity have often been attributed Saint Paul's dictum that women should neither teach nor preach: "Let women keep silence in the churches, for it is not permitted for them to speak, but let them be submissive" (I Cor. 14: 34–35); "I do not allow a woman to teach, or to exercise authority over men; but she is to keep quiet" (I Tim. 2:11–12). Much has been written about how the Pauline dictum served as a vehicle for repressing women, who were excluded from attending university and, in most cases, from participating in government, practicing medicine in an official capacity, or pursuing professions in literature and painting. Yet recent research shows that some early modern women, particularly those of the upper classes, were more intellectually active than previously thought. During the past few decades, scores of women's texts have been rescued from oblivion and become the subject of study. In their new collection, *Las escritoras españolas de la Edad Moderna. Historia y guía para la investigación*, editors Nieves Baranda Leturio and Anne J. Cruz present a panoply of materials illustrating ways to approach this subject.

In an important study on literacy in early modern Europe, Baranda Leturio points out that literacy rates grew steadily in the sixteenth century among both men and women, and by the early seventeenth century, about a quarter of the women in Ávila, for example, could read although not necessarily write ("L'Education des Femmes"). Grace Coolidge notes that, in early modern Spain, childhood was viewed as a separate, distinct period during which the young were to be educated for their future roles in life. For people of means, this often included teaching their offspring—male and female—to read and write. A popular religious image of the time shows Saint Anne teaching the Virgin to read. Although this image has generated diverse and contradictory interpretations, Coolidge believes that "Spanish women and girls favored the subject, and found inspiration in it" (107). Emilie Bergmann adds that, "This depiction of the Virgin's acquisition of literacy through mother-daughter bonding suggests a maternal genealogy of wisdom, as well as acknowledging the roles of mothers as teachers" (244). Despite the Pauline dictum, as Elizabeth Teresa Howe explains, women did teach, and mothers were often the primary educators of their daughters. Even Vives recognized the value of women teaching other women (*Education of a Christian Woman* 123–37).

Poor peasants of both sexes were nearly always illiterate, although the urban poor sometimes received an education. Howe notes in *Education and Women in the Early Modern Hispanic World* that schools for indigent foundlings, including girls, existed in some large cities and that even secular schools such as the Colegio de Nobles Doncellas did not limit admission to aristocrats (107–20). Many girls of the artisan and merchant classes received at least rudimentary instruction, and female aristocrats often had tutors who provided a well-rounded, classical education, despite the depiction by mid-twentieth-century historians of upper-class Spanish women as voiceless prisoners in their own homes. Helen Nader states that in many noble families, "educating girls seemed simple and natural" (6). That is, girls were educated as a matter of course. Nader's study of the formation of the Mendoza women and Howe's and Mujica's studies of María de San José, who was educated in the palace of Doña Luisa de la Cerda, show that aristocratic women of the highest social strata learned Latin, modern languages, mathematics, and the sciences (Nader 6; Howe 75–80; Mujica, "Guiding the Sisters"). While, according to Electa Arenal and Stacey Schlau, learned women were often treated as "freaks" at court (4), by the seventeenth century, a few aristocratic women had achieved acclaim for their writing, among them, María de Zayas Sotomayor and Mariana de Carvajal. Studies by Marina Brownlee, Margaret Greer, Rhodes, Vollendorf, and Eavan O'Brien have shed light on the cultural ambience in which Zayas wrote, her literary prowess, and her views on women. *Zayas and Her Sisters*, an anthology of novellas by early modern women, and *Zayas and Her Sisters 2*, an accompanying collection of essays, edited by Judith A. Whitenack and Gwyn E. Campbell, have expanded our access to and knowledge of not only Zayas and Carvajal but also Leonor de Meneses and Ana Francisca Abarca de Bolea y Mar. Mujica's *Women Writers of Early Modern Spain: Sophia's Daughters* includes an extensive general introduction on early modern women, information on fifteen female authors, and examples of their writing.

A few non-aristocratic women also received humanistic educations. Margaret Boyle discusses the upbringing of sisters Cecilia del Nacimiento and María de San Alberto, whose mother, Cecilia Morilla, the wife of a university professor, gave them a broad education that included foreign languages, poetics, geography, and mathematics (293–306; cf. Arenal and Schlau 129–41). Although women were admonished not to indulge in reading for pleasure, many struggled to achieve high levels of intellectual competence, says Anne Cruz

(*Women's Literacy* 1). Even women who did not own books could sometimes augment their knowledge through access to the extensive private libraries of male relatives or friends (Cruz, "Reading over Men's Shoulders," 41–58).

Convents were significant centers of female learning in early modern Spain, where nuns constituted the largest group of educated women and produced the largest cohort of female authors (Baranda Leturio and Marín Pina 11). From the Middle Ages, certain convents had fostered female literacy, but in most cases, their curricula were extremely limited (Arenal and Schlau 4). Medieval nuns such as Hildegard of Bingham, Catherine of Siena, and Teresa de Cartagena wrote on a variety of subjects, but as Danielle Régnier-Bohler points out, it was not always easy to distinguish women's authentic voices, even in female authored documents, as priests sometimes censured or rewrote materials (428). Yet, Baranda Leturio and María Carmen Marín Pina argue in *Letras en la celda: Cultura escrita de los conventos de la España moderna* that even though many nuns wrote on command by priests, many did not, and even those who did exercised considerable agency over their production. Indeed, many convents created their own distinct literary cultures with procedures for producing, revising, and distributing texts. Unfortunately, convent writing rarely appears in literary anthologies, and the vast majority of it has been lost.

Convents were usually as hierarchical as the outside world, with aristocratic women enjoying special privileges. Arenal and Schlau note that, "For women of a certain rank the opportunity to study and learn was one of the important advantages of convent life" (4). During the sixteenth century, educational prospects in convents increased. Teresa of Ávila, founder of the Discalced Carmelites, stipulated in the Constitutions of the order that her nuns were to learn to read (although not necessarily to write), and that the prioress was to supply them with inspirational books. Motivated by the example of Saint Teresa de Ávila, who composed a *Vida* (spiritual memoir) and three other treatises, as well as perhaps thousands of letters, short prose pieces, and poetry, many nuns wrote about their spiritual experiences. Some dictated their stories to an amanuensis or reported them to confessors who wrote them down. Isabelle Poutrin argues that some convents were veritable beehives of literary activity. In their groundbreaking anthology, *Untold Sisters: Hispanic Nuns in Their Own Words*, Arenal and Schlau brought together the writings of early modern Spanish and Spanish-American nuns, demonstrating the richness and variety of their writing and inspiring countless books and articles on convent culture. For example, Elizabeth Lehfeldt's *Religious Women in Golden Age Spain: The Permeable Cloister* describes the freedom late medieval nuns enjoyed to conduct business and interact with the community, and the various and contradictory consequences of religious reform.

In 1563, the Council of Trent reinstated the medieval rule of female claustration that had been ignored by many orders for decades. Yet, some brave nuns risked their lives to found convents in war-torn areas of Portugal, France, and the Low Countries. Bárbara Mujica's archival research on the next generation of Carmelite nuns after Teresa de Ávila shows that early modern women sometimes displayed tremendous independence and valor, challenging religious superiors and facing enemy attacks for the faith (see *Lettered Women*).

Another group of early modern women who distinguished themselves as warriors are those Spanish nuns who founded convents in the Americas. These courageous women crossed the Atlantic to advance Christianity. Several newer books elucidate the lives of women religious in Colonial America. *Colonial Angels* by Elisa Sampson Vera Tudela shows how Colonial nuns transformed traditional Spanish religious institutions, integrating indigenous American outlooks and customs. *A Wild Country Out in the Garden*, edited by Kathleen A. Myers and Amanda Powell, is a compendium of the writings of María de San José, a late seventeenth-century nun living in a convent in Puebla, Mexico, whose vivid imagination began to worry her confessor. The book offers a vivid portrait of life in a Mexican convent, in particular the relationship between nuns and male authorities. *Brides of Christ* by Asunción Lavrín also provides a detailed description of convent life in Colonial Mexico, including information on governance, prayer practices, and relationships between nuns and priests. Of particular interest with regard to women's writing are Lavrín's observations on the constraints on such writing, which were so strict that "no woman that we know of wrote any literary work or spiritual tract" (312). With the exception of Juana Inés de la Cruz, the seventeenth-century nuns who bucked this tendency did so anonymously and sometimes at considerable risk.

Much of the research on early modern religious women has focused on Teresa de Ávila. Jody Bilinkoff's study of sixteenth-century Ávila offers a vivid portrait of the thriving city of "new men"—ambitious merchants and government officials, many of them *conversos*—in which Teresa grew up, and her position as the daughter and granddaughter of *conversos* in a society obsessed with "blood purity." Teófanes Egido López provides documentation of Teresa's *converso* background and a detailed discussion of her family's efforts to distance themselves from their roots in the study *El Linaje judeoconverso de Santa Teresa*. Alison Weber examines in *Teresa de Avila and the Rhetoric of Feminin-*

ity how Teresa used rhetorical devices to avoid censure for her mystical claims. Mujica elucidates Teresa's use of both the apophatic and kataphatic spiritual traditions ("Beyond Image"), and the feminist aspects of her thought (*Teresa de Jesús; Teresa de Ávila, Lettered Woman;* "Was Saint Teresa a Feminist?"), while Gillian T. W. Ahlgren explores Teresa's spirituality and its practical application in today's world (*Enkindling Love*). These are only a few of the countless books and articles on Teresa that scholars have produced since the 1980s.

Extra-conventual religious life has become another focus of research. Mary Elizabeth Perry's work on *beatas*, religious women who lived alone or in independent communities unaffiliated with any convent, has shown that these women exercised considerable influence on their communities through preaching, writing, prophesizing, and teaching disciples. Because they were not cloistered or subject to an order, they traveled freely throughout cities, often serving the poor and infirm. Their independence and practice of interacting directly with the people caused religious authorities to view them as a menace, and the Inquisition persecuted them vigorously. More recently, Alison Weber has shown in *Devout Laywomen in the Early Modern World* that both Catholic and Protestant laywomen from all parts of Europe exercised agency by serving as healers, educators, and organizers of faith communities.

Although few early modern women wrote for publication, many articulated their opinions in letters, spiritual journals, and memoirs—important vehicles for female expression inside and beyond the convent. Until recently, this material, considered outside the parameters of literature, was overlooked by literary scholars. Today, it is an important subject of investigation, as scholars have come to appreciate not only its cultural and historical value, but also some of its high esthetic quality. In *Women's Letters Across Europe: 1400–1700*, Jane Couchman and Ann Crabb include essays on the ways that early modern women used letters to achieve their goals and make their voices heard. In *Teresa de Ávila, Lettered Woman*, Mujica shows how Saint Teresa used letters to both religious and laypeople to guide the Carmelite reform, manage convents from afar, and provide spiritual guidance for men as well as women.

Convents offered women opportunities to practice occupations from which they would have been discouraged in the outside world. Significant research has been done in recent years on convent chroniclers, musicians, composers, playwrights, and artists. For example, Colleen Baade has elucidated the function of music and prohibitions against certain forms of song in Spanish convents; Susan M. Smith and Georgina Sabat de Rivers have published the plays of Sister Marcela de San Félix, daughter of Lope de Vega, and written about her theater; Anna-Lisa Halling has also explored convent theater, including the use of *villancicos* [folk songs] as performance pieces (*Feminine Voice and Space*; "Space, Performance, and Subversion"); and Mindy Nancarrow Taggard has studied convent painting, including that of Cecilia del Nacimiento.

Care of the sick was central to convent life on both sides of the Atlantic. The practice of medicine in the convent has been investigated relatively little, but Mujica has explored the healing methods of Ana de San Bartolomé, Teresa de Ávila's nurse, and her use of homeopathic remedies ("Healing on the Margins"). In their collection *Women of the Iberian Atlantic*, Sarah E. Owens and Jane E. Mangan include several articles on women as healers, both in convents and in other settings. For example, Nuria Salazar Simarro and Owens examine the integration of Amerindian and Spanish medical treatment in the Americas, in particular in the Convent of Jesús María in Mexico, while Timothy D. Walker and Hugh Glenn Cagle elucidate the role of female healers in Brazil.

Of course, nearly all married women practiced medicine informally at home, attending to the health of their husbands and children with traditional remedies. However, some women practiced medicine outside the home and convent as well. Although women were barred from receiving a university medical education, they had been healers in Spain since the Middle Ages. In the early modern period, some routinely practiced medicine without official authorization, according to Michele L. Clouse. In fact, in a few cases, they acquired enough knowledge and experience through apprenticeships that they passed the necessary exams and obtained a medical license (24). However, as medicine became increasingly professionalized in the sixteenth century, women were gradually excluded from practicing in the large cities, although they continued to practice in rural areas. Even obstetrics or midwifery, considered women's domain since biblical times, evolved into a medical specialization reserved for university-educated male physicians. In general, women were kept at the periphery of scientific activity, as we saw in the case of Oliva Sabuco, rarely achieving public acclaim for their accomplishments.

In contrast, theater was a field in which women excelled openly. Although moralists such as Juan de Mariana condemned actresses, women were a staple of the early modern *comedia*. They appeared onstage as early as the mid-sixteenth century. Elizabeth Cruz Petersen provides a meticulous description of the rigorous preparation of early modern actresses, showing that these women spent hours training, memorizing roles, exercising their bodies, and rehearsing. She argues that even though these women nearly always played roles created by men, they provided alternative models of comportment for women, not only by challenging mores and performing in public, but also by representing characters that defied norms. Some female actors went on to manage their own theater companies, joining theater guilds and even assuming leadership positions.

Within the past thirty years, archival research has led to the discovery of several plays written by early modern women. Editions published by Lola Luna in 1993 of Ana Caro's *Valor, agravio y mujer* [Valor, Offence, and Woman] and *El conde Partinuplés* [Count Partinuplés] made readily available for the first time plays by an early modern *dramaturga*. Although Caro's works had appeared in earlier editions by Mesonero Romanos (1853) and Serrano y Sanz (1903), now they could be taught in university courses. Shortly afterward, Amy Williamsen founded, with others, the Asociación de Escritoras de España y las Américas (AEEA); later, Grupo de Estudios sobre la Mujer en España y Las Américas (GEMELA). A plethora of new editions and studies appeared, including an anthology of women playwrights by Teresa Soufas, accompanied by a critical study of their works (published as *Dramas of Distinction* and *Women's Acts*); as did a bilingual edition of María de Zayas's *Traición en la amistad* [Friendship Betrayed] by Valerie Hegstrom and Catherine Larson. Hegstrom and Williamsen edited *Engendering the Early Modern Stage: Women Playwrights of the Spanish Empire*, a groundbreaking collection of essays on *dramaturgas*. The plays by Caro and Zayas were performed for the first time for a modern audience as part of a joint conference of the Association for Hispanic Classical Theater (AHCT) and GEMELA at Georgetown University in 2006, organized by Mujica, then president of AHCT. Caro's play first appeared in a general theater anthology, *A New Anthology of Early Modern Spanish Theater: Play and Playtext*, edited by Mujica.

Early modern Spain was replete with *mujeres varoniles*, manly women, who challenged the notion that women could have no agency. Being *varonil* did not necessarily mean engaging in masculine pursuits. Teresa de Ávila routinely urged her nuns to be "strong soldiers" or "steadfast men," by which she meant simply that they should display those characteristics traditionally associated with men: perseverance, clear-sightedness, determination, and valor. Women warriors were those who had goals and strove to achieve them, whether in the household, in the convent, on the stage, or at their writing desks. However, women warriors were not all writers, artists, or nuns. Queens and other aristocratic women often had political voice and agency (see Earenfight). And, as Mujica explains, ordinary women could also defy the prototypical image of the ineffectual, voiceless woman. She argues, "In the artisan and merchant classes, city women ... worked as butchers, chandlers, shoemakers, silk weavers, embroiderers, lace makers, and smiths. Some were highly skilled artisans"

(*Sophia's Daughters* xliv). Although women were usually excluded from guilds, some found ways to circumvent the rules: "Knowing a craft and carrying out business independently gave women prestige, power, and wealth" (xliv). Such women certainly constituted a minority, yet they show that women warriors could come from any social class.

About This Volume

Women Warriors in Early Modern Spain: A Tribute to Bárbara Mujica is a cohesive collection with a clearly defined focus. Mujica, whose career this book celebrates, is a highly respected scholar whose research has advanced the fields of Spanish literature, theater, and women's studies. The volume includes articles by fourteen outstanding scholars who examine works by or about exceptional women from diverse walks of life—from queens to poets, from actors to saints. Together, these essays suggest the variety of female types who inhabited early modern Spain and who, in some way, defied cultural norms. Some were aristocratic intellectuals, but some were working women—impresarios or spiritual leaders who managed complex organizations. Emily C. Francomano finds heretofore unsuspected evidence of female *cancionero* poets. Gillian T. W. Ahlgren shows how Teresa de Ávila defied clerics and championed female spirituality. Elizabeth Cruz Petersen and Susan Paun de García bring to light new information about women's participation in running theater companies and training actresses. The image of the late medieval and early modern woman that emerges from this book is one of strength and agency, although the abuse to which women could be subjected is not glossed over. The contributors to this volume approach their material from different perspectives. Most are literary scholars, but others are translators or theater professionals. The volume concludes with an original composition by award-winning Chilean poet Marjorie Agosín.

Part I of this volume, "Women as Dramatic Subjects," emphasizes an area to which Mujica has made major contributions.[1] The scholars represented in this section celebrate the women warriors of early modern Spanish theater, from fictional rebels to queens. In his "Self-Fashion Show: Women in the Plays of Cervantes and Significant Others," Edward H. Friedman explores the roles of women in full-length plays such as *El cerco de Numancia* [The Siege of Numancia], *El laberinto de amor* [The Labyrinth of Love], and *Pedro de Urdemalas* [*Pedro, the Great Pretender,* as translated for the Royal Shakespeare Company production of the play in 2004]. Friedman argues that, although the Roman attack on the town of Numancia awakens the courage of the men, it is the women who move them to action by urging them to protect their female relatives and children. The pleas of the maiden Lira, the embodiment of the spirit of the town, finally motivate them to act decisively. In *El laberinto del amor*, three bright, ambitious young women work together to secure marriages with the men of their choosing, demonstrating exceptional cleverness and adeptness at role-playing. *Pedro de Urdemalas* features a noblewoman who has been raised by gypsies and displays amazing dexterity in moving from one world to the other.

Frederick A. de Armas discusses a historical queen as depicted on the Spanish stage in "Chained by Her Words: Calderón's *La gran Cenobia* and the Perils of the Sublime." Cenobia, the warrior queen of Palmyra, was a well-known figure in seventeenth-century Spain. Pedro Calderón de la Barca and his contemporaries believed she had been educated by Longinus, author of the treatise *On the Sublime*, a story that has since been proven untrue. De Armas argues that the motivating force in Cenobia's actions is the *sublime*. Longinus's book provides the model she must follow.

Emilie L. Bergmann analyzes another bellicose female protagonist in "Folklore as Queer: Vélez de Guevara's *La Serrana de la Vera*." *La Serrana* features a strong, masculine woman who is the pride of her town because of her physical prowess. When an army officer jilts her, she becomes so enraged with men that she vows to kill as many as she can. While most critics have analyzed *La Serrana* in the light of gender transgression, Bergmann considers the play's uniqueness through Vélez's appropriation of local ballads and folktales from the mountainous region of Extremaduras, some of which are savagely violent. Bergmann finds the villagers' lexicon of monstrosity in Vélez's play extremely pertinent, as it encodes their notion of the protagonist's hybrid sexuality and of her horrific execution.

In "*Mujer vestida de hombre* to the Extreme: Catalina de Erauso in Montalbán's *La monja alférez*," Teresa Scott Soufas compares the portrait of the "lieutenant nun"—an actual woman warrior—in the popular early modern play by Juan Pérez de Montalbán to the historical figure who inspired it, underscoring the inevitable ambiguity that is intrinsic to such a comparison. The real Erauso was a Basque noblewoman who became a soldier known for her aggressiveness and violence. Soufas shows that the play is replete with contradictions and falsehoods, but this opacity is, Soufas believes, at the core of the work's greatness.

Part II of this book, "Women *in* the Theater: Actors, Producers, Constructed Subjectivity," connects with Mujica's experience as a theater practitioner.[2] The first two articles focus on female theater professionals. In "Career-

Oriented Women in the Theater: María Álvarez, Bárbara Coronel, Fabiana Laura," Elizabeth Cruz Petersen studies three *autoras* (owner-producers/impresarios) and shows how they overcame the legal and social obstacles they confronted. A significant number of female actors became *autoras* after retirement from the stage, and their companies became virtual schools where a new generation of women gained acting experience and learned entrepreneurship. Bárbara Coronel, María Álvarez, and Fabiana Laura are three examples of "women warriors" in the realm of theater. They managed acting schools that provided women with a sense of community and the resources they needed to forge careers in a society that was hostile to female entrepreneurs.

Susan Paun de García also writes about actors and *autoras*, but shifts focus to the beginning of the eighteenth century. In "Women in Charge: *Autoras* and Actresses in the Reign of Felipe V," Paun de García points out that the advent of the Bourbon dynasty in Spain did not radically change the tastes of the general theater-going public, although new trends, facilitated by women, began to take form. The increasing importance of music and comedy provided new opportunities for women, both as performers and managers. The growing popularity of opera and *zarzuela* [operetta], and the Spanish distaste for *castrati*, meant more roles for women became available. As in the previous century, female theater professionals had to have a connection with a male thespian to secure employment, and many *autoras* were married to *autores* with whom they co-managed their companies, often taking over after the husband's death. However, there are records of *autoras* who achieved their position through other means.

The section ends with Isaac Benabu's contribution, "Lope de Vega's 'Warring' Female Characters." The author challenges the notion that the *comedia* is populated by helpless, vulnerable female characters, citing several examples of strong, determined women in Golden Age plays. Although the character of Casandra in Lope de Vega's *El castigo sin venganza* [Punishment Without Revenge] is not usually cited as an example of combativeness, Benabu argues that her defiance of her husband and her relationship with his son are indeed acts of belligerence. In constructing her subjectivity, he offers a "theatrical reading" that aims to bridge the distance between character analysis in the academy and on the stage, between a dramatic reading and a theatrical one.

Part III of this volume, "Women in Literature and Culture: Poets, Readers, Holy Subjects," focuses on the role of women in the production and consumption of literature, and as the inspiration for literary works, for even when women did not actively write, they influenced what men wrote. In "'Entre las otras sois vos': The *Cancionero de Herberay* and Women's Cultural Production," Emily C. Francomano argues that, although only five women writers appear in the vast corpus of late medieval poetry that comprises the *cancionero*, female input may be greater than previously thought. By concentrating only on the text of the *cancionero* as it appears in modern editions and anthologies, scholars have overlooked signs of women's participation that appear in manuscripts. Using material hermeneutics, Francomano analyzes the *Cancionero de Herberay*, a manuscript compiled around 1463 in honor of Leonor de Navarre, and finds evidence that some of the poetry in it may have been composed by women. Francomano suggests that Leonor is perhaps "*the* historical 'precursory author' of the anthology of poems in her honor" for, as patron, she helped shape the form and content of the work and functions as a "lyrically constructed character." Francomano posits that some of the poems signed by men may actually have been written by women who assumed masculine *personae*.

Charles Victor Ganelin's "Sense(s) and Sensibility in Two Sonnets of Catalina Clara Rodríguez de Guzmán" centers on one of Spain's most pugnacious women poets, one who rivals Quevedo in her genius for satire. However, Ganelin concentrates not on her lampoons of Spanish mores, but on her use of the senses and silence to convey human longing. Through silence—the absence of voice—the poet suggests the privation of companionship and profound loneliness. Ganelin relates her use of sibilants to the meditational poetry of mystics, thereby revealing a profound sensitivity in her work that previous critics have hardly noticed.

"Women's Vision, Women's Truth: Teresa de Ávila's Defense of Women's Access to God," by Gillian T. W. Ahlgren, highlights Saint Teresa's "warrior" facet. After the 1559 Valdés Index of Forbidden Books forbade most Spanish translations of the Bible and many inspirational books, the vast majority of women, who knew no Latin, could not rely on intellectual sources for knowledge of God. Many women already practiced affective spirituality, which Teresa fostered in her convents by encouraging interiority, meditation, and mental prayer. Male clerics generally found affective spirituality suspect, believing women incapable of discerning an authentic spiritual experience. Teresa defied the authorities, argues Ahlgren, writing the *Interior Castle* to teach women discernment of spirits, which gave them the language they needed to validate their experiences. Sharon Voros also writes about Teresa de Ávila, here in reference to her reading of the *Song of Songs*, a highly controversial text considered unsuitable for women by many theologians. In "Teresa of Ávila and Jeanne Guyon Read the *Song of Songs*," Voros notes that the French mystic Jeanne-Marie Guyon, who lived a century after Teresa, was also a reader of the *Song of Songs,* and that both women developed strategies that demonstrate their understanding of this provocative biblical text.

Teresa de Ávila has been not only a research topic for Mujica, but also the subject of one of her novels.[3] In fact, from the early seventeenth century to our own times, Saint Teresa has inspired poets, playwrights, and novelists. Mujica's *Sister Teresa: The Woman Who Became Saint Teresa of Ávila* was described by *Entertainment Weekly* as "a rich, gritty" novel whose protagonist is a "vibrant and fully fleshed woman not above vanity, deceit, and a little preconvent hanky-panky." The novel was adapted for the stage by Coco Blignaut at the Actors Studio in Los Angeles and premiered in November 2013. A Spanish edition, *Hermana Teresa,* appeared in 2017.[4]

Unsurprisingly, Part IV of this volume, "Teresa de Ávila Refashioned on the Stage and on the Page," focuses on creative writing inspired by Saint Teresa de Jesús. In "Vision, Vulnerability, and the Provocative 'Higas' in Lope de Vega's *Santa Teresa de Jesús,*" Sherry Velasco considers why the "fig-hand" gesture, by which Teresa's confessor urged her to scare away the devil, does not appear in Teresian iconography, yet is depicted in Lope's play. Considered extremely insulting (something akin to "the finger"), the fig-hand would surely have upset audiences. Velasco argues that Lope linked the gesture to primal fears about the susceptibility to adversity ascribed to the evil eye, and it was believed that older women were those most likely to infect others with the evil eye. Velasco explains that the fact that Teresa was approaching her late forties when she was forced to make the controversial sign surely increased the problematic nature of the episode. However, Lope resolves the issue by transforming Teresa's disturbing experience into a pious moment, and the fig-hand into a protective amulet.

Susan L. Fischer provides an analysis of the novel *Sister Teresa* in "Teresa of Ávila, Spiritual Warrior Secularized: Going for the Subjective in Bárbara Mujica's Biographical Fiction." Fischer explains how the author builds alternate perspectives into the novel using an unreliable narrator, Angélica, to underscore the subjectivity of both the fictional and historical (or "official") voices. She shows that Mujica draws on her long, scholarly career—including her knowledge of Cervantes's novelistic technique and of Teresa's letters—to structure her novel and build a complex character that speaks to the modern reader. Mujica also relies on her knowledge of convent culture to construct a fictional community of sisters, women who can be catty and cruel, but who can also become warrior women, sisters-in-arms, who protect each other from abusive priests.

Alison Weber brings the Teresa legend into modern Spain in her analysis of *Malas palabras* by Cristina Morales (2012), and *Un corazón tan recio* by Alicia Dujovne Ortiz (2014). In "Revisionism, Prolepsis, and Anachronism: Two Contemporary Spanish Novels About Teresa of Ávila," Weber avers that the main attractions of historical fiction are the opportunity to learn "what happened" and to fill in the gaps about "what might have happened." Weber shows that these novels are "revisionist" in that they challenge traditional narratives about Teresa, depicting her as a real human being with passions, fears, and doubts. They are "proleptic" in that they show Teresa to be ahead of her time, displaying enlightened attitudes toward gender and race.

Sisters in Arms: A Final Call

Early modern Spain was replete with women warriors—women who battled the status quo, defended causes, challenged authority, and broke barriers. Furthermore, the spiritual guidance of prioresses in convents, the treatises they wrote, and the proselyting of *beatas* in public streets certainly constitute preaching. Although earlier scholars often depicted early modern Spanish women as victims (and many were), today's investigators tend to focus on women's agency. Indeed, the history and fiction of the period are filled with examples of women who found ways to defend their God-given right to make their own decisions, to define their own identities, and to encourage their sisters to do the same. The fourteen essays contained in *Women Warriors in Early Modern Spain* make this point patently clear.

Certainly, books and articles on women's everyday pursuits already exist, but most are limited to one aspect of female activity—for example, education, writing, or healing. The essays included here show how many different models of female behavior actually existed for the women of late medieval and early modern Spain. Taken as a whole, *Women Warriors* illustrates the spiritual and psychological power of early modern women, many of whom continue to speak to us today.

Notes

1. Mujica is the author of scores of articles on early modern Spanish theater and editor or co-editor of several collections of essays on theater. Her topics include, but are not limited to, the philosophical and theological underpinnings of Pedro Calderón de la Barca's plays; Calderón's female characters; staging early modern plays; Cervantes's *entremeses*; the Golden Age canon; the theater of Lope de Vega, Tirso de Molina, Agustín Moreto, and Guillén de Castro; female actors; and women playwrights.

2. Mujica's *A New Anthology of Early Modern Spanish Theater: Play and Playtext* was the first major anthology of Golden Age plays published since 1979 and the first performance-based collection ever published. Rather than a mere compendium of texts, it is an in-depth study of Spanish theater, with a meaty introduction to *comedia* performance from the 1500s until the present, substantive introductions to the plays with particular attention to performance issues, and an ample bibliography. Mujica is not only a theater scholar, but also a director who has staged plays by Calderón, Cervantes, Lope de Rueda, and Leandro Fernández de Moratín, as well as scores of modern Spanish and Spanish-American playwrights. She is founder and editor of the journal *Comedia Performance*, president emerita of AHCT, and a member of the board of GALA Hispanic Theater in Washington, D.C. In 2017, the AHCT honored Mujica with the Donald T. Dietz Service Award.

3. Mujica has written extensively on Teresa de Ávila—her youth, letters, spirituality, feminism, relationships with friends, relevance for today's readers, and Lope's plays about her. She has also studied Teresa's followers, Ana de San Bartolomé, Ana de Jesús, and Cecilia del Nacimiento. A forthcoming book, *Lettered Women: The Disciples of Teresa de Ávila*, follows the careers of the Carmelite nuns María de San José, Ana de Jesús, and Ana de San Bartolomé, who brought the Carmelite Reform to Portugal, France, and the Low Countries; it contains many heretofore unpublished documents by and about these women. Mujica's *Women Writers of Early Modern Spain* makes a variety of women authors available to modern audiences, while her studies of the pastoral novel highlight female figures in this understudied genre.

4. That Mujica is a bestselling writer of fiction is also apparent from the success of other novels of hers in which she writes about strong, defiant women who make their own way in a man's world. *Frida*, published in seventeen languages, is based on the Mexican painter Frida Kahlo, while *I Am Venus* centers on forceful women in the life of seventeenth-century Spanish painter Diego Velázquez. *I Am Venus* was a winner of the Maryland Writers' Association National Fiction Competition in 2012, and her novel *Lola in Paradise* was a winner in 2016. Her book-length fiction also includes two collections of short stories. In addition to those mentioned above, Mujica has won other awards for her writing, among them the E. L. Doctorow International Fiction Competition, the Pangolin Prize, the Theodore Christian Hoepfner Award, the Trailblazer's Award from Dialog on Diversity, and first place in the Maryland Writers' Association National Short Fiction Competition. She is a two-time Pushcart Prize nominee. She is also author of two collections of short stories, *Sanchez Across the Street* and *Far from My Mother's Home*, the latter of which has been published in Spanish and French. Many of her more recent stories have appeared in literary magazines.

References

Agrippa, Henricus Cornelius. *Declamation on the Preeminence and Nobility of the Female Sex*. 1529. Edited and translated by Albert Rabil, Jr. University of Chicago Press, 1996.

Ahlgren, Gillian T. W. *Enkindling Love: The Legacy of Teresa of Avila and John of the Cross*. Fortress Press, 2016.

Arenal, Electa, and Stacey Schlau. *Untold Sisters: Hispanic Nuns in Their Own Works*. 1989. Translations by Amanda Powell. University of New Mexico Press, 2010.

Baade, Colleen. "Convent Theatre and Music-Making: Music and Misgiving in Female Monasteries in Early Modern Spain." In *Female Monasticism in Early Modern Europe: An Interdisciplinary View*, edited by Cordula van Wyhe, Ashgate, 2008, 81–95.

Baranda Leturio, Nieves. "L'Education des femmes dans l'Espagne post-tridentine." In *Genre et identités aux Pays-Bas méridionaux: l'education religieuse des femmes après le concile de Trente*, edited by Silvia Mostaccio, Louvain-la-Neuve, Belgium: Academia, 2010, 29–63.

———. "Women's Reading Habits: Book Dedicatons to Female Patrons in Early Modern Spain." In *Women's Literacy in Early Modern Spain and the New World*, edited by Anne J. Cruz and Rosalie Hernández, Ashgate, 2011, 19–39.

Baranda Leturio, Nieves, and María Carmen Marín Pina, eds. *Letras en la celda: Cultura escrita de los conventos de la España moderna*. Madrid: Iberoamericana-Vervuert, 2014.

Baranda Leturio, Nieves, and Anne J. Cruz. *Las escritoras españolas de la Edad Moderna. Historia y guía para la investigación*. Madrid: UNED, 2018.

———. *The Routledge Research Companion to Early Modern Spanish Women Writers*. Routledge, 2018.

Bergmann, Emilie. "Learning at Her Mother's Knee? Saint Anne, the Virgin Mary, and the Iconography of Women's Literacy." In *Women's Literacy in Early Modern Spain and the New World*, edited by Anne J. Cruz and Rosalie Hernández, Ashgate, 2011, 243–61.

Black, Georgina Dopico. *Perfect Wives, Other Women: Adultery and Inquisition in Early Modern Spain*. Duke University Press, 2001.

Bilinkoff, Jody. *The Avila of Saint Teresa: Religious Reform in a Sixteenth-Century City*. Cornell University Press, 1989.

Boyle, Margaret. *Unruly Women: Performance, Penitence, and Punishment in Early Modern Spain*. University of Toronto Press, 2015.

Brownlee, Marina. *The Cultural Labyrinth of María de Zayas*. University of Pennsylvania Press, 2000.

Caro, Ana. *El conde Partinuplés*. Edited by Lola Luna, Kassel, Germany: Edition Reichenberger, 1993.

———. *Valor, agravio y mujer*. Edited by Lola Luna, Madrid: Castalia, 1993.

Clouse, Michele L. *Medicine, Government and Public Health in Philip II's Spain: Shared Interests, Competing Authorities*. Ashgate, 2011.

Coolidge, Grace E. *The Formation of the Child in Early Modern Spain*. Ashgate, 2014.

Couchman, Jane and Ann Crabb, eds. *Women's Letters Across Europe, 1400–1700*. Ashgate, 2005.

Cruz, Anne. Introduction to *Women's Literacy in Early Modern Spain and the New World*. Ashgate, 2011.

———. "Reading over Men's Shoulders: Noblewomen's Libraries and Reading Practices." In *Women's Literacy in Early Modern Spain and the New World*. Ashgate, 2011, 41–58.

Defourneaux, Marcelin. *Daily Life in Spain in the Golden Age*. Stanford University Press, 1971.

Earenfight, Teresa. *Queenship and Political Power in Medieval and Early Modern Spain*. Ashgate, 2005.

Egido López, Teófanes. *El Linaje judeoconverso de Santa Teresa: pleito de hidalguía de los Cepeda*. Madrid: Editorial de Espiritualidad, 1986.

El Saffar, Ruth. "Literary Reflections on the 'New Man': Changes in Consciousness in Early Modern Europe." *Revista de Estudios Hispánicos* 22 (1989), no. 2: 1–23.

———. *Rapture Encaged: The Suppression of the Feminine in Western Culture*. Routledge, 1994.

Elliott, J. H. *Imperial Spain: 1469–1716*. New American Library, 1963.

Erasmus, Desiderius. *Christiani matrimonii institutio* [The Institution of Christian Marriage] Basileæ: Apud J. Frobenium, 1526.

Fink De Backer, Stephanie. *Widowhood in Early Modern Spain: Protectors, Proprietors, and Patrons*. Brill, 2010.

Greer, Margaret. *María de Zayas Tells Baroque Tales of Love and the Cruelty of Men*. Pennsylvania State University Press, 2000.

Halling, Anna-Lisa. *Feminine Voice and Space in Early Modern Iberian Convent Theater*. PhD diss., Vanderbilt University, 2012.

———. "Space, Performance, and Subversion in Soror Violante do Ceu's *Villancicos*." *Comedia Performance* 14 (2017), no. 1: 71–105.

Hegstrom, Valerie, and Catherine Larson, eds. *Traición en la amistad*. Bucknell University Press, 1999.

Hegstrom, Valerie, and Amy Williamsen, eds. *Engendering the Early Modern Stage: Women Playwrights of the Spanish Empire*. University Press of the South, 1999.

Howe, Elizabeth Teresa. *Education and Women in the Early Modern Hispanic World*. Ashgate, 2008.

Huarte de San Juan, Juan. *Examen de ingenios para las ciencias* [Examination of Wits]. 1575. Madrid: *Biblioteca de Autores Españoles*, LXV, 1953.

Jordan, Constance. *Renaissance Feminism: Literary Texts and Political Models*. Cornell University Press, 1990.

Kelly-Gadol, Joan. "Did Women Have a Renaissance?" In *Becoming Visible: Women in European History*, edited by Renate Bridenthal and Claudia Koonz, Houghton Mifflin, 1977, 175–201.

Kung, Michelle. Review of *Sister Teresa*, by Bárbara Mujica. *Entertainment Weekly*. 16 March 2007, ew.com/article/2007/03/16/sister-teresa/.

Lavrín, Asunción. *Brides of Christ*. Stanford University Press, 2008.

Lehfeldt, Elizabeth A. *Religious Women in Golden Age Spain: The Permeable Cloister*. Ashgate, 2005.

Leon, Fray Luis de. *Obras completas castellanas I*. Madrid: Biblioteca de autores cristianos, 1967.

María de San José. *A Wild Country Out in the Garden: The Spiritual Journal of a Mexican Nun*. Edited by Kathleen A. Myers and Amanda Powell, Indiana University Press, 1999.

Mujica, Bárbara. "Actresses as Athletes and Acrobats." In *Prismatic Reflections on Spanish Golden Age Theater*, edited by Gwyn Campbell and Amy Williamsen, Peter Lang, 2015, 229–42.

———. "Allegories of Faith: Lope's Two Plays on Teresa de Ávila." In *Religious and Secular Theater in Golden Age Spain: Essays in Honor of Donald T. Dietz*, edited by Donald Larson and Susan Paun de García, Peter Lang, 2018, 63–76.

———. "Antonio Güirau's *Refundiciones* of *La dama duende*: Genre and Music." In *Diálogos sobre teatro español: Entre siglos*, edited by Martha Halsey and Phyllis Zatlin, Estreno/Pennsylvania State University Press, 1999, 353–65.

———. "Beyond Image: The Apophatic-Kataphatic Dialectic in Teresa de Avila." *Hispania* 84, no. 4: 741–48.

———. "Calderón para ateos: La producción de *Sueño* de José Carrasquillo." In *Calderón y su puesta en escena a través de los siglos*, edited by Manfred Tietz, Stuttgart: Franz Steiner, 2003, 329–42.

———. *Calderón's Characters: An Existential Point of View*. Barcelona: Ediciones Puvill, 1980.

———. "Calderón's *La vida es sueño* and the Skeptic Revival." In *Texto y espectáculo: Nuevas dimensiones críticas de la "comedia,"* edited by Arturo Pérez-Pisonero, SLUSA, Mason Groves School of the Arts, Office of Hispanic Arts-University of Texas at El Paso, 1990, 23–32.

———. "Cecilia del Nacimiento." *Oxford Bibliographies in Renaissance and Reformation*, 2016, www.oxfordbibliographies.com/.

———. "Cervantes' Use of Skepticism in *El Retablo de las maravillas*." In *Looking at the Comedia in the Year of the Quintencennial*, edited by Barbara Mujica and Sharon Voros, University Press of America, 1993, 149–57.

———. "Comedia Actresses, Then and Now: The Case of Ana Caro's *Valor, agravio y mujer*." In *Remaking the Comedia: Spanish Classical Theater in Adaptation*, edited by Harley Erdman and Susan Paun de García, Tamesis, 2015, 189–96.

———. "Corpus Sanus, Mens Sana, Spiritus Sanus: Cuerpo, mente y espíritu en las cartas de Teresa de Jesús." In *Los cinco sentidos del convento*, edited by Josefina López, Caracas, Venezuela: Publicaciones UCAB [Universidad Católica Andrés Bello], 2009, 13–23.

———. *The Deaths of Don Bernardo* (novel). Los Angeles: Floricanto, 1990. Anthologized in *The Global Anthology of Jewish Women Writers*, edited by Robert and Roberta Kalechofsky, Micah Publications, 1990, 249–60.

———. "Encuentro de santos: Francisco de Borja y Teresa de Jesús." In *Francisco de Borja y su tiempo*, edited by Enrique García Hernán and María Pilar Ryan, Rome: Albatros-Institutum Historicum Societatis Iesu, 2011, 745–53.

———. "The End: Staging the Final Scenes of El Burlador de Sevilla." *Bulletin of the Comediantes* 47, no. 2 (Winter 1995): 201–22.

———. "Evil Within, Evil Without: Teresa of Avila Battles the Devil." In *The History of Evil in the Early Modern Age (1450–1700)*, edited by Daniel Robinson, Durham, UK: Routledge, 2018, 95–112. History of Evil Series, Chad Meister and Charles Taliaferro, general editors.

———. "Facing the Music: Introducing Song into the Comedia." In *Shakespeare and the Spanish Comedia: Translation, Interpretation, Performance*, edited by Bárbara Mujica, Bucknell University Press, 2013, 221–38.

———. *Far from My Mother's Home* (short stories). Mountain View, CA: Floricanto Press, 1999. [Spanish edition, *Lejos de la casa de mi madre*. Floricanto, 2019.]

———. *Frida: A Novel*. Overlook, 2001.

———. "From *Comedia* to *Zarzuela*: The Generic Transformation of Calderon's *La dama duende*." *Indiana Journal of Hispanic Literatures* 10–11 (1997): 17–35.

———. "Golden Age/Early Modern Theater: *Comedia* Studies at the End of the Century." *Hispania* 82, no. 3, 397–407. [Special Issue: *Comedia Studies at the End of the Century*, edited by Bárbara Mujica.]

———. "Guiding the Sisters: Carmelite *Suavedad* and Ana de San Bartolomé's *Meditaciones sobre el camino de Cristo*." In *The Sword: A Journal of Historical, Spiritual, and Contemporary Carmelite Issues* 77 (2017), no. 1: 91–105.

———. "Guillén de Castro." In *Major Spanish Dramatists: A Bio-Critical Guide to the History of the Spanish Theater: 1500 to Today*, edited by Mary Parker, Greenwood Publishing, 1998, 51–62.

———. "Healing on the Margins: Ana de San Bartolomé, Convent Nurse." *Early Modern Studies Journal* 6 (2014), www.earlymodernstudiesjournal.org/review_articles/healing-margins-ana-de-san-bartolome-convent-nurse/.

———. *Hispania* 82, no. 3. Special Issue: *Comedia Studies at the End of the Century*. Edited by Bárbara Mujica.

———. "Honor from a Comic Perspective: Calderón's *Comedias de Capa y Espada*." *Bulletin of the Comediantes* 38 (1986), no. 1: 7–24.

———. *I Am Venus*. Overlook, 2013.

———. "Keeping the Canon Alive: A Washington Performance of *La vida es sueño*." In *Texto y Espectáculo: Proceedings of the 1993 Symposium on Golden Age Drama*, edited by José Luis Suárez, York, SC: Spanish Literature Publications, 1995, 63–68.

———. *Lettered Women: The Disciples of Teresa de Ávila*, forthcoming.

———. "Letters to Friend and Foe: Ana de Jesús in France and the Low Countries." In *Festschrift in Honor of Professor Robert L. Fiore*, edited by Julia Domínguez and Chad Gasta, Newark, DE: Juan de la Cuesta Hispanic Monographs, 2009, 327–46.

———. "Lope de Vega's *El Castigo sin venganza*: What Do Readers Know and When Do They Know It?" *Comedia Performance* 12 (2015), no. 1: 50–79. [Guest edited by Susan Paun de García and Donald Larson]

———. "María de San José in Portugal: Life in the Lisbon Carmel." In *Miríada Hispánica* (2018): 121–34. [Special issue in honor of Alison Weber]

———. "María de Zayas's *Friendship Betrayed* à la Hollywood: Translation, Transculturation, and Production." In *The Spanish Comedia in English: Translation and*

Performance, edited by Donald Larson and Susan Paun de García, Tamesis, 2008, 240–53.

———. *A New Anthology of Early Modern Spanish Theater: Play and Playtext*. Yale University Press, 2014.

———. "The Ones Who Stayed Behind: The Letters of Catalina de Cristo to Ana de San Bartolomé." *The Sword: A Journal of Historical, Spiritual and Contemporary Carmelite Issues* 78 (2018).

———. "Outsiders: Why Mysticism Matters." *Commonweal* (26 Feb 2010): 15–18.

———. "Paco Portes y el arte de la comedia de figurón: *El lindo don Diego*." In *Del texto al Espectáculo. Homenaje a Francisco Portes*, edited by Ysla Campbell, Juárez, Mexico: Prensa de la Universidad de Juárez, 2009, 49–64.

———. "Paul the Enchanter: Jerónimo Gracián and Teresa's Vow of Obedience." *The Heirs of St. Teresa*, edited by Christopher Wilson, Washington D.C.: Institute of Carmelite Studies, 2005, 21–44.

———. "Performing Sanctity: Lope's Use of Teresian Iconography in *Santa Teresa de Jesús*." In *A Companion to Lope de Vega*, edited by Alexander Samson and Jonathan Thacker, Tamesis, 2008, 183–98.

———. "Problemas de representación: lo erótico en *La vida es sueño*." In *Deseo, sexualidad y afectos en la obra de Calderón*, edited by Manfred Tietz, Stuttgart: Franz Steiner, 2001, 139–49.

———. "El público moderno y el auto sacramental: *El gran Mercado del mundo*, de Calderón." In *Calderón: Protagonista eminente del barroco europeo*, edited by Kurt Reichenberger, Kassel, Germany: Reichenberger, 2000, 43–64.

———. "The Rapist and His Victim: Calderón's *No hay cosa como callar*." *Hispania* 62, no. 1 (March 1979): 30–46.

———. *Sanchez Across the Street* (short stories). Sarasota, FL: Florida Literary Foundation, 1997.

———, ed. *Shakespeare and the Spanish* Comedia: *Translation, Interpretation, Performance*. Bucknell University Press, 2013.

———. *Sister Teresa: The Woman Who Became Saint Teresa of Ávila*. Overlook, 2007. [Spanish edition, *Hermana Teresa*. Santiago de Chile: Cuarto Propio, 2018.]

———. "The Skeptical Premises of Calderón's *En esta vida todo es verdad y todo mentira*." In *Texto y espectáculo: Selected Proceedings of the Symposium on Spanish and Golden Age Theater, March, 1987*, edited by Bárbara Mujica, University Press of America, 1989, 117–26.

———. "Skepticism and Mysticism in Golden Age Spain: Teresa de Avila's Combative Stance." In *Women in the Discourse of Early Modern Spain*, edited by Joan Cammarata, University of Florida Press, 2001, 54–76.

———. "Staging Calderón's *El gran teatro del mundo* for a Modern Audience." In *Homage to Bruno Damiani*, edited by Filippo María Toscano, University Press of America, 1994, 213–25.

———. "Teaching Literature: Canon, Controversy, and the Literary Anthology." *Hispania* 80, no. 2 (May 1997): 203–15.

———. *Teresa de Ávila, Lettered Woman*. Nashville: Vanderbilt University Press, 2009.

———. "Teresa de Avila: Portrait of the Saint as a Young Woman." *Romance Quarterly* 63 (1): 30–39. [Special issue in commemoration of the fifth centenary of Saint Teresa's birth]

———. *Teresa de Jesús: Espiritualidad y feminismo*. Madrid: Ediciones del Orto / University of Minnesota, 2006.

———. "Three Sisters of Carmen: The Youths of Teresa de Jesús, María de San José, Ana de San Bartolomé." In *Youth of Early Modern Women*, edited by Elizabeth Cohen and Margaret Reeves, Amsterdam University Press, 2018, 137–58.

———. "Time Warp: Tiempo y temporalidad en una producción de *El caballero de milagro*, de Lope de Vega." In *El texto puesto en escena*, edited by Bárbara Mujica and Anita Stoll, Tamesis, 2000, 164–73.

———. "Tragic Elements in Calderón's *La dama duende*." *Kentucky Romance Quarterly* 16 (1969), no. 4: 303–23.

———. "Was Saint Teresa a Feminist?" In *Approaches to Teaching Teresa of Avila and the Spanish Mystics*, edited by Alison Weber, Modern Language Association, 2009, 74–82.

———. "Wisdom Onstage: The Evolution of Sabiduría in Calderón's *autos sacramentales*." In *Studies in Honor of Donald W. Cruikshank*, edited by Grace Magnier. *Bulletin of Spanish Studies* 90 (4–5): 787–806.

———. "Women Directing Women: Ana Caro's *Valor, agravio y mujer* as Performance Text." In *Engendering the Early Modern Stage: Women Playwrights of the Spanish Empire*, edited by Amy Williamsen and Valerie Hegstrom, University Press of the South, 1999, 19–50.

———. *Women Writers of Early Modern Spain: Sophia's Daughters*. Yale University Press, 2004.

Nader, Helen. *Power and Gender in Renaissance Spain: Eight Women of the Mendoza Family, 1450–1650*. University of Illinois Press, 2004.

O'Brien, Eavan. *Women in the Prose of María de Zayas*. Tamesis, 2010.

Owens, Sarah and Jane E. Mangan, eds. *Women of the Iberian Atlantic*. Louisiana State University Press, 2012.

Perry, Mary Elizabeth. "*Beatas* and the Inquisition in Seville." In *The Inquisition and Society in Early Modern Europe*, edited by Stephen Haliczer, Barnes & Noble, 1987, 147–68.

Petersen, Elizabeth Marie Cruz. *Women's Somatic Training in Early Modern Spanish Theater*. Routledge, 2017.

Poska, Allyson, Jane Couchman, and Katherine McIver. *Ashgate Research Companion to Women and Gender in Early Modern Europe*. Ashgate, 2013.

Poutrin, Isabelle. *Le Voile et la plume: Autobiographie et sainteté féminine dans l'Espagne moderne*. Casa de Velázquez, 1995.

Régnier-Bohler, Danielle. *Women in the West: Silences of the Middle Ages*. Belknap Press of Harvard University, 1992.

Rhodes, Elizabeth. *Dressed to Kill: Death and Meaning in Zayas's Desengaños*. University of Toronto Press, 2011.
Smith, Paul Julian. *The Body Hispanic: Gender and Sexuality in Spanish and Spanish-American Literature*. Oxford University Press, 1989.
———. *Representing the Other: "Race," Text, and Gender in Spanish and Spanish-American Narrative*. Clarendon Press, 1992.
Smith, Susan M. and Georgina Sabat de Rivers, eds. *Los coloquios del Alma: Cuatro dramas alegóricos de Sor Marcela de San Félix, hija de Lope de Vega*. Newark, DE: Juan de La Cuesta Hispanic Monographs, 2006.
Soufas, Teresa Scott, ed. *Dramas of Distinction: A Study of Plays by Golden Age Women*. University of Kentucky Press, 1997.
———, ed. *Women's Acts: Plays by Women Dramatists of Spain's Golden Age*. University of Kentucky Press, 1997.
Stoll, Anita K., and Dawn L. Smith. *Gender, Identity, and Representation in Spain's Golden Age*. Associated University Presses, 2000.
Taggard, Mindy Nancarrow. "Picturing Intimacy in a Spanish Golden Age Convent." *Oxford Art Journal* 23 (2007), no. 1: 97–112.
Teresa de Jesus. *Libro de la Vida*. Edited by Damaso Chicharro, Madrid: Cátedra, 1993.
Tudela, Elisa S.V. *Colonial Angels: Narratives of Gender and Spirituality in Mexico, 1580–1750*. University of Texas Press, 2014.
Vives, Juan Luis. *The Education of a Christian Woman: A Sixteenth-Century Manual*. 1524. Edited and translated by Charles Fantazzi. University of Chicago Press, 2000.
Vollendorf, Lisa. *The Lives of Women: A New History of Inquisitional Spain*. Vanderbilt University Press, 2005.
———. *Reclaiming the Body: María de Zayas's Early Modern Feminism*. North Carolina Studies in the Romance Languages, 2001.
Weber, Alison, ed. *Devout Laywomen in the Early Modern World*. Routledge, 2016.
———. *Teresa de Avila and the Rhetoric of Femininity*. Princeton University Press, 1990.
Whitenack, Judith A., and Gwyn E. Campbell, eds. *Zayas and Her Sisters*. Pegasus, 2000.
———. *Zayas and Her Sisters 2: Essays on Novelas by 17th-Century Spanish Women*. Global Publications, 2001.

Part I

Women as Dramatic Subjects

EDWARD H. FRIEDMAN

Self-Fashion Show
Women in the Plays of Cervantes and Significant Others

MIGUEL DE CERVANTES was, in his own time, and to state the case as accurately as possible, a marginal playwright, or at least a marginalized playwright. Some scholars have endeavored to redeem his dramatic works, while others have continued to foster the image of a narrative genius with creative skills not particularly suited for the stage. The focus here will be on women in Cervantes's *comedias*, his ten full-length plays, with respect to early modern Spanish society and in light of the dramatic formula of Lope de Vega. Lope's model for the "new art of writing plays," the *comedia nueva*, defined the national theater in the seventeenth century, up to the time of Pedro Calderón de la Barca and the dramatists of his school. First, I would like to submit certain generalizations, as an attempt at contextualization—in reverse, it might be argued—and then move to the plays of Cervantes per se and to the women inscribed therein.[1]

As a rule, women were subordinate to men in early modern Spanish society. They enjoyed fewer privileges, and their status was routinely precarious, since their finances, their alternatives, and, indeed, their happiness was dependent on their fathers and brothers before marriage and on their husbands after marriage. Unmarried women were at the mercy of their families, and they consistently ended up in convents, as nuns or laywomen. Some did venture forth into unknown territories and craft new roles for themselves. In short, the prospects for women, if not black and white, could be classified as dark gray. Early modern Spanish drama—the *comedia*—regularly used the concept of honor (*la honra*) to symbolize the difficult situation of women in society. Within the conventions of honor, a woman's well-being was predicated on the honor of her family or her husband. If her honor was tarnished in any way, the honor of the man or men who were her guardians was tarnished. Dishonor could result from appearances. Within this system, appearance was synonymous with reality; that is, appearances constituted reality. An innocent woman who was deemed to be guilty could be punished, including by death, in order to preserve the honor of her husband or the men in her family. Dramas such as Calderón's *El médico de su honra* and *El pintor de su deshonra*—with the respective husbands as "doctor of his honor" and "painter of his dishonor"—figure among the best-known examples of the wife-murder (uxoricide) plays. Because honor has such a substantial role in the serious plays, one might observe that the plays reflect the male perspective. Men are subjects, whereas women become objects. There are notable exceptions, of course, including plays that deal with especially laudable female characters, such as women of historical importance and figures from the Bible.

The most obviously assertive women in the *comedia* are found in comic plays. From classical antiquity onward, comedy has presented a world turned upside down. Comedy need not emulate reality, and, thus, in a topsy-turvy universe, women can be represented as seizing control. The archetypal comic structure, in this instance, is for women to plot to marry the men that they (and not their fathers and brothers) choose. The female protagonists of the comedies are almost always unmarried. As in the case of the "designing women" of the comedies, many characters in early modern Spanish drama devote themselves to *metatheater* (see Abel). They become metaphorical playwrights, inventing scripts that deviate from the plans of the men who have authority over them. These plays-within-plays project the theme of "the world as stage." The characters challenge the status quo. There is hardly a *comedia* in which one cannot discern the presence of metatheater, and this includes the best-known Spanish plays of the period: Lope's *Fuenteovejuna*, Tirso de Molina's *El burlador de Sevilla* [The Trickster of Seville], and Calderón's *La vida es sueño* [Life Is a Dream].

As would seem logical, some of the most women-friendly plays are by women dramatists, including María de Zayas, Ana Caro, and the Mexican nun Sor Juana Inés de la Cruz. Their female characters are highly articulate and successful as plotters of their own success. The playwrights follow the protocols established by Lope de Vega for the *comedia nueva*, but they add depth to the discourse and actions of women characters. An ironic element of this scheme is that, in the *comedia*, women who set out to help themselves—more often than not to redeem lost honor—cross-dress so that they can travel more safely. There is a suspension of disbelief here, in that women dressed as men are taken to be men. A forceful example is in Ana Caro's *Valor, agravio y mujer* [Valor, Grievance, and Woman], where the lead character spends most of the play in male garb and wins the heart of a woman desired by three men. (She comprehends the psychology of women, but she is also good with a sword.)

A key irony related to the role of women in the *comedia* is that the goal of comic plays—the happy ending—is marriage, while the leading female roles in serious and tragic plays are those of married women (Wardropper, "Lope's *La dama boba*"). One conceivably could see the progression from comedy to tragedy as a figurative six-act play in which the marriage or marriage proposals at the end of Act 3 become, in extreme cases, the death of the married woman at the end of Act 6. Lope de Vega emphasizes the preponderant scheme as *tragicomedia*—with tragedy averted in the serious plays, but the threat of dishonor lurking in the comic plays—but, in some cases, tragedy averted can mean a restoration of honor in the wake of a purification that can denote the death of an apparently guilty or compromised, yet faultless, wife.

The roles of women in Spanish drama, unlike in Elizabethan English drama, were played by women. The theater in Spain offered rich roles for women, including leading roles, supporting roles (such as maids), and character roles. María de Zayas's *La traición en la amistad* [The Betrayal of Friendship], for example, includes a female Don Juan who stands in contrast to the loyal "community of women" who act in unison to win the day over a group of men who elect to proceed independently. (Note that women were not seated with men in the Spanish public theaters, as they were, for example, in the Globe Theatre.) Cross-dressing as men on the Elizabethan stage was a curious enterprise, because the actors in the britches roles were young men. This paradoxically might have served the cause of verisimilitude, but the Spanish women dressed as men were actually women, a fact that may stretch the imagination but seems somehow more legitimate within theater practice. Although respect for actresses was by no means a given, it seems poetically just that women play the female roles, for which they can seek empathy, inflection, physical presence, and, thereby, a measure of realism.

It is interesting to contemplate the playwright's task. A play does not usually have a narrator, so the speeches of the actors are extremely significant in that regard. The playwright, needless to say, must write the dialogue for all characters; therefore, men write women's roles, and women write men's roles. When we talk about strong women characters, strong women's voices, and strong feminine or feminist perspectives, we have to give credit to male dramatists who create the characters, their discourse, and the plot mechanisms. Naturally, the inverse is true. Additionally, even though the Spanish *comedia* seems to foreground the male perspective, one may prefer to read "against the grain." If one sees reading and analyzing a play a bit like directing a play, then the result may be a selection of some elements over others, that is, a highlighting of—or a focus on—aspects of the play that may be more implicit than explicit. The "direction" of a play may provide the "missing" perspective or point of view associated with narrative.

For instance, there is something highly conventional about the Spanish *comedia*, yet it is important to look at how playwrights inject their unique signatures into their creations, at how they recreate the recourses of the genre while establishing new ways of representing reality, social and theatrical. Within each category and subgenre, the artist finds ways of building upon precedent. Likewise, the reader or critic (and, in a sense, all readers are critics) seeks the essence of the work while putting her/his mark on analysis and interpretation. Admirable women (playwrights and characters) contribute considerably to this process. From the late sixteenth to the seventeenth centuries, the *comedia nueva* placed women in leading and subordinate roles and in conditions that replicated and strayed from the social norm. The most common weak spot for female characters stems from honor—a crucial determinant of plot and dénouement—as a function of the male domain. Whether married or unmarried, women in the *comedia nueva* are ruled by fathers, brothers, other family members, guardians, or husbands. Only in the realm of comedy, of make-believe, can a woman thrive in society, most resoundingly by breaking the rules of decorum.

Cervantes wrote *comedias* before and during the successful reign of Lope de Vega as the most prominent theatrical figure in Spain. His plays, accordingly, occupy a dual position in literary history. In 1615—and due, in large measure, to the overwhelming critical and popular success of *Don Quijote*—Cervantes published eight full-length plays and eight dramatic interludes, the *Ocho comedias y ocho entremeses*, which bears the telling subtitle "nunca representados," never presented on stage. The most famous Spanish writer and one of the most famous writers of all times was a late bloomer. He was fifty-eight when Part One of *Don Quijote* was published in 1605 and sixty-eight when Part Two was published ten years later, and he was, alas, a frustrated playwright. Cervantes avowed to have written some twenty or thirty plays during his first period, of which only two plays survive: *El cerco de Numancia* and *Los tratos de Argel*, about the siege by Roman troops of a small Spanish town and about Christian captives in Algiers, respectively. While the *entremeses* have received considerable praise, the *comedias*—with the exception of *La Numancia*—have, in general, been negatively critiqued or ignored. Multiple reasons have been posited for this value judgment and neglect, including, of course, the quality of the works. Another reason relates to timing. Cervantes stands between the sixteenth-century attempts to recreate classical tragedy, the dramatic turn of Lope de Vega, and the emergence of an innovative strategy for playwriting: the *Arte nuevo de hacer comedias*, a blueprint that impressed and pleased the theater-going public and critics from the end of the sixteenth century through the seventeenth century, and that produced such playwrights as Tirso de Molina, Juan Ruiz de Alarcón, Guillén de Castro, Mira de Amescua, Pedro Calderón de la Barca, Agustín Moreto, Francisco de Rojas Zorrilla, María de Zayas, and Ana Caro.

In the distinction between "ancients," those most disposed to exalt the forms of classical antiquity, and the "moderns," those who concede the legitimacy of change, Lope de Vega falls among the "moderns." He encouraged the creation of tragicomedy and emphasized the unity of action rather than that of time and place. He mixed verse forms and character types while promoting the criterion of decorum. He wisely advocated attention to the wishes and responses of spectators. Lope was a brilliant and prolific poet, as were many of his followers, most notably Calderón, author of Spain's most celebrated play, *La vida es sueño*. In the anniversary year of 2016, as the life and the art of Cervantes was commemorated (and it is still commemorated), so was (and is) William Shakespeare, his contemporary and a playwright with possible ties to him as well as to Lope, if one bears in mind the enigmatic *Cardenio*, purportedly a "lost"—or, for some, "recovered"—play by Shakespeare and John Fletcher. The title figure is based on the character Cardenio, who first appears in chapter 23 of *Don Quijote*, Part 1 (see, for example, Chartier).

Cervantes was, in effect, a master of revisionism. He was a literary alchemist, who often started with preexisting models and reinvented them. *Don Quijote* depends on the romances of chivalry for its direction, but contains a paradigm shift that marks an adjustment in style, purpose, tone, and comprehensive design. Within *Don Quijote*, intertexts—prior texts and codes—are constantly evoked and remade. The Marcela and Grisóstomo episode in Part One of *Don Quijote*, for example, recasts pastoral romance as a feminist discourse on freedom and as a decentering of the male perspective. The point of view of the defenders of Grisóstomo, and the dying declaration of the self-appointed shepherd himself, serve to supplement, and to reorient, what could be labeled the deep structure of the archetypal pastoral. At the end of the episode, Don Quijote sides with and protects Marcela, after her delivery of the well-known "Don't hate me because I'm beautiful" speech (Cervantes, *Don Quijote de la Mancha*, 125–28 [I, 14]).

In *La Numancia*, Cervantes accentuates multiperspectivism, the construction of history, and self-consciousness toward one's role in the historical record. The perspectives, and the fluctuating vantage points, of the Romans, the Numantians, and the sixteenth-century Spaniard are interspersed in the shaping of the play. Arguably, the dominant feature of the play—and another link to *Don Quijote*—is the intensity of its irony. Cervantes's verses may not have the beauty or elegance of Lope's or Calderón's, but the poetic discourse possesses an almost overwhelming rhetorical energy, in keeping with the play's epic thrust. Directors frequently employ the term "spine" to signal what they perceive to be the driving force of a specific play, and this determination becomes the backbone of the staging (see Clurman 78–79, passim). One might deem the paradoxical "victory in defeat" as the spine of *La Numancia*, the link among the disparate facets of the play. Scipio's pride leads to arrogance. The vulnerability of the Numantians leads to a decisive plan. Spain and the other allegorical figures expand the frame of the siege and its aftermath. The sacrifice is magnified, historicized, and brought into the present of the composition, in which a unified Spain is the ultimate metonym. Cervantes's rewriting of tragedy is unabashedly patriotic, with no concealed critique or satirical edge, and any historical revisionism serves the laudatory tenor of the play. Multiperspectivism fosters a lofty cause, while in *Don Quijote* it resolutely, and commendably, muddies the waters. Theme and discourse coalesce in *La Numancia*. Cervantes replicates the tragic overtones, the irony (dramatic irony that presupposes the spectator's knowledge of the dénouement), and—in a pre-Christian setting—the *fate* of classical antiquity, but with a recontextualization that assimilates the Spanish imperial landscape, literally and figuratively. The tragedy of Numancia moves from microcosm to macrocosm, from destruction to rebirth, and from pagan hopelessness to the earthly and spiritual rewards of the Catholic faith.

The female presence in *La Numancia* is affecting, if understated. The resistance of Numancia to the Roman siege elicits the indisputable courage of the men of the town, who are primed as warriors, but it is the women who remind them that they must be protectors as well. In Act 3, three unidentified women stirringly and eloquently reason that the men cannot leave their wives, female relatives, and children defenseless. The maiden Lira reiterates their pleas, and this motivates the leaders to elaborate a different and conclusive maneuver. Lira underscores the suffering of the Numantians by personalizing their pain. The three women who speak are abstractions; she is concrete, a specific example of the trauma and the valor of the townspeople. Her lover Marandro, linked to Leonicio in the "two friends" tradition, dies after having stolen bread from the Roman camp for her. Lira's young brother enters to announce the death of their mother and the imminent death of their father, and the boy himself dies onstage. With Bariato, the last living inhabitant of Numancia, Lira becomes the emblem of the town, which in turn becomes the emblem of imperial Spain. The personified España merges time and space, converting the defeat into a victory for the ages, a spiritual victory that anticipates the triumph of Catholicism. Sensing the symbolic aura of maternity, of the motherland, a director may opt to cast a woman in the role of España.

The prolific and much-appreciated Miguel de Unamuno, who was less successful as a playwright than as a writer of fiction and essays and an all-purpose polemicist, claimed on numerous occasions to prefer that his plays be heard rather than seen—"Prefiero un público de ciegos a un público sordo" [I prefer a blind audience to a deaf audience] (qtd. in Zavala 129)—and the same might apply to *La Numancia* and to the other extant play of Cervantes's first period, *Los tratos de Argel* [The Negotiations in Algiers]. *Los tratos de Argel*, sometimes listed as *El trato de Argel*, has a counterpart in Cervantes's 1615 collection: *Los baños de Argel* [The Prisons of Algiers]. The two plays center on captivity and on the struggles of Spaniards who must now live among the enemy. The axes of similitude and difference between the *Argel* plays are revealing. Both conceptualize the motif of captivity and find an element of unity in the roles of characters as prisoners of the Muslims, prisoners of love, and Catholics imprisoned in the body until the soul is freed from its earthly constraints. *Los tratos de Argel* is filled with soliloquies and narratives about actions rather than the direct representation of actions. The structure is more conceptual and more abstract, more rhetorical, than dramatic per se. It is a dramatic edifice built around an idea and around parallel motifs. *Los baños de Argel* shows the influence of Lope de Vega's "arte nuevo." Set against *Los tratos de Argel*, the later play presents more action onstage and seeks to link the discrete plot elements. *Los baños de Argel* stresses character development and trades allegorical and supernatural figures for human beings. A horizontal movement replaces—to a degree, at least—the primarily vertical structure of *Los tratos de Argel*.

What remains a constant in Cervantes's dramaturgy, however, is the use of the analogue as a structuring principle: the theme of sacrifice, the theme of captivity, the connections among associative fields, what can be called the "unifying concept" as a connecting thread. Lope, like Shakespeare, draws upon the Aristotelian emphasis on the unity of action. Many of Lope's plays have secondary plots that mirror the main plot—the tyrant in *Fuenteovejuna*, for example, betrays the Catholic Monarchs Fernando and Isabel as he violates the women of the village—but Cervantes never loses sight of the seemingly independent events that interact conceptually and reflect a unity of thought rather than a unity of action.

In the *Argel* plays, Cervantes dramatizes the imprisonment of Christians by their Muslim captors by showing characters in conflicts that include political, religious, and psychological components. Contrasts between the two groups are amplified by struggles in the areas of love and passion. In *Los tratos de Argel*, for example, the Spanish captive Aurelio is separated from his beloved Silvia and pursued by the Muslim Zahara, who puts desire before faith. Silvia, in matching fashion, must resist the fervent advances of the Muslim Yzuf. Here, and throughout the play, Cervantes demonstrates the moral superiority of the Spaniards as he allows human emotion to frame the ideological content. The Zahara of *Los baños de Argel* is a Christian convert who, like Zoraida in the captive's tale of *Don Quijote*, helps a Spanish prisoner (Don Lope) to escape. A series of interrelated love intrigues heightens suspense and moves the action forward. The female characters—Christian and Muslim, moral and immoral—are fundamental to the message systems of the plays, because, within a fixed structure of priorities, each is personalized, figurative, and dramatically relevant.

It is fascinating to compare Miguel de Cervantes's two extant early plays, *La Numancia* and *Los tratos de Argel*, with sixteenth-century plays by writers such as Lupercio Leonardo de Argensola, Gaspar de Aguilar, and Francisco Agustín Tárrega—those mentioned and praised in chapter 48 of Part One of *Don Quijote*.[2] These playwrights are associated with the neo-Aristotelian preceptists, and Cervantes—as a dramatist and as a commentator on drama—is situated between them and the "comedia nueva" originated by Lope de Vega. Somewhat more fascinating, in my opinion, is the "dynamic tension"—a phrase coined by Charles Atlas in a totally unrelated context—between Cervantes and Lope. When one contemplates the structure of Cervantes's *comedias*, Lope can be seen as the proverbial "elephant in the room." The juxtaposition is valid to an extent because Cervantes replies to Lope in the dialogue of the priest and the canon in *Don Quijote* (I, 48), and, more appreciably, in the plays themselves. A pivotal moment comes when the personified *Comedia* addresses the personified Curiosity in the opening scene of Act 2 of *El rufián dichoso* [The Fortunate Ruffian] with the words "Los tiempos mudan las cosas / y perficionan las artes" (Cervantes, *Comedias y tragedias*, I: 414, vv. 1229–30) [Times change things and perfect the arts].

The modified "ancient" posture is now decidedly "modern," the consequence, no doubt, of a reality check. Yet Cervantes is never content with imitation. He inserts himself into any mimetic equation. That is why the implicit presence of Lope in some, if not all, of Cervantes's eight *comedias* is ripe for an examination of the push-and-pull of similitude and difference. In *El rufián dichoso*—tracing the progression of the main character, Cristóbal de Lugo, from sinner to saint—Cervantes blends unity of action with analogues on the theme of identity. There is one character, but a range of identities, each enacted self-consciously. As the Dominican friar Cristóbal de la Cruz, the protagonist professes to be devout, proves to be devout, and ultimately achieves sainthood. The structure of *El rufián dichoso* documents, on one level, salvation and a heavenly ascent and, on another, Cervantes's coming to terms with the "comedia nueva." He cedes dramatic space to his adversary without eliding his own technique and his own literary identity.

In *El rufián dichoso*, Cervantes uses the three-act structure to depict three stages of a transformation, much as Lope does, for example, in the conversion of Finea from simpleton to prudent lady in *La dama boba* [The Foolish Lady], or Calderón does in the conversion of Segismundo from "monster" to perfect prince in *La vida es sueño*. In Act 1 of *El rufián dichoso*, two female characters, an adulteress and a prostitute, align themselves with Cristóbal de Lugo. In Act 2, the moribund young Doña Ana Treviño cannot reconcile her bad fortune with faith in eternal life. She refuses to take confession from Fray Cristóbal de la Cruz, and he determines to sacrifice himself to convince her of the theological imperative. He dies a painful death from leprosy, but he fights demons on Doña Ana's behalf and realizes the ultimate goal, in a move from vice and the lower depths to saintliness and eternity.

Cervantes returns to the staging of captivity in other plays: *El gallardo español*, about a gallant Spaniard and his exploits in love, war, and imprisonment; and *La gran sultana*, about a Spanish Christian woman who wins the heart, and the subservience, of a sultan. Yet, each of Cervantes's plays is, first and foremost, whether comic, serious, or in-between, a new "take" on the question of identity, a subject, not coincidentally, at the core of *Don Quijote*. *El gallardo español* contraposes a Spanish couple with a Muslim couple. Don Fernando and Doña Margarita are metatheatrical figures who end up in Orán, where they place their honor and their lives in jeopardy. The Muslims are foes on diverse levels. Cervantes relies on the power of speech—mythologizing—to initiate the plot. Oropesa, a Spanish prisoner, tells his mistress Arlaja tales of the valiant Don Fernando, and she beseeches her suitor Alimuzel to capture the Spaniard and to bring him before her. The action may hinge less on male heroics than on female aggressiveness, for it is the enamored women—antithetical characters—who push the storyline forward. History in *El gallardo español* is, in a double sense, peculiar. It is surpassed by fiction, yet firmly acknowledged in the background and outranked only by dramatic exigencies and pragmatism.

Doña Catalina de Oviedo, the protagonist of *La gran sultana*, is not only the thematic center of the play, but also an exemplar of ironic self-fashioning. Renowned for her beauty and for her devotion to Catholicism, she has lived for six years as a captive in the Turkish court undetected by the Gran Turco. Exposed by a troublemaker, she is introduced to the Gran Turco, master of a grand harem, who immediately falls deeply in love with her. Doña Catalina is vulnerable, but true to her faith. She is tested on all sides. The Gran Turco proposes marriage, with a concession: she will not have to forfeit her religion. As she considers the proposal, she is reproached by her father, also held prisoner. Her abiding commitment to Christianity could lead to an automatic refusal, but she justifies the marriage as an earthly form of martyrdom through which she can assist other Christian captives, among them Clara and Lamberto, the latter disguised as a woman (Zelinda) desired by the Gran Turco. Doña Catalina is a complex—one might be inclined to say captivating—character because her steadfastness must be qualified, rationalized. She wants to be an ideal Christian, and, at the same time, she wants to live; she redefines martyrdom to suit the predicament into which she is thrown. She saves herself and others, yet the play blurs the lines between the absolute and the relative and between constancy and self-preservation. Doña Catalina promises the Gran Turco an heir. What will be the religion of their son? Will the capricious husband maintain his harem?

Doña Catalina's dilemma is the crux of the play, but Cervantes creates a vivid panorama of the court of the Gran Turco and its wide array of characters, including a good number of women. The court is a site of chaos and of contradictory persuasions and temperaments: tolerance and intolerance, lucidity and misunderstanding, self-awareness and camouflage, conviction and skepticism, and so forth. *La gran sultana* seems to generate a confusion of values alongside a palpable gender confusion. The play may be not so much about grandeur as about human nature, indecisiveness, and the disorder of things. Religious zeal operates amid a stream of transgressive acts and attitudes, and it appears that the turmoil and misperception exhibited in the plot will prevail after the play concludes.

Identity in plays is inseparable from metatheater, because role-playing as fact and fiction can lead to self-discovery, to hidden truths, and to higher orders. *El laberinto de amor* [The Labyrinth of Love] and *La entretenida* [The Entertaining Play] revise the *comedia nueva*'s archetypal comic plot, wherein a quick-thinking woman can defy her father or brothers by devising a script that will permit her to select a spouse on her own. The labyrinthine social universe of *El laberinto de amor* exaggerates the traditional plot by featuring three main female protagonists and unanimously successful matches, and, as a counterpoint, *La entretenida* "entertains" by frustrating the matrimonial hopes of all the characters, who represent several social strata. In *El laberinto de amor*, three exceptionally bright and ambitious young women—Rosamira, Julia, and Porcia—join forces to secure marriages with the men of their choosing. They accomplish this objective through agility of mind and body, since role-playing—taken to extreme limits—is essential to their success. The labyrinth fabricated by Cervantes is a study in paradox, for much of the derring-do of the women involves their dressing, and acting, as men. Of equal importance is the play's treatment of female bonding. Through collaboration, reciprocal respect, and the meeting of minds, they constitute a community of women similar to that of María de Zayas's *La traición en la amistad*.

The focal figure of *La entretenida* is Cristina, a young lady of modest means, who, like the antiheroes and antiheroines of picaresque narrative, hopes to improve her lot within an inflexible hierarchy. She is misled—by literary romance, by the happy endings of comedies, and by her role as a director of a "real" theatrical piece—into overestimating her control of the outcome. She and everyone around her are thwarted in their nuptial goals. In the end, histrionics get them nowhere. This is the downside of metatheater. Some view the message as theological: the characters have not been true to their authentic selves and cannot prosper. Others may judge the moral as lighter, as an antidote to the prototypical comic ending, illustrated hyperbolically in *El laberinto de amor*. Whatever the critical consensus, one can note that the protagonist of *La entretenida* is a woman who is neither wealthy nor noble. She may be accused of overstepping, but she dominates the dramatic configuration. The other female characters are mere cogs in the machinery of the collective failure. Although Cristina's destiny is predetermined by the playwright and by society, she is, it would seem, ahead of her time, a sign, or harbinger perchance, of the rising middle class and the increased interest in equity in social transactions.

If *El laberinto de amor* and *La entretenida* reluctantly admit that Lope's prescription for playwriting is the new standard while teasing its conventions, then *La casa de los celos y selvas de Ardenia* [The House of Jealousy and the Arden Forest] would seem to revert to Cervantes's pre-Lope writing for the stage, and it definitely could have been written far earlier than its publication date. The play is unlike the others, a miscellany of chivalric characters, motifs, and permutations. When I first began to think about the play—decades ago—I was struck by something akin to poststructuralist decentering, in which historicism and realism defer to a multiperspectivism derived from levels of fiction. The Carolingian dynasty is rendered as chivalric romance, with knights and their ladies, allegorical figures, magicians, endless supporting players, and an enchanted forest. Roldán, Reynaldos, Angélica, Bernardo del Carpio, the emperor Charlemagne, Merlin, Venus, Cupid, Castilla, Fear, Curiosity, Desperation, Jealousy, Fame, Notoriety, and shepherds borrowed from pastoral romance "strut and fret" their minutes on the page. The lady Angélica, whose intertextual credentials are eminent, is the primary object of prey. She has combative tendencies, but is outmatched by the woman warrior Marfisa—a bellicose avenger, with an intertext of her own—who does not let her gender interfere with a craving for warfare. That *La casa de los celos* is a splendid anomaly is a certainty. So is its dependence on analogues and episodes that stem and digress from the love triangle that serves as its foundation but, conspicuously, is not resolved. Unity of action seems to have been left offstage. The play's spine could be its exploration of intertextuality, of how texts procreate and tell stories that commend literature's ability to capture history and human behavior in its own terms and through inward movement. Reality is the decentered "Other" that is made present through its absence. As in *Don Quijote*, history in *La casa de los celos* becomes the microcosm to fiction's macrocosm.

Cervantes's plays are not as formulaic as those of Lope de Vega and his successors, but the approach via a "unifying concept" covers his plays in a general way, most discernibly in the works that do not evoke the *comedia nueva*. I would maintain that the most noteworthy play of the eight *comedias* of 1615 (accepting *noteworthy* as an open adjective, but referring in part to its adherence to a more strictly Cervantine *mode* or *mold*) is *Pedro de Urdemalas*, which is neither the best-known nor the most revered in the corpus. The title character is based on a legendary trickster. Cervantes's Pedro de Urdemalas is both good-hearted and unscrupulous, a schemer and scammer. He helps a mayor who lacks the knowledge of the law to make judgments. He helps lovers settle spats, stay together, and get the best of those who object to their union. He swindles a widow and a farmer, with no apparent remorse. He is friendly with a group of gypsies, to whose leader he recounts the story of his life. His link with the gypsies allows his personal narrative to intersect with that of the beautiful young and desirable gypsy Belica, whose modus operandi is equally bold. Belica does not feel comfortable in her, if you will, gypsy skin.

A feeling of superiority inflects her every move. Performing a dance—one of her specialties—she makes a play for the king, to the wrath of the queen. The movement of the *comedia* validates Belica's unflinching assertions: she is, in fact, a noblewoman born out of wedlock to a mother who gave her as a baby to a band of gypsies. Belica is, moreover, the niece of the king. She readily adapts to her new circumstances and lifestyle, completely disdaining the habits, customs, and friendships of the gypsies and erasing them from her purview. Pedro de Urdemalas is the epitome of protean. His adaptability is admirable, although this means can be anything but. The protean label extends to morality, which weaves in and out of Pedro's actions. The definitive juncture in the play is the meeting of Pedro with a theater manager who is traveling with his company and, recognizing talent when he sees it, invites Pedro to join the troupe. In sum, Belica—now Isabel—is meant to be a noblewoman, and, correspondingly, acting is the ideal vocation for Pedro.

In *Pedro de Urdemalas*, Cervantes takes the theme of identity from opposing angles to construct a commentary on role-playing, class, and literary invention. This may be his broadest statement on the concept of the *theatrum mundi*, seen as a kind of *mise-en-abyme* with endless mirror images. Cervantes creates two plots—each with a unity of action—that add perspectivism to the dramatic vision. The Belica/Isabel plot brings "the force of blood" and social determinism into the picture. The Pedro de Urdemalas plot takes metatheater to its farthest reaches, as the consummate actor on the stage of life becomes a professional actor, with the opportunity to interpret, before spectators, highborn roles comparable to that of Isabel. Identity is flexible, mutable, and as likely to be misused and compromised as it is to be proven genuine. Cervantes's recourse to metaphor, metonymy, synecdoche, paradox, and the synthetic trope of irony puts identity—one might say—in the spotlight, as an innate and sought-after attribute when it is legitimate and as illusory and deceptive when it is not. In a study of Cervantes's theater, I began the title of one chapter with the phrase "The World as Stage" and another with "The Stage as World." The first dealt with *El laberinto de amor* and *La entretenida*, the second with *La casa de los celos*. The wording distinguishes representation (the microcosm) from substitution (the macrocosm). "The world as stage" conforms to a hierarchy in which the theater is a subject, a *signifier*. "The stage as world" supplants hierarchy and makes theater the *signified* (Friedman, *The Unifying Concept*, 103–32). With its twofold plot and sets of conceptual interconnections, *Pedro de Urdemalas* encompasses both the theological and the secular, the sublime and the ridiculous, and points in between.

Cervantes alternates a continuous series of brief episodes with the principal plotlines of Belica's corroboration of her noble lineage and Pedro's conversion of improvised theatrical performances into sanctioned theatrical performances. Cervantes keeps the analogical form that marks his dramaturgy and doubles the unity of action of Lope's "arte nuevo," hence modifying it. *Pedro de Urdemalas* is irrefutably about identity and human psychology. The "case studies" reveal that identity can be seen as predetermined, self-determined, or indeterminate. Belica/Isabel is born to be a blue blood, to disdain those who rank below her. As himself, Pedro is helpful to some, hurtful to others. He aids women who undergo the tribulations of courtship, but he is not above deceiving and mocking women. In the future, he will follow the scripts of fellow dramatists. His identity—ironically, before *and* after his career change—is predicated on his malleability, or, as structuralists might have argued, on his function within a given system. He is an empty vessel unless he has a role to play. Belica's intuition and the sense that she has been miscast in society hasten her transition from gypsy to aristocrat. The concealment of her identity precedes Isabel's stepping into her role. Pedro is a character in search of the means to accommodate his capricious temperament. Each of the episodes prior to his encounter with the theater manager is a miniature production in which Pedro "auditions" for the "real" audience in preparation for his formal interview. The comic spirit of *Pedro de Urdemalas* does not hide the importance of the figurative aims and allusions in the play. Identity and theatricality are conjoined in metaphorical realms that summon the here-and-now and what lies beyond. The theater revels in upstaging itself, in intimating that *all* theater has traces of metatheater, and that reality and allegory are never mutually exclusive. In the various planes of the dramatic performance, the protagonist Pedro is *always* with other actors, as are we the audience—Cervantes seems to imply—as we engage in the act of reflecting and refracting physical and mental images. The role of history, so basic to *Don Quijote*, *La Numancia*, and the plays on captivity, is absent in *Pedro de Urdemalas*, in which the timeline is the temporary yet infinite period between the curtain going up and it coming down.

The female characters in Cervantes's *comedias* exemplify the breadth of women's roles in drama and in society. There is an intricacy to the characters in both major and minor parts, because Cervantes seeks innovative options for characterization, new ways of casting traditional stories, and surprises for the reader/spectator. Love may be the common denominator in his plays, but the backdrop varies tremendously. Heroism, rivalry, class-consciousness, loyalty, literary precedent, metatheater, feminism (or, for some, pre-feminism), and other factors guide the playwright in his portrayal of women. His characters are, in general, emotional, meditative, and complexly drawn, and they never are duplicates of their predecessors. As in his narrative fictions, women in his plays invite close readings of texts and subtexts. There is much food for thought—and much that remains elusive—when one evaluates Cervantes's *comedias*. The plays merit scrutiny. They are compelling, but they can be hard to categorize and hard to analyze. In his last speech, Pedro de Urdemalas refers to a *comedia* to be performed by his company, one that will defy the norms of writing for the theater. He delights in the difference between his work and those of others, and so can we.

Notes

1. For commentary on the plays of Cervantes, among other notable studies, see Arboleda; Brioso Santos; Canavaggio; Casalduero; Cotarelo y Valledor; de la Granja; García Aguilar, Gómez Canseco, and Sáez; García Martín; Maestro; Marrast; McKendrick; Pedraza Jiménez; Rey Hazas; Sánchez; Spadaccini and Talens; Wardropper, "Comedias"; Ynduráin; and Zimic, as well as the introductions to the editions of Cervantes's theater by Sevilla Arroyo and Rey Hazas, and by Gómez Canseco. For a consideration of women in Cervantes's theater, see Anderson. See also Friedman (*The Unifying Concept*; "Perspectivism on Stage"; "Miguel de Cervantes Saavedra").

2. Alfredo Hermenegildo provides a thorough survey of Spanish recreations of classical tragedies. For a survey of Renaissance literary theory, see Weinberg. For application to Spanish theorists, see Moir and Sánchez Escribano and Porqueras Mayo.

References

Abel, Lionel. *Metatheatre: A New View of Dramatic Form*. Hill and Wang, 1963.
Anderson, Ellen M. "Mothers of Invention: Toward a Reevaluation of Cervantine Dramatic Heroines." *Bulletin of the Comediantes* 62 (2010), no. 2: 1–44.
Arboleda, Carlos Arturo. *Teoría y forma del metateatro en Cervantes*. Universidad de Salamanca, 1991.
Brioso Santos, Héctor, coord. *Cervantes y el mundo del teatro*. Kassel, Germany: Reichenberger, 2007.
Canavaggio, Jean. *Cervantès dramaturge. Un théâtre à naître*. Presses Universitaires de France, 1977.
Casalduero, Joaquín. *Sentido y forma del teatro de Cervantes*. Madrid: Gredos, 1966.
Cervantes, Miguel de. *Comedias y tragedias*, 2 vols. Coordinated by Luis Gómez Canseco, Madrid: Real Academia Española, 2015.
———. *Don Quijote de la Mancha*, 2 vols., edition of the Instituto Cervantes. Directed by Francisco Rico, Madrid: Real Academia Español, 2015.
———. *Teatro completo*. Edited by Florencio Sevilla Arroyo and Antonio Rey Hazas, Barcelona: Planeta, 1987.

Chartier, Roger. *Cardenio between Cervantes and Shakespeare: The Story of a Lost Play.* Cambridge: Polity Press, 2013.
Clurman, Harold. *On Directing.* Fireside, 1997.
Cotarelo y Valledor, Armando. *El teatro de Cervantes.* Madrid: Tip. de *Revista de Archivos, Bibliotecas y Museos*, 1915.
de la Granja, Agustín. "Apogeo, decadencia y estimación de las comedias de Cervantes." In *Cervantes*, Alcalá: Centro de Estudios Cervantinos, 1995, 225–54.
Friedman, Edward H. "Miguel de Cervantes Saavedra (1547–1616)." In *Spanish Dramatists of the Golden Age*, edited by Mary Parker, Garland, 1998, 63–74.
———. "Perspectivism on Stage: *Don Quijote* and the Mediated Vision of Cervantes' Comedias." *Ideologies and Literature*, Nueva época, 2 (1986), no. 1: 69–86.
———. *The Unifying Concept: Approaches to Cervantes' Comedias.* York, SC: Spanish Literature Publications, 1981.
García Aguilar, Ignacio, Luis Gómez Canseco, and Adrián J. Sáez. *El teatro de Miguel de Cervantes.* Madrid: Visor, 2016.
García Martín, Manuel. *Cervantes y la comedia española en el siglo XVII.* Universidad de Salamanca, 1980.
Hermenegildo, Alfredo. *La tragedia en el Renacimiento español.* Barcelona: Planeta, 1973.
Maestro, Jesús G. *La escena imaginaria: poética del teatro de Miguel de Cervantes.* Madrid: Iberoamericana-Vervuert, 2000.
Marrast, Robert. *Cervantès dramaturge.* Paris: L'Arche, 1957.
McKendrick, Melveena. "Writings for the Stage." In *The Cambridge Companion to Cervantes*, edited by Anthony J. Cascardi, Cambridge University Press, 2002, 131–59.
Moir, Duncan. "The Classical Tradition in Spanish Dramatic Theory and Practice in the Seventeenth Century." In *Classical Drama and Its Influence: Essays Presented to H. D. F. Kitto*, edited by M. J. Anderson, Barnes and Noble, 1965, 193–227.
Pedraza Jiménez, Felipe B. "El teatro mayor de Cervantes: comentarios a contrapelo." In *Actas del VIII Coloquio Internacional de la Asociación de Cervantistas*, edited by José Ramón Fernández de Cano y Martín, El Toboso, Spain: Ayuntamiento del Toboso, 1998, 19–38.
Rey Hazas, Antonio. "Cervantes y el teatro." *Cuadernos de Teatro Clásico* 20 (2005): 21–96.
Sánchez, Alberto. "Aproximación al teatro de Cervantes." *Cuadernos de Teatro Clásico* 7 (1992): 11–30.
Sánchez Escribano, Federico, and Alberto Porqueras Mayo, eds. *Preceptiva dramática española del Renacimiento y el Barroco*, 2nd expanded ed. Madrid: Gredos, 1972.
Spadaccini, Nicholas, and Jenaro Talens. "On Theater as Narrativity." In *Through the Shattering Glass: Cervantes and the Self-Made World*, University of Minnesota Press, 1993, 64–108.
Vega, Lope de. *Arte nuevo de hacer comedias.* Edited by Enrique García Santo-Tomás, Madrid: Cátedra, 2009.
Wardropper, Bruce W. "Comedias." In *Suma cervantina*, edited by Juan Bautista Avalle-Arce and E. C. Riley, Tamesis, 1973, 147–69.

———. "Lope's *La dama boba* and Baroque Comedy." *Bulletin of the Comediantes* 13 (1961): 1–3.
Weinberg, Bernard. *A History of Literary Criticism in the Italian Renaissance*, 2 vols. University of Chicago Press, 1961.
Ynduráin, Francisco. "Cervantes y el teatro." In *Relección de clásicos*, Madrid: Editorial Prensa Española, 1969, 87–112.
Zavala, Iris M. *Unamuno y su teatro de conciencia*. Universidad de Salamanca, 1963.
Zimic, Stanislav. *El teatro de Cervantes*. Madrid: Castalia, 1992.

FREDERICK A. DE ARMAS

Chained by Her Words
Calderón's *La gran Cenobia* and the Perils of the Sublime

CENOBIA (ZENOBIA), Queen of Palmyra, was one of the great warrior queens and examples of wisdom and wise rule in the ancient world. Although biographies of Cenobia were well known during the Renaissance, her story had yet to be the object of a major literary work or even of a finished work of art until Pedro Calderón de la Barca, still a young man at the age of twenty-five, decided to write a striking play, *La gran Cenobia* [*The Great Zenobia*].[1] Curiously, this work remains rather unknown even to this day. In a way, this shroud of invisibility may be related to the play's very subject. Cenobia was said to be tutored by Longinus, who was reputedly the author of *On the Sublime*. Ernst Robert Curtius decried how the Western tradition has relegated almost to oblivion this Greek text, since it "has never found a congenial spirit" (400), and Michel Deguy adds that "this work has managed to avoid being appropriated and capitalized on," saying it has gotten lost since its "'discourse of exaltation' would necessarily defy interpretation as the most elevated peak defies and discourages ascent" (6). Its author has also disappeared from sight, since we can no longer ascribe the treatise to Cenobia's tutor. Thus, this triple invisibility (of work, concept, and authorship), I would argue, contributes to the veiling of Calderón's work.

And yet, this invisibility in the Renaissance may have been due to critical neglect. We do know from Bernard Weinberg that *On the Sublime* was translated and commented upon during the Renaissance (141–51); and we know from the articles of Gustavo Costa (such as "The Latin Translations of Longinus' *Peri Ypsous* in Renaissance Italy") that its impact was felt by a number of theorists, who would have read Francesco Robortello's first edition of 1554.[2] Translations into Latin appeared as early as 1566 and 1572, and an Italian translation (unpublished) was produced in 1575 (Refini 35–36). Most recently, a volume of collected essays has shown that: "Contrary to widely held assumptions, its early modern revival did not begin with the adaptation published by Boileau in 1674; it was not connected solely with the early Greek editions which began to appear from 1554; nor was its impact limited to rhetoric and literature" (van Eck, Bussels, Delbeke, and Pieters 1). The editors of the volume do acknowledge that: "Neither have the ways the sublime was used, in rhetoric and literature, but also in the arts, architecture and the theater, been studied in any systematic way" (1–2). My purpose here is to unveil some of *La gran Cenobia*'s sublimity, which, as Deguy states, is the very opposite of grandiloquence. In doing so, I hope to bring to light the striking figure of the Queen of Palmyra as envisioned by Calderón.

Starting with the Middle Ages, Cenobia was often included in catalogues of famous women. Brief mentions or short biographies of her life and deeds appeared in texts such as Boccaccio's *Famous Women* (ca. 1362), Petrarch's *Triumphs* (1351/1374), Alvaro de Luna's *Book of Virtuous and Famous Women* (1446), Fernán Pérez de Guzmán's *Generations and Portraits* (1450), Juan Luis Vives's *Instructions for the Christian Woman* (1524), and Antonio de Guevara's *Familiar Epistles* (1539).[3] In spite of her fame, European authors stopped short of writing lengthy or fictional works about her or drawing her likeness. During the Renaissance, Michelangelo made a drawing of her,[4] but the first actual painting of her dates from the eighteenth century: Giovanni Battista Tiepolo's *Queen Zenobia Addressing her Soldiers* (1725–1730).

Let us recall how she appeared in the literary tradition. As a child, Cenobia was said to delight in the hunt and, as she grew older, she went after more dangerous prey: "dared to confront bears and to pursue, lie in wait for, capture, and kill leopards and lions" (Boccaccio 439). Soon, she became knowledgeable in the arts of war, writing, and ruling. Together with her husband Odaenathus, she defeated the Persians and rescued Emperor Valerian. When Odaenathus died and her husband's son Maeonius was killed by soldiers, "she draped the imperial mantle around her shoulders" (431). Declaring herself ruler of the Palmyrene Empire, no emperor dared challenge her for a very long time: "neither the emperor Gallienus nor the emperor Claudius after him dared make any attempt against her" (431) knowing of her wisdom and courage. It is this Cenobia that is at times alluded to in early modern Spanish plays such as Lope de Vega's *La doncella Teodor* (1610–1612) and *La fe rompida* (1614).[5]

The striking geography of Cenobia's faraway lands constitutes a second important element in her depiction. Although Palmyra had been described by Pliny in his *Natural History*, it was not until the seventeenth century that Europeans traveled there and came back with accounts of it. Pietro della Valle returned to Rome in 1626 but did not publish his three volumes of voyages (including his trip to Palmyra) until 1652; and the Frenchman Jean Baptiste Tavernier published his adventures in 1676. Very much like Pliny the Elder, both expressed their amazement at the beauty of the city (Southern 13). But it is to the English that we owe a debt for producing the first drawings of the ruins of this mysterious site. They can be found in *The Antiquities of Palmyra* by Abednego Sellers (1696) and *The Ruins of Palmyra* (1751), based on the expedition by Robert Woods and James Dawkins (Southern 14). Thus, Western Europeans could view the remains of the city's illustrious colonnade, the Temple of Baalshami, and the Baths of Diocletian, together with depictions of the city's dramatic location in the midst of a desert with the mountains as background. In chapter 25 of the fifth book of his *Natural History*, Pliny had long before expressed amazement at Palmyra's natural streams and as to how its crops end in a circle or compass of sand. Although the city underwent two destructions, one by the Romans in 273 and a second by the Timurids in 1400, much of its ruins were excavated and continued to exhibit their ancient splendor until many of its famous monuments were deliberately destroyed by ISIL in 2015. Retaken by the Syrian army and with the help of Russian forces, the diminished remains of its ancient glory can be viewed again. Russia's top orchestra was sent to play a concert on the very site where ISIL executed its prisoners and where the ancient Roman amphitheater still stands.[6] We can ask of such moments if they are grandiloquent or sublime. Can the city of Palmyra, at such moments, still evoke the writer of a treatise that may never have gone there?

When Calderón de la Barca decided to turn to this city and its queen to write his 1625 play *La gran Cenobia*, he would not have been able to view any of the drawings mentioned above, nor could he have read contemporary travelers' descriptions of this faraway and enchanting site, nor were there any plays on the subject that preceded his.[7] He did have available, as mentioned, a number of short biographies, which were often part of catalogues of famous women. He also employed some historical accounts,[8] in particular the *Historia Augusta*, a collection of biographies of Roman Emperors from 117 to 284. Seemingly a compilation from six different authors, it was analyzed and edited by Isaac Casaubon in 1603. Critical neglect of Calderón's play is rather puzzling since he draws a strong and enticing portrait of the Warrior Queen as well as constructing an impactful figure of the hubristic Emperor Aurelius (Aureliano), her foe. Perhaps Menéndez Pelayo's early assessment of the play turned critics' attention away from it, since he labeled it "una de sus obras más absurdas..." [one of his most ridiculous works] (360). The dozen or so essays that have been written on *La gran Cenobia* foreground the dramatic complexity and dynamism of the work and deal with diverse topics.[9] At the same time, Melveena McKendrick, although praising the character of Cenobia, sees the work itself in a less favorable light: "Calderón's attitude to Cenobia is one of unequivocal admiration." But then she argues that, "The issues are too clear cut, the contrasts too extreme, the protagonist too blandly perfect" (200–201).[10] I would argue for the sublimity of the character rather than her perfection. After all, many conflictive passions overtake her and she has other flaws, as we shall see. I also believe that the play is carefully constructed, beginning with the rise of a new emperor (Aureliano) while holding back the appearance of Cenobia, who is first shown as Warrior Queen, triumphing over a Roman general. The contrasts between them may be at times pronounced, but they are striking and they rise out of the very passions of the characters.

The sublime, I would argue, is that which impels the action of *La gran Cenobia* and drives the queen to greatness. Let us remember that Cenobia's tutor and adviser at court was thought to be none other than the Longinus to whom the famous treatise *On the Sublime* was attributed.[11] Although today we know that this is not the case (we refer to its author as Pseudo-Longinus), Calderón and any contemporaries familiar with the story or anyone reading Boccaccio, Luna, and others would have believed this to be factual.[12] And yet, Pseudo-Longinus is never mentioned in Calderón's play. This absence may well be due to Calderón's appropriation of the book as an invisible model that Cenobia must follow, and as a text that could help in the creation of a work that seeks to utilize the sublime through language and passion in order to contrast Aureliano and Cenobia. The sublime in Pseudo-Longinus's usage may refer to a work, its style, and also to specific passages in a work. It has been described as a moment that "induces amazement, wonder or awe, in virtue of its ambition, scope or a passion that seems to drive it," having "the power to 'entrance' us, to 'transport us with wonder' as opposed to merely persuading or pleasing us" (Pateman 169).[13] More than technique, it is based on grand conceptions and nobility of thought ([Pseudo-]Longinus 9.2). And what grander conception could there be than that portraying a woman (considered in the past to be weaker than a man) as a Warrior Queen, as someone who could withstand the power of the Roman Empire and its male rulers?[14] If there is one word that is repeated as much as "sublime" in the treatise, it is "striking."

And there is no doubt that both Aureliano and Cenobia are striking but in many different ways.

The beginning of *La gran Cenobia* is certainly striking. Aureliano, a Roman general who is dressed in skins, has a dream where a bloodied emperor hands him the signs of power, a laurel crown and a scepter, telling him, "serás emperador de Roma" [you will be emperor of Rome] (Calderón de la Barca 311). Aureliano concludes that this is mere wish-fulfilment: "cuya voz en el viento desatada / sombra fue de mi dicha imaginada" [whose voice released by the wind was but a shadow of my imagined good fortune] (311). While Pseudo-Longinus argues against "outbursts of emotion which the subject no longer warrants" (3.5), here an audience can easily come to understand Aureliano's misfortune, his great ambition, and his dejection at having his desires vanish as part of a dream. And yet, he soon beholds the crown and scepter on the branch of a tree, taking them for himself. Even as he does, there is some doubt that lingers: "Pero ¿qué es lo que veo? / O los ojos me mienten o el deseo"] (Calderón de la Barca 312) [But what do I see? Either my eyes deceive me or desire does so]. Speaking of the importance of props on the stage, María Cristina Quintero emphasizes that "textual signifiers are translated into concrete objects upon the stage" and are experienced "in three dimensions" by the audience ("The Things They Carried" 83). And yet, the fact that Aureliano is dressed in skins and takes the objects for himself also points to his bestial side, to being unfit to govern others since he cannot control himself.[15] While Quintero is particularly interested in material objects that circulate upon the stage, Pseudo-Longinus points out that one of the techniques for reaching sublimity is visualization or *phantasia*, to "see what you describe and bring it vividly before the eyes of your audience" (15.1–2). Calderón does this in a triple movement, first through a dream, then through the actual objects that Aureliano beholds, and third in the way he grabs them. Holding the objects of power lead him to increment his passion and dispel his hesitation. Touching them, he believes in their reality rather than their deceitfulness.

As in *La vida es sueño* [Life Is a Dream], this play underlines over and over again the importance of earthly power as a dream. In this scene, power thus brings together two important aspects of the sublime: the ability to make passion credible and present, and the visualization of that passion. Eugenio Refini, in discussing Pseudo-Longinus's visualization explains: "Knowing that men are struck by strong feelings, Longinus confirms that image-production aims at the emotional involvement of the audience" (48). The way in which the objects are concretized from phantom-like origins is bound to arouse emotions in Calderón's audience. There is yet one more element that confirms the sublime. The priestess Astraea enters the scene leading Roman soldiers, claiming that she has been brought there by Apollo to confirm his role as emperor. The sublime for Pseudo-Longinus is what brings us closest to the gods, and here Astraea seems to be underlining that Aureliano's actions have been decreed by Apollo.

And yet, while the scene seems to point to the sublime through the authenticity of passion, through the coming together of gods and men, through power and visualization, Calderón subtly undermines the sublime as related to Aureliano. There is a key passage in Pseudo-Longinus's treatise that must be quoted at length:

> We must realize, dear friend, that as in our everyday life nothing is really great which it is a mark of greatness to despise. I mean, for instance, wealth, position, reputation, sovereignty, and all other things which possess a very good exterior, nor would a wise man think things supremely good, contempt for which is itself eminently good— certainly men feel less admiration for men who have these things than for those who could have them but are big enough to slight them. (7.1)

The speed with which Aureliano grabs for power, for position, and for sovereignty is a clear indication that his thought is not sublime and that his actions lack sublimity. More than sublime he may be seen as "bathetic" (7.3), his actions turning a potentially sublime moment into something puerile and almost trivial. Indeed, his fate may be that of Narcissus. In yet another moment of bathetic visualization, the new emperor looks at himself in a fountain and finds nothing but praise for his figure and motivation. Just as the mythological figure was "de su misma belleza enamorado" [enamored of his own beauty] (Calderón de la Barca 313), here Aureliano, drunk with power and glory, viewing his "sacred" silhouette, avows: "Narciso pienso ser en mi fiereza" [I will be Narcissus in my fierceness] (313). His boastfulness, his savagery, and his pride will be his triple tragic hamartia.[16]

As if to contrast with this moment of pride and elevation, the next scene portrays the arrival of the Roman general Decio (a figure invented by Calderón), who comes to report that he has lost a battle to Queen Cenobia. The description he makes of her lands, of her beauty, and of her power may cause wonderment in the reader or audience, but not in Aureliano, who now believes that failure is impossible, that his dream of power cannot be shattered. The images evoked by Decio are so striking that they are far from grandiloquent and may well partake of the sublime, as when he refers to the sunrise in the Orient as "diluvios de fuego" [floods of fire] (Calderón de la Barca 319); or as when he describes the city of Palmyra and its fertile fields emerging from the sands. The sublimity of speech is lost on Aureliano, who humbles Decio: "Arrójale a sus pies y pónele el pie encima" [Aureliano shoves Decio to the ground and places his foot on top of his body] (322). He even takes away Decio's sword and swears that his first task will be to defeat Cenobia. In Pseudo-Longinus's treatise, frigidity of speech is explained when a writer is "keenly critical of others' faults, he is blind to his own" (4.1). In a similar manner, Aureliano seems to find fault with Decio, and with Cenobia and her kingdom, but never seeks introspection.

The play carefully conceals Cenobia from us, although providing indications of her greatness in Decio's description. As Ignacio Arellano states: "Para Aureliano Roma está al servicio de sus pasiones. Para Cenobia la reina debe estar al servicio de su pueblo" [For Aureliano, Rome is there to serve his passions. For Cenobia, a Queen must serve her people] (10). Her beauty is such that it cannot be depicted, thus toying with the link between visualization and the sublime, while nodding to silence as the greater grandeur ([Pseudo-] Longinus 9.3).[17] All the benefic influence of the seven planets is reflected in the queen, who becomes a microcosm, a perfected being who is a mirror of the universe.[18] While Aureliano is deceived by the gods in the guise of the seer and priestess Astraea, Cenobia holds within herself the gifts of the planetary gods of old and is thus in tune with divine sublimity. Indeed, she is a Pallas in battle (Calderón de la Barca 322). And while Decio attempts to teach Aureliano about the reverses of fortune, the new emperor can only condemn Cenobia through the equation of weakness-woman-fortune (de Armas, *El retorno de Astrea*, 75).

Having presented Aureliano as a narcissistic, bathetic, savage, and flawed hero, whose ideals are far from representing the sublime, and having provided hints of Cenobia's sublimity, Calderón now shifts the scene to Palmyra. Here, Libio plots with Irene to murder the queen's husband Abdenato. He fears that if they do not accomplish this with celerity, the people will realize her worth and allow her to be queen even though she is a woman and this contravenes the customs of Palmyra. And yet, Cenobia seems not to understand fully the machinations of others. When a coward named Persio takes on the identity of the valiant Andronio, the queen rewards him even if the stories he tells seem ridiculous. Indeed, she fails to be a good judge of character. Daniel L. Heiple explains that: "the buffoon she trusts to protect her is a cowardly imposter, and Libio and Irene, her confidants, are murderers and traitors" (16).

Pseudo-Longinus, in the very first pages of his treatise, makes an important allusion: "Speaking of the common life of men Demosthenes declares that the greatest of all blessings is good fortune, and that next comes good judgment which is indeed quite as important, since the lack of it often completely cancels the advantage of the former" (2.3). Cenobia has the gift of fortune (Jupiter) but lacks judgment on how to pick her advisers and defenders. Although her flaw causes her much suffering, she strives to triumph since she not only has the gifts of Jupiter, but also is shown with two objects onstage, props very different from those of Aureliano. After her husband's murder she appears on stage "con armas negras, vestida de luto, leyendo un libro" [with embossed armor with raised designs (becoming black from the hammer),[19] dressed in mourning, reading a book] (Calderón de la Barca 343). Her mourning attire reflects that, with her husband dead, she now is alone as a woman who must fight the mightiest of empires. Book and sword (armor) are emblematic representations of *sapientia* (wisdom and cleverness) and *fortitudo* (valor), the two key virtues of the epic hero as portrayed in Ulysses and Achilles (Curtius 170–77; de Armas, "Homer," 97–115). Indeed, Pseudo-Longinus finds a vast number of examples of the sublime in the Homeric poems, particularly in the *Iliad,* from whence the opposition and confluence of qualities in *La gran Cenobia* arises.

The siege of Palmyra seems to be as difficult a task as the taking of Troy, thus acquiring Homeric overtones. Indeed, the siege has already been recorded in a book that Cenobia reads:

> Que, viendo a Decio vencido,
> vino al Oriente Aureliano
> con todo el poder romano
> de su poder ofendido;
> y que, habiéndola cercado
> enemiga, la asaltó
> tres veces, y tres volvió
> rompido y desbaratado,
> tanto que le fue forzoso
> retirarse ...
>   (Calderón de la Barca 344)

[Seeing that Decio had been vanquished, Aureliano came to the Orient with all of Rome's power, offended by her power. Having laid siege, he attacked the city three times, three times were he and his armies broken and wrecked to such an extent that he was forced to draw back.][20]

Pseudo-Longinus asserts: "Homer had done his best to make the men of the *Iliad* gods and the gods men" (9.7). Cenobia takes on the qualities of the Homeric hero, and shows that as a woman she may well embody many of the traits of heroes and gods. If "sublimity is the echo of a noble mind" (9.2), then Cenobia, with book in hand, evinces her sublime qualities as she is able to fight Aureliano and the Roman Army, even in the midst of treachery and deceit at her own court of Palmyra. But she is also seen as a new Amazon (Calderón de la Barca 319), and we know from Homer that the Amazon Penthesilea went to serve King Priam of Troy during the Trojan War. Achilles wounded her in the right breast, but was smitten by her great beauty. There may well be a hidden equation in the play between Decio and Cenobia and Achilles and Penthesilea. Decio is smitten by Cenobia's beauty, but his honor and the emperor's pledge to give him an equal place in the Roman Empire force him to fight against her. Decio places himself in front of a bridge, and in the manner of the chivalric romances, challenges the army of Palmyra. The deceitful Aureliano also promises his own crown to the traitorous Libio. While Decio cannot truly fight Cenobia, Libio can use treachery. The emperor thus wins through deceit: when Libio brings Cenobia to him, he gives Libio a crown but orders that he be thrown off a cliff.[21] We imagine that a similar promise made to Decio, one of co-rule, would have also been retracted.

The third act begins with the representation of Aureliano's triumph, as the emperor enters Rome. The stage directions are clear: "Suena la música y entran soldados delante, y detrás un carro triunfal, en el cual viene Aureliano, emperador, y a sus pies Cenobia, muy bizarra, atadas las manos y, tirando del carro, cautivos y detrás gente" (Calderón de la Barca 373) [Music is heard and soldiers enter first; and behind them is shown a triumphal carriage on which stands the Emperor Aureliano; and, at his feet, Cenobia, with elaborate attire, her hands tied; and pulling the cart, a number of captives; and behind, more people]. It is as if we are witnessing a tragic fall, the fall of Cenobia. Given the many prophecies, laments, and changes in fortune, a spectator could conclude that the play as tragedy should end here. Fausta Antonucci believes that in this work, Calderón is returning to sixteenth-century tragedy and mentions, among others, the following traits: "en los campos semánticos del horror, del miedo, del llanto, de la muerte, la sangre y la violencia; la concepción de la peripecia como mudanza de fortuna; una intriga relativamente sencilla" ("Calderón riscrittore" 150) [in the semantic field, there is horror, fright, weeping, death, blood and violence; the notion of the peripety is tied to a change in fortune; there is also a plot that is relatively simple]. Although I would underline that the first two acts may stand as tragic with the fall of Cenobia, Antonucci rightly sees a lesser form of tragedy in the play as a whole where, in the end, the arrogant and savage Aureliano, a character that seems to emerge from Senecan tragedy, meets his deserved end, while Cenobia is rescued from her tragic plight.

Together with the visual representation of Aureliano's triumph and Cenobia's fall, the play provides a description by Decio of Aureliano's triumphant entry into Rome, thus putting into words what is occurring onstage. Visualization is foregrounded to such an extent that it overcomes sight, the image previously presented. Decio's emotions, as he tells of the triumph, point to the sublime: "where, inspired by strong emotion, you seem to see what you describe and bring it vividly before the eyes" ([Pseudo-]Longinus 15.2). The triumphal car with Cenobia at the emperor's feet is described so vividly and with such emotion that it may recall the carriage led by Phaeton as described in Euripides, which Pseudo-Longinus uses as an example of the sublime (15.4). Calderón, signaling that the emperor's stance is "a imitación / hermosa de algún planeta" [in beautiful imitation of a planet] (372), may well be recalling Phaeton's attempt to maneuver the carriage of the Sun. The sublimity here cloaks the danger to come: Phaeton, like Aureliano, will fail and fall. Indeed, the emperor's speech pales before that of Cenobia. Her response arouses emotions in her Roman audience, and would most certainly have done so in an audience that viewed *La gran Cenobia*. They knew her worth and related her exalted words with her nobility: "Sublimity is the echo of a noble mind" ([Pseudo-]Longinus 9.2). Pointing to the dying of the sun every night, to the tempestuous sea that seeks to quell the stars, Cenobia reaches sublimity through a double method. First, because what she says is "apt to the situation" (40.3); and secondly "because it is always the unusual which wins our wonder" (35.5). Nothing that Aureliano says afterward comes close to Cenobia's sublime words.

Just as visions and phantasms began the work, as Aureliano sought to take a crown shown to him in his dreams, now, seated on the throne, the emperor again believes he sees phantoms and visions, this time of Libio and Astrea, people he thought he had killed and who appear in front of him with daggers, as many around him seek to avenge themselves or simply kill a tyrant, a cruel and arrogant ruler:

> Sombras ¿qué me perseguis?;
> fantasmas ¿qué me quereis?
> Libio, yo te di la muerte;
> Astrea, yo te maté.
>   (Calderón de la Barca 392)

[Why do you pursue me, shadows? What do you seek, ghosts? Libio, I killed you, and Astraea I killed you too.]

But in the end, it is Decio who murders Aureliano. The emperor dies at his feet, raging against the gods, thus underlining his lack of sublimity, his lack of connection with the divine. As the soldiers arrive, Decio confesses that he has killed the emperor to regain his honor. The soldiers, instead of arresting him, proclaim him Caesar. He then declares that Cenobia will be his queen, as Astrea appears in order to validate this moment and to recall to the spectator that she had predicted this moment, acting as beneficent messenger from the gods. It may well be that some of the elements of the play strain the audience's sense of reality. Although Menéndez Pelayo once railed against the play's absurdities, it is important to recall that "sublime literature looks for something higher than realistic imitation" (Refini 50). Calderón seeks to represent wonder through sublime and striking moments where the audience can visualize nearly impossible feats and stances, imperfect characters, and seemingly rare and vivified statues exhibiting wondrous objects that reflect their souls.[22]

Very much as in the beginning of the play, Cenobia, although invoked, is not present. She need not speak, she need not appear at this point since, as Pseudo-Longinus explains: "And so even without being spoken the bare idea often of itself wins admiration for its inherent grandeur" (9.2). The idea of Cenobia becoming a Warrior Queen and defying the Roman Empire is of itself sublime. From the farthest outposts of empire, from a land of beauty and wonder, this sublime figure must suffer and fall so that in the end she may rule, not in Palmyra, but in Rome, thus reuniting East and West in a sublime moment of concordance. Cenobia, following the notions of Longinus (a figure that although said to be the counselor of the queen is absent from the play), has been chained by her sublime words, has been imprisoned by the grandiloquent and arrogant Aureliano, only to triumph in the end. Her triumph is also that of Pseudo-Longinus, who always seeks the remarkable, the noble, the wondrous. And his triumph is that of Calderón, who wrote a striking and forceful play about a forgotten Warrior Queen.

Notes

1. Rina Walthaus reminds us that Calderón's was the only play on the subject of Cenobia in early modern Spanish theater ("La fortaleza de Cenobia" 109–28).

2. For an overview of Costa's research, see Mattioli, 139–55. On Robortello's edition, see also Refini, 35.

3. Petrarch includes Cenobia in his *Triumph of Fame*, along with women like Cleopatra and Semiramis. Alvaro de Luna takes most of his information from Boccaccio, but divides his work in three parts: Biblical, Classical, and Christian Women. She is said to be of high lineage, descending from the Ptolemies, rulers of Egypt (Luna 442; Boccaccio 429). She has shied away from men since she took pride in her virginity (Luna 443). Even when she marries she practices sexual continence. Her prowess in battle in soon evinced as she and her husband rescue emperor Valerianus from the Persians. But when her husband dies, she declares herself ruler of the Eastern Empire, and no Roman emperor dares to oppose her (449). The work ends with her praises and leaves out the last section of Boccaccio's biography, where she is indeed conquered by Emperor Aurelius. Vives's text, although following a similar line, is said to depart from Renaissance ideals of womanhood: "no se ajusta a los preceptos humanistas sobre la importancia del recogimiento y domesticidad femenina, en tanto que garantes del orden social: si por una parte Zenobia ejemplifica la virtud cardinal de la mujer—la castidad—por otra parte, esta aparece ligada al desempeño del poder político" (Peraita 21) [it does not follow humanistic precepts on the importance of female seclusion and domesticity as key to social order. If, on the one hand, Zenobia exemplifies chastity, the cardinal virtue in a woman, on the other hand, this virtue seems to be tied to the wielding of political power.]

4. It has been argued that Michelangelo was influenced by Longinus's sublime through a manuscript translated from the Greek by Fulvio Orsini: "the circulation of Longinus in the Farnesian entourage during the last years of the artist's life may have played an important role in the predilection for Buonarroti's art, as well as in the interpretation of his artistic experience in terms of sublimity" (Refini 36). Refini is here summarizing Gustavo Costa's argument (224–38). Was Michelangelo's portrait of Cenobia influenced by conceptions of the sublime?

5. Calderón also refers to Cenobia in *Darlo todo y no dar nada* (1636).

6. "Where the Islamic State (IS) spilled blood, Russia played Bach. As the chords of the Mariinsky Theatre orchestra filled the Roman amphitheatre of Palmyra, an ancient city that was an IS stronghold until March, the music's message was clear: there is civilization and there is barbarism; stand with Russia on the side of the good. The Russian government had sent one of the country's top orchestras from St Petersburg to the Syrian desert to deliver that message" (*The Economist*, 6 May 2016).

7. Two early modern works written after Calderón's play proved more successful:

Francois Hébelin, Abbé d'Aubignac's tragedy *Zenobie* (1647), written in order to learn how to use the classical unities (Bourque 71–77); and *Zenobia Regina de Palmireni*, an opera staged in Venice in 1694 with a libretto by Antonio Marchi and music by Tomasso Albinoni. They may hide Calderón since the Spanish work may have been rendered invisible through sublimity.

8. Ignacio Arellano asserts that he also used "la *Historia Nova* de Zósimo, historiador griego del siglo V, que utiliza obras anteriores de Pollione y Vopisco" (2) [the *Historia Nova* by Zosimus, a Greek historian of the fifth century, that utilizes previous works by Pollione and Vopisco]. His *Historia Nova* was written in Constantinople, in six books. For a complete list of ancient sources for the Cenobia story, see Stoneman.

9. These topics include: the role of Fortuna (Arellano; de Armas, *El retorno de Astrea*; de Armas, *The Return of Astraea*; Gómez; Valbuena Briones; Walthaus, "La fortaleza de Cenobia"; Walthaus, "'Representar tragedias así la Fortuna sabe'"); the question of tyranny (Hollman); the work as mirror of princes to instruct Philip IV (Walthaus, "'Representar tragedias así la Fortuna sabe'"); the dual performance of power, contrasting "wise and disastrous models of monarchy" (Quintero, *Gendering the Crown*, 54); the visionary and ghostly quality of the work (Arellano); the uses of classical mythology and particularly of Astraea (de Armas, *The Return of Astraea*); tragic elements (Antonucci, "Calderón riscrittore"; Antonucci, "Algunas calas"); and the importance of material culture (Quintero, "The Things They Carried").

10. María Cristina Quintero echoes this assessment but partially disagrees: "What makes the play particularly appealing to modern sensibilities is that, in the almost Manichean opposition between enlightened and disastrous models of authority, the positive exemplar is a woman" ("The Things They Carried" 83).

11. She learned the Egyptian and Greek languages from Longinus: "Zenobia's knowledge of these languages enabled her to read voraciously and commit to memory all the Latin, Greek and barbarian histories. Moreover, she is believed to have composed epitomes of these works" (Boccaccio 435).

12. "[W]e do know from his book that he lived in the first century, in the depaganized Roman Empire ... and at a distance of centuries from the Homeric world, where, as he nostalgically recounts, there had still been intercourse between gods and men" (Deguy 6).

13. "For the effect of genius is not to persuade the audience but rather to transport them out of themselves. Invariably what leads to wonder, with its power of amazing us, always prevails over what is merely convincing and pleasing" ([Pseudo-]Longinus 1.4).

14. Cenobia is very much like the women warriors admired by Bárbara Mujica. See, for example, her essay on Angeles Mastretta, where she quotes the Mexican author as saying: "I can tell you that there's no way that during the forties and fifties Mexican women had as much freedom as during the twenties. Because when a war is going on, people don't care who you make love with, if you get married or you don't, if you're living with someone with or without papers. Those things become absolutely secondary" ("Angeles Mastretta" n.p.). See also her review of Kristen Downey's *Isabella the Warrior Queen*. Here, Mujica is as laudatory as Downey regarding Isabella's achievements. Dis-

cussing the war against Granada, Mujica argues: "In the 10-year conflict that followed, Isabella and Ferdinand worked as a team. Ferdinand led the troops in battle, while Isabella secured supplies and managed camp hospitals.

15. "His attire is an early indication that he will embody an uncivilized and dangerous force" (Quintero, "The Things They Carried," 83); "he is closer to the passionate beast than to a rational being" (de Armas, *The Return of Astraea*, 73).

16. Ignacio Arellano uses this scene to point to Aureliano's inability to read signs. Although fountains and mirrors may point to either vanity or self-knowledge, Aureliano shows "ignoracia de si mismo" [lack of knowledge of his self] (6).

17. "And so even without being spoken the bare idea often of itself wins admiration for its inherent grandeur. How grand, for instance, is the silence of Ajax in the Summoning of the Ghosts" ([Pseudo-]Longinus 9.2–3). Let us recall that in the Odyssey, Ajax in Hades will not speak to Odysseus since he is still angry that he was awarded Achilles's armor.

18. For example, Mercury gives her wit, Jupiter gifts her with luck or good fortune, Mars endows her with Valor and Venus with beauty (Calderón de la Barca 319).

19. For this interpretation of "armas negras," see Frieder 213.

20. As Quintero points out, there seems to be a second book, the *Historia Oriental*, which she is writing. Indeed, when she writes the name "Libio" it somehow becomes written in blood: "The paper covered with blood is evidence of the crime that Libio has already committed—he has murdered Cenobia's husband Abdenato.... It is also a premonition of future crimes—the blood that will be shed when Aureliano attacks Palmyra after Libio betrays the queen" (*Gendering the Crown* 90).

21. Aureliano is actually following an ancient tradition here, which counsels the ruler to use a traitor for gain, but then punish him. A similar situation occurs with the rebel soldier in *La vida es sueño*. The classical model is found in Plutarch's *Life of Romulus* (Heiple 3).

22. "Sublimity does not necessarily coincide with perfection ... while statues are expected to have human form (that is, more generally to reproduce reality), sublime literature looks for something higher than realistic imitation" (Refini 50).

References

Antonucci, Fausta. "Algunas calas en el tratamiento del modelo trágico por el jóven Calderón." *Mélanges de la Casa Velázquez* 42 (2012), no. 1: 145–62.

———. "Calderón riscrittore: il caso de La vida es sueño." In *Teatri del Mediterraneo. Riscritture e ricodificazioni tra '500 e '600*, edited by Valentina Nider, Università degli Studi di Trento, 2004, 45–57.

Arellano, Ignacio. "Glosas a La gran Cenobia de Calderón." *Acotaciones: Revista de investigación teatral* 18 (2007): 9–32.

Boccaccio, Giovanni. "Zenobia Queen of Palmyra." In *Famous Women*, translated by Virginia Brown, Harvard University Press, 2001, 427–37.

Bourque, Bernard J. *All the Abbé's Women: Power and Misogyny in Seventeenth-Century France*. Tübingen: Narr Francke Attempto Verlag, 2015.
Calderón de la Barca, Pedro. *Comedias, I: primera parte de comedias*. Edited by Luis Iglesias Feijoo, Madrid: Fundación José Antonio de Castro, 2006.
Costa, Gustavo. "The Latin Translations of Longinus' *Peri Ypsous* in Renaissance Italy." In *Acta Conventus Neo-Latini Bononiensis. Proceedings of the Fourth International Congress of Neo-Latin Studies, Bologna, 26 August to 1 September 1979*, edited by R. J. Schoeck, Binghamton, NY: Center for Medieval and Early Renaissance Studies, 1985, 224–38.
Curtius, Ernst Robert. *European Literature and the Latin Middle Ages*. Translated by Willard R. Trask. Harper & Row, 1973.
De Armas, Frederick A. "Homer: An Epic Contest." In *Cervantes, Raphael and the Classics*, edited by Frederick A. de Armas, Cambridge University Press, 1998, 97–115.
———. *El retorno de Astrea: astrología, mito e imperio en Calderón*. Iberoamericana/Vervuert, 2016.
———. *The Return of Astraea: An Astral-Imperial Myth in Calderón*. University of Kentucky Press, 1986.
Deguy, Michel. "The Discourse of Exaltation: Contributions to a Re-reading of Pseudo-Longinus." In *On the Sublime: Presence in Question*, translated by Jeffrey S. Librett, State University of New York Press, 1993, 5–24.
Economist. "A Russian Orchestra plays Bach and Prokofiev in the Ruins of Palmyra," 6 May 2016, www.economist.com/news/europe/21698422-russian-government-sent-one-countrys-top-orchestras-syrian-desert.
Frieder, Braden. *Chivalry and the Perfect Prince: Tournaments, Art and Armor in the Spanish Habsburg Court*. Truman State University Press, 2008.
Gómez, Juan Manuel. "Fortune and Responsibility in Calderón's *La gran Cenobia*." *Hispania* 94 (2011), no. 1: 63–73.
Heiple, Daniel L. "The Tradition behind the Punishment of the Rebel Soldier in *La vida es sueño*." *Bulletin of Hispanic Studies* 50 (1973): 1–17.
Hollman, Hildegard. "El retrato del tirano Aurelio en *La gran Cenobia*." In *Hacia Calderón: Cuarto Coloquio Anglogermano*. Edited by Hans Flasche, Karl-Hermann Körner, and Hans Mattauch, Walter de Gruyter, 1979.
Luna, Alvaro de. *Libro de las virtuosas e claras mugeres*. Edited by Julio Vélez-Sainz, Madrid: Cátedra, 2009.
McKendrick, Melveena. *Women and Society in the Spanish Golden Age*. Cambridge University Press, 1981.
Mattioli, Emilio. "Gli studi di Gustavo Costa su Sublime in Italia." *Studi e problemi di critica testuale* 36 (1988): 139–55.
Menéndez Pelayo, Marcelino. *Calderón y su teatro*. Madrid: Revista de Archivos, 1910.
Mujica, Bárbara. "Angeles Mastretta: Women of Will in Love and War." *Americas* 49 (1997), no 4.
———. "Review of Kirstin Downey's *Isabella the Warrior Queen*." *Washington Indepen-*

dent, 23 January 2015. *Review of Books*, www.washingtonindependentreviewofbooks.com/bookreview/isabella-the-warrior-queen.

Pateman, Trevor. *Key Concepts: A Guide to Aesthetics, Criticism and the Arts in Education.* Routledge, 2016.

Peraita, Carmen. "¿Zenobia humanista o Zenobia domesticada? Los ejemplos de las claras mujeres en el *De institutione foeminae christianae* de Juan Luis Vives (1524)." *Bulletin Hispanique* 101 (1999): 19–39.

[Pseudo-]Longinus. *On the Sublime.* Translated by H. L. Havell. MacMillan, 1890.

Quintero, María Cristina. *Gendering the Crown in the Spanish Baroque Comedia.* Routledge, 2012.

———. "The Things They Carried: Sovereign Objects in Calderón de la Barca's *La gran Cenobia*." In *Objects of Culture in the Literature of Imperial Spain*, edited by Mary E. Barnard and Frederick A. de Armas, University of Toronto Press, 2013, 80–98.

Refini, Eugenio. "Longinus and Poetic Imagination in Late Renaissance Literary Theory." In *Translations of the Sublime: The Early Modern Reception and Dissemination of Longinus Peri Hupsous in Rhetoric, the Visual Arts, Architecture and Theater*, edited by Caroline van Eck, Stijn Bussels, Maarten Delbeke, and Jurgern Pieters, Brill, 2012, 33–54.

Southern, Pat. *Empress Zenobia: Palmyra's Rebel Queen.* Continuum, 2008.

Stoneman, Richard. *Palmyra and Its Empire: Zenobia's Revolt Against Rome.* University of Michigan Press, 1992.

Valbuena Briones, Ángel. "El tema de la fortuna en *La gran Cenobia*." *Quaderni Ibero Americani* 45–46 (1975): 217–23.

Van Eck, Caroline Stijn Bussels, Maarten Delbeke, and Jurgern Pieters. Introduction to *Translations of the Sublime: The Early Modern Reception and Dissemination of Longinus Peri Hupsous in Rhetoric, the Visual Arts, Architecture and Theater*, edited by Caroline van Eck, Stijn Bussels, Maarten Delbeke and Jurgern Pieters, Brill, 2012, 1–10.

Walthaus, Rina. "La fortaleza de Cenobia y la mutabilidad de Fortuna: dos emblemas femeninos en *La gran Cenobia* de Calderón." In *Que toda la vida es sueño y los sueños, sueños son: Homenaje a don Pedro Calderón de la Barca*, edited by Ysla Campbell, Ciudad Juárez: Universidad Autónoma de Ciudad Juárez, 2000, 109–28.

———. "'Representar tragedias así la Fortuna sabe': La representación de Fortuna en dos comedias tempranas de Calderón (*Saber del mal y del bien y La gran Cenobia*)." In *Calderón 2000. Actas del Congreso Internacional IV Centenario del nacimiento de Calderón*, edited by Ignacio Arellano, Kassel, Germany: Reichenberger, 2002, 397–409.

Weinberg, Bernard. "Translations and Commentaries of Longinus *On the Sublime* to 1600: A Bibliography." *Modern Philology* 47 (1950): 141–51.

EMILIE L. BERGMANN

Folklore as Queer
Vélez de Guevara's *La serrana de la Vera*

AMONG THE WORKS of the highly prolific Luis Vélez de Guevara (1579–1644), *La serrana de la Vera* [The Mountain Girl of la Vera] has accrued significant scholarly attention since around 1990, becoming one of his best-known dramatic works. The protagonist's violent deeds and the staging of her equally violent execution present a rare exception to the marriage plot, in which even the most defiant *mujer varonil* (masculine woman, a stock character in seventeenth–century Spanish theater) conforms to her gender role by the third act. Vélez's *serrana* disrupts binary categories of gender identity and sexuality from the first scene, and by Act 3, she has murdered two thousand men. Contrary to the ending of a conventional *comedia* marriage plot, Vélez's *La serrana de la Vera* ends with the spectacle of execution by garroting and a volley of arrows, ordered by the Santa Hermandad [Holy Brotherhood] with the approval of the Catholic monarchs and the entire community of Garganta la Olla, including the protagonist's father. The display of Gila the *serrana's* mutilated body on stage creates effects of horror and pity and lends a dimension of public expiation to the violence of the play.

The potential for theatrical excess is obvious throughout, and the actor who plays the part of Gila has the rare opportunity to exhibit her strength and agility on stage. The autograph manuscript of Vélez's play specifies that he wrote the part of Gila for the actor Jusepa Vaca to display her beauty and prowess as a swashbuckling *bandolera* [female bandit] (Vélez de Guevara, *La Serrana de la Vera* [2002], 79, 187). The playwright's classification of his work as a tragedy signals the intensity of emotion that he anticipated on the part of the audience (Parr and Albuixech 27–30; Vélez de Guevara, *La Serrana de la Vera* [1982], 22–25). Adrienne L. Martín speculates on the calculated effect of the final scene in which the *serrana*'s mutilated body is displayed: "Whether the protagonist was interpreted as a cruelly and unjustly martyred victim or as a deservedly punished assassin, the mix of violence and eroticism must have been a tremendous draw" (167).

While most scholarly approaches to the play analyze the relationship between the play's violence and the protagonist's non–normative gender and sexuality, attention to spectacle is essential to an understanding of the play's popularity and the representation of non–normative gender. Alert to the dramatic potential of the execution scene, Bárbara Mujica faults Radio Televisión Española's film version of the play as disappointingly "bland" and "sanitized" (233). Not only is the execution narrated by a town crier, but it is also out of sequence: it is displaced from the climactic end of the action to function as a prologue, thereby defusing the suspense. The conflicting emotional effects are essential to the audience's experience of Vélez's play as tragedy, distinguishing it from the conventions of Spanish *comedias* in which violence is a transient threat, dispelled by the resolution of conflict through marriage.

Lope de Vega, in his *Arte nuevo de hacer comedias en este reino* [New Theatrical Art], remarks upon the popularity of these characters: "suele / el disfraz varonil agradar mucho" [masculine disguise is a crowd–pleaser], but in the following lines, he stipulates, "si mudaren traje, sea de modo / que pueda perdonarse" [cross–dressing must have a plausible justification] (Vega Carpio, lines 283–84). The ideal pretext for "pardoning" female cross–dressing is its instrumentality in resolving plot complications that obstruct the female protagonist's marriage. Gila, the protagonist of Vélez's *La serrana de la Vera*, does not dress as a man, and her marriage does not end the play; instead, the promise of marriage, followed by Gila's deception and dishonor, is the catalyst for the violent outcome.

Lope's version of *La serrana de la Vera* (1595–1598) and his *Las dos bandoleras y fundación de la Santa Hermandad de Toledo* [The two female bandits and foundation of the Holy Brotherhood of Toledo] (1597–1603) established the characteristics of the subgenre of *bandolera* plays, in which women turn to violent crime against men to avenge their dishonor. With the exception of Vélez de Guevara's protagonist, Gila, the *bandoleras* of the *comedia* suspend their violence in moments of compassion, and are reintegrated into their communities when they exhibit "complete repentance and surrender to the divine will" (McKendrick 112). Although other *bandoleras* "delight in enumerating their victims," who number, at most, in the dozens, their statistics pale beside Gila's extreme violence—she murders two thousand men—and her spectacular punishment (113, 115).

That Gila does not cross–dress is not exceptional among theatrical *mujeres varoniles*. Francisco Ortiz observed in his *Apología en defensa de las comedias que se representan en España* [Defense of plays performed in Spain] (1614) that male disguise was not always necessary; the boldness of these characters' words and gestures was sufficient to quicken the pulse of male viewers: "Pues ha de ser más que de hielo el hombre que no se abrase de lujuria viendo una mujer desenfadada y desenvuelta, y algunas veces, para este efecto, vestida como hombre" [A man would have to be made of ice not to be inflamed with lust upon seeing a woman moving freely and, at times, dressed as a man] (cited in Velasco 209–10). Melveena McKendrick's study of the "mujer varonil" focuses on dozens of plays whose female protagonists defy the constraints of gender in their behavior and speech. Whether or not they avail themselves of the liberating disguise of masculine attire, these characters' agency is circumscribed, as the challenge to the patriarchal gender hierarchy is effectively disarmed by heterosexual love in the third act. Matthew Stroud however, proposes that the "fears of sexual fluidity, of transgression, of perversion, of women usurping the power of men, of the traps of sexual expectation, of desire out of control" that are resolved through the marriage plot, are "intentional misdirection," arguing for "the ability of art to send multiple, contradictory messages that will simultaneously uphold and subvert the symbolic, heterosexual culture" (83–84). Catherine Connor posits that early modern audiences perceived the marriages that end most *comedia* plots in terms of a "range of possible meanings" not exclusively subversive or hegemonic (27). Gila is represented as having feminine beauty, hypermasculinity, and autonomy. She is also depicted as a dutiful daughter, and, finally, as dishonored, sexually seductive, and murderous. The "range of possible meanings" in Vélez's play involves complex perceptions of gender and sexuality.

Gila's strength and autonomy exemplify McKendrick's distinction between the *mujer vestida de hombre* and the *mujer varonil* (x–xi). There can be no doubt, however, that Gila is an exception to both categories. Although her masculine pursuits—hunting and plowing the fields—benefit her aging father, they are inadequate justification for her hypermasculinity. They fall short of Lope's requirement for cross–dressing: "de modo / que pueda perdonarse." Her homicidal vengeance for her dishonor is so excessive that pardon is out of the question. *Comedia* scholars have made numerous attempts to categorize the *serrana's* gender and sexuality. Ruth Lundelius highlighted Gila's self–identity as male by observing that in the late twentieth century she would be "recognized as a transsexual" (222); while Mujica calls her a "hermaphroditic character," and "butch rather than just *varonil*" (226, 230). J. A. Drinkwater diagnoses her as a "classic hysteric" (80). These scholars, and others, have attempted to explain the extraordinarily violent outcome of Vélez's play, and its relationship to the character of Gila, from the perspectives of the literary conventions of the *comedia*, gender and psychoanalytic theory, and the patriarchal ideology of the Baroque. Although their studies draw attention to the importance of the play in depicting gender transgression, I propose to address the play's uniqueness through its appropriation of local ballads and folktales of the "Serrana de la Vera" from the mountainous terrain of the Extremaduran province of Cáceres.[1] In their early twentieth–century edition of the play, Ramón Menéndez Pidal and María Goyri studied twenty-one versions of the *romance* (134) and found that Vélez's play followed them more closely than Lope's (136–43). McKendrick suggests that "[i]t is quite conceivable that, wanting to write a play after the manner of Lope, [Vélez] referred back to the original ballad in order to refresh his memory" (278); of greater interest to McKendrick than the play's sources, however, is how the play generates "an atmosphere of savagery and violence of its own" (115).

The *serrana's* strength, in legends and in Vélez's play, is superhuman. Vélez adds details to the legend: his character, Gila, can stop a team of oxen or a mill wheel, and she can out-fight any man in her home town of Garganta la Olla or in neighboring, rival towns. In the first scene of the play, before Gila has appeared on stage, her father wields the reputation of her strength and courage to deflect the military captain, Don Lucas, who is determined to lodge his troops in the elderly peasant's house. Giraldo's boasting that his daughter is worth two sons becomes reality upon Gila's triumphal return from a hunt, surrounded by an entourage of cheering townspeople and companions bearing the severed heads and pelts of the ferocious predatory animals she has just killed: a wolf, a bear, and a wild boar. In lines 205–44, the villagers of Garganta la Olla celebrate her uniqueness, cheering her on with the refrain, "¡Quién como ella, / la Serrana de la Vera!" [There's none like her], and a lengthy paean that concludes with the community's wish for her wellbeing and for a young man for her to marry (Vélez de Guevara, *La Serrana de la Vera* [2002], lines 87–88).[2]

Vélez's stage directions specify Gila's entrance on horseback, with hair loosened around her shoulders, "vestida a lo serrano de mujer, con sayuelo y muchas patenas" [dressed as a woman of the mountains, with the medallions typical of costumes worn by peasant women for festive occasions] (86). With her peasant woman's hunting dress, plumed hat, and rifle, she embodies feminine beauty and masculine strength simultaneously. The effect of the impaled heads of ferocious animals is to clothe her in a particularly bloodthirsty version of peasant masculinity. Gila explicitly claims a male gender identity: upon meeting Gila, Don Lucas, the captain who will leave her dishonored in Act 2, declares that he has never seen such a woman. She replies in lines 350–52,

> Si imagináis
> que lo soy, os engañáis,
> que soy muy hombre.
>   (Vélez de Guevara 91)
>
> [If you imagine that I'm a woman, you're mistaken, for I'm very much a man.]

Later, in line 773, when she takes up the sword, inappropriate for a woman as well as a peasant, she refers to her female attire as her only feminine attribute: "Mujer soy sólo en la saya" [My skirts are my only womanly attribute] (105).

At a fair in Plasencia in Act 1, Gila disrupts ritualized male bonding in tests of strength, and puts to shame a group of men from Chinchón, notorious for their toughness. She defies her father's threat to break his staff over her head, rendering him symbolically impotent, and goes on to reiterate her description of her skill in hunting, as well as her ability to break men's bones, reduce swords to splinters, and wrestle a bull to the ground with her bare hands (lines 806–56). Not only does she claim the right to call herself a man; she defines manhood itself. In lines 823 and 834, she accuses other men of being not just "gallinas" [hens] but "gallinas mojadas" [wet hens] and inflicts humiliating "coscorrones" [blows to the head] (107–8). As if this display were not daring enough, she expresses same-sex desire. Her object is no mere peasant woman who might be courted by one of the men she defeats in tests of strength; it is the most powerful woman in the realm, Queen Isabel. The marriage plots of other *comedias* involving the *mujer varonil* also offer the spectacle of female characters not only claiming masculine autonomy but also attracting the sexual desires of other female characters. However, those plots end with a return to gender normativity and the homosocial exchange of women in the marriage of the protagonist.

Before meeting the Queen, Gila declares her preference for powerful women (lines 633–44):

después de dezir que es bella,
dizen que es brava muger,
que al lado de su marido,
que le guarde Dios mil años,
le ven hazer hechos estraños
. . . .
Madalena, en viendo yo
mugeres desta manera,
me vuelvo de gusto loca.
   (lines 633–440; Vélez de Guevara 100)

[After praising her beauty, they say she is a fierce woman; that, accompanied by her husband, may God keep him a thousand years, she is seen to achieve amazing feats. . . . Madalena, when I see women like her, I go mad with pleasure.]

Upon meeting Isabel, she goes further to declare, "Que de vos, alta señora, / a muchos días que estoy / enamorada" [Your highness, for many days I have been enamoured of you] (lines 871–73), and in the same long monologue (lines 847–99),

si hombre fuera,
por vos sola, me perdiera,
y aún así lo estoy, ¡por Dios!
   (lines 888–90; Vélez de Guevara 109)

[If I were a man, I'd lose myself for you alone and I have, by God!]

After Gila throws a bull to the ground, Isabel remarks, "Loca aquella labradora" (line 923) [That farm girl is crazy], and later, "Enamora / verla tan valiente y bella" (lines 937–38) (Vélez de Guevara 111) [It makes one fall in love with her to see her so brave and beautiful]. In light of common twentieth-century usage, it is possible to speculate that the repeated use of the term "loca" to describe Gila may encode a reference to homosexuality. More to the point, Stroud interprets as "code for lesbianism or transsexualism" the *gracioso* Mingo's reference to rumors of "faltas secretas" [secret faults] (Act 2, 1170) (Vélez de Guevara 118) in reporting gossip circulating among men whom Gila has rejected.

Stroud points out that the denial that same-sex desire could have been imagined by playwrights or audiences shaped twentieth-century approaches to the *comedia*, including studies by gay scholars (19). Nearly half a century earlier, however, Ashcom had asserted that "[t]he Lesbian motif is implicit in most of the plots involving masculine women" (59). In response to Ashcom, McKendrick contends that "the so-called lesbian motif . . . simply did not occur," even to "over-vigilant moralists" much less to playwrights or audiences (319). Reconfirming Ashcom's view with historical and theoretical arguments, Gail Bradbury, Dámaris Otero-Torres, Stroud, and François Delpech ("La 'doncella guerrera'") have produced convincing arguments that Gila's adulation of Queen Isabel is homoerotic and would have been perceived as such by Vélez's audience. Lundelius notes the implicit lesbian desire in Gila's "amorous assertions" and "erotic feeling" expressed directly to Queen Isabel, commenting on the audience's fascination with the "aura of unconventional sexuality" and "erotic ambiguities" surrounding the character of the *mujer varonil* in general. She states that "the suspicion of deviant sexuality was one ploy Vélez counted on to attract and hold his audience" (230–33).

Stroud cites historical research that reveals "a wealth of information about same-sex relationships and the official reaction to them" (17–19). Studies by Israel Burshatin, Rafael Carrasco, José Cartagena-Calderón, Mary Elizabeth Perry, and Sherry Velasco, as well as the essays in collections edited by Josiah Blackmore and Gregory Hutcheson and by Alain Saint-Saens and María José Delgado, have added to the irrefutable evidence that *comedia* audiences were well aware of the everyday realities of boundary-crossing and the blurring of gender identities and sexual desire. I would suggest that, as current concepts of gender identities and sexualities acknowledge the inadequacy of binary categories and incorporate a diverse spectrum of desires, we may read medieval and early modern literature more accurately and better approximate the perspective of early modern *comedia* audiences. The historical documentation of the cases of Catalina de Erauso, known as the "Monja Alférez" (Lieutenant Nun) and Elena/Eleno de Céspedes reveal more than rebellion by women against the roles imposed on them; they also reveal an instability of gender roles that literary critics have traditionally dismissed as inconceivable.

The *serrana* who embodies gender hybridity is a familiar figure from medieval and early modern lyric. Louise Vásvari calls the burly, excessively hairy *serranas* in stanzas 950–1042 of Juan Ruiz's *Libro de buen amor* "predatory virilized wild mountain girls" who sexually humiliate the Arcipreste "with the aid of their powerful prosthetic penile attributes" (131). Although the narrator in the *Libro de buen amor* claims to have been terrified, the scenes of female sexual aggression are comic (145). Vélez, in contrast, creates a seductively feminine protagonist who uses her beauty, rather than her physical force, to lure her victims. Gila turns the comic threat and sexual aggression of earlier *serranas* into tragedy.

In the theatrical context of the *mujer varonil*, Gila's exceptional status is rooted in another folkloric tradition, the ballads and legends of the "Serrana de la Vera" from the mountainous area surrounding the town of Garganta la Olla near Plasencia. Vélez borrowed the general outline of the plot and the ballads' description of the protagonist as beautiful seductress and homicidal monster in lines 2202–5 of the play (Vélez de Guevara 149), which are also the first four lines of the ballad:

Allá en Garganta la Olla
en la Vera de Plasencia,
salteóme una serrana
blanca, rubia, ojimorena;
trae recogidos los rizos
debajo de la montera;
al uso de cazadora
gasta falda a media pierna,
botín alto y argentado
y en el hombro una ballesta.
    (Menéndez Pidal 298)

[There in Garganta la Olla in the area of Plasencia a serrana assaulted me: fair–skinned, blonde, with dark eyes; she hides her curls under her hunting cap, wears a short skirt, high boots with silver ornaments, and on her shoulder a crossbow.]

In Menéndez Pidal and María Goyri's notes to their edition of the play, their first collaborative edition of a *comedia* for the Centro de Estudios Históricos, they mention twenty-one versions of the *romance*, from the seventeenth century to the twentieth (134). Since then, Julio Caro Baroja, Jesús Antonio Cid, and other folklorists have collected numerous variants. The *serrana* of the ballads and legends combines exceptional beauty, seductiveness, and sexual appetite with superhuman strength and pitiless cruelty toward all men, fueled by a desire for revenge against the man who dishonored her.

The first printed version of the *romance* was published by Azedo de la Berrueza in 1667, decades after Lope de Vega's *La serrana de la Vera* (1595–

1598) and Vélez's play. Delpech ("La leyenda de la serrana de la Vera") posits that the published version may have been influenced by Lope's and Vélez's dramatizations. In it, he finds that the *serrana*'s "biography" includes the key episodes of the young woman's conflicts with her parents regarding her marriage, and the defiance that leads her to the mountains; in addition, it offers a psychological explanation for her actions (26). It includes the motifs of the *serrana*'s feminine allure and athleticism, in particular the shortened skirt that allowed freedom of movement, her attempted seduction of a young man, and his narrow escape.

In most versions of the ballad, the *serrana* offers a sexually suggestive supper of "perdices y conejos" [partridges and hares], which does nothing to calm her would-be victim's apprehension at seeing crosses or skulls on the way to her *choza* or cave:

—¿Cuyos son aquestos huesos?
¿Cuyas estas calaveras?
—Hombres son que he matado
por que no me descubieran.

["Whose bones are those? Whose skulls?" "Men I have killed so they wouldn't give away my hiding place."]

As he escapes, she pursues him, "bramando como una fiera" [bellowing like a wild animal] (Menéndez Pidal 299–300). Her visitor, identified as a "pastor" or "leñador" [shepherd or woodcutter] in some versions, manages to escape by outwitting her, leaving the door ajar and waiting until she falls asleep. In Menéndez Pidal's version, she asks her visitor to play a "rabelillo" (a small stringed instrument, played with a bow), while she strums a "vihuela"; in the 1667 version, and others, she falls asleep like a stereotypical male post-coitus, "[c]ansada de sus deleites" [Exhausted from her pleasures] (Caro Baroja 271–72). As her intended victim escapes through the forest, she uses a sling to hurl a stone at him, knocking off his hunting cap; he wisely abandons a symbol of his masculinity in order to save his life. Some versions include the *serrana*'s request that her visitor take a message to her father (Caro Baroja 272); the version published in *Flor nueva* ends with her fear of being discovered, and the traveler's equivocation:

—¡Ay de mí, triste cuitada,
por ti seré descubierta!

—Descubierta no serás ...
hasta la venta primera.
   (Menendez Pidal 300)

["Alas, you'll betray me!" "You won't be betrayed until I arrive at the first inn."]

Although it does not include the episodes of the *serrana*'s arrest and execution, the ending of this variant signals the destruction of the menacing female figure.

Despite the impossibly hyperbolic qualities of the *serrana*, generations of inhabitants of the region have given her the name Isabel Carvajal, daughter of a distinguished local family, and designated a house in Garganta la Olla as her birthplace, while specific topographic features are associated with her legend. Caro Baroja's fieldwork in 1973 located the mountains, streams, caves, and passes in the wilderness surrounding Garganta la Olla, features of the landscape that older residents still referred to as inhabited by the Serrana, for example, the eponymous cavern known as the "Cueva de la Serrana." The anthropologist posits a "reverse Euhemerism" that transformed myth into history. He refers to Gila's folkloric counterpart as a mythical "númen folklórico" [folkloric spirit], "una especie de Polifemo hembra" [a kind of female Polyphemus] (280). The phantasmatic presence of this legendary character has become a tourist attraction in recent years, with an annual reenactment of scenes from Vélez's play; its longevity may be attributed to its embodiment of the perils and the fascination of transgressing the gender binary.

Although the oral tradition of the "Serrana de la Vera" is characterized by its topographic specificity in the Sierra de Tormantos, Pedro Manuel Piñero and Virtudes Atero collected Andalusian variants of the *romance* in Tarifa and Algeciras, versions in which the intended victim finds the *serrana* in a pine tree, combing her abundant tresses. He informs the authorities in the nearest town, and upon returning shoots her in the face with a musket—or shoots first, and reports the incident afterward. A unique feature of these variants is the narrator's discovery of the *serrana*'s monstrous physiology:

De la cintura pa arriba
de persona humana era,
de la cintura pa abajo,
era estatura de yegua.
   (Piñero and Atero 403)

[From the waist up she was a human being, but from the waist down, a mare.]

These ballads may derive from legends in which the *serrana* is only partially human, a monster born of a shepherd and a mare (Caro Baroja 281, 285). The Andalusian variants provide a maternal genealogical explanation for the *serrana*'s superhuman strength and unruliness. Her human-equine hybridity is emblematic of her indeterminate sexual identity: neither male nor female, but both, she represents such a threat to the social order that there is no question of a return to the community through a change in behavior or clothing. Because her challenge to gender roles is not a temporary disguise that can be discarded, the *serrana*, unlike the other *bandoleras* of the *comedia*, cannot be reintegrated into the social order.

Having introduced the *romance* in lines 2202–5, Vélez continues the episode of the *serrana*'s ambush of a peasant who wandered too close to her rustic abode, sung by a group of peasants, in Act 3, lines 2656–69: "Salteóme la serrana / juntico al pie de la cabaña..." (Vélez de Guevara 165) [The *serrana* assaulted me right next to her cabin]. A few lines after the peasants sing the *romance*, Gila interrogates Pascuala, a peasant girl who informs her that she has displaced the real and imaginary threats that instill fear in the peasant community: the bogeymen who inhabit children's nightmares as well as predatory animals and storms that can destroy the peasants' livestock and crops. Among the meanings of the terms Pascuala uses are specific references to gender and sexuality in lines 2697–2709:

> *Gila:* ¿Qué dicen en el lugar
> de mí?
> *Pascuala:* Que eres Locifer,
> saltabardales, machorra,
> el coco de las consejas,
> el lobo de sus ovejas,
> de las gallinas, la zorra.
> Los niños callan contigo,
> los hombres huyen de ti,
> los viejos dicen que así
> fue la Cava de Rodrigo,
> las mozas, que otra pareja
> no tuvo el mundo, y el cura

como ñublo te conjura
la puerta de la igreja.
  (Vélez de Guevara 166)

["What do they say about me in the village?" "That you're Lucifer; audacious; a tomboy; the bogeyman of fables; the wolf who threatens their sheep; the fox in the henhouse. You terrify the children into silence; men flee from you; old people say that you're like the woman who inspired lust in Rodrigo the last Gothic king; young women say you have no counterpart; and the priest stands at the church door, trying to ward you off like a hailstorm."]

Opening with an identification of Gila as the personification of evil, Pascuala follows up with three terms associated with a range of hetero- and homosexual transgression: "saltabardales," "machorra," and "la Cava de Rodrigo." Both "saltabardales" and "machorra" appear to have connoted lesbianism or female masculinity in the early modern period.[3] Menéndez Pidal and Goyri clarify line 2698 by citing early usages (160). Gonzalo Correas defines "saltabardales" as "mujerota inquieta y marimacho" (565), a woman who figuratively jumps the fence between traditional feminine gender and sexual roles. In the *Diccionario de autoridades* (1726), "Salta bardales," as two words, appears under "bardal" [fence] and, instead of referring to feminine masculinity, includes male and female youth, "vivos y alocados, que no tienen asiento en parte alguna, andando en todas con indiscreción y desenvoltura" (1:560) [wild and reckless, who don't settle anywhere, wandering about carelessly].

None of the three editions I consulted annotate "machorra," perhaps because its meaning seems obvious. It is, however, a term that has been variously defined across the centuries, with three distinct meanings pertinent to Gila's dramatic role. The most common meaning is sterility in a woman or a female animal, and this is the only definition given in the *Diccionario de autoridades*: "la oveja estéril, y por extensión se llama así la mujer u otro animal del sexo femenino que no pare" [the barren sheep, and by extension the woman or other female animal that does not give birth] (1:446). Twentieth-century dictionaries began to list one of the meanings as "marimacho" (dyke), albeit as a Mexican usage (Alemany Bolúfer 1060). Paul Julian Smith notes that the washerwomen in Federico García Lorca's *Yerma* call the protagonist "machorra," meaning both sterile and "virilized" (31). The current English translation in the online *Collins Spanish–English Dictionary* is "dyke (*vulg.*)" or "lesbian," without the reference to sterility.[4] In 1925, the Real Academia added a meaning associated with rural life in the province of Salamanca: "oveja que en festividades o bodas matan en los pueblos para celebrar la fiesta" (Real Academic Española 3:761) [sheep that is slaughtered in village festivals or weddings], in other words, a scapegoat. This usage suggests a lexical connection between Gila's hypermasculinity as transgressive excess and the communal spectacle of her destruction to restore the social order. In Pascuala's litany of vituperation, the audience could hear an additional emphasis on the fate already known from the *romance*.

In the lines that follow, Pascuala reports that, in addition to an association with the threat of predatory animals in the rural experience, Gila has acquired a mythical dimension, as "el coco de las consejas," the bogeyman or ogre of folktales. On the surface, "la Cava de Rodrigo" signifies the woman who was to blame for the downfall of Christian kingdoms in the Iberian Peninsula, but the injustice of blaming her for the violation by Rodrigo, the last Gothic king, is also encoded in this reference. Pascuala's diatribe ends with an identification of Gila as a force of nature—"como ñublo"—like the hailstorms that terrify farming communities. At this point, civil authority seems as overwhelmed as the priest at the church door, confronting the power of wind, rain, and hail, but the weather is about to change as the town reclaims its power.

The play's dialogue addresses the causes of Gila's tragedy, a combination of nature and nurture. To achieve the effects of tragedy, Vélez added a backstory to the elements of the ballad tradition by introducing the self–deception of Gila's aging father. He is essential to the dramatization of the fantastic legends and ballads of the brawny seductress. Vélez recreates her character as a daughter nurtured by a father and a community who collaborate in transforming her into the admirable monster of the first scenes. Comments by her friend Madalena and by the protagonist herself attribute Gila's strength and masculine gender identity to nature, but the plot and Gila's final exchange with her father blame him for treating her as a son. In Act I, Gila agrees with Madalena's observation in lines 659–60 regarding the disparity between the masculinity of her gender identity and her female body: "Erró la naturaleza, / Gila, en no herte varón" (Vélez de Guevara 101) [Nature erred, Gila, in not making you a man]. In Act 2, when Giraldo complains that Gila's ambitions are excessive for a peasant woman, she counters with "Pedilde, padre, cuenta a las estrellas / de esa altivez, pues ellas son la causa" (lines 1565–66) [Father, you can blame the stars for this ambition, for they are the cause], echoing Madalena's earlier comment about Nature's error (Vélez de Guevara 130). In view of the consequences of Gila's crimes, Madalena concludes in lines 3271–72, "Esta fue tu Estrella amarga; / nunca nazieras al mundo" (Vélez de Guevara 185) [This was your bitter fate; you should never have been born].

In Act 2, when Giraldo announces that Gila has been granted the greatest happiness possible for any woman, he invalidates her claims to masculinity. He seems oblivious to the irony of his arrangement of Gila's marriage to the captain, Don Lucas, whom she had chased from the town at musket-point in Act 1, lines 1553–54. She asks, ironically, if her father is about to tell her that she has been chosen for an exclusively male position of authority: general, king, bishop, or Pope. When he reveals his plan, Gila protests in lines 1584–88:

> No me quiero casar, padre, que creo
> que mientras no me caso que soy hombre.
> No quiero que nadie me sujete.
> No quiero que ninguno se imagine
> dueño de mí; la libertad pretendo.
>   (Vélez de Guevara 134)

> [Father, I don't want to marry; as long as I'm unmarried I am a man. I don't want anyone to dominate me. I don't want any man to imagine he owns me; I aspire to freedom].

Drinkwater points out that this is the turning point of the play, overlooked by other critics, "when Don Lucas and Giraldo shake hands over Gila" (79). I would add that this gesture revokes not only Giraldo's and the townspeople's acceptance of Gila as a man, but also her relationship to Giraldo as a son. The stage has already been set by Giraldo and Gila's self–deceiving collaboration in transforming a daughter, whose value was symbolic and realized only in exchanges between men, into a son who enjoyed the privileges of autonomy and actions having value in themselves. Drinkwater points out that, in patriarchal society, Gila exemplifies a bitter lesson: "that women who defy the established order face social marginalization and death" (83). George Mariscal finds that Gila combines the traditional, sexually aggressive *serrana* of medieval poetry and legend with "the much more threatening figure of a woman who demands the kind of complete autonomy associated in the seventeenth century with heretics and madmen" (150). Although Gila was able to force Don Lucas to retreat in their first skirmish, he manipulates Giraldo to agree to let him marry her, and seduces Gila through her ambition to emulate the Queen, the "mujer brava" she most admires, as well as other powerful women of antiquity whose marriages, she observes, enhanced their authority. Don

Lucas's deception reduces her not simply to the devalued status of a woman, but to a dishonored one.

In Act 3, as the Santa Hermandad arrests her, Gila appeals to Giraldo as a daughter, but he refuses to recognize her as his offspring. She shows her loyalty by refusing to give up her arms to the captain: "aunque vos sois caballero, / para mí es mi padre más" (lines 3112–13) [although you are a nobleman, to me, my father has higher authority]. Earlier, after her father had disowned her, Gila attempted to explain her actions as the result of her dishonor:

Gila: Tu hija pienso que soy.
Giraldo: Ese nombre no te doy
por las crueldades que has hecho ...
Gila: ¿Por qué no?
si me ha forzado mi afrenta.
   (lines 3089–96; Vélez de Guevara 178–79)

["I consider myself your daughter." "I deny you that name, for your cruelties." "Why not? Since they were the result of my dishonor."]

Despite his rejection, she surrenders only to his authority.

As she faces execution for her crimes, however, she calls to him as if she were about to whisper an important final message, and then savagely bites his ear. Gila justifies her final violent act in lines 3251–55 by accusing her father of shirking his duty as a parent:

que esto mereze quien pasa
por las libertades todas
de los hijos. Si tú usaras
rigor conmigo al principio
de mi inclinación gallarda,
yo no llegara a este extremo.
   (Vélez de Guevara 184)

[This is the just retribution for the parent who gives complete freedom to his children. If you had punished my first inclinations of arrogance, I wouldn't have arrived at this extreme].[5]

Giraldo accepts his daughter's "justa paga / a mi descuido" [fair punishment for my carelessness]. From the first act, the play has depicted him as incapable of controlling his wayward daughter, in part because he benefits from her masculine behavior. The moment that she is discovered and taken prisoner, she boasts that she has avenged her honor, claiming it as her own, without mentioning her father's right to seek vengeance or legal redress (Vélez de Guevara 180).

The play's demonization of a woman who rejects feminine gender roles, and her brutal execution, justified by Gila herself as a warning to parents (lines 3257–58) (Vélez de Guevara 184) and to the King, Fernando de Aragón, as "memoria / que de exemplo sirva a España" [memorable example for Spain] (lines 3296–97) would seem to exemplify José Antonio Maravall's characterization of Spanish *comedia* as an instrument of authoritarian ideology. He refers specifically to the representation of female banditry in plays by Lope, Mira de Amescua, and Vélez, and observes: "not even the extreme (i.e. criminal) 'deviation' of the bandit escapes integration into baroque society, fulfilling in a certain way his role in it; he does not break down the values on which society is based, but rather recognizes them as fully prevailing" (48). The violence of the final scenes of *La serrana de la Vera* illustrate Maravall's analysis that the function of violence in the arts was to "terrify people and in this way to succeed more efficiently in subjecting them to their place within the order" (163).

A curiously erotic exchange between Fernando and Isabel in lines 3128–45, after Gila's arrest by the Santa Hermandad but before the royal pair are informed of it, might seem to support Maravall's argument. The passage reasserts normative heterosexuality together with the sexual subordination of peasants, while the audience is aware of Gila's fate and the reinstatement of order. The dialogue's incongruous lightness of tone contrasts with its verse form, endecasyllabic tercets, appropriate for "cosas graves" [serious topics] according to Lope's *Arte nuevo* (line 311). Fernando praises Gila's beauty and courage, prompting Isabel to claim, facetiously, to be jealous, while at the same time reducing Gila to a tasty dish for the jaded palates of the ruling class:

> Tal vez suele agradar una villana
> como tosco manjar, que por antojos
> da el harto del faisán al apetito.
>   (lines 3133–35; Vélez de Guevara 180)

[Perhaps a peasant woman would please your palate, a rustic whimsy to pique the pheasant–weary appetite.]

In response, Fernando denies any sexual attraction to such "enojos" [aggravations], an obvious understatement. Before returning to the seriousness of

Gila's threat to the civil order, he embraces Isabel and refers to two of their daughters, affirming his devotion to family (lines 3136–45). The introduction of a brief, playful interlude, as well as the contrast between the play's action and the awareness of the rulers, subverts their authority and the values they symbolize.

In their interpretations of Vélez's play, however, Mariscal and Otero-Torres argue for complex, negotiated identities and power structures. Otero-Torres cites critical perspectives that reveal "fuerzas centrífugas" (centrifugal forces) rather than terms like "subversion" or "resistance." She finds in Vélez's play that the dominant discourses of religious unity and political power are riddled with fissures that disrupt the illusion of splendor. She aims to reveal what Gila's punishment intends to silence: the presence of a body that transgresses the natural and symbolic limits between femininity and masculinity (132–33). One of the shadows that may accompany the body so emphatically present in the *serrana*'s displays of physical strength, and in the spectacle of her execution, is the hybrid creature born of a mare in the Andalusian variants of the "Serrana de la Vera" ballad.

Mariscal's Gramscian approach to Vélez's *La serrana de la Vera* views the female monster in the Baroque cultural context of hegemonic appropriation of the marginal. In his analysis of the play, Gila's execution ensures not merely the restoration of the patriarchal social hierarchy, but also its enhancement. He argues that the "violent removal" of marginal and subordinate protagonists in this and other plays serves "not merely to assert the hegemony of the dominant class but in order to reinvigorate that class and its increasingly contested ideologies ... [It is] a sign that the dominant had begun to make modifications in its basic ideological apparatus in order to consolidate its hegemonic position', a position that encompassed religious as well as political discourses" (145). For Mariscal, the play is "a screen–allegory for the pressing issue of how to theorize the new state" and "insure the continued hegemony" of the ruling class (166). "Gila enters into direct conflict with both her father and the king, but is eventually recuperated through the discourse of martyrdom" (150), and Gila's execution "transformed the figure of the manly–woman into that of the womanish–man (St. Sebastian)" (152). For Mariscal, it is no coincidence that the captain whose betrayal provokes Gila's homicidal rage is on his way to join the Christian attack on Granada. He interprets the assimilation of the violently transgressive, marginalized *serrana* through martyrdom in terms of Baroque religious ideology.

Mariscal's view of the relationship between the sacred and the destruction of an unassimilable other is corroborated by Caro Baroja's anthropological research on present-day folklore. In 1946, he published a study of the legends of the *serrana* in the town of Garganta la Olla, and in 1973, he returned with folklorist Jesús Antonio Cid and published an essay on the ballad and the legends associating place names and objects with the *serrana*. Caro Baroja notes that local tradition claims that the town's baptismal font was hewn from the stone the *serrana* used to seal the opening of the cave where she murdered her male victims, a six-hundred-pound boulder "que manejaba como nosotros podemos manejar una naranja" (285, citing Hurtado 70–74) [that she handled the way we would handle an orange]. Thus, a symbol of the legendary *serrana*'s unassimilable monstrosity becomes the means by which newborns are integrated into Roman Catholic orthodoxy. Delpech concludes his analysis of Vélez's play by reflecting on myth: "Primero se trata de un mito sacrificial: eliminación del obstáculo—aquí un monstruo en forma de mujer—que impide el paso de la vida salvaje a la cultura" ("La leyenda de la serrana de la Vera" 16–17) [This is primarily a sacrificial myth: the elimination of the obstacle— here a monster in female form—that obstructs the passage from primeval life to culture].

My approach to *La serrana de la Vera* began with a question: why did the *mujer varonil* become one of the most popular motifs, not only in Spanish *comedia* but also in other cultures, while another folkloric character, who does not cross-dress but uniquely embodies normative characteristics of masculinity and femininity, is depicted as a monstrous threat that must be violently destroyed? My study of the play attempts to frame this question in terms of "genealogical critique" as Judith Butler defines it: not as "a search for the origins of gender, the inner truth of female desire, a genuine or authentic sexual identity that repression has kept from view," but as an investigation of "identity categories that are in fact the effects of institutions, practices, discourses with multiple and diffuse points of origin" (x–xi). The institutions, practices, and discourses in this case are those of early modern Spanish theater, folktales, and ballads, narratives that continue to circulate orally but that also began to appear in print in the sixteenth century.

The contradictory figure, the *mujer varonil* of the *comedia* who abandons masculine attire and resumes conformity to gender roles, also has a folkloric background, but it is transcultural rather than local. Elsewhere, I have contrasted Gila's story with the marriage plot of the far more cheerful ballad tradition of the *doncella guerrera* [woman warrior] (see Bergmann). McKendrick recognizes that "there is nothing quite like [the plot of the ballad of the *doncella guerrera*] in the drama but the *romance* is obviously a significant predecessor" (298). The Spanish and Ladino ballad tradition of the *doncella guerrera* is one of the most widely distributed in the Peninsula and in Sephardic communities throughout the Mediterranean. Ballads celebrating the daring and skill of warrior women date from the sixth-century "Ballad of Hua Mulan" in China and are found in a wide range of cultures.

Unique to both Chinese and Spanish versions of the ballad of the woman warrior is the filial piety that motivates her masculine disguise: in the absence of a son, the *doncella guerrera* volunteers to replace her aging father in the king's armies. She is motivated by family loyalty, her behavior is circumscribed by masculine power, and her gender-crossing is as playfully reversible as a change of costume. Martín observes that the initial narrative element of the ballad "display[s] a complete evacuation of the male role. The impotent father has not produced a son; instead, he has produced a strong-willed and competent daughter who has effectively replaced him as a soldier in the king's army and displaced him as paterfamilias by arranging her own marriage" (128). By volunteering for military duty in her father's place, the young woman transforms herself into a son, but only temporarily. The filial piety essential to Spanish and Chinese women warriors is not part of the oral tradition of the *serrana* of la Vera. The father-daughter backstory that Vélez added in the process of dramatizing the legend may link it with this specifically Spanish version of the woman warrior. Thus, the legends collected by folklorists suggest possible cross-pollination between the oral and dramatic traditions.

Delpech interprets the *doncella guerrera*'s gender inversion in terms of the social function of rites of initiation, courtship, and marriage customs—the rituals of human life—as opposed to the mythic bisexuality or androgyny in religious observances or cyclical, seasonal rituals ("La Doncella guerrera" 79). In contrast to the reversible transformation of the *doncella guerrera*, Delpech finds elements of mythic sacrifice and rites of passage in the folkloric narratives that inspired Vélez's play (27). To add to McKendrick's psychological approach, Mariscal's analysis of political power, and Caro Baroja and Delpech's anthropological perspectives, I would argue that the ludic eroticism of the *doncella* of the ballads and her theatrical counterparts mask the anxiety provoked by the possibility of uncoupling the masculine from the male body, a possibility made explicit in the irrevocably masculine, sexually potent figure of the mountain woman from Garganta la Olla.

The *serrana* lurks in an isolated wilderness while the ballads celebrating women warriors circulate everywhere. She is unique, in contrast to the multitude of female characters in the *comedia* who might don male attire, hone their self-defense skills, and become *guerreras* for a time. The *serrana*'s location is inscribed in the lines of her ballad and in the title of Vélez's and Lope's plays:

La Vera and Garganta la Olla, the latter a place name that refers to the gorges of the region and suggests the narrow passage and enclosed space of female reproductive physiology. An imposing bronze statue in homage to the Serrana de la Vera overlooks the town of Garganta la Olla. She carries a crossbow over her shoulder and a large knife on her belt; the allure described in the ballads and Vélez's play is missing from the stodgy figure in wellingtons and a frumpy dress hemmed well below the knee, her alluring *melenas* bound in a thick braid down her back. After venturing so far beyond the prescribed limits of feminine behavior, however, she cannot be constrained so easily. In the imagination of the local inhabitants, the cries of her victims can be heard in the howling winds in the mountains (González Terriza 24). Pascuala sketched the profile of the formidable neighbor who haunted the imagination of the local community: a vengeful gender outlaw, a predator who turned the tables and targeted men. Centuries later, the conundrum of the *serrana*'s sexuality and her gender identity continues to trouble the readers of Vélez's play.

Notes

1. Capitalization of "serrana" varies among editions and studies: folklorists capitalize the full phrase "Serrana de la Vera" with reference to the legendary figure, in contrast to most literary critics, who refer to the *comedia* character in lower case, with the exception of the editors Ramón Ménendez Pidal and Maria Goyri de Menéndez Pidal, and William Manson and George Peale, in their editions of the play from 1916 and 2002, respectively.

2. All further page references to the play are from Manson and Peale's 2002 edition. I thank George Peale for granting permission to reproduce passages of the play. All translations are mine.

3. For a discussion of terms that denoted masculine femininity and connoted lesbianism in the early modern lexicon, see Mary Gossy, "Aldonza Lorenzo as Butch," 20–22.

4. According to the same source, the recorded usage of "machorra" peaked around 1800, suggesting that the association with the fertility of farm animals was more common in earlier periods than the reference to human sexuality.

5. Menéndez Pidal and Goyri de Menéndez Pidal note that numerous editions of *Ysopet*, beginning in 1489, popularized another version of a scene in which a son bites his mother's ear (160).

References

Ashcom, B. "Concerning 'La mujer en hábito de hombre' in the *Comedia*." *Hispanic Review* 28 (1960): 45–62.

Alemany Bolúfer, José. *Diccionario de la lengua española*. Barcelona: R. Sopena, 1917.

Bergmann, Emilie L. "Tame and Untamed: Two Dutiful Daughters in the *Romance de la doncella guerrera* and Luis Vélez de Guevara's *La serrana de la Vera*." In *Shakespeare and the Spanish Comedia: Translation, Interpretation, Performance (Essays in Honor of Susan L. Fischer)*, edited by Bárbara J. Mujica, Bucknell University Press, 2013, 149–63.

Blackmore, Josiah, and Gregory Hutcheson, eds. *Queer Iberia: Sexualities, Cultures, and Crossings from the Middle Ages to the Renaissance*. Duke University Press, 1999.

Bradbury, Gail. "Irregular Sexuality in the Spanish *Comedia*." *Modern Language Review* 76 (1981): 566–80.

Burshatin, Israel. "Written on the Body: Slave or Hermaphrodite in Sixteenth-Century Spain." In *Queer Iberia: Sexualities, Cultures, and Crossings from the Middle Ages to the Renaissance*, edited by Josiah Blackmore and Gregory Hutcheson, Duke University Press, 1999, 420–56.

Butler, Judith. *Gender Trouble: Feminism and the Subversion of Identity*. Routledge, 1990.

Caro Baroja, Julio. "La Serrana de la Vera o un pueblo analizado en conceptos y símbolos inactuales." In *Ritos y Mitos equívocos*, edited by Julio Caro Baroja, Madrid: Istmo, 1974, 259–337.

Carrasco, Rafael. *Inquisición y represión sexual en Valencia: Historia de los sodomitas, 1565–1785*. Barcelona: Laertes, 1985.

Cartagena-Calderón, José. *Masculinidades en obras: El drama de la hombría en la España imperial*. Newark, DE: Juan de la Cuesta, 2008.

Connor, Catherine. "Marriage and Subversion in *Comedia* Endings: Problems in Art and Society." In *Gender, Identity, and Representation in Spain's Golden Age*, edited by Dawn L. Smith and Anita K. Stoll, Bucknell University Press, 2000, 23–46.

Correas, Gonzalo. *Refranes y frases proverbiales*. Madrid: Ratés, 1906.

Delpech, François. "La 'doncella guerrera': Chansons, contes, rituels." In *Formas breves del relato: Coloquio Casa de Velázquez-Departamento de Literatura Española de la Universidad de Zaragoza, Madrid, Febrero De 1985*, edited by Yves-René Fonquerne, Aurora Egido, and Leonardo Romero, Zaragoza, Spain: Secretariado de Publicaciones de la Universidad de Zaragoza, 1986, 57–86.

———. "La leyenda de la serrana de la Vera: las adaptaciones teatrales." In *La mujer en el teatro y la novela del siglo XVII: Actas del II Coloquio del Grupo de Estudios sobre Teatro Español Toulouse, 16–17 noviembre, 1978*, edited by Yves-René Fonquerne, Institut d'Études Hispaniques et Hispano-Américaines, Université de Toulouse–Le Mirail, 1979, 23–38.

Diccionario de autoridades, 3 vols. 1726. Madrid: Gredos, 1969.

Drinkwater, J. A. "*La serrana de la Vera* and the 'Mystifying Charms of Fiction.'" *Forum for Modern Language Studies* 28 (1992), no. 1: 75–85.

González Terriza, Alejandro Arturo. "La Serrana de la Vera: constantes y variaciones de un personaje legendario." *Culturas Populares. Revista Electrónica* 4 (2007), www.culturaspopulares.org/textos4/articulos/gonzalezt.htm.

Gossy, Mary. "Aldonza Lorenzo as Butch." *¿Entiendes? Queer Readings, Hispanic Writings*, edited by Emilie L. Bergmann and Paul Julian Smith, Duke University Press, 17–28.

Hurtado, Publio. *Supersticiones extremeñas.* Cáceres, n.p, 1902.
Lundelius, Ruth. "Paradox and Role Reversal in *La Serrana de la Vera.*" In *The Perception of Women in Spanish Theater of the Golden Age,* edited by Anita K. Stoll and Dawn L. Smith, Bucknell University Press, 1991, 220–44.
"Machorra." *Collins Online Spanish–English Dictionary,* www.collinsdictionary.com/dictionary/spanish-english/machorra.
Maravall, José Antonio. *Culture of the Baroque: Analysis of a Historical Structure.* Translated by Terry Cochran, University of Minnesota Press, 1986. Originally published as *La Cultura del Barroco: Análisis de una estructura histórica.* Barcelona: Ariel, 1975.
Mariscal, George. "Symbolic Capital in the Spanish *Comedia.*" *Renaissance Drama* 21 (1990): 143–69.
Martín, Adrienne Laskier. *An Erotic Philology of Golden Age Spain.* Vanderbilt University Press, 2008.
McKendrick, Melveena. *Woman and Society in the Spanish Drama of the Golden Age: A Study of the "Mujer Varonil."* Cambridge University Press, 1974.
Menéndez Pidal, Ramón. *Flor nueva de romances viejos.* Madrid: Espasa-Calpe, 1959.
Menéndez Pidal, Ramón, and María Goyri de Menéndez Pidal. "Observaciones y notas." In Luis Vélez de Guevara, *La serrana de la Vera,* edited by Ramón Menéndez Pidal and María Goyri de Menéndez Pidal, Madrid: Teatro Antiguo Español, 1916, 125–69.
Mujica, Bárbara. *A New Anthology of Early Modern Spanish Theater.* Yale University Press, 2015.
Otero-Torres, Dámaris. "Historia, ortodoxia y praxis teatral: el homoerotismo femenino en *La serrana de la Vera.*" In *El escritor y la escena V. Estudios sobre teatro español y novohispano de los Siglos de Oro: Homenaje a Marc Vitse,* edited by Ysla Campbell, Ciudad Juárez, Mexico: Universidad Autónoma de Ciudad Juárez, 1997, 131–39.
Parr, James A., and Mercedes Albuixech. "Estudio introductorio." In Luis Vélez de Guevara. *La Serrana de la Vera,* edited by William R. Manson and George Peale, Newark, DE: Juan de la Cuesta, 2002, 15–40.
Perry, Mary Elizabeth. *Gender and Disorder in Early Modern Seville.* Princeton University Press, 1999.
Piñero, Pedro Manuel, and Virtudes Atero. "El Romance de La Serrana de la Vera: La Pervivencia de un mito en la tradición del Sur." *Dicenda: Cuadernos de Filología Hispánica* 6 (1987): 399–418.
Real Academia Española. *Diccionario de la lengua española,* 15th ed. Madrid: Espasa-Calpe, 1925.
Saint-Saens, Alain, and María José Delgado, eds. *Lesbianism and Homosexuality in Early Modern Spain: Literature and Theater in Context.* University Press of the South, 2000.
Smith, Paul Julian. *The Theatre of García Lorca: Text, Performance, Psychoanalysis.* Cambridge University Press, 1998.
Stroud, Matthew. *Plot Twists and Critical Turns: Queer Approaches to Early Modern Spanish Theater.* Bucknell University Press, 2007.

Vásvari, Louise. "The Semiotics of Phallic Aggression and Anal Penetration as Male Agonistic Ritual in the *Libro de buen amor*." In *Queer Iberia: Sexualities, Cultures, and Crossings from the Middle Ages to the Renaissance*, edited by Josiah Blackmore and Gregory S. Hutcheson, Duke University Press, 1999, 130–56.

Vega Carpio, Lope de. 2002. *El arte nuevo de hacer comedias. Significado y doctrina del arte nuevo de Lope de Vega*. Edited by Juan Manuel Rozas, Biblioteca Virtual Miguel de Cervantes, www.cervantesvirtual.com/obra-visor/arte-nuevo-de-hacer-comedias-en-este-tiempo-0/html/.

Velasco, Sherry. *Lesbians in Early Modern Spain*. Vanderbilt University Press, 2001.

Vélez de Guevara, Luis. *La Serrana de la Vera*. Edited by Ramón Menéndez Pidal and María Goyri de Menéndez Pidal, Madrid: Teatro Antiguo Español, 1916.

———. *La serrana de la Vera*, 2nd ed. Edited by Enrique Rodríguez Cepeda, Madrid: Cátedra, 1982.

———. *La Serrana de la Vera*. Edited by William R. Manson and George Peale, Newark, DE: Juan de la Cuesta, 2002.

TERESA SCOTT SOUFAS

Mujer vestida de hombre to the Extreme
Catalina de Erauso in Montalbán's *La monja alférez*

J UAN PÉREZ DE MONTALBÁN (1602–1638) is credited by most critics with contributing *La monja alférez* [The Lieutenant Nun] to the theater of seventeenth-century Spain. It is a play that defies categories and definition, and is about what the main character is not. It weaves together contradictions and misinformation, and blends the theatrical world with that of the spectators. The real woman, the so-called "monja alférez," was Catalina de Erauso from the Basque region. At a young age, she escaped from the convent into which her family had placed her as a child and, according to the description found in what is purported to be her memoir, *Historia de la Monja Alférez escrita por ella misma* [History of the Lieutenant Nun Written by Herself], she cut her hair, donned male clothing, and spent years living as a man whose exploits, especially among the Spanish ranks in battles in the New World, brought her a reputation for bravery and violence. Catalina de Erauso's presence in Madrid in the mid-1620s coincided with Montalbán's decision to write a play about this figure, whose fame had spread and was of sensational interest to the public. He created a play that has some characteristics of a *comedia de capa y espada* [cloak and sword play]: complicated elements of a love story including some from the real Erauso's life and others from his own imagination, complete with love triangles and deceptions.[1]

In concert with the ideas of scholars who have written on *La monja alférez*,[2] I propose to foreground its salient aspects, focusing on the masterful ambiguity that is its main component. It presents a fascinating blend of opposites, incongruities, and falsehoods: the gender identity of the main character, the distance or lack thereof between the real Erauso and the fictional one, the identity of a *monja* and the title of *alférez*, geographical locations distant from each other, and the *monja's* act of conquering that takes a different turn in the last scene of the play—all of which make the work unstable. I shall elaborate upon these and other ambiguities and contradictions in the play, which for me are its most important underlying qualities and what make it a striking work.

In addition to the many ambiguities, the question of authorship has been raised with respect to both the play and Erauso's memoirs. Jack Parker notes: "Unfortunately for the Montalván canon, this play may be by Luis Belmonte Bermúdez" (64). While there is some uncertainty about the origin of the theatrical version that portrays her, what we know about the living Catalina de Erauso is from her purported autobiography. Erauso supposedly dictated her autobiography, but the oldest extant text of *Vida i sucesos de la Monja Alférez* [Life and Accounts of the Lieutenant Nun] dates to a collection of 1784 edited by Joaquín Bautista Muñoz. Luzmila Camacho Platero outlines the problem with the authenticity of the autobiographical text (13–15). Among the issues so involved are the loss of the original seventeenth-century manuscript and the discrepancy between date information given in the eighteenth-century text and that which appears on her baptismal document.

In terms of Montalban's play, it is easy to understand that it is about someone whose depiction is not identifiable as authentic. The dramatized story begins in Lima where doña Ana lives and is verbally courted by Alonso Guzmán, la *monja alférez*, in the guise of a soldier and lieutenant. Don Diego, a friend and fellow officer of the protagonist, also interacts with him and is likewise a hopeful suitor of Ana. Don Miguel, the biological brother of Guzmán, also garrisoned with the troops, reveals at one point that he is determined to find his missing sister whom their father has sought over the years.

The first act continues with mishaps at the gambling table where Miguel and Guzmán are playing with others including el Nuevo Cid. When a brawl breaks out, Guzmán wounds the latter and impresses his brother Miguel with his fighting skills. But Guzmán has lost considerable money at the gambling table, and he visits Doña Ana ostensibly, at least as far as she believes, to have a romantic rendezvous. His visit with her ends when she goes inside to extinguish lights, in preparation for what she anticipates will be their tryst. When Guzmán and his servant Machín hear others approaching, Guzmán is pleased:

Ayudar
mis intentos han querido
los cielos con la verdad,
ven.
   (1, 523–26)

[The heavens have desired to help my plans with the truth, come on.]³

Ana returns after having made arrangements for him to enter and unwittingly grabs the hand of the man she thinks is Guzmán, although he is really the suitor Don Diego. Because he is deeply attracted to Ana, Diego accepts the unexpected opportunity to go to her chambers and to make love to her there. This ambiguity is not out of keeping with other *capa y espada* dramatizations. We later learn why Ana has allowed this charade to continue to its fulfillment, and why she did not reveal what had happened to anyone.

As the second act begins, Guzmán returns to Lima after a three-year absence during which Ana and Machín did not know where he was or why he had left. Upon his return, he explains:

salí al campo con Miguel
de Erauso, y riñendo con él,
fue el Alférez desdichado
más que yo, pues de una herida
penetrante que le di,
entre la sangre le vi
casi despedir la vida.
   (2, 864–70)

[I left for the countryside with Miguel de Erauso, and fighting with him, it was he who was more unfortunate than I, since penetrated by one of my thrusts, I saw him bleeding and losing his life.]

Their altercation was over Miguel's ongoing suspicion that Guzmán was really his sister. Guzmán explains that, thinking he had killed his brother, he was afraid to write to Ana or to Machín for fear of being traced to Arauco in Chile, where he was hiding. But again, the play presents the opposite of what appears to be true. Guzmán finally learned that Miguel had recovered from his wounds but died later of an illness. Knowing that he had not committed fratricide and was not in danger of being arrested, he felt free to return to Lima.

Then it is Ana's turn to tell Guzmán about what happened the last night they had seen each other:

> Después que de la ventana
> me aparté, Guzmán, y muertas
> las luces, mi casa toda
> ocuparon las tinieblas.
> A cumplir lo concertado
> contigo, volví a la puerta
> de la calle, abrí, y dos hombres
> hallé parados en ella.
>   (2, 903–10)

[After leaving the window, Guzmán, and with the lights darkened, my whole house was in shadows. In order to arrange our tryst, I returned to the front door, opened it, and found two men waiting there.]

The men she allowed into her house, however, were not Guzmán and his servant, whom she was awaiting. She then reveals the deceptive actions of the man who entered and took advantage of her while her maid Inés entertained the other male.

Ana's explanation indicates that, by noting differences in body size and other physical details, she had understood what was happening. The discrepancy involved in her identification of Guzmán, not as a woman but as a male suitor, is heightened through her statement. But not wanting to make known her dishonor, and seeking to protect her elderly father from a confrontation with much younger and stronger men, she did not resist. She also explains that, because she did not know who this man was, she kept "una prenda" (2, 1018) [a piece of clothing] that could identify him in the future: a pair of gloves that the unknown man had left behind, the very gloves that Guzmán had given as a gift to his friend Diego earlier. Guzmán thus decides to restore Ana's honor by revealing to Diego the truth of his identity as a woman, so as to eliminate any feelings of competition Diego's part for Ana's affection and to move Ana and Diego toward marriage.

Guzmán shows Diego the gloves as proof that he knows where he had left them and what he had done that night. With this information, which can be interpreted as a threat, Guzmán informs his friend that he has concocted a solution for the problem: "el remedio es ser marido / de quien el honor debéis" (2, 1275–76) [the remedy is to marry the woman to whom her honor you owe]. Diego resists, proclaiming the reason for his doubts: "en casarme pretendáis / con quien tuvo otro galán" (2, 1283–84) [you intend that I marry a woman who has another lover]; he knows that Ana was awaiting someone else that night. Upon hearing that Guzmán was to be her partner in the tryst, Diego again resists, assuming that because she was willing to admit Guzmán into her chambers, she would be willing to do so even after marriage.

At this point, Guzmán makes the first declaration about the truth of "his" gender in order to calm Diego's doubts about his relationship with Ana, though he does not refer to the female identity as also being that of a rejected category of nun. Extracting a promise from Diego to keep secret what he is about to say, Guzmán states: "Sabed, pues, don Diego amigo, / que yo soy mujer" (2, 1333–34) [Understand then, Diego my friend, that I am a woman]. Obviously surprised over this information, Diego expresses his wonder over how Guzmán could have hidden as a man for so long and participated so aggressively in warfare, but he articulates his real astonishment in the following way:

> he de creer,
> que amáis siendo mujer,
> otra mujer? No queráis
> acreditar
> imposibles.
> (2, 1350–53)

[you expect me to believe that you love another woman when you are a woman? Don't believe impossibilities.]

This statement has triggered much critical commentary over what some consider the existence of a lesbian relationship between Guzmán and Ana.

There are many strands in this interpretation of these two characters. Critics, as Bárbara Mujica (558–59) points out, have addressed the potential reception of a representation of romantic love between two women in seventeenth-century Spain. Lisa Vollendorf, for example, introduces one element: "We cannot know with any precision the extent which homoeroticism, particularly female homoeroticism, was intelligible to early modern readers" (64). And Judith Brown puts it this way: "Europeans had long found it difficult to accept that women could actually be attracted to other women. Their view of human sexuality was phallocentric—women might be attracted to men and men might be attracted to men, but there was nothing in a woman that could sustain ... the sexual desires of another woman" (6). Relying, however, on the play's dialogue, Mujica outlines the critical position taken by other scholars, which supports what some understand as the lesbian nature of the relationship between the protagonist and Ana. As Act 1 begins, Guzmán and Ana are saying their goodbyes due to his imminent departure for the port of Callao near Lima to undertake military duty. She expresses her fears about his ability to stay faithful to her, while he urges her to have faith in his dedication. She bestows upon him the gift of a chain as a sign of her affection. Guzmán addresses Ana as "mi doña Ana" [my lady Ann] (2, 20) and "mi bien" [my dearest] (1, 448) and says: "Esta eslabona recibo / más que por sus eslabones / manifiestan las prisiones / en que enamorado vivo" (1, 93–96) [This chain I receive as more than its links but as the prisons of love in which I live]. There is also a reference to a relationship between the two women when Guzmán responds to Diego's surprise at hearing that his friend is a woman:

> ... venirme a Lima, Don Diego,
> a donde Doña Ana bella,
> juzgándome por varón
> amor y afición me muestra.
> Gocé un año sus favores.
>   (2, 1473–77)

> [... I came to Lima, Diego, where beautiful lady Ann, judging me a man, shows me love and affection. I enjoyed her favors for one year.]

But much later in Act 3, he states, "que sólo cupo en su pecho / mi amor" (2, 2472–73) [but my love only existed in her heart].

Sherry Velasco contends that Guzmán is genuinely in love with Ana but with an eye to the playwright's mitigation of "the lesbian question in a number of ways" (62). Primary is the fact that Guzmán's vow of chastity assures that there is no sexual activity ascribable to him. Thus, the performative identity (*alferéz*) and the rejected identity (*monja*) do overlap in certain ways. The fact that Guzmán is a woman as well as a virgin—physical qualities the character shares with the real Catalina de Erauso—"partially desexualizes the character, making his relationship with Doña Ana less disturbing" (Mujica 558). Mujica presents competing interpretations of this aspect of *La monja alférez*, contending that "Pérez de Montalbán leaves the door open for a nonlesbian reading, according to which Guzmán's courtship of Doña Ana is nothing more than a facet of his masculine charade, not the result of a real passion. In other words, Guzmán courts Doña Ana because that's what men do; he may feel real affection for her, but he is not in love with her" (559). My own reading of the play does not admit the presentation of a lesbian love affair but rather emphasizes Guzmán as a suitor within the performance of masculinity, which is sustained throughout. Lesbian love (that may or may not be in the play) is thus another feature of the contradictions and discrepancies that are the basis of the whole work.

The second act ends with an encounter between Guzmán and the authorities, who have come to force the protagonist to assume both female clothing (but not a nun's habit) and an identity as a woman. Finally, Guzmán makes strong statements about his refusal to live as a woman, thereby reinforcing the element of the performance undertaken by him and that continues throughout the play. When an arresting *alcalde* (mayor) orders Guzmán, "Vístase la ropa, amigo" [Put on this clothing] (2, 1647), the *monja alférez* responds: "Qué ropa? yo soy soldado, y en mi traje han de llevarme" (2, 1648–51) [What clothing? I am a soldier and in my uniform you have to take me away].[4] His alarm is registered in an aside as follows:

(¿Pues yo que dejo quitarme
la vida por no decir
que soy mujer, ni traer
faldas, había de querer
llevarlas para morir?)
    (2, 1654–58)

[(Will I who allows that I be killed for not saying that I am a woman nor wearing women's skirts have to wear them in order to die?)]

In a following aside, he says: "(Por no parecer mujer; / todo lo quiero perder / fuera del alma)" (2, 1664–66) [(In order not to appear as a woman, I want to lose everything except my soul)]. However, the echo of the religious vows taken by Guzmán as a youth does not erase his performed identity as a man. For men, too, can believe and live (or die) according to Church doctrine and teachings.

Here, of course, Guzmán is on the brink of abandoning the masculine identity. Or so it seems. But Don Juan, another friend of Diego and Guzmán, explains:

> La sentencia ha suspendido
> el Virrey, porque ha sabido
> de vuestro amigo don Diego
> que sois mujer.
> (2, 1668–71)

[The Viceroy has suspended the death sentence because he has learned from your friend Diego that you are a woman.]

Guzmán immediately counters with another set of lies:

> Mujer yo?
> Miente, mande su Excelencia
> ejecutar la sentencia,
> que don Diego le engañó
> por excusarme la muerte.
> (2, 1671–75)

[I a woman? He lies; let his Excellence execute the sentence, for Diego deceived him in order to spare me death.]

The third act, now set in Spain, creates a complex web of repeated information as well as added details of what has transpired between the second and third sections of the play. For instance, the first long dialogue delivered by friend Diego opens with reference to the arrest of Guzmán, but with the additional revelation that the Virrey (Viceroy) of Lima, upon further investigation of the killing of el Nuevo Cid by the *alférez*, had found that Diego had provoked the *monja alférez*'s attack. Likewise, Diego provides a description of Guzmán's unhappy stay in a Trinitarian monastery to which the protagonist was relegated after he/she was arrested and knowledge of his/her true gender identification was made public "por la fama / que tiene de religiosa" [for her reputation as a nun] (2, 1707–8). Diego explains that a Basque sister undertook to support her countrywoman and nominated her/him for a higher position in the community. This was unacceptable to Guzmán, and so the nun received a terrible beating, becoming a victim of his non-fatal violence. The nuns of the community were so offended by this behavior that they demanded Guzmán's expulsion from the convent—exactly as the *monja alférez* wished.

From Diego's speech, we learn that the trip to Spain could have ended with more misfortune for the protagonist due to the Bishop of Alcides's negative reaction to the again masculine-dressed Guzmán. The Bishop's opinion changed, however, when he learned of the bravery and the "hazañas heroicas" (3, 1752) [heroic feats] Guzmán had displayed. Guzmán was even awarded "dineros and joyas" (3, 1756) [money and jewels] by this religious authority, who treated the protagonist as a composite of the two gender identities. Next, Diego affirms his reasons for breaking his promise to Guzmán not to reveal the secret of his gender. Diego adds that he wanted to remove "sospechas" (3, 1781) [suspicions] and "murmuración" (3, 1782) [gossip] that could impede his marriage to Ana, the woman he loves.

As Act 3 progresses, there are conflictive emotions, even negative ones, primarily expressed against Guzmán by Ana, who is furious with him for having abandoned her. It is thus clear that she believed him to be a man, that she did not penetrate his disguise. She expresses hope, in an aside, that Diego will take revenge on Guzmán for what she perceives as her grievance and dishonor:

> Ojalá
> vengue este infame pecho
> su agravio, y mi deshonor.
>   (3, 2362–64)

[Oh that this take revenge on this infamous breast for his grievance and my dishonor.]

Guzmán then accuses Diego of having broken a promise not to reveal the female identity of the *monja alférez*; when Diego says he did so "Por daros vida" (3, 2386) [To save your life], Guzmán reiterates his disgust with the outcome of Diego's revelation:

> El celo
> de librarme, no era justo
> que os obligar a romperlo,
> habiéndoos yo prevenido,
> que sintiera mucho menos
> la muerte, que publicar
> que era mujer.
>   (3, 2386–92)

[Your desire to liberate me was not just, since I warned that I would suffer death much less than making public that I was a woman.]

Guzmán attacks Diego for having caused him so much anguish and embarrassment, but friend Don Juan gets between the two combatants and explains that his purpose is to "castigar una *mujer / atrevida*" [punish a bold *woman*] (3, 2414, emphasis added).

There is then a change in demeanor on the part of the *monja alférez* as he explains to Ana that he had previously revealed his real gender identity to Diego to preserve her honor. Guzmán continues with what many critics, including myself, consider his major conquest: the self-conquest of admitting that he is a woman. Confirming what we have known about his vow of chastity, he alludes clearly to the non-physical relationship he has had with Ana:

> Y así, don Diego, ya es justo
> restituir lo que debo
> a doña Ana, declarando,
> que sólo cupo en su pecho
> mi amor.
>   (3, 2469–74)

[And so, Diego, it is just that I restore to lady Ann what I owe, declaring that my love only existed in her heart.]

Guzmán then kneels at Diego's feet. This is all part of her performance of masculinity, which is consciously upheld by the *monja alférez*; he does not don women's clothes at this point. In fact, he had requested earlier that he be allowed to continue wearing men's clothing and enlist to fight in Flanders in the service of Spain. The marriage between Ana and Diego is understood as forthcoming, and the message of the play, the conquest of the self, is voiced by the Vizconde [Viscount] de Zolina: "Nunca has mostrado el valor / como ahora de tu pecho" [Never have you shown valor like you are doing now] (3, 2507–8); and by Sebastián de Ilumbre, a *hidalgo* or gentleman:

> Más has ganado vencida
> de ti misma, que venciendo
> ejércitos de enemigos.
>   (3, 2509–11)

[You have won more defeating yourself than by defeating enemy armies.]

The title of the play exhibits the contradiction in the protagonist's identity—*La monja alférez*—and is a dichotomy in and of itself. The first term labels a woman who dedicates herself to a life of religious contemplation and service. There is, of course, nothing of such a lifestyle in the depiction of Guzmán, except for the report of the disastrous stay he had in a convent in Lima. (We know that in real life, Erauso, as a young girl, ran away from a convent and from existence as a nun.) Guzmán's and Erauso's fulfillment of the title of "lieutenant" on stage and in life is both real and yet impossible. During the early modern period a woman never would have been allowed to be an officer in the armies; thus, she had to perform her "duties" through a performance of masculinity. A component of that performance is underscored more than once when others make Guzmán's beardlessness a topic of observation. For example, his servant Machín inquires of him: "qué baños, / qué ungüentos, qué drogas / tienes para no barbar?" (1, 805–7) [what baths, what creams, what drugs do you have that prevent growing a beard?]. Among the bodily characteristics that Ana notes in her experience with Diego in her bedroom is that the man in question indeed has a beard: "tócole el rostro, y las señas / varoniles hallo en él, / que tu poca edad te niega" (2, 948–50) [I touch his face, and I find manly signs there that your young age denies you]. When Guzmán returns from Lima after three years, Machín notes his beardlessness: "y te vienes / tras la ausencia de tres años, / calvo la barba?" (2, 803–5). After Guzmán's first altercation with el Nuevo Cid, for which he suffers no retribution from the authorities, a soldier gives this description of him: "información ha hecho, / que es el lampiño, hombre de pelo en pecho" [it is known that the unbearded man is a man of chest hair] (1, 340–41).

As we have seen throughout this essay, one of the issues that critics must confront when writing about *La monja alférez* is, as Mujica queries, "how to refer to the protagonist grammatically. Should one say 'he' or 'she,' or in Spanish, should one use masculine or feminine adjectives?" (557). Further, my own reading supports Mujica's observation that "in the play itself references to Guzmán are inconsistent. When referring to the character's sex, the feminine is used; otherwise, the masculine is used" (557).[5] It is likewise noteworthy that on three occasions, two characters refer to Guzmán not as the *monja alférez* but as the *alférez monja*, thereby emphasizing the performative instability of his/her identity. Twice in his long dialogue during his conversation with the Vizconde de Zolina, Diego refers to him in this way (3, 1800 and 1893), and after a few more lines, he alternately speaks of him with the usual title of *Monja Alférez* (1898), but then reverses the order again in his first conversation with

Ana in Madrid (3, 2144). And in his closing speech, the Vizconde speaks of "el Alférez Monja" (3, 2517). Instability is woven throughout the play.

Interestingly, only Guzmán's brother Miguel suspects that he is actually his sister Catalina, in part due to a picture and his father's letter; this idea is reinforced because Guzmán does not respond to overtures made by a prostitute at Miguel's bidding. Catalina's performance as Guzmán does not really end, for the protagonist is still in soldier's garb at the close of the play, and we know that the historical Catalina de Erauso went to Rome and received the Pope's permission to live out her life wearing men's clothing. Moreover, the play does not truly close because, in the last address to the audience, the Vizconde promises a second part if circumstances warrant it:

> Con aquesto, y pidiendo
> perdón, tenga fin aquí
> este caso verdadero,
> donde llega la comedia
> han llegado los sucesos;
> que hoy está el Alférez Monja
> en Roma, y si casos nuevos
> dieren materia a la pluma,
> segunda parte se promote.
>   (3, 2512–20)

[With this and asking for pardon, this true case comes to an end, where the play and the happenings here have arrived; for today the Lieutenant Nun is in Rome, and if new experiences occur to be written about, a second part is promised.]

The conflation of the dramatized character and the real one in this speech is another of the inconsistencies represented in the play. This reference to the world beyond the stage reveals a potential dependency on the world of the spectators. If Catalina's real-life parents and Guzmán's parents referred to in the play determined to install Catalina/Guzmán in the female religious life, person and character rejected such a life entirely. But the salvation of his/her soul is of greatest importance to the *monja* who lives as an *alférez*, thus establishing the blend of identities attributable to the living and the dramatized Catalina de Guzmán. Nothing is stable, and a subsequent dramatization of the protagonist would perhaps follow more activity and reports about the real/fictional Catalina/Guzmán—or perhaps not.

Notes

I am grateful to Susan L. Fischer for her astute editorial suggestions.

1. Bárbara Mujica states in the introduction to her edition of the play in *A New Anthology of Early Modern Spanish Theater: Play and Playtext*: "By the time Juan Pérez de Montalbán wrote his play in 1626, Erauso was already a celebrity. Upon her return to Spain, she traveled around the country on what might be compared to a modern-day publicity tour, promoting her feats as a female virgin *alférez*. A curious public was anxious to learn more about her, and Pérez de Montalbán knew how to exploit the market" (554).
2. See, for example, Jack Parker, Sara Taddeo, Mary Elizabeth Perry, Irma Vélez, Sherry Velasco, Jules Whicker, Christian Andrés, Luzmila Camacho Platero, and Mujica.
3. All quotations from the play are taken from Mujica's 2014 edition and are given by act and line in the text; and all translations are mine.
4. Luzmila Camacho Platero considers the importance of clothing, which "funciona como significante del sexo biológico" [functions as a signifier of biological sex]. See also Traub, "The Insignificance of 'Lesbian' Desire," and Garber, *Vested Interests*.
5. I was tempted to refer to Guzmán through the combination of pronouns him/her, but in deference to the tedium it might have caused to my readers, I decided to follow the general critical practice of referring to the protagonist in the masculine.

References

Andrés, Christian. "Historicidad, Mito y Teatralidad en el personaje de La Monja Alférez (según la comedia de Juan Pérez de Montalbán)." In *Memoria de la palabra: Actas del VI congreso de la Asociación Internacional Siglo de Oro*, coordinated by Francisco Domínguez Matito and María Luisa Lobato López, Iberoamericana Vervuert, 2004, 251–61.
Brown, Judith. *Immodest Acts: The Life of a Lesbian Nun in Renaissance Italy*. Oxford University Press, 1986.
Camacho Platero, Luzmila. "Estudio crítico." In *Juan Pérez de Montalbán, La monja alférez*, edited by Luzmila Camacho Platero, Newark, DE: Juan de la Cuesta, 2007, 17–28.
Garber, Marjorie. *Vested Interests: Cross-Dressing and Cultural Anxiety*. Routledge, 1992.
Mujica, Bárbara. "The Allure of Scandal: *La monja alférez*." In *A New Anthology of Early Modern Spanish Theater: Play and Playtext*, edited by Bárbara Mujica, Yale University Press, 2014, 554–60.
Parker, Jack. *Juan Pérez de Montalván*. Twayne, 1975.
Pérez de Montalbán, Juan. "La monja alférez." In *A New Anthology of Early Modern Spanish Theater: Play and Playtext*, edited by Bárbara Mujica, Yale University Press, 2014, 561–98.

Perry, Mary Elizabeth. "*La monja alférez*: Myth, Gender, and the Manly Woman in a Spanish Renaissance Drama." Paper presented at the Eighth Louisiana Conference on Hispanic Languages and Literatures (LA CHISPA), Tulane University, New Orleans, 1987.

Taddeo, Sara A. "'Mentís que no soy mujer mientras empuño este acero': Verdad, engaño y valor in *La monja alférez*." *Looking at the Comedia in the Year of the Quincentennial: Proceedings of the 1992 Symposium on Golden Age Drama*, edited by Barbara Mujica and Sharon D. Voros, University of Texas Press, 1992, 111–20.

Traub, Valerie. "The Insignificance of 'Lesbian' Desire in Early Modern England." In *Queering the Renaissance*, edited by Jonathan Goldberg, Duke University Press, 1994, 62–83.

Velasco, Sherry. *The Lieutenant Nun: Transgenderism, Lesbian Desire, and Catalina de Erauso*. University of Texas Press, 2000.

Vélez, Irma. "Vida I sucesos de la Monja Alférez: Un caso de travestismo sexual y textual." In *La seducción de la escritura: Los discursos de la escritura hoy*, edited by Rosaura Hernández and Manuel F. Medina, Mexico City: Pagination, [1996], 391–401.

Vollendorf, Lisa. *The Lives of Women: A New History of Inquisitional Spain*. Vanderbilt University Press, 2005.

Whicker, Jules. "La virtud militar y el diseño moral de *La monja alférez* de Montalbán." In *Memoria de la palabra: Actas del VI Congreso de la Asociación Internacional Siglo de Oro*, coordinated by Francisco Domínguez Matito and María Luisa Lobato López, Iberoamericana Vervuert, 2004, 1851–60.

Part II

Women *in* the Theater

Actors, Producers, Constructed Subjectivity

ELIZABETH CRUZ PETERSEN

Career-Oriented Women in the Theater
María Álvarez, Bárbara Coronel, Fabiana Laura

RESEARCHERS CONTINUE to piece together historical bits to present the numerous facets that made up the lives of women of the theater in early modern Spain. In presenting the extraordinary accomplishments of these women, we are reminded by Jean-Philippe Deranty and Andrew Dunstall that, as scholars, we have the duty "to bear witness" to the struggles and achievements of our predecessors in a way that does "not double an oppression" (828). Fortunately, current scholarship by historians such as Carmen Sanz Ayán and Teresa Ferrer Valls allows us to relate to the legacy of these theater professionals beyond their often-relegated subaltern status. These studies elucidate how *autoras* [managers/directors] overcame legal and social obstacles placed before them to secure a position in history. For instance, Ferrer Valls and her team of scholars created a vast database, *Diccionario Biográfico de actores del teatro clásico español* (DICAT), which contains entries collected from historical documents, court records, and critical sources that chronicle the lives of actresses and *autoras* who surpassed cultural barriers to become leaders.[1] In the wake of these recent studies, three women of Spain's early modern theater prominently stand out: María Álvarez, Bárbara Coronel, and Fabiana Laura, whose careers "allow us to form a more accurate notion of early modern Spanish society. They provide us with alternate outlooks" (Mujica ix–x). These women emerge from anonymity, surpassing cultural barriers by becoming leaders in their own right. As career-oriented women, Álvarez, Coronel, and Laura reinvented themselves as directors, impresarios, and mentors, establishing a network of women theater professionals in the process. As artistic directors and executive administrators, they managed schools that fostered an awareness of autonomy in their young apprentices, producing a sense of community among women in their field.

María Álvarez, also known as *La Perendenga*, began her theater career in 1664 as a member of Juan Francisco Ortiz's acting company. She was admitted into the actors' guild that same year and then again in 1665 along with her first husband Francisco Correa. After her husband's death in 1670, she continued acting in the *corrales* [playhouses] and palaces. By 1677, she wore two hats, those of co-*autora* and actor. She operated as manager and administrator in Félix Pascual's company, while he handled the directing responsibilities. The following year, she entered the company of Agustín Manuel (de Castillo). And by the time she ascended to being an *autora autónoma* [autonomous manager/director], she had become a well-respected and celebrated actor, playing primarily lead roles in *comedias* and *autos sacramentales* [plays on religious and moral themes]. Álvarez established her first professional enterprise in 1679, and ran it for three years before she took a break to work as an actor during the 1682–1683 theater season. She appears again in historical documents dated 1688, with the prestigious title of *autora de comedias por Su Majestad* [director of plays for His Majesty], a title she held until 1692.

As a product of a family that was a theatrical dynasty, Bárbara Coronel followed a different course from that of Álvarez. Born in Valencia in 1632, she was the daughter of Agustín Coronel, *autor de comedias por Su Majestad*, and the actress María Coronel, as well as the niece of the famous actor Cosme Pérez, better known as Juan Rana. Bárbara Coronel entered the actors' guild at the tender age of ten, and by age eleven she was a regular on stage, performing for her father's company during the Corpus Festival in Úbeda and, later that year, in the Coliseo de Sevilla. She reappeared thirteen years later in Córdoba as a lead actor, famous for her role as *la mujer vestida de hombre* [woman dressed as a man], a role in which both Álvarez and Laura also excelled (González 907). By age 35, Coronel had established her own company, managing and directing plays in 1667, 1669, and 1670. We find her again in 1676, performing with her company in Valencia. She continued to perform through 1678, retiring at age 48.

Born into a wealthy family in Granada, Fabiana Laura followed a unique path to becoming an illustrious director, impresario, and manager. Her father Matías Andreas de Eslava was a physician and her mother Salvadora Hurtado was the daughter of a respectable pharmacist. At a young age, Laura moved in with her aunt, who loved the theater and oftentimes sponsored performances at her residence. Growing up around the arts, Laura fell in love with the theater, as well as with one of the actors who frequented her aunt's house. While still in her teens, she ran away to join the traveling theater company run by Francisca López Sustaete, eventually marrying Miguel Bermúdez (de Castro), one of the actors in the group. Their marriage ended in divorce shortly thereafter. Laura then joined another company, traveling to Italy via Córdoba. She was honored with the title of *autora de comedias por Su Majestad* in 1669. For the next three years, she and her company traveled to cities such as Valencia, Málaga, and Madrid, where critics applauded her and her group of actors for their performances. From 1672 through 1688, Laura earned high praise as leading lady for other professional companies, becoming one of the most celebrated and sought-after actresses of her time. In 1691, she and her second husband, actor Manuel Ángel, established a new organization wherein they shared the roles of director and manager. Due to her success as an *autora* and his lack of directorial experience, Laura most likely played the larger role in the management of their theater company, which produced winning plays.

Staging the *comedia* as a play where tragedy and comedy coexist was a commercial venture that, in order to succeed, required entrepreneurial and leadership skills from those in positions of authority. One alternative career path for women actors was that of manager/director of one's own company, which, according to some contemporary writers, was believed to be lucrative enough to keep one well fed, as Luis Quiñónes de Benavente indicated in one of his *Loas* or prologues: "Usase ya en nuestros tiempos/Ser los autores muy gordos" (31) [Nowadays directors tend to be very fat]. Ferrer Valls in her paper "Actors and Theatrical Documentation in Spain in the Sixteenth and Seventeenth Centuries" defines *autores* as those who legally formed and ran theater companies as bona fide businesspersons. *Autores* (both men and women) were responsible for negotiating contracts with actors, playwrights, stage crews, and the managers of the *corrales*. They also commissioned plays, scheduled and secured rehearsal and performance venues, hired actors and crew members, reviewed promotional materials, and handled the bookkeeping, which leads one to believe that, as young girls, these women must have been taught at least basic arithmetic. In fact, DICAT lists thirteen women who held the position of *cobradora*, responsible for collecting entrance fees at the playhouses. As heads of their organizations, they executed all aspects of theater productions. These businesspersons acted as dramaturges, designers, and directors, buying and modifying scripts, designing stage sets (including scenery, furniture, props), and directing plays according to the venue and audience.

Apparently, women who ascended to the position of *autoras* also wore several hats in order for the *comedias* to thrive. Normally, a woman acquired the role of *autora* by one of three means: the first method was by functioning as a *co-autora* [co-director] in her husband's company, the second was by acquiring ownership of her husband's company after his death, and the third was by ascending to director on her own merit—what Mimma De Salvo labels "*autónoma*" [autonomous]. In the early 1600s, women usually inherited the job from their husbands as *viudas* [widows] or rose to the position of *co-autoras* sharing equal management responsibilities with their spouses. As a rule, women as daughters of actors or *autores* did not inherit the position of *autora*. Manuela (de) Escamilla was the one exception found in the historical documents (see De Salvo). Although there were occasions before the 1600s where women directed alongside their husbands, for example, Juana Manzano in 1585 and Juana Bautista de Leon in 1571 (Sanz Ayán, "Las 'autoras' en comedias," 549–50; Sanz Ayán, "More Than Faded Beauties," 116), they were the exceptions to the rule.

However, the dawn of the seventeenth century witnessed an emergence of *co-autoras* who either worked as co-directors with their husbands or with other *autores* unrelated to them. Sanz Ayán reckons, "in these years, given the scenic needs of the plays represented and the important role of music and dance, sharing directorial duties with experienced *autoras* would have been a good alternative, not to mention that some were well-known and their names as directors would have added value to the company" ("Las 'autoras' en comedias" 559).[2] By the second half of the seventeenth-century, women worked their way up the hierarchies of the theater community to become successful *autoras autónomas* on their own merit. According to Sanz Ayán, these actresses generally acquired the role of *autoras* at the pinnacle of their stage careers or after accumulating ample knowledge of the theater business ("Las 'autoras' en comedias" 554). In other words, it took more than just celebrity status to qualify one as an *autora*. Experience and intricate knowledge of the theater industry often determined the type of license granted to a director. The official license of *autora de comedia por Su Majestad*, as opposed to just *autora*, conceded special benefits to the director and her company. Once established, a commercial theater fell under one of two categories: *compañías de título o reales* [royal or titled companies], theater companies with official licenses from the Royal Council to perform in a league of major towns and cities, or *compañías de la legua* [companies of league], those who were prohibited from performing within said "league" (Ferrer Valls, "Actors and Theatrical Documentation").

Directors of commercial theaters who were granted the official title were given exclusive rights to perform secular plays in the city's *corrales* from Easter to Corpus and then *autos* during Corpus Christi festivities (Ferrer Valls, "Actors and Theatrical Documentation"). This privilege provided actors a platform for the prospect of diverging from social norms, especially if one considers, from a postmodern perspective, that these practices "initially pursued for representational ends often produce inner feelings that are then sought for their own experiential sake" (Shusterman 26); a way of empowering women actors with "aesthetic agency." In addition, as members of an acting guild, women exerted "economic agency" usually reserved for men (Daniels 165), a way of having a place and opportunity to work their way up the ranks. Thirty-two women are said to have ascended to the role of *autoras autónomas* between 1643 and 1706.[3] Álvarez, Coronel, and Laura, who count among the members of this elite group and whose function equaled that of their male counterparts, went on to hold the title of *autora de comedia por Su Majestad*.

As impresarios, *autoras de comedia por Su Majestad* held the most important position in their organizations, as aforementioned, possessing legal authority and responsibility for all aspects of the theater. The jobs of the owners of the acting companies comprised administrative, managerial, and directing duties. During the forty-day observation of Lent, they negotiated contracts and established their company's repertoire and secured the plays and performance venues for the theatrical year, which began at Easter or soon thereafter and lasted until Carnival the following year, ending on Shrove Tuesday. This task was often daunting since *autores* normally booked roughly twenty performances a month. Documents show, for example, that during March 1670, Laura and her group participated in fifty performances in Málaga, which included dances, music, *entremeses* [interludes], and *sainetes* [one-act farces]. In 1676, Coronel and her company gave forty-two performances at the *casa de comedias de la Olivera de Valencia* from May 30 to July 30. And from April through May of 1690, Álvarez and her troupe presented forty-four shows, including dances for the royal family at the Palace in Valladolid and *autos* during the Corpus Christi festival.

Comedias along with historical documents provide a glimpse into the lives of actors and *autores*. By way of illustration, in *Lo fingido verdadero* [The True Deceiver], Lope de Vega highlights the problems a director encounters in mounting various productions. Through the voice of his protagonist Ginés, Lope explains how the *autor* feels pressured to find actors that can memorize several plays at once, such as *comedias, loas, entremeses,* and *autos*. Due to the complexity of the plays, he also has to hire a prompter in case actors forget their lines. And finally, the *autor* contracts a *guardarropa* to ensure that costumes and props are properly maintained and set before each performance. In addition, unforeseen events can cause directors undue stress, especially with the absence of actors or musicians due to illness or lateness, as Ginés laments in Act 2, Scene 2:

> Ginés: ¿Los músicos?
> Pinabelo: Florisén dijo que luego vendría.
> Ginés: ¡Harto bien, por vida mía! Siempre nos ha de faltar un músico.
>   (*Lo fingido verdadero* 234)
>
> ["And the musicians?" "Florisen said he'd be right along." "A fine state of affairs, upon my life! We're always short a musician." (Vega Carpio, *Acting Is Believing*, 70–71)]

The summoning of acting companies or particular actors to perform in court added to an *autora*'s frustrations. Unforeseen situations oftentimes had immediate and disastrous effects on a company's finances. For example, in 1691, Álvarez suffered financial hardship after she was ordered to return to Madrid to perform for the royal family. Lost fees from canceled performances far exceeded the payment she received for the performance at the Buen Retiro (Sanz Ayán, "Las 'autoras' en comedias," 570). Therefore, in order to safeguard against capital losses, managers frequently scheduled more than one or two shows a day, which put a burden on the actors to memorize several plays at once; Álvarez's company in fact performed three plays in four days in March 1690: they presented *El secreto a voces* [The Secret in Words] on March 27 and 28; performances were canceled on March 29 due to "mal día y no aver jente" [bad weather and no audience]; then they put on *Caso con dos puertas* [House of Two Doors] on the March 30; and *La fuerza de la ley* [The Force of the Law] on March 31. That same year, Álvarez's company performed a two-day run of five plays (a combination of *comedias* and *autos*) in Peñeranda beginning on May 29. They ended the run on June 1 with two *comedias*, one performed in the morning and another in the afternoon.

Spanish playwrights depended on the actors' skill to read and understand their work before interpreting their roles on stage. Evidence of this is found in contracts that required actors to study the plays, musical numbers, and so forth provided by the *autor/a* (Miguel Gallo 289). Therefore, part of an acting company's program required actors to familiarize themselves intimately with the company's large repertoire. This meant that actors and directors invested many hours studying and rehearsing, as witnessed by Agustín de

Rojas Villandrando, who in his 1603 *El viaje entretenido* wrote: "Estos representantes/antes que Dios amanece/escribiendo y estudiando . . . / se están ensayando siempre" [These actors, who rise before dawn, are writing and studying . . . / they're always rehearsing] (90). During rehearsals, actors normally read and made changes to scripts according to the *autora*'s directions, which indicates that most must have known how to read and write. According to my assessment, out of the 1,571 actresses listed in DICAT, only thirty-six are noted as *not* being able to write. It is questionable whether five of these thirty-six women were even actresses. Seventy-nine of all of the women listed were musicians, three of whom were illiterate. And of the sixty-eight actresses that had acquired the title of *autora*, only two could not write, which does not mean that they could not read. For instance, in 1691, when Laura co-directed with her husband, four of the five women employed by their company did not know how to write (again, this does not indicate an inability to read): Bonifacia Camacho, Francisca Pampanón, Feliciana María Suárez, and Teodora Vázquez. Yet from 1691 through 1692, they presented seventy plays, twenty of which were new.

The intense routines cultivated work habits that became ingrained in the actors' daily régime, a lifestyle admired by Rojas Villandrando:

Yo me admiro
cómo es posible que pueden
estudiar toda su vida
    (302)

[I admire how they study their entire lives.]

Furthermore, actors rarely rested in between performances, as demonstrated in a scene in *Lo fingido verdadero*. In the midst of a run, Marcela insists that her fellow actors continue to "study" and "prepare" for future performances:

Remédiese otra comedia,
que mientras éstas se hacen
estudiaremos algunas
para hacerlas adelante.
    (*Lo fingido verdadero* 285)

[We'll have to prepare a new play but, in the meantime, we'll study some old plays for future performances].

In most cases, actors performed several roles in one season, as Fray Juan de Mariana observed of the women on stage: "Estas mujeres no sólo hacen personajes de mujeres, sino de soldados también, de rufianes y de esclavos, vestidas a la manera de los hombres" (Bravo Villasante 151) [These women not only play female characters, but also soldiers, hooligans, and slaves, dressed in male garb]. This was a feat not easily accomplished, especially considering that once the theatrical season began, companies had short lead times before opening a show. Historical records show that, in 1692, Álvarez and her company committed to rehearsing fifteen plays in less than two weeks (see Ferrer Valls, et al.). In addition, *autores* expected their actors to commit to memory writings of considerable sophistication, as in the aforementioned case of Álvarez's company, whose repertoire of *comedias* included *Cueva y castillo de Amor* [Cave and Castle of Love], *El tercero de su afrenta*, *Mejor está que estaba* [The Third Offence, Better Never to Have Been], *Psiquis y Cupido* [Psyche and Cupid], and *Travesuras son valor* [Bravery in Mischiefs].

Many of the actors came from working middle-class families who hired tutors to teach their daughters to read and write as, for example, in Lope's (1981) *La dama boba* [Lady Simpleton]. Other actors belonged to theatrical families who made a reasonably comfortable living in the theater (McKendrick 84). Therefore, it stands to reason that they would have had the means to hire a tutor for their daughters. It made sense for them to invest in their daughters' education, especially if the girls followed their parents into the profession; it increased their chances of becoming prosperous actors and even *autoras*. Moreover, theater companies also functioned as schools. In addition to acting, women were trained as singers, dancers, and even musicians. For instance, Josefa Ramón, a musician, also played a male *gracioso* [comic character, fool].

Consequently, this type of learning environment cultivated critical thinking skills for the actors. In addition to memorizing highly complicated scripts, these young women also had to evaluate how best to perform them (McKendrick 91). In the process of learning and interpreting their roles, actors actively and skillfully engaged in conceptualizing, analyzing, and applying the information they gathered not only from the plays they read, but also from their own observations, experiences, reflections, reasoning, or communication with others in and out of their theater companies. On many occasions, women in positions of authority, in this case *autoras*, served as models for young apprentices.

A woman in a leadership position must have instilled a feeling of empowerment in young actresses, especially if one considers, as Melveena McKendrick posits, that if women actors "took being able to read for granted, then it is fair to assume that other forms of untraditional female behavior would have seemed more comprehensible and acceptable to them" (91), such as those of businesswomen. As members of acting companies, many of these young actors acquired administrative and directing skills fundamental to running an organization (see De Salvo). Furthermore, the association of theater companies with the acting guild from 1631 opened doors for women to pursue a career path. Hence, young, unmarried women seeking a vocation in the theater could maneuver themselves into roles of authority and influence.

When hiring young, single, female actors, many *autores* faced the task of overcoming the prohibition against unmarried women working on stage. In 1587, the courts reversed a decree that had banned women actors from participating in *comedias*, but the law, which followed the strict social codes set by the Church and the State, only allowed married actresses accompanied by their husbands to perform on stage. The law also prohibited women and men from dressing in a manner that represented anything other than their own gender or status position, which led to several injunctions against improper attire. From 1563 to 1691, sixteen luxury laws were passed in Spain (Martínez Bermejo 97).

The exercise of cultivating habits of certain individuals or groups of people to comply with or diverge from social norms played an important role in early modern Spain, where treatises and devotional works regarding social decorum circulated. Treatises that advised their readers on proper dress codes and conduct include: Juan Luis Vives's *De institutione feminae christianae* [The Education of a Christian Woman], Fray Luis de León's *La perfecta casada* [The Perfect Wife], Francisco de Osuna's *Norte de los estados* [The North Star of Ranks], and Antonio de Guevara's 1868 *Letra para recien casados* [Letter to Newlyweds]. Since actors altered their external appearance through costume, makeup, or hairstyle to change or enhance a character's physical traits, sumptuary laws were put in place to control their dress. The 1615 decree, for instance, prohibited women actors from dressing provocatively, including as a man (Bravo Villasante 152). The prohibition of plays due to concern with actors' costumes (especially with women dressing as men) led to the closing of the *corrales* in 1644 and 1646. Even though the sumptuary laws were largely ignored, the possibility of fines or imprisonment loomed large at every performance.

Nonetheless, the *autoras* in question employed both married and single women actors to play roles such as *la mujer vestida de hombre*, and many women who studied under them became *autoras* on their own merits. By the second half of the seventeenth century, the majority of *autoras* had worked previously for companies directed by women, which were essentially acting schools (Sanz Ayán, "Las 'autoras' en comedias," 546; Sanz Ayán, "More Than Faded Beauties," 118–19). These schools offered actresses instructions and hands-on experience in the arts of acting and entrepreneurship. At times the *autoras* conceded the position of *primera dama* [leading lady] for ancillary roles in order to devote more time to directing and mentorship. One such model was Álvarez, who, in 1690, yielded her role as *primera dama* to Águeda Francisca. Álvarez's attitude, according to Sanz Ayán, "indicates that she possessed an incipient entrepreneurial approach as she sought to make the company function well as a whole, regardless of her celebrated status" ("Las 'autoras' en comedias" 567). Moreover, even the women who never worked directly with *autoras* would have at some point in their careers witnessed women directing, negotiating, and managing every aspect of productions. No doubt, these models inspired in women a prospect of becoming entrepreneurs and operating companies of their own ("Las 'autoras' en comedias" 562).

Some of these women excelled as entrepreneurs, and they even ran for the guilds' high-ranking office of *mayordoma*. Ana Isabel de Castro was elected in 1686, and María de Navas in 1697, to that position. They belonged to powerful institutions, such as the *Cofradía* [Guild] *de Nuestra Señora de la Novena*, which protected their status as professionals, increasing both married and unmarried women's chances for success. From the mid-1600s, various records listed unmarried women actors and directors as members of acting companies, a far cry from the court orders that once had prevented single women from gracing the stage (Sanz Ayán, "Las 'autoras' en comedias," 559–62). And even though the aforementioned 1587 decree that prohibited unmarried women from working in acting companies was still in effect, respectable companies continued to hire them.

All three of the *autoras* featured in this essay employed single female actors in their companies. In 1667, Coronel employed Ana María, who enjoyed a long career in theater, and then Josefa de Guzmán, who played *segunda dama*, from 1669–1670. It is unclear if any of the women in Coronel's company in 1676—for example, Josefa de Salazar (also known as Pingorrongo), Manuela de Arias, Ana María Santa, and María Navarro (who later established her own theater company as well as trained future *autoras*)—ever married. In 1669, Laura employed Hipólita María de Quiñones, who was single at the time. She married an actor from Manuel Vallejo's company the following year. Quiñones worked until the age of seventy, and was ninety when she died. Margarita Zuazo, who never married, went on to run her own company and to tutor other young women to become *autoras*. Notably, Álvarez employed the highest number of single actresses. Schooled by Álvarez in 1692, most of the following women continued to enjoy long careers in the theater: Josefa Laura (or de Cabia) earned enough money to support her family and a servant; Juana Laura remained active in theater until 1695; Sabina Pascual, daughter of the *autor* Félix Pascual and the actor Manuela Bustamente (La Mentrilla), was elevated to *autora* in 1706; Catalina Antonia, a musician and an actor, continued to earn a living in theater for many years; and María Antonia enjoyed a long career in theater playing *quinta* and *tercera damas* [fifth and third female roles] (1690–1706). The success of the actors attests to the *autoras*' exceptional direction and mentorship.

As masters of their craft, moreover, *autoras* played a critical part in the evolution of the theater, fostering collaboration and connections with each other and with other women in their profession. Andrea de Salazar, a well-respected *autora* whose company specialized in elaborate palace productions in 1695 and 1696 (Sanz Ayán, "Las 'autoras' en comedias," 565), worked side-by-side with Álvarez in Manuel Vallejo's company for a few years before they became licensed *autoras*. Álvarez also worked together with Laura in the company of Jerónimo García. Laura shared the role of *primera dama* with Teresa de Robles, another celebrated actor and *autora*, as members of Agustín Manuel de Castilla's company in 1679. In 1684, Laura and her apprentice María de Escamilla took turns playing the lead role in Manuel de Vallejo's acting company. Together, they served as career-minded models for a new generation of women actors, who also established a network of women professionals by hiring and schooling young women in the business of theater.

Hiring and working with fellow colleagues and apprentices became a frequent practice in the second half of the seventeenth century. For instance, Andrea de Salazar hired Águeda Francisca as her leading lady in 1695 and 1696, a role she played for Álvarez in 1690. Ana Hipólita (Vaquero), Francisca's sister, worked as an understudy for Álvarez in 1690 and gained employment in Laura's acting company for the next several years. Hipólita continued an active theater career until 1709. Bonifacia Camacho (o López) was *primera dama* in Álvarez's company in 1690. Camacho then entered Laura's company in 1691 and 1692 (as *tercera dama*). Josefa de Guzmán who, as mentioned above, worked for Coronel in 1669 and 1670, continued to work for *autoras* such as Margarita Zuazo (1673–1676), who studied under Laura, and Ángela Barba (1684–1685), who trained with Coronel. Guzmán entered Barba's company as *segunda dama* and later advanced to leading lady under her tutelage.

Others moved up the social and economic hierarchy by managing and directing their own acting companies. Ana Isabel de Castro rose to the position of *autora* soon after working for Álvarez in 1692. Castro began her own enterprise in 1693 and ran it until 1696. Sabina Pascual, another acting student of Álvarez, became *autora* in 1706 and also in 1719. Barba, a member of Coronel's 1676 organization, became *autora de comedias* in 1683 and *autora de comedias por Su Majestad* in 1684–1685. From 1687 to 1688, Barba formed another company in which she shared directing responsibilities with Hipólito de Olmedo. María Navarro, an understudy for Coronel in 1676, started her own acting school in 1701 with one of her students, Mariana de Prado, graduating to *autora* in 1703. Margarita Zuazo, a product of Fabiana Laura's tutelage from 1669 to 1671, also exemplifies the role of mentor and impresario. Zuazo established her own enterprises as a single woman, gainfully employing and training young women such as Guzmán (mentioned earlier), and Jerónima de Sandoval, who later established her own company in 1701. Therefore, by the second half of the 1600s, the majority of the *autoras* who had previously worked for companies directed by women created schools of their own, where women received instruction and hands-on experience in acting and entrepreneurship.

Early modern Spanish history offers us strong-minded and career-oriented women, such as María Álvarez, Bárbara Coronel, and Fabiana Laura who, along with other theater *colegas*, reinvented themselves as artistic directors and executive administrators. They managed schools that fostered an awareness of autonomy in their young apprentices, producing a sense of community among women in their discipline. Attracting the collaboration of fellow actors and directors, they established a network of women theater professionals who would become *autoras autónomas*—directors, entrepreneurs, and mentors in their own right.

Notes

1. Unless otherwise noted, the data on all the *autoras* and actors mentioned in this essay are extracted from DICAT.

2. All translations are mine, unless otherwise indicated.

3. Mimma De Salvo lists in the Appendix of her dissertation the following women as having ascended to the role of *autoras autónomas*: María Álvarez, Ángela Barba, Francisca Bezón, María de la O (Bustamante, y), Isabel de Castro, Juana (María) de Cisneros, Juana Coloma, Bárbara Coronel, Ana María Craso, María de la Cruz, Ángela Drago, María Enríquez, Catalina Esteban, Josefa María (Fernández), Inés Gallo, Fabiana Laura, Ángela León, Manuela Liñán, Francisca López (de) (Sustaete) (*viuda o autónoma*), Magdalena López, Petronila Antonia (Lugo, de), María Jacinta, María (Manuela) Navarro, María Navas, Juana Ortiz, Juana Peres, Juana de los Reyes, Teresa de Robles,

Jerónima Sandoval, Manuela Serafina, Antonia Manuela (Sevillano, Galindo), and Margarita Zuazo.

References

Bravo Villasante, Carmen. *La mujer vestida de hombre en el teatro español: Siglos xvi–xvii.* Madrid: Revista de Occidente, 1955.
Daniels, Mary Blythe. "Re-visioning Gender on the Seventeenth-Century Spanish Stage: A Study of Actresses and *Autoras*." PhD diss., University of Kentucky, 1998.
Deranty, Jean-Philippe, and Andrew Dunstall. "Doing Justice to the Past: Critical Theory and the Problems of Historicism." *Philosophy and Social Criticism* 43.8 (2007): 812–36.
De Salvo, Mimma. "La mujer en la práctica escénica de los Siglos de Oro: la búsqueda de un espacio profesional." PhD diss., Universitat de València. Midesa s.r.l., 2008, www.midesa.it/.
Ferrer Valls, Teresa. "Actors and Theatrical Documentation in Spain in the Sixteenth and Seventeenth Centuries." Paper presented at the VII World Shakespeare Congress: Shakespeare and the Mediterranean. Valencia, Spain: Universitat de València, April 18–23, 2001, www.uv.es/entresiglos.
———. *Diccionario Biográfico de actores del teatro clásico español (DICAT).* Kassel, Germany: Edition Reichenberger, 2008.
Ferrer Valls, Teresa, et al. *Base de datos de comedias mencionadas en la documentación teatral (1540–1700).* Universitat de València, 2016.
González, Lola. "La mujer vestida de hombre. Aproximación a una revisión de tópico a la luz de la práctica escénica." *AISO. Actas VI* (2002): 905–16, www.cervantes.es.
Guevara, Antonio. *A los recien casados. letra para Mosen Puche, valenciano, en la cual se toca largamente como el marido con la mujer y la mujer con el marido se han de haber.* Madrid: A Durán, 1868.
León, Fray Luis de. *La perfecta casada.* Madrid: Porrúa, 1999.
Martínez Bermejo, Saúl. "Beyond Luxury: Sumptuary Legislation in 17th-Century Castile." In *Making, Using and Resisting the Law in European History.* Edited by G. Lottes, E. Medijainen, and J. Viðar Sigurðsson, Pisa University Press, 2008.
McKendrick, Melveena. "Representing their Sex: Actresses in Seventeenth-Century Spain." In *Rhetoric and Reality in Early Modern Spain*, edited by Richard Pym, Tamesis, 2006, 72–91.
Miguel Gallo, Ignacio Javier de. *El teatro en Burgos, 1550–1752: el patio de comedias, las compañías y la actividad escénica: estudio y documentos.* Burgos: EXCMO. Ayuntamiento de Burgos, 1994.
Mujica, Bárbara. Preface to *Women Writers of Early Modern Spain: Sophia's Daughters*, ix–xiii. Yale University Press, 2004.
Osuna, Francisco de. *Norte de los estados, en que se da regla de bivir a los mancebos y a los casados y a los bindos y a todos los continentes, y se tratan muy por estenso los remedios del desastrado casamiento.* 1541. Burgos: Juan de Junta, 2014.

Quiñónes de Benavente, Luis. *Colección de piezas dramáticas, entremeses, loas y jácaras escritas*. Edited by Cayetano Rosell and Manuel A. Vargas, Madrid: A. Durán, 1872.

Rojas Villandrando, Agustín de. *El viaje entretenido*, Madrid: B. Rodríguez Serra, 1901.

Sanz Ayán, Carmen. "Las 'autoras' en comedias en el siglo XVII: empresarias teatrales en tiempos de Calderón." *Calderón de la Barca y la España del barroco* 2 (2001): 543–79. Madrid: Centro de estudios Políticos y Constitucionales.

———. "More Than Faded Beauties: Women Theater Managers of Early Modern Spain." *Early Modern Women: An Interdisciplinary Journal* 10, no. 1 (2015): 114–21.

Shusterman, Richard. *Body Consciousness: A Philosophy of Mindfulness and Somaesthetics*. Cambridge University Press, 2008.

Vega Carpio, Lope de. *Acting Is Believing: A Tragicomedy in Three Acts by Lope de Vega (c 1607–1608)*. Translated by Michael D. McGaha, Trinity University Press, 1986.

———. *La dama boba*. Edited by Diego Marín. Madrid: Cátedra, 1981.

———. *Lo fingido verdadero. Comedias Vol. 1*. Edited by Luis Guarner, Barcelona: Iberia, 1967, 191–287.

Vives, Juan Luis. *De Institutione Feminae Christianae (Selected Works of Juan Luis Vives)*. Translated by Charles Fantazzi, edited by Charles Fantazzi and Constatinus Matheeussen, Brill, 1996–1998.

SUSAN PAUN DE GARCÍA

Women in Charge
Autoras and Actresses in the Reign of Felipe V

THANKS TO THE WORK of literary scholars, musicologists, and historians who have built upon the early work of Emilio Cotarelo y Mori, as well as the archival efforts of Norman Shergold, John Varey, and their various collaborators, we now understand a great deal more about the theatrical profession in general in Spain's sixteenth and seventeenth centuries—both on and off the stage—than we did a short while ago, and much more about women in the profession in particular (see Sanz Ayán; and Ferrer Valls, "La mujer sobre el tablado"). Most studies, however, stop at the year 1700, a date that, while convenient, might give the impression that a change of dynasty led to immediate alterations in popular taste and theatrical practice. While the new royals imported their own artistic preferences,[1] audiences in the public theaters remained faithful to Spanish traditions. Nevertheless, alternatives to old traditions gradually made inroads, facilitated by women in charge. With the increasing importance of both music and comedy on the stage, women came into their own in the eighteenth century, both as managers and as performers.

Of particular interest are stars of the stage and *autoras*, or owner-directors of companies. Women such as María de Navas, Teresa de Robles, Sabina Pascual, Juana de Orozco, or Petronila Jibaja (or Xibaja/Gibaja) ran companies with star performers like Francisca de Castro and Rosa Rodríguez, who performed in the commercial theaters (Cruz and Príncipe) and also in royal command performances. A closer look at their circumstances and their work lends insight into the limitations imposed upon women in the profession as well as into situations that allowed them to rise to the top. The familial nature and structure of the theatrical profession provided apprenticeship opportunities through which the traditional modes and models of performance were continued, despite the forces of change that pushed Spanish theatrical culture toward modernization or "Europeization" in the eighteenth century.

Family Ties

Perhaps the fact that women in the theater were required to have some connection, by family or by marriage, to a male can account for the "dynastic" nature of performing companies (so characterized by Charles Davis and John Varey [174]). Many *hijos/hijas de la comedia* [sons/daughters of the stage] "inherited" their profession; Davis and Varey list nine families that accounted for over half of the actors and actresses in Spain in the first two decades of the eighteenth century (183–86).[2] Family ties led not only to roles on the stage but also to positions of authority, as *autor/as* or manager-impresarios. The family was the ideal trampoline to launch a career and was a veritable guild of professional formation. A case in point is that of Teresa de Robles, whose trajectory as a *graciosa* [a comic figure, often a servant or soubrette] can be traced all the way back to Cosme Pérez, who trained her grandfather, Antonio de Escamilla. Antonio then trained his daughter Manuela to play the role of Juan Ranilla, and his granddaughter Teresa to master the role of the *alcalde burlesco* [buffoonish mayor] in *mojigangas* and *entremeses* [mummeries and interludes] (Buezo, "Mujer y desgobierno," 107–19). Both Teresa and her mother specialized as *terceras damas* [third part actresses], or *graciosas*, comic roles that often involved singing in shorter pieces. Notably, Robles carried on the family tradition in another facet of the theater, as "director" of a company. Her grandfather Antonio, her stepfather, José Verdugo de la Cuesta, and her aunt Manuela had all been *autores* (De Salvo, "La importancia de las sagas familiares," 196–97).

The case of Teresa de Robles was certainly not unique. Of the approximately 1350 documented actresses who were active between the end of the sixteenth century and the first decade of the eighteenth, ninety-six, in addition to being actresses, during some time in their career were also *autoras de comedias*, directing or sharing the direction of a theatrical company in the capacity of impresario, compared to 660 male *autores* in the same period (De Salvo, "La búsqueda de un espacio profesional," 457). Even if the "falsas autoras" — women to whom the term was applied simply to mean "wife of the *autor*" — are eliminated, the number of *autoras* during that time is still eighty-six. Most of them, however, did not rise to the top of the profession; that is, they were not in possession of the "título de Su Majestad" [royal title] giving them license to perform in the theaters of Madrid during the season and at royal command performances. Documents reveal only eight such *autoras de título* ("La búsqueda de un espacio profesional" 473).

What Did the *Autores* Do?

The bureaucracy of theater administration in the early eighteenth century had not changed since 1632, when the Ayuntamiento de Madrid [town council] created the Junta de teatros, a hierarchical body whose authority extended over all actors and theaters in Spain and its colonies. The Junta, consisting of a judge protector of the theaters, a magistrate, and two commissioners of theaters, controlled the formation of companies, the care of scripts and scores, the maintenance of theaters, as well as the conduct (professional and personal) of actors. During Lent, the Juez Protector [Judge Protector] selected the *autores* of the two companies that would play in the court during the next season, which started on Easter Sunday and continued through Shrove Tuesday. The *autor* had to present the judge with a list of company members (usually between twenty-five and thirty actors, musicians, copyists, prompters, box office managers, and wardrobe managers), bring problems to his attention, and consult with civil and religious authorities to find solutions to problems.

As head of the company, the *autor/a* often played principal roles as well. A company normally had around six (but sometimes as many as ten) *galanes* [leading men] and *damas* [leading ladies] each, ranked from first to sixth according to prestige, pay, and specialization. Rounding out the troupe were *barbas* [authority figures], *vejetes* [old men], and *graciosos* and *graciosas*. Traditionally, the *tercera dama* played comic roles, sometimes earning as much as the *primera* [first] *dama*. All *damas* often sang, but *galanes* rarely did; *graciosas* and *graciosos* usually both sang and danced.

In a season of nine months, a company could perform seventy or eighty plays besides *entremeses, loas, mojigangas, sainetes* [interludes, prologues, mummeries, one-act farces], etc. Most were in repertory and needed little rehearsal, but the public demanded new plays; the authorities increasingly sought to satisfy their demand (in order to maximize ticket sales) by limiting any previously performed works, although sometimes the *autores* could get away with changing a work's title or using its less familiar subtitle (e.g., *El alcalde de*

Zalamea y El garrote más bien dado) [The Mayor of Zalamea and The Most Deserved Garrote].

The responsibilities of an *autora* were not easy, as can be seen in the case of Juana de Orozco, one of the most important *autoras* of the eighteenth century. Varey, N.D. Shergold, and Charles Davis (160–63) provide documents that show her as one of the *autores de titulo* of 1728. Her company is cited as having been that of Antonio Vela, so Orozco followed the custom of the widow taking over the company upon the death of her husband. (Vela was still noted as *autor* on July 11, but Orozco is listed as *autora* on July 26, 1728.)

Almost immediately, Orozco had to face legal suits and staffing issues. In August 1728, Josefa Sanz, *sexta dama* [sixth part] in the then Juana de Orozco company, asked to be released from her contract. The tribunal of medical examiners refused to examine her husband, a medical student, for his degree while his wife was employed as an actress. Orozco maintained that Sanz should be required to finish out the year, given that she sang soprano and her absence from the stage would severely hamper the company. The decision came down in favor of Sanz because, as a *sexta dama*, her roles were minor and her singing was not part of her contract but voluntary. Her continued presence on the stage would have destroyed her husband's career possibilities for life, and she would have become the breadwinner of the family, which would be "en la malicia común" [in common or popular spiteful gossip] seen as indecent.

Evidently, Orozco did not enjoy hiring members of the company. In 1729, faced with increasing losses of revenue due to a lack of actors (*gracioso, segundo músico, segunda barba, dama música, sobresaliente* [musical actress, supernumerary]), she asked to be released from the position of *autora* and to have the Junta name someone else. The petition was denied (Varey, Shergold, and Davis 171–72). In 1738, Orozco again tangled with the bureaucracy, facing a problem caused by a new rule designed to increase the number of new plays. When she brought a list to the commission for approval, she was ordered to remove from it forty-eight plays that had previously been performed since 1732 (see Hormigón, *Catálogo de directoras*, 901–2). And in 1739, Orozco had to seek permission for the eleven-year-old Catalina Pacheco to wear the traditional costume for the part of Trufaldín, which would show her legs (893).

How Did Women Become *Autoras?*

The paths to becoming an *autora* did not change for the most part from the seventeenth to the eighteenth century (Ferrer Valls, "La incorporación de la mujer," and "La mujer sobre el tablado"; see also De Salvo, "La búsqueda de un espacio profesional," 497–508). The position was closely linked to having a connected male family member (father, brother, son) or husband.³ While sometimes "autora" designated the state of being married to an *autor*, the term could also refer to a married couple that worked as collaborators or co-managers. *Co-autoras* could undertake business in their husbands' place, dealing with legal, economic, or contractual issues, as well as payments and receipts, essentially representing the husbands, who might be the official directors in name. De Salvo ("La búsqueda de un espacio profesional" 497) lists fifty *co-autoras* between the last decade of the sixteenth century and the first decade of the eighteenth. Of these, eighteen took over the company after the death of their husband.

From 1660 on, we begin to find greater numbers of *autoras* working alone, not connected to husbands, either because they were not married (or had been widowed for years), or because even though they might have been married, their lives and impresarial activities were conducted independently of their husbands, who in many cases were not *autores*. In effect, even though actresses were legally required to be married and to work with their spouses, these women somehow managed to get around this. Some of these *autoras autónomas* worked with "título official," among whom Teresa de Robles and María de Navas functioned as *autoras* in the first decade of the eighteenth century, with Sabina Pascual in the 1710s, Juana de Orozco in the 1720 and 1730s, and Petronila Jibaja in the 1740s functioning as an autonomous *autoras* ("La búsqueda de un espacio professional" 475).

Although most independent *autoras* had entrepreneurial careers that could be called unstable or transitory, they still managed to gain fame both as actresses and *autoras*; their talents were sought after in the major cities of Spain and Portugal, and for the most prestigious theatrical events of their time ("La búsqueda de un espacio profesional" 516). Their fame also opened the doors to important positions such as the honorary annual *mayordomía* [stewardship] of the Cofradia de Nuestra Señora de la Novena.⁴

While we know very little about most of the *autoras*, what we do know indicates that they held long careers within the family of the theater. María de Navas and Teresa de Robles led eventful lives, coping with changes in political and personal fortunes, working their way to success, often in spite of themselves. They are the most mentioned in Shergold and Varey's *Genealogía*⁵ and have been studied thoroughly by Catalina Buezo. The others, while mentioned in the *Genealogía* and listed often in documents, have less information available about their lives and careers. Nonetheless, they are frequently noted as important figures.

A brief review of what key sources reveal about seven women — as *autoras*, as actresses, and as important figures in the theater of their time — is provided in the Appendix. Some were active in the late seventeenth century, but all had to contend with the changes in organization and taste that occurred in the eighteenth century with the advent of the new Bourbon dynasty.

Felipe V: Changes in Dynasty and Taste

When the seventeen-year-old Bourbon king Felipe V arrived in 1701, he knew no Spanish and neither did his thirteen-year-old queen Maria Luisa Gabriela de Saboya. The young Bourbon king's preference for Italian theater, and opera in particular, was clearly influential. When he was in Italy, Felipe V had enjoyed musical performances, including operas, as well as plays in Italian. As the royal couple struggled to learn the Spanish language, they preferred Italian plays and Spanish plays with music. In 1703, the king brought an Italian troupe with him to Madrid and gave them use of its best theater, el Coliseo del Real Sitio del Buen Retiro. The company became known as Los Trufaldines, and they built their own *corral* in the calle Alcalá.[6] The two official Spanish companies complained, and with good reason. The Italians played daily, except on Friday and for command performances. Their shows began at 6 pm, and men and women sat together, which took away audiences from the Spanish troupes. The Italians also did not pay taxes to support the hospitals.[7] Known as "cómicos y operistas," starting in 1705 they moved to their own theater, the former *lavadero* [public washhouse] de los Caños del Peral, where they paid no rent for nine years (Cotarelo y Mori, *Historia de la zarzuela*, 26–36).

After the arrival in Spain of Isabel de Farnesio, who married Felipe V shortly after the death of María Luisa de Saboya in 1714, Italian courtiers and artists came to dominate court life in Madrid. In 1719, the newly arrived Italian Marqués de Scotti, named director of the Caños del Peral, set about making changes to benefit the Italians, concentrating on developing a repertory of Italian operas. Given his "virtually unlimited economic and political freedom to champion his Italian opera company," the city either had to accede to the Italians, or "beat them at their own game by competing directly with Scotti's troupe" (Buck 74). During most of the 1720s, the Italians dominated the operatic scene, and the Spanish theater troupes "concentrated on traditional Spanish forms of spectacle and musical theater: the *zarzuela*, the *comedia de magia* (plays featuring magician heroes), and the *comedia de santo* (plays about saints and their miracles)" (74).

Opera: the Road to Fame and Fortune

One of the most important changes in performing arts from the seventeenth century to the eighteenth was the increasing importance and weight of music in the theater and the consequent increasing importance of women in positions of power and leadership:

> "Commercial" court theater, i.e., performances designed for the palace but adapted to the "corrales" or public courtyards, included lengthy singing and dancing roles that called attention to the actresses. Their visibility and popularity opened doors for them in management, and enabled them to circumvent legal controls that heretofore prevented women from independently assuming these professional responsibilities. (Sanz Ayán 119)

The culmination of the trend—opera—is illustrative of these changes for both theater and women performers.

The practice of including music in the *comedia* and related genres became standard during the seventeenth century, but "[p]erhaps more than any other form, the *zarzuela* acted as a kind of mirror of eighteenth-century Spanish culture, reflecting both Iberian tradition and foreign fashion" (Bussey 9). Usually performed first for a royal audience, *zarzuelas* were often later adapted for the public theaters, the initial production expenses having been assumed by the court (17). These long and elaborate two-act productions, with plots based on mythology, often with allegorical overtones, differed from Italian opera in that almost all alternated spoken dialogue with sung portions. While the musical numbers included Italian styles such as *da capo* arias, duets, and ensembles, they also included Spanish forms such as *coplas, jotas,* and *seguidillas* (34–36).

One essential difference between the Italian *opera seria* and the Spanish *zarzuela* was the latter's relative lack of recitatives. Writing in 1796, the musicologist and defender of the *zarzuela* Antonio Eximeno noted the predilection of the Spanish public for theatrical music, but on its own terms:

> Spaniards love music in the theater passionately; but they do not sacrifice reason to this passion; they have small pieces of music that serve as interludes, and they also present musical dramas, that they call zarzuelas, in which scenes are recited and one only sings when the music is required, that is, the passages in which a passion burns. In this way spectators are not annoyed by the insufferable monotony of

the Italian recitative. Instead, the whole story is spoken, the characters, the customs, etc., so that the pleasure of the ear is conciliated with the instruction of the mind. (cited by Cotarelo y Mori, *Historia de la zarzuela*, 1911; translation mine)

As we will see, Spaniards had definite preferences in terms not only of form but also of performance.

Both the early eighteenth-century Spanish *zarzuela* and the Italian *opera seria* included arias with high vocal tessitura, but in Spain, they were sung by women. The castrati, "so popular in Italian opera, [seem] never to have gained acceptance" with the Spanish public, who preferred the "soprano-dominated texture... typical of the early eighteenth-century *zarzuela*.... [T]he Spanish solution was to cast women in male roles" (Bussey 112). While men sang in the chorus or played *barbas* or *graciosos*, women, not castrati, sang the plum roles in the Spanish musical theater, until the arrival in the 1740s of Farinelli, whose direction of the court musical scene saw the ascendance of the Italian style over the Spanish. Between 1710 and 1740, nevertheless, the "Italian Invasion"[8] had begun, and Italian influence pervaded every aspect of theatrical life.

Both William Bussey and Donald C. Buck have noted political as well as artistic ramifications of the "Italian Invasion." Spanish actors saw themselves being progressively replaced by the Italians, first in the palace productions (starting in 1703) and then in the *corrales*. The competition between the Spanish actors and musicians and their Italian counterparts affected the former adversely in some ways, although, according to Bussey, the Spanish companies were financially healthy, and their size grew (129–30).

While the upper classes began to favor opera instead of *zarzuelas*, eventually the popular classes were attracted by the spectacles, made possible by the construction of Italianate theaters to replace the *corrales*:

> During the decade between 1735 and 1745... the old *corrales* in Madrid were torn down. The theatres... that had not changed significantly for approximately 150 years, suddenly ceased to exist. In their place stood Italianate buildings that could have been opera houses in Milan or Naples.... The lavish spectacles like the zarzuela that had always been financed by the court in the seventeenth and early eighteenth centuries had gradually become a product of the public *corrales* as royal support of Italian opera grew. Zarzuelas were now commissioned by the public theatres, not the royal ones, and public taste began to be more important than that of the court. (Bussey 189–90)

Various events took the court from Madrid to Badajoz and then to Seville from January 7, 1729 until 1733. This absence of the court from Madrid, and with the court, the Italians, changed things. At first, the lack of performances at court translated to losses at the box office, prompting theater administrators to look for a way to attract greater audiences: "They found an answer in musical theater: *zarzuelas, comedias con música* [and] operas in the Italian style, with texts by the most popular Spanish dramatists, and sung in Spanish. Between 1728 and 1733 there was a significant increase in the number and cost of these lavish musical productions in Madrid's two *corrales*" (Buck 74). The success of musical theater can be appreciated in two Spanish productions. In 1728, Juana de Orozco's company performed the *zarzuela Hercules furente y matarse por no morirse* [Hercules Enraged and to Kill Oneself to Avoid Dying] twelve times, with a 1729 revival—an eleven-day run—plus two more performances during the summer of 1731. The investment in lavish costumes and sets amounted to a significant commitment on the part of Orozco's company, especially in a time of slumping ticket sales, but the success was encouraging and led to more extravagant productions of *zarzuelas*. Orozco's company produced the *melodrama harmónico Con amor no hay libertad* [With Love There is No Freedom] in 1731, and revived it later in the same year and again in 1732. Orozco's successor, Ignacio Cerquera, revived it again in 1734. Clearly, musical works appealed to the public, and the traditional *zarzuela* form, "updated" in the Italian manner, proved to be a formula for success: "the Vela-Orozco-Cerquera company in particular, boasting a roster rich in talented singers, saw the opportunity to cultivate the Italian style [to] develop ... a new audience for native musical theater, one dependent not on the court but on the mainstream public of Madrid" (Buck 75–77).

Another "lucky break" for the Spanish companies came in 1735, when the Italian company went to Lisbon. Taking advantage of their absence, a specialized Spanish troupe of singer-actresses formed with the best from the Cruz and Príncipe companies took over the Caños del Peral. Again, Juana de Orozco directed this special company of "operatistas" in productions of two operas[9] during the 1735 summer season, to great success. In the fall, the regular companies reformed, both ending their season with musical works. The San Miguel troupe presented an *ópera* in the Cruz, and the Cerquera company performed a *melodrama harmónico* in the Príncipe. Judging from the expenses recorded for these productions, "they must have been the most lavish and spectacular performances yet staged by the Spanish companies" (Buck 78).

This new formula for success did not mean that the public no longer supported traditional drama. They wanted both, so for the 1737–1738 season, one company (Ignacio Cerquera's) performed dramas, while the other (Juana de

Orozco's) mounted operas. The Sr. Obispo Gobernador del Consejo ordered the formation of a "Compañía de músicas"[10] to perform four or five operas between Easter of 1737 and Shrove Tuesday of 1738. Juana de Orozco's company took over the Cruz in a special season of seven operas (staged in May, August, September, October, and November of 1737, and January and February of 1738), most of them just as lavishly produced, as Buck details.

Singer-Actresses

Although music had been an integral part of the early modern Spanish theatrical tradition since its beginnings, the appearance of professional singers did not occur until the eighteenth century, when a distinction between actress and singer appeared. Cast lists distinguished between actresses who specialized in declamation, *de lo representado*, and actresses who specialized in singing, *de lo cantado*. When music was no longer solely at the service of the text but became a feature in its own right, greater expression and vocal technique was required on the part of the singers, whose "quiebros," "pasos" or "pasajes" [quavers or passaggios] of the throat are frequently mentioned in the texts themselves (Flórez Asensio 524). Despite their training and experience, singers sometimes fell victim to rising demands, for extending both their vocal range and the tessitura of the music they were required to sing, and increasing the amount of singing they were required to do. Maladies of the throat could end a career, as was the case for Rosa Rodríguez, who died in 1749 of a throat infection (Cotarelo y Mori, "Actores famosos del siglo XVII," 68).

One of the most popular of the singing actresses was Francisca de Castro, the *primera dama* of the 1737 opera company. Also part of the company of nineteen women were Juana de Orozco, Rosa Rodríguez, and Bernarda de Villaflor, the young daughter of Francisca de Castro. Their success, however, proved ephemeral. Castro was seriously ill during much of the 1737–1738 season, causing performances to be postponed for several days at a time. Perhaps the physical demands were too much for her; only two months after the season ended, she died. Even though the Spanish companies continued to perform, Castro's death "seems to have dampened the ambition of the singers and actresses to undertake another season of opera on the same scale. Nothing approaching the impact of the 1737 season, with its political and aesthetic implications, was to occur in the theatrical life of Madrid for decades to come" (Buck 85–86). Nevertheless, we note that Petronila Jibaja continued the trend of influential *autoras* to the end of Felipe V's reign.

In fact, Elisabeth Le Guin notes the increasing popularity throughout the eighteenth century of "Teatro de Mujeres," in which the entire cast of a *comedia* or opera, as well as of *entremeses*, was made up of women (330). By the 1730s, a new generation of actresses and *autoras* took control and, taking advantage of changes in public taste, seized opportunities to put women in charge. As the Appendix shows, these women, sometimes in spite of themselves, rose to positions of power and fame. Having inherited a tradition of entrepreneurship and performance, they left an indelible mark on the history of the theater in Spain.

Appendix: *Autoras* and Actresses in the time of Felipe V

MARIA DE NAVAS

Described as "actriz protea" [protean actress], María de Navas played both *damas* and *galanes*. Her date of birth is unknown, probably around 1670 in Milan (Hormigón, *Autoras en la historia*, 587). Daughter of harpist Alonso de Navas and his wife Ana, María went to Spain at the age of twelve with her parents, first to Barcelona and then to Valencia. In 1683, she married Francisco Moreno, an actor who had previously been a friar (Shergold and Varey I: 538). For reasons unknown, she fled or was exiled to Lisbon in 1695, giving rise to a series of scandals and libels about an unwanted pregnancy. Not even thirty years old when she arrived in Lisbon, she is described as an *autora* (Buezo, "María de Navas," 279–80). After her marriage to Moreno was annulled, she married the *apuntador* [prompter] Buenaventura Castro, with whom she had a son, Manuel de Castro. She separated from him in 1700 (he died in 1709) and retired to a convent; however, a short while later she returned to the stage. When she died in Madrid on March 9, 1721, she was *primera dama* in the company of José de Prado (husband of Petronila Jibaja).

Catalina Buezo documents her presence on the stage at least from 1678, appearing in various guises, from "loca" [lunatic] to soldier to husband to "viejo venerable" [venerable old man], often with Teresa de Robles in the cast ("María de Navas"). From 1688 to 1694, she played *damas* in Madrid in Agustín Manuel's company (*DICAT*). Between 1697 and 1702, Navas had her own company in Valencia (Shergold and Varey I: 551); in 1703, she was playing both *damas* and *galanes* in her own company in Barcelona when it was brought to Madrid by petition of the king. She returned to Valencia in 1703, playing roles of *dama* and *galán*. The Junta de corrales again required the presence of her company in 1704, since the Madrid companies were missing first *damas*. She claimed insolvency, so the Junta gave her 150 *doblones*[11] for her debts and another 150 for the trip (Buezo, "Juan Rana en Teresa de Robles," 281–82).

Between 1706 and 1709, she was playing first *damas* with the company of Juan Bautista Chavarría. At the same time, she had her company in Valencia, which came to Madrid to play Calderón de la Barca's *El pleito matrimonial* in the prestigious Corpus celebrations (Sabina Pascual's company played Calderón's *auto El primero y segundo Isaac*). Perhaps because she specialized in roles of *mujer varonil* or *mujer vestido de hombre* [virile woman, woman dressed as a man], some biographers suggest that she participated as a soldier in the War of Succession under the banner of the Archduke Carlos, but Hormigón discounts this idea (*Autoras en la historia* 587). According to rumors, María de Navas had arrived in Zaragoza in 1710 following the retreat of Archduke Carlos of Austria, who disputed the Spanish crown with Felipe V de Borbón in the War of Succession. In Zaragoza, Navas repented her disloyalty; she was pardoned and retired to a religious community in Zaragoza until she was summoned to Madrid to play *damas* in 1712 (Pellicer 107). Other reports cite her intention of taking vows in the convent of Santa Catalina de Siena in Madrid, for which she sought donations. Once she had collected a tidy sum, her devotion cooled and she returned to the stage, playing *damas*—in José de Prado's company according to Casiano Pellicer (107), in her own company according to Buezo ("María de Navas" 285)—from 1720 until her death a year later, on March 5, 1721.

TERESA DE ROBLES

The *Genealogía* tells us that Teresa de Robles was the daughter of the *cobrador* [collector] Juan Luis Robles and actress Ana de Escamilla.[12] At some point before 1686, she married the Galician *autor* Rosendo López de Estrada[13] and had two daughters, both of whom went on to have careers on the stage.

Teresa began acting in the company of her grandfather, Antonio de Escamilla, in 1675 and 1676, "playing fifth parts; in 1678 she was in Agustín Manuel's company, in 1679 with José de Prado, and in 1681 with Carvajal" (Rennert 149). She left Madrid and was retired for a time in Valencia, but "after the motive for her retirement ceased," she returned to the stage (Shergold and Varey II: 567). She specialized in *terceras damas*, playing to great applause, especially in musical roles, and formed part of the companies of Escamilla and Manuel Vallejo, beginning her second phase on the stage in 1683 in Valencia. She was in Madrid playing *terceras damas* with Agustín Manuel in 1687. Between 1692 and 1699, her name appears on cast lists of the companies of Damián Polop, Manuel Vallejo, Agustín Manuel, and Carlos Vallejo. *Genealogía* states that she was in her husband's company, but leaves the year she was in the company blank, though *DICAT* speculates the year as being sometime in the 1690s. She played in her own company in 1700 and 1701, and subsequently, until 1706, with *autores* Gregorio Antonio, Juan Baptista Chavarría, Antonio Ruiz, and again with Juan Bautista Chavarría. In 1705, the Cabildo named her *mayordoma* of the Cofradía, but her brother Bartolomé de Robles served in her place (Shergold and Varey II: 567).

As granddaughter of Antonio de Escamilla, she was, according to Buezo ("Juan Rana en Teresa de Robles") and Hormigón (*Catálogo de directoras* 1176–78), heir to the tradition of Juan Rana and practically owned the role of "alcalde burlesco" [comic mayor] in the last third of the seventeenth century. Cosme Pérez had no male descendants; his daughter was not an actress, and his niece, Barbara Coronel, opted for other kinds of roles. In *El triunfo de Juan Rana*, Escamilla affirmed his inheritance of Cosme Pérez's role, but he, like Pérez, had no male descendents, so his craft was passed to his daughter Manuela, who played "Juan Ranillas," and to his granddaughter, Teresa de Robles (Buezo, "Juan Rana en Teresa de Robles," 270). Specializing in comic roles as a *tercera dama*, she also appeared in *zarzuelas*, playing Jupiter in the 1699 production of *Júpiter y Yoo*, with Sabina Pascual as Corina, and playing Galatea in the 1708 production of *Acis y Galatea*, with Pascual as Doris (Cotarelo y Mori, "Actores famosos del siglo XVII," 57n1, 42n1).

Teresa de Robles supposedly retired from the stage toward the end of the second decade of the eighteenth century. Varey, Shergold, and Davis note that she was receiving a "ración" [ration] of two *reales* in 1726 (137)[14]; she must have been of an advanced age by then, having begun her career in the 1670s.

JUANA DE OROZCO

Daughter of the Alicantino Miguel de Orozco and Sebastiana Giménez, Juana de Orozco was the second wife of Antonio Vela, whom she married in Tarragona in 1704. Vela had been in María de Navas's company in Valencia in 1702 (Shergold and Varey I: 952). *Genealogía* offers little information about her other than that she played *quintas damas* [fifth parts] in Madrid in the company of Juan Bautista Chavarría in 1708 and 1709 (II: 902). And yet she became one of the most important *autoras* of her time. From other sources, we can see her influence on the musical scene, and we can appreciate some of the problems and headaches that *autores* had to face.

Like most, she began as an actress. In 1713, she was part of the José Garcés company, playing *cuarta dama* [fourth part] *de lo representado* [acting], but playing *tercera dama* [third part] *de lo cantado* [singing] in the Cañizares/ Literes *zarzuela Acis y Galatea* (Flórez Asensio 533–34). This experience was important preparation for her time later as *autora* of an all-female opera company. She played *terceras damas* in José Ferrer's company in Lisbon both in 1715 and 1719 along with her husband (*DICAT*).

Over the next decade or so, until 1743, Juana de Orozco alternated between the roles of actress and *autora*, leading her own company in Madrid in the seasons of 1729–1734 and 1738–1739 (Hormigón, *Catálogo de directoras*, 1132–55). Her presence and expertise were crucial for the success of the all-female opera company's season in 1737–1738. Her last engagement was as *autora* of a summer company that traveled to Valladolid and Burgos during July and August of 1743.

SABINA PASCUAL

Born in Barcelona, Sabina Pascual was the daughter of Valencian *autor* Félix Pascual and actress Manuela Bustamante, "La Mentirilla" ["The Fibber"] (Shergold and Varey I: 9; II: 565). She married the Valencian musician Manuel de Villaflor; one of their two sons, Ramón de Villaflor married actress-singer Francisca de Castro (I: 798). After the death of Villaflor in 1707, she became the second wife of actor Antonio Quirante. She was widowed again when Quirante died in 1712 (I: 1145; II: 565).

By 1687, she was playing *segundas damas* [second parts] in Valencia in the company of Isidoro Ruano (II: 565, 688). Two years later, she was in Granada, playing *sextas damas* [sixth parts] in her father's company. She was a *sobresaliente* [supernumerary] in Madrid in Agustín Manuel's company in 1689 and played *segundas damas* with the same *autor* in Madrid in 1692 and 1695–1699, though it is not clear if she played *segundas damas* all those years. The year 1700 found her in Madrid, in Juan de Cárdenas's company. The *Genealogía* at one point (I: 1137) describes Sabina Pascual as the wife of the *autor* Manuel de Villaflor in 1703, and from 1701 to 1706 until 1712, she was part of "her husband's" company (II: 565). But if Villaflor died in 1707, was the "husband" in whose company she played Antonio Quirante? Or was she an *autora* in her own right? Just when she took over the company is unclear.

In 1709, her company was one of the two selected to perform *autos* during the Corpus festivities (María de Navas was the other *autora* selected). Since only Calderón de la Barca's *autos* had been performed since his death in 1681, the companies decided to perform newly written works. It was a disastrous experiment, and both companies had to close their theaters due to lack of ticket sales. Both *autoras* finally got permission to perform the traditional Calderón *autos*, to great and lasting success (Hormigón, *Catálogo de directoras*, 1159). There seems to have been a hiatus in her function as *autora* until 1719, when there was mention of the "company of Sabina" (Shergold and Varey I: 911, 921).

Varey, Shergold, and Davis reproduce a document committing Sabina Pascual as *autora* to a season beginning September 1, 1719 and ending on Shrove Tuesday of 1720, during which time the company promises to present ten new plays not performed in the previous ten years (77–79). Hormigón produces lists of *comedias* her company performed in the Cruz and Príncipe during the 1719–1720 season (*Catálogo de directoras* 1160–63). A letter dated April 5, 1727, ordering Sabina and others to return to Madrid from Lisbon, is one of the last records we have of her as *autora* (Varey, Shergold, and Davis 144), but her presence on the musical stage continued.

PETRONILA JIBAJA

Illegitimate daughter of actor Pedro Quirante and Rosa María Sancho y Valderrama (not in the theater), Petronila Jibaja (or Gibaja/Xibaja) married Joseph de Prado (Cotarelo y Mori, "Actores famosos del siglo XVII," 184). Known as "la Portuguesa" due to a long residence in Lisbon, she was celebrated in the court there for her beauty and her acting (Pellicer 119). She is reported to have spent much time in Lisbon, and it was said she was a mistress of the king, for which reason she was not in the confidence of the queen (Shergold and Varey II: 950). This probably occasioned her departure from Lisbon. When she arrived in Madrid, she brought such good jewelry and fine clothes that audiences came to her performances just to see them.

By 1721, she had joined the company of José de Prado and married him; that same year she gave birth to a "niño monstruo" [freak child] that lived but a short time.[15] A second son became Capellán of the so-called "chapel of the actors" (Pellicer 119). The date of Prado's death is not clear. In official records, Petronila appears as Prado's wife in 1723, but in 1724 and 1725, she is listed as his widow (Varey, Shergold, and Davis 125, 133). Her acting career continued into the 1730s: in 1733, in the company of Manuel de San Miguel, sharing the roles of *primeras damas* with Juana de Orozco; in 1735, in the same company; and playing *primeras damas* in the company of José Garcés in 1737 (215, 227, 264–65).

Exactly when she started her own company is not clear. Cotarelo y Mori notes performances of the *zarzuela Margarita de Cortona* in the Príncipe during Christmas of 1745, "por la Compañía de [by the company of] Petronila Gibaja." In discussing music written for operas, *comedias*, and *autos* in 1746, he lists at least five that were performed by this same company before July 9, when theaters were closed due to the death of Felipe V. She retired from the stage in 1750 at the age of fifty-eight (Cotarelo y Mori, *Orígenes y establecimiento de la ópera*, 65n1). Pellicer supposes that she died around 1762 (119), but

Cotarelo y Mori maintains that she died suddenly on October 23, 1763, leaving a son, Juan Antonio Gibaja, a *capellán* of the Cofradía de Nuestra Señora de la Novena, whose father was not her husband Prado ("Actores famosos del siglo XVII" 185).

FRANCISCA DE CASTRO

Daughter of famous character actor Fernando de Castro and Manuela Labaña, the most famous singer in Spain in the new century until her death in 1738 (Cotarelo y Mori, *Orígenes y establecimiento de la ópera*, 66), Francisca de Castro, married the actor Ramón de Villaflor, son of Manuel de Villaflor and Sabina Pascual (Shergold and Varey I: 198, 557).

She earned fame as the kind of actress that today is called a "triple threat": she could sing, dance, and act. Cotarelo y Mori finds her doing all three in the 1724 production of *Fieras afemina amor* [Love Tames Wild Beasts], mounted in the Buen Retiro to celebrate the royal acclamation of Luis I (*Orígenes y establecimiento de la ópera* 62n1). In 1732, she appeared with the San Miguel company in the *zarzuela Milagro es hallar verdad* [It's a Miracle to Find the Truth] as part of a nearly all-female cast (64n1). Like many artists, Francisca de Castro toured Portugal, where she and her husband spent more than forty days in 1727. And as happened with others, when her presence was required in Madrid, she had to return, at considerable expense (Varey, Shergold, and Davis 146). Writers of her time lauded her in prose and verse, saying she sang like a goldfinch; they praised the sweetness of her voice in comparison to the Italian "sopranistas" or castrati. Like Petronila Jibaja, she dressed in the velvets, silks, and damasks prohibited by sumptuary laws, as evidenced by official inventories in 1728 and 1730 (Cotarelo y Mori, *Orígenes y establecimiento de la ópera*, 67). In 1735, she played *terceras damas* in the company of Ignacio Cerquera (Varey, Shergold, and Davis 227), and in the 1735–1736 and 1736–1737 seasons, she performed in the all-female opera company. Her recurring illness in 1738 occasioned several cancellations of performances. Though she might not be called ill-fated, she certainly died before her time (Cotarelo y Mori, *Orígenes y establecimiento de la ópera*, 67).

ROSA RODRÍGUEZ

Rosa Rodríguez probably started her career in theater in Galicia or Portugal before coming to Madrid and joining the company of José de Prado in 1720 as *sexta dama* or *cantante sobresaliente* [supernumerary singer]. Her rise was steady. By 1721 she was *cuarta dama* when she went with the company to Portugal, where she stayed for two years, acting as *tercera dama graciosa* in Spanish plays performed in the capital.

Initially, she did not perform musical solos, as the following anecdote illustrates. In 1724, along with two other actresses in Petronila Jibaja's company (Francisca de Castro and María de San Miguel), Rodríguez wrote a short comic interlude by way of a *baile cómico* [comic dance] in which she played herself, coming onstage with a knife to kill the "poeta," who had not given her any arias to sing in the play. As Rodríguez broke into song, Francisca de Castro protested in jealousy. Her singing career was launched when she stepped in to replace the actress who played Cibele in Calderón's *Fieras afemina amor* [Love Tames Wild Beasts], singing the arias to great acclaim (López Alemany 11–12).

She had a second stay in Lisbon from 1726 to 1728, and was celebrated as the best Spanish singer at a time when others, like Francisca de Castro, had left Portugal. In January 1728, she had the leading role in the opera *Amor aumenta el valor* [Love Increases Courage], performed at the Spanish embassy in Lisbon to celebrate the marriage of crown prince Fernando to the princess María Bárbara (de Braganza) (Bec 24). Although she returned to Spain in 1729, she evidently went back to Portugal before her appearance on the Madrid stage in 1735. In November of 1734, the *autor* Manuel de San Miguel petitioned that Rodríguez, "La Gallega," be brought from Portugal to replace Isabel Vela, who retired to a convent in Pinto and left vacant the critical musical role of *tercera dama* (Varey, Shergold, and Davis 216). In 1737, she was in the company of José Garcés playing *terceras damas*, specializing in comic and singing roles (264–65).

Rodríguez was particularly active in lyric drama performed at the court as well as in public theaters, and formed part of the company of *operatistas* that brought together the most famous and best actress-singers of the moment.[16] She often played *tercera dama* in the companies of Ygnacio de Cerquera, Manuel de San Miguel, and José Parra (Bec 25). At the beginning of 1748, she became gravely ill; nodes on her vocal cords made it impossible for her to sing. As Farinelli remarked, her absence from the stage meant that "la pobre Gallega" [the poor girl from Galicia] would be sorely missed (Cotarelo y Mori, *Orígenes y establecimiento de la ópera*, 135). Unfortunately, she died soon after, in Madrid on May 28, 1749 (Bec 26).

Like Teresa de Robles, Rosa Rodríguez played *tercera dama* in the *Siglo de Oro* tradition, and played both male and female comic roles in *entremeses* (Bec 27). And like Francisca de Castro, Rodríguez became the object of praise among poets and writers who praised her natural grace, her excellence, and her mastery of her craft, crowning her "reina" or queen. Caroline Bec notes, however, that she was "desmesurada y licenciosa" [immoderate and licentious] on stage as *graciosa*, which evidently gave rise to libels, as suggested by the poem "Mariquilla Rodríguez, ya parió" [Mariquilla gave birth] (37). She had the ability to be both comic and serious, a very Spanish mixture, especially when compared to serious French and Italian works (34–35). Given her facility with languages—Gallego, Portuguese, Castilian, and Italian—she often played burlesque roles or caricatures of ethnic types. As a singer, she was evidently a contralto or a mezzo, with a big vocal range, making her great in both female and male roles. In the company of the *Operatistas*, she earned higher salaries than average and was probably worth it, since she could act, do comedy, and sing (28–29).

Notes

1. For a concise yet thorough discussion of Felipe V's impact on the theater, especially musical theater, see Donald C. Buck's "Aesthetics, Politics, and Opera in the Vernacular: Madrid, 1737."

2. Family trees reveal a veritable web of relationships, just in terms of the few women highlighted in this essay. María de Navas married Ventura de Castro, uncle to Francisca de Castro by her father's second marriage, which produced five sons; one, Fernando, married Manuela Vela y Labaña, parents to Francisca de Castro. Francisca's mother, Manuela, was sister to Antonio Vela, who married Juana de Orozco. Francisca's husband, Ramón de Villaflor, was the son of Manuel de Villaflor and Sabina Pascual. Sabina's second husband, Antonio Quirante, was the son of Pedro Quirante, who sired an illegitimate daughter, Petronila Quirante, better known as Petronila Jibaja, who became the second wife of José de Prado.

3. María de Navas was the sister of *autor* Juan de Navas; Teresa de Robles was the stepdaughter of *autor* José Verdugo and granddaughter of Antonio de Escamilla, while at the same time niece of actress and *autora* Manuela de Escamilla and wife of *autor* Rosendo López Estrada; Sabina Pascual was the daughter of *autor* Félix Pascual (De Salvo, "La búsqueda de un espacio profesional," 488–93). Juana de Orozco married *autor* Antonio Vela, and Petronila Jibaja married *autor* José de Prado.

4. The Cofradía de Nuestra Señora de la Novena [Confraternity of Our Lady of the Novena] was established in 1631 as the official guild of actors and playwrights. In 1687, María de Navas sought and was elected to the position of mayordomo, but delegated her brother Juan. Teresa de Robles did the same in 1705, although she delegated her brother Bartolomé (Shergold and Varey I: 476). Carmen Sanz Ayán wonders if there was some kind of impediment that might prevent a woman from actually performing the duties, or if it was a function of them having to be gone on tour so much.

5. The Shergold and Varey (1985) edition brings together the two parts of the *Geneaología*. References will specify the item number, and will indicate from which of the two volumes the information is taken.

6. For a thorough study of Los Trufaldines, see Doménech Rico.

7. Since the 1560s, certain *cofradías* [charitable brotherhoods] had maintained hospitals for the needy in Madrid and had built *corral* stages as a way to raise money to support them. The ensuing popularity of theater benefited both the performing companies and the hospitals, which depended on a portion of the revenue from their performances.

8. Traditionally, when speaking about music, the progressive Italianization of Spanish music was seen as a key to its "decadencia." More recent scholarship, however, rejects the notions of "foreign invasion," "modernization," or "Europeization" as encompassing a valuation of the foreign as a threat to identity. In fact, Buck finds the *zarzuela* uniquely indicative of a mixture of "indigenous and foreign elements. Perhaps more than any other form, the *zarzuela* acted as a kind of mirror of eighteenth-century Spanish culture, reflecting both Iberian tradition and foreign fashion" (8–9).

9. "*Trajano en Dacia y cumplir con amor y honor* [Trajan in Dacia, and Comply with Love and Honor] was dedicated to the future queen, María Bárbara de Braganza. *La cautela en la amistad y robo de las Sabinas* [Caution in Friendship, and the Abduction of the Sabine Women] bore a dedication to the Spanish Infanta María Teresa" (Buck 78).

10. Varey, Shergold, and Davis (266) list artists and their wages. Francisca de Castro was the highest paid (1,100 ducados), followed by Rosa Rodríguez (1,000 ducados for comic roles) and Juana de Orozco (900 ducados). The "Salarios de operistas" are listed in Reales: Castro 14,880, Rodriguez 11,000, Orozco 9,900. Jibaja was given an "ayuda de costa of 3,220, and Rodriguez 3,000 (277). Another list shows "Ymporte de las operistas y demás empleados en las comedias de música." Francisca de Castro was paid 12,775 reales for 257 performances, eighty of which were operas, Rosa Rodríguez was paid 12,100 for her salary and a costume, and Juana de Orozco was paid 9,900 for salary (279).

11. Charts from *The Bankers' Magazine, and Statistical Register* (104) value a *doblón* as being worth five dollars. In 1871, 150 *doblones* would have been worth about ninety-eight dollars. Given inflation, today the sum would be considerably greater.

12. According to *Genealogía* (Shergold and Varey II: 241), Ana de Escamilla was part of a company called *Las muchachas*. The Marqués de Liche retired her from the stage, but she returned later (no dates are given).

13. In documents listing members of Rosendo López's company in 1686, Teresa de Robles figures as "autora," meaning wife of the *autor* (De Salvo, "La búsqueda de un espacio profesional," 470–71). *Genealogía* (Shergold and Varey I: 876) tells us that Rosendo López retired from the theater to become a *Corregidor* [alcalde mayor] in Galicia, taking his wife along; however, due to "su mala conduta y tontería" [bad behavior and foolishness], he was stripped of the office and returned to the boards. He died in 1702.

14. Charts from *The Bankers' Magazine, and Statistical Register* (117) value a *real* as being worth one-twentieth of a dollar, or five cents.

15. *Genealogia* (Shergold and Varey II: 950) records that, in 1721, Jibaja gave birth to a male child with no brain or buttocks, and with undescended testicles.

16. During the 1737–1738 season, seven operas were performed by singers such as Francisca de Castro, Ysabel Vela, Rita de Orozco, María Antonia de Castro, Juana de Orozco, and Bernarda de Villaflor. A second attempt at a season of operas (1743–1744), with Juana de Orozco and Bernarda de Villaflor, was less successful.

References

The Bankers' Magazine, and Statistical Register, Vol. 25. Edited by I. Smith, Homans. Wm. Crosby and H.P. Nicholes, 1871.

Bec, Caroline. "La Comédienne-Chanteuse Rosa Rodríguez: Une *Graciosa* dans les drames lyriques madrilènes (1720–1746)." *Cuadernos dieciochistas* 16 (2015): 21–38.

Buck, Donald C. "Aesthetics, Politics, and Opera in the Vernacular: Madrid, 1737." *The Opera Quarterly* 10 (1994), no. 3: 71–91.

Buezo, Catalina. "La mujer vestida de hombre en el teatro del siglo XVII: María de Navas, itinerario vital de una 'autora' aventurera." In *Autoras y actrices en la historia del teatro español*, edited by Luciano García Lorenzo, Universidad de Murcia, 2000, 267–86.

———. "Mujer y desgobierno en el teatro breve del siglo XVII: el legado de Juan Rana en Teresa de Robles, alcalde gracioso y 'autora' de comedias." In *Teatro y poder: VI y VII Jornadas de Teatro Universidad de Burgos*, edited by José Ignacio Blanco Pérez, Universidad de Burgos, 1998, 107–20.

Bussey, William. "Foreign Influence on the Zarzuela: 1700–1779 (Volumes I and II)." PhD diss., University of Michigan, 1980.

Cotarelo y Mori, Emilio. "Actores famosos del siglo XVII: Sebastián de Prado y su mujer Bernarda Ramírez." *Boletín de la Real Academia Española* 3 (1916): 3–38.

———. *Historia de la zarzuela, o sea el drama lírico en España, desde su origen a fines del siglo XIX*. Madrid: Tipografía de Archivos, 1934.

———. *Orígenes y establecimiento de la ópera en España hasta 1800*. Revista de Archivos, Bibliotecas y Museos, 1917. Facsimile edition with introduction by Juan J. Carreras, Madrid: Instituto Complutense de Ciencias Musicales, 2004.

Davis, Charles and John Varey. "Las compañías de actores de los corrales de comedias de Madrid: 1708–1719." In *En torno al teatro del siglo de oro: actas de las jornadas I–VI*, edited by Heraclia Castellón Alcalá, Agustín de la Granja, and Antonio Serrano Agulló, Almería, Spain: Instituto de Estudios Almerienses, 1991, 163–86.

De Salvo, Mimma. "La importancia de las sagas familiares en la transmisión del oficio teatral en la España del Siglo de Oro: el caso de las actrices." In *Líneas actuales de investigación literaria*. ALEPH Asociación de Jóvenes Investigadores de la Literatura Hispánica, Universitat de València, 2004, 187–98, dialnet.unirioja.es/descarga/libro/569132.pdf.

———. "La mujer en la práctica escénica de los siglos de oro: La búsqueda de un espacio profesional." PhD diss., Universidad de Valencia, 2006.

Diccionario biográfico de actores del teatro clásico español (DICAT). Edited by Teresa Ferrer Valls, Kassel, Germany: Reichenberger, 2008.

Doménech Rico, Fernando. *Los Trufaldines y el Teatro de los Caños del Peral (La Commedia dell'arte en la España de Felipe V)*. Madrid: Fundamentos Colección Arte, 2007.

Ferrer Valls, Teresa. "La incorporación de la mujer en la empresa teatral: actrices, *autoras* y compañías en el Siglo de Oro." In *Calderón entre veras y burlas. Actas de las II y III Jornadas de Teatro Clásico de la Universidad de la Rioja*, edited by F. Domínguez Matito and J. Bravo Vega, Logroño, Spain: Universidad de la Rioja, 2002, 139–60.

———. "La mujer sobre el tablado en el siglo XVII: de actriz a *autora*." In *Damas en el tablado. Actas de las XXXI Jornadas Internacionales de teatro clásico de Almagro (1–3 de julio de 2008)*, edited by Felipe B. Pedraza, Rafael González Cañal, and Almudena García González, Cuenca, Spain: Universidad de Castilla-La Mancha, 2009, 83–100.

Flórez Asensio, María Asunción. "Los vientos se paran oyendo su voz: de 'partes de música' a 'damas de lo cantado.' Sobre la evolución de la técnica vocal en el teatro español de los siglos XVII y XVIII." *Revista de Musicología* 29 (2006), no. 2: 521–36.

Hormigón, Juan Antonio, ed. *Autoras en la historia del teatro español*, Vol. 1. Serie Teoría y práctica del teatro No. 10. Madrid: Publicaciones de la Asociación de Directores de Escena de España, 1996.

———. *Catálogo de directoras en la historia del teatro español (1550–2002)*, Vol. I (1550–1930). Serie Teoría y Práctica del Teatro No. 21. Madrid: Publicaciones de la Asociación de Directores de Escena de España, 2003.

Le Guin, Elisabeth. *The Tonadilla in Performance: Lyric Comedy in Enlightenment Spain*. University of California Press, 2013.

López Alemany, Ignacio. "La representación de *Fieras afemina Amor* en la proclamación de Luis I (1724)." *Hispanófila* 169 (2013): 3–17.

Pellicer, Casiano. *Tratado histórico sobre el origen y progresos de la comedia y del histrionismo en España: y con la noticia de algunos célebres comediantes y comediantas así antiguos como modernos*. Madrid: Imprenta de la Administración del Real Arbitrio de Beneficiencia, 1804.

Rennert, Hugo. *The Spanish Stage in the Time of Lope de Vega*. The Hispanic Society of America, 1909.

Sanz Ayán, Carmen. "More Than Faded Beauties: Women Theater Managers of Early Modern Spain." *Early Modern Women: An Interdisciplinary Journal* 10 (2015), no. 1: 114–21.

Shergold, Norman, and John Varey, eds. *Genealogía, origen y noticias de los comediantes de España*. Fuentes para la Historia del Teatro en España. Tamesis, 1985.

Varey, John, N. D. Shergold, and Charles Davis, eds. *Teatros y comedias en Madrid: 1719–1745. Estudio y documentos*. Fuentes para la Historia del Teatro en España XII. Tamesis, 1994.

ISAAC BENABU

Lope de Vega's "Warring" Female Characters

MEMORABLE AMONG the "warring women" in the Spanish *comedia* is Laurencia in Lope de Vega's *Fuenteovejuna*. She is not merely a strategist, but also a warrior; and an accomplished actor to boot. The playtext does not supply any direction as to how she is to deliver her monologue in Act 3 (ll. 1714–17, 1725–95), in which she attempts to convince the men of Fuenteovejuna that she was raped by the Commander, and her words leave no doubt as to how she intends them to be greeted by her audience. Her powerful attack on the virility of the men of Fuenteovejuna is intended to stir the menfolk in her village to rise against their overlord, and it is motivated by a desire to deliver her husband Frondoso from the Commander's order that he be hanged. Not only does the delivery of the words in Lope's text demand that the actor use her talents to rouse her audience, but also her costume underscores the theatricality of her performance, as does Lope's stage direction that she appear *"desmelenada"* (3, 1713). Her disheveled appearance also constitutes part of the artifice she contrives: for she dresses (or rather undresses) for the part:

> Mis cabellos, ¿no lo dicen?
> ¿No se ven aquí los golpes,
> de la sangre y las señales?
> (3, 1752–74)

[Doesn't my hair proclaim it? Can't you see here the blows, and the bloodstains?]

However, Frondoso's declaration to the Queen at the end of the play confirms that Laurencia was not raped by the Commander: "y a no saberse guarder / ella . . ." (3, 2413) [if she hadn't known how to protect herself]. There is a clear motivation in the strong language she uses, as that of any female character who puts on a performance in order to convince the men listening to her. (I am reminded here of Katherine's final speech in Shakespeare's *The Taming of the Shrew* [5.2.140–83].)

We turn now to the case of Casandra in Lope's *El Castigo sin venganza* (henceforth *Castigo*), the main female character studied in this essay. Judging by the impression she gives upon first appearing, the character has often not been perceived as either a strategist or a warrior. But her passionate unmasking at the start of the second *jornada* [act] of the play, and her calculated strategies all through it, leave no doubt about her capacity to do battle in order to get what she wants. And, as I shall show, Casandra's talent at putting on an act is evident throughout the play. I preface my analysis of her with a few general points about reading stage characters.

In bridging the distance between character analysis in the academy and on the stage, I set out the following five points to outline in brief the methodology of theatrical reading.

First, to construct a dramatic text in order to stage it in the theater, or when deconstructing it in the academy, it is advisable to read the text from the end to the beginning, as it were, because all action is directed toward the ending, the point where everything is revealed and resolved. As such, it constitutes the most informative point to begin sketching characterization; doing so enables measuring the pace of the action throughout, and it also facilitates an analysis of the moods prevailing on stage at the opening and beyond.

Second, a characteristic of theatrical writing is its *spatial* quality: spatial because theatrical writing assumes *ab initio* that the playtext contains spaces that must be filled by the actor/director. In other words, this characteristic, which is particular to theatrical writing, is the result of a playwright's awareness that the written text will be interpreted by an actor and/or director, and so theatrical writing must leave a space for their own particular contributions in bringing the play to the stage. The playwright thus defines the limits of the action she or he has designed, but there is a certain openness or space in the writing that allows director and actor to interpret; always, however, *within the certain limits set by the playwright.*

Third, the words of the playtext are intended to be translated into action, and actions are usually conditioned by the characters' state of mind. Tracing the motivation underlying all stage discourse is therefore essential.

Fourth, a point that expands on the third. A character's discourse imitates human speech. However fast our thought processes may be, in general we think first and then we give verbal expression to our thoughts. In a character's discourse, we should not ask what the written word conveys. Rather, we should ask what thoughts underlie what the character expresses or conceals. André Helbo has suggested a way in which theatrical discourse might be analyzed: not merely as words on a page, but as the translation of thoughts first conceived in the mind and only then communicated through speech. The context in which these words are spoken, therefore, is all important: "[we should,] given the discourse/actions attributed to the character, . . . look for whatever may elucidate his/her discourse, in other words, *the conditions that govern the character's speech*" (Helbo et al. 145, emphasis mine).

Fifth, the theatrical analysis of a playtext, therefore, requires that a distinction be made between three important perspectives: (1) what the playwright writes in his or her playtext; (2) how the actor interprets the part, i.e., what is performed on the stage; and (3) the spectator's perspective, to which (1) and (2) are directed; or the way stage-action is designed and its perception by the spectator.

There follow some theatrical parameters that are specific to the construction of a performance that a playwright provides by implicit instructions in the playtext. For the playwright, the opening of a play poses challenges unsensed by an expectant audience at the beginning of a play. The opening is the result of careful preparation and focus, and audience involvement in what follows depends on the successful channeling of energies from the start. Looked at from this perspective, an opening only constitutes an artificial beginning in that it is constructed with the end in sight. It is, arguably, the most difficult point at which to begin a study of the playtext, with the considerable problems it poses to the reader for immersion in the text. Perhaps a study of the ending, where all is revealed and understood, the point at which the entire plot is aimed and where it unfolds, is a more reliable starting point for a critical reading (Benabu, *Reading for the Stage*, 64).

Furthermore, there are features already alluded to that are inscribed in the playtext to trace the development of the action, such as pacing, which requires an actor/director to measure the way the action develops with the precision with which a musician interprets rhythmic development. Establishing mood on stage is also essential so as to ensure the desired engagement of a spectator from the inception of a tragedy, which is the genre of the play under discussion. A serious and even somber mood at the opening intensifies as the action unfolds, evoking strong emotions in the spectator, frequently by means of dramatic irony. As the action progresses, the spectator acquires an increasing awareness of the danger that threatens, and gradually gains the impression that the conflict presented on stage is insoluble and that catastrophe cannot be averted.

To exemplify these ideas that have generally been recognized, let us contrast briefly the function of the honor theme, so prevalent in the Spanish Golden Age *comedia* in both comedy and tragedy. In a tragedy, a preoccupation with honor generates situations that produce grave consequences, as when a character's suspicions lead to violent actions. With regard to characterization, playwrights constructing characters in a tragedy usually invest them with complexity, and the characters are often nuanced. In comedy, however threatening an honor conflict may appear, it is resolved by the play's close.

Some of these theoretical considerations underpin the present contribution to the analysis of Casandra, the adulterous wife of the Duke of Ferrara, in Lope's *Castigo*. *Castigo* is a *comedia palaciega*, which means that it was intended for presentation before a sophisticated audience. Its composition reflects an elevated style of performance, and the playtext contains many classical allusions. There are aria-like sequences (noted by Victor Dixon in "Manuel Vallejo," 64) especially between Casandra and Federico, whose roles require stylized acting. Character groupings at either end of the stage demand that two characters engage in dialogue while attention shifts subsequently to another character group in dialogue, and back to the first group. An example of this is found in the second *jornada* of *Castigo* when Casandra and Lucrecia are talking on one side of the stage (from the beginning of Act 2, 994–1113), while the Duke and Federico talk on the opposite side (Act 2, 1114–31).[1] As Casandra and Lucrecia leave the stage at Act 2, line 1137, focus returns to the dialogue between the Duke and Federico (Act 2, 1138–94).

In addition, there are behavioral styles associated with the court to be taken into account in the construction of the characters: masking personality, ceremony, intrigue, etc. Finally, the adulterous pair, Casandra and Federico, are fully drawn characters with enough psychological detail to allow the critic to construct the character. Casandra's behavior, restrained at first, is soon followed by anger, a desire for vengeance, and a surrender to passion; in Federico's case, his melancholy, impulsiveness, and passion, are eventually followed by despair.

Past criticism of the play has tended to see Casandra in two opposing ways: sympathetically or unsympathetically. Often, her character has been constructed based upon an analysis of her first appearance in the text, much as the Duke's has been constructed in the opening scene (see Benabu, "La construcción del personaje teatral"). The bibliography on this play is considerable, so I have selected a number of representative views on Casandra. Edward M. Wilson shared a sympathetic view of the character. As she was a stranger to Ferrara, he considers the young Casandra to have been the victim of her husband's abandonment shortly after their marriage. For this reason, Wilson suggests that "her reactions are more comprehensible to a modern reader" (167). This may be so, but they could also mislead a contemporary reader influenced, say, by feminist concerns. However, the play was composed for a seventeenth-century audience, when political correctness was not uppermost on a spectator's mind. Antonio Carreño affirms his view of Casandra in his article "La 'sin venganza' como violencia," supported by the exchange between Casandra and Lucrecia at the opening of the second *jornada*, as being "sexualmente frustrada" [sexually frustrated]. Later, Carreño considers her actions toward the Duke as motivated by the predicament in which she finds herself—as "[una] esposa desdeñada" ("La sangre" 254) [a disdained wife]— to whom he attributes "la llama de la pasión implacable" (257) [the flame of an implacable passion]. Gwynne Edwards also seems to absolve Casandra of any responsibility for submitting to her passion for Federico: "By spurning Casandra and driving her into Federico's arms, the Duke creates a further set of circumstances whose repercussions cannot be avoided" (113).

T. E. May, on the other hand, while devoting his article to the Duke, has no doubt in asserting that "Casandra must be accused of adultery, revengefulness, and deceit" (155). This is how May sums up the character: "One is bound to say that there is something repellent about Casandra and even that she is as hard as flint. . . . Her constant self-deceit is apparent in her oscillations as to her motives. She has no more than glimpses of herself as she truly is; her words go outwards in the service of an aggressive self-defence, are all insidious persuasions of herself and others" (157). More recently, Edward H. Friedman appears to underscore May's negative view of Casandra, but he tones down his evaluation of the character: "Although preserving her good name is of the utmost importance, she cannot refrain from reflecting on love and vengeance" (220).

All of these views of Casandra, however contradictory, cannot be resolved by relegating the problem of constructing her character to the particular choices of a director, as Bárbara Mujica has suggested.² The notion that a director is entitled to resolve characterization according to his or her own lights, countering the instructions supplied by the playwright, was dismissed by Helen Gardner in a discussion of how Shakespeare's plays were directed before the heyday of postmodernism. Gardner questions the validity of a belief that playscripts contain a myriad of significations that a director chooses to adopt when preparing a play for performance, a view that concurs with the postmodernist notion that an author's intention may often be ignored in favor of the critic's interpretation.³ Herein lies my basic disagreement with those critics who uphold that contemporary directors have license to interpret playtexts that are not of their own composition by reading into them choices that only reflect a personal preference.

To preface my construction of Casandra, I restate that in an earlier study on the Duke, I was struck by Casandra's insincerity: "the vengeance she persuades herself to wreak on the Duke is a cover for her growing passion for Federico" (Benabu, *Reading for the Stage*, 211). I take this opportunity to enlarge on this view by adopting the approach facilitated by theatrical reading.

Reading from her last appearance in Lope's mature tragedy back to her first gives us a clue as to how to construct the character of Casandra. By the third *jornada*, it is clear that Casandra and Federico have been consorting in the Duke's absence. Those passionate verses that close the second *jornada* and function like an operatic duet provide all the evidence needed to inform the spectator as to what has transpired between the adulterous pair from the end of the second to the beginning of the third *jornada*. And what may have appeared in the opening soliloquy of the second *jornada* to express Casandra's ploy to avenge herself on the Duke, as well as in her later soliloquy at Act 3, 1811–55, is shown in the third *jornada* to have grown into a full-blooded passion that proves irresistible for both Casandra and Federico. For in the third *jornada*, Casandra shows her true colors. Overcome by their guilt, Casandra and Federico quake at the announcement of the Duke's return to Ferrara. But Casandra only regrets that she will not be able to meet Federico as openly as she had done during the Duke's absence:

Muriendo estoy de pesar
de que ya no podré verte
como solía.
   (3, 2257–59)

[I am dying from the pain that I shall not be able to meet you as we used to.]

Federico's weak plan to feign love for Aurora before his father in order to camouflage his affair with Casandra meets with a sudden, violent reaction from Casandra that denotes a mind beginning to lose self-awareness, overawed as it is by a sense of guilt and despair at losing her lover. Federico's plan only consists in keeping the affair from being discovered:

Asegurar pretendí
al Duque, y asegurar
nuestra vida.
   (3, 2720–23)

[I only sought to reassure the Duke and thus protect our own lives.]

Yet Casandra feels threatened by it, and taking offense at his suggestion, accuses him of initiating the affair (it is made perfectly clear in the second *jornada* that the initiative was hers [3, 1821–30]):

Casandra: ¿Qué? Vive Dios,
que si te burlas de mí
después que has sido ocasión
desta desdicha, que a voces
diga, ¡o que mal me conoces!
tu maldad, y mi traición.
Federico: Señora.
Casandra: No hay que tratar.
Federico: Que te oirán.
Casandra: Que no me impidas.
Quíteme el Duque mil vidas,
pero no te has de casar.
   (Act 3, 2279–88)

[*Casandra:* By God, if you deceive me after having been the cause of
   my misfortunes. How little you know me! I shall proclaim aloud
   your wickedness and my betrayal.
Federico: Madam.
Casandra: No compromise.

Federico: You will be overheard.
Casandra: Don't try to stop me. The Duke may kill me a thousand times over, but you shall not marry.]

As the third *jornada* unfolds, the Duke (his suspicions about the adulterous affair aroused) hopes to catch Casandra by informing her that he is determined to have Aurora marry Federico. Hiding her emotions, Casandra hypocritically preaches prudence to the Duke:

Señor,
no uséis del poder, que amor
es gusto, y no ha de forzarse.
    (3, 2693–95)

[Sir, don't exercise your power. To love is a pleasure that should not be forced.]

As soon as the Duke exits, Casandra, alone on the stage, openly discloses her true motives in having offered such sensible advice; in fact, the volatility of her feelings have so disturbed her that she appears to have forgotten that the proposed marriage of Aurora to Federico was part of Federico's plan to dispel suspicion about their affair: "¡Ay de mí, que se ha cansado / el traidor Conde de mí!" (3, 2696–97) [Heavens, that treacherous Count has grown tired of me!]

Once more her imagined fears about betrayal are unleashed, this time taking the form of jealousy. In this disturbed frame of mind, she accuses Federico of spurning her love, unaware that the Duke is overhearing this conversation that confirms his worst suspicions. It is her last encounter with Federico, and because she begins by accusing him of disloyalty, it seems that she is all too quickly appeased by his assurances that his feelings remain unchanged. Is Casandra only donning the mask of outrage? In fact, what their exchange evidences is Casandra's ability to manipulate Federico so as to get her own way, because, as I have suggested above, the transition from grave offense to reassurance is too quick to be convincing:

Federico: Digo, señora, que haré
todo lo que tú quisieres,
y esta palabra te doy.
Casandra: ¿Será verdad?

Federico: Infalible.
Casandra: Pues no hay a amor imposible.
Tuya he sido, y tuya soy.
No ha de faltar invención
para vernos cada día.
    (3, 2762–69)

[*Federico:* I swear, Madam, that I shall fulfill your every wish.
Casandra: Can this be true?
Federico: Unfailingly.
Casandra: Well, love knows no boundaries. I have always been yours and am still. There's nothing we won't think of doing so as to see one another everyday.]

For Casandra this is a triumphant and self-assured final exit from the stage. Clearly, her mood swings all through the third *jornada* are evidence of a mind under pressure: she is determined never to relinquish her unquenchable passion for Federico and is equally resolved to avert her husband's suspicions. But these swings also confirm her talent in manipulating a melancholic Federico. To the end she fights hard for the gratification of her deepest desires. In conforming with the demands of tragedy, Lope shows Casandra in her final appearance in an ironical light, deluding herself that she will be able to keep her lover without being discovered.

Reading back to the second *jornada*, which opens shortly after her marriage to the Duke, the actor discovers essential markers in order to "unmask" Casandra and help construct the character throughout. By the beginning of the second *jornada*, the civility Casandra shows in the first *jornada* has worn thin: she gives full vent to her frustration, attributing it to having been abandoned by her husband after their wedding night. She complains bitterly (and justifiably) about her husband's behavior toward her. She regrets having left her father's house and envies the simple pleasures of humble women whose love is reciprocated by their husbands. She is also explicit about both her sexual and maternal expectations of marriage. There can be no doubt that the Duke's abandonment of his young wife is reprehensible. (We remember that he only agreed to marry because of the pressure exerted by his subjects that he should father a legitimate heir.) But Casandra's tirade to Lucrecia at the beginning of the second *jornada* affirms in strong language that her honor has been compromised by the Duke's abandonment.

However, by applying what has been stated above about the motivation underlying a character's words specifically to those in Casandra's long and embittered soliloquies at Act 2, 994–1073 and 1532–91, I suggest that the subtext of these speeches gives grounds for suspecting that her passionate anger may not simply be attributable to the Duke's abandonment. Given the passion with which the speeches are delivered, they more likely conceal an underlying conflict she does not know how to resolve: I am referring to the insinuations of her attraction to Federico that she admits to Lucrecia, and that Lope placed in the first *jornada*. Consequently, in a long exchange in the second *jornada* that marks the center-point of the play, Casandra coaxes Federico to confess his secret passion, suspecting that she herself is the object of his affliction. And by the time she pronounces the first of her two soliloquies in the second *jornada*, she links her designs on Federico with a risky plan that will wreak revenge on the Duke. Her first reaction, however, is to dismiss her adulterous thoughts:

> Cuando a imaginar me inclino
> que soy lo que quiere el Conde,
> el mismo engaño responde
> que lo imposible imagino.
> . . . .
> Los imposibles parecen
> fáciles, y yo, engañada
> ya pienso que estoy vengada.
>   (2, 1552–55, 1566–68)

[When I dare to imagine that I am the object of the Count's affections, this self-deception informs me that I am imagining what is impossible.... The impossible appears easy, and I, deceived, believe I am already avenged.]

By the time she pronounces the second soliloquy, her plans have solidified and she dispels any semblance of reserve. No subtext here, for she bluntly spells out her plan of action:

> Al galán Conde y discreto,
> y su hijo, ya permito
> para mi venganza efeto.
>   (2, 1826–28)

[I now allow myself to use the gallant and discreet Count as the object of my revenge.]

And then, convincing herself that she is justified in following her plan, she adds:

> dándome el Duque ocasión,
> que hay dentro de mí quien dice
> que si es amor, no es traición.
>   (2, 1838–40)

[since the Duke has given me occasion for doing so, there is something within me that says that if it's love, then it cannot be treason.]

Thus, by the end of the *jornada*, both lovers openly confess their feelings to one another in a series of operatic asides.

Turning now to the first *jornada*, and considering Lope's development of Casandra in the course of the play, it seems misguided to construct the character basing it on the civilities she displays on first appearing. These correspond to conventions that an aristocrat should observe on her first visit to Ferrara where she is to make her home. Yet, the initial speeches of Casandra and Federico may contain indications of what is to follow through the suggestive powers of metaphor. Casandra admits that she has been somewhat inattentive in leaving her party and attempting to approach the river alone, thus getting herself into deep waters (1, 374–85).

Casandra's attraction for Federico is clearly insinuated in the first *jornada*, before her marriage to the Duke, at Act 1, 591–600, and visually for the spectator in the two embraces that she gives Federico at Act 1, 409–10 and 887–80. A mutual attraction grows steadily in the course of their meeting in the first *jornada*, and is first expressed in mild terms when she is rescued by Federico and carried onstage in his arms. Lope intimates this nascent attraction by means of poetic wordplay that marks the impact that Federico has on Casandra:

> Dicha ha sido haber errado
> el camino que seguí,
> pues más presto os conocí
> por yerro tan acertado.
>   (1, 478–81)

[Mistaking the road I was following was fortunate for me, since through so fortunate a mistake, I met you all the sooner.]

Left alone by the male characters on stage and in the presence of her maid Lucrecia, Casandra admits that she is marrying against her will to comply with her father's wishes. What is more, she openly confesses to her maid her regret that she is not marrying Federico instead of the Duke. In a cautious verbal exchange, the mistress asks her maid for her impressions of Federico:

Casandra: Mientras los dos hablan, dime
qué te parece, Lucrecia,
de Federico.
Lucrecia: Señora,
Si tú me dieses licencia,
mi parecer diría.
Casandra: Aunque ya no sin sospecha,
yo te la doy.
Lucrecia: Pues yo digo . . .
Casandra: Di.
Lucrecia: que más dichosa fueras
si se trocara la suerte.
Casandra: Aciertas, Lucrecia, y yerra
mi fortuna.
  (1, 582–92)

[*Casandra:* While they are engaged in conversation, tell me, Lucrecia, what you think of Federico?
Lucrecia: Madam, if you'd allow me to say what I think, I'd tell you.
Casandra: Though I suspect what you are going to say, you have my permission.
Lucrecia: So I'll tell you . . .
Casandra: Speak!
Lucrecia: that you'd be happier if the roles could be reversed.
Casandra: You are right, Lucrecia, for my fortune has erred.]

Furthermore, there are cracks visible in Casandra's "innocent" composure in the first *jornada:* her willingness to flirt with Federico, and her lack of any resistance in allowing herself to be attracted to Federico even after she discovers that he is to be her stepson. She even invites him to leave his horse and travel together with her in her coach. And in a later scene, in the Duke's presence, she refuses to allow Federico to kiss her hand and instead insists on embracing him (1, 862–88). In much the same way as Lucrecia did with her mistress, servant Batín teases the truth out of a lovelorn Federico at the end of the first *jornada* (1, 978–80). And through the rhapsodic speeches exchanged between Casandra and Federico, on the stage the actors underline the way in which these characters react to one another by displaying appropriate facial and bodily expressions (see Fischer 142–46). Lope intimates their growing attraction and supplies dramatic tension for an audience who senses that their attraction can only lead to forbidden pleasures.

In her study about the power in the use of language and silence in *Castigo*, Melveena McKendrick analyzed the Duke's language, but her observations may also be applied to the constrained language used by both Casandra and Federico in the first *jornada* (see, for example, Federico's masked declaration as he kisses Casandra's hand at Act 1, 871–86).

In my construction of Casandra's character, all of the evidence adduced suggests that we should not ignore Lope's instructions as to her true identity. However demurely Casandra may act in public on her first appearance as the shy and discreet bride-to-be, her passionate nature surfaces as she openly admits to her maid the attraction she feels for Federico, and the fact that she would have preferred him to be her husband. And a concern for reputation in admitting that it is too late to refuse to marry the Duke only appears to be an excuse for the sublimation of those feelings Federico has awakened in her:

> ... mas ya es hecho,
> porque cuando yo quisiera,
> fingiendo alguna invención
> volver a Mantua, estoy cierta
> que me matara mi padre,
> y por toda Italia fuera
> fábula mi desatino.
>   (1, 592–98)

[... but it is already done, for should I want to return to Mantua under some imagined pretext, I feel certain that my father would kill me. And this senseless act would be publicized throughout Italy.]

From this point in the first *jornada* until her last appearance, Casandra increasingly shows herself to be in the grip of passion, and she behaves manipulatively, especially when she forces Federico to confess his love in the second *jornada*, and when she demands in the third *jornada* an assurance from him that they should continue to meet. She goes so far her as to suggest to the Duke that Aurora should marry the Marquis, thus ensuring that Federico will not marry Aurora.

To summarize: I have suggested that Casandra's indignation at the start of the second *jornada* cannot be read in isolation, forgetting that Lope has intimated the attraction she felt for Federico at their first meeting. She persuades herself in her soliloquy in the second *jornada* (2, 1811–55) that her growing passion for Federico is only a way of wreaking vengeance on the Duke:

> ... loca imagino
> hallar venganzas y gustos
> en el mayor destino.
> Al galán Conde y discreto,
> y su hijo, ya permito
> para mi venganza efeto.
>   (2, 1823–28)

[... possessed, I imagine I'll find vengeance and pleasure by committing the greatest folly. I'll allow myself to seduce the gallant and discreet Count in order to give vent to my vengeance.]

But a spectator will easily see through her ruse as a cover for her passion. (Compare hers to the development of the character of Federico's former betrothed, Aurora, who is consistently honest and obliging throughout, even though she too suffers from unsatisfied love.)

In this play, all three protagonists—the Duke, Casandra, and Federico—are tragic because they lose themselves in a labyrinth of heightened emotions. Furthermore, in convincing herself that her manipulations will succeed, is Casandra not rehearsing the Duke's self-imposed blindness when judging the adulterous pair under the pressure of his disgrace and dishonor by assigning to himself the powers of Heaven (see Benabu, "La construcción del personaje teatral")? Casandra and Federico's submission to their illicit passion is adequately drawn by all those who have studied the play. This essay has attempted to show that, underlying Casandra's initial modesty, there lies the passionate and vengeful nature of a "warring" character. And the construction of the character has been eked out by tracing the indirect directions contained in Lope's playtext.

Notes

1. The English prose translations of Lope's play are my own. All citations from the play refer to the 1966 edition by Cyril A. Jones.

2. See Mujica's article, "Lope de Vega's *El castigo sin venganza*: What do Viewers Know and How They Know It?" To counter the view about the choices given to directors, David Lodge writes: "Most producers and directors secretly despise writers, regarding them as mere drudges whose job it is to provide the raw material for the exercise of their own creativity, necessary evils who must be kept firmly in their place. Actors, however, regard writers with respect, even a certain awe. They know that the Writer is the ultimate source of the lines without which they themselves are impotent" (55).

3. See Gardner's article, "Shakespeare in the Directors' Theatre," in her collection *In Defence of the Imagination*. More recently, this critical fad has been humorously derided by R. A. Foakes, commenting on how some postmodern critics disregard the instructions contained in a Shakespearean playtext while protecting their own authorship. In his example, Foakes quotes Margaret De Grazia and Peter Stallybrass: "From a deconstructionist viewpoint, ... an emphasis on material practices rather than the author tends to elide the notion of authorial intention in the belief that whatever they may do, authors do not write books" (273). Foakes adds: "The academic critics who deal in such matters nonetheless proclaim their agency and their authorship of the books they write in order to advance their careers" (48).

References

Benabu, Isaac. "La construcción del personaje teatral: el duque de Ferrara en *El castigo sin venganza*." In *El patrimonio del teatro clásico español: actualidad y perspectivas*, edited by Germán Vega, Héctor Urzáiz, and Pedro Conde, Valladolid, Spain: Universidad de Valladolid y Ayuntamiento de Olmedo, 2015, 233–42.

——— . *Reading for the Stage: Calderón and His Contemporaries*. Tamesis, 2003

Carreño, Antonio. "'La sangre / muere en las venas heladas': tragedia en *El castigo sin venganza*, de Lope de Vega." *Revista canadiense de estudios hispánicos* 21 (1997), no. 2: 253–71.

——— . "La 'sin venganza' como violencia: *El castigo sin venganza* de Lope de Vega." *Hispanic Review* 59 (1991), no. 4: 379–400.

De Grazia, Margaret, and Peter Stallybrass. "The Materiality of the Shakespearean Text." *Shakespeare Quarterly* 44 (1993): 255–83.

Dixon, Victor. "Manuel Vallejo, *Un actor se prepara*: un comediante del siglo de oro ante un texto (*El castigo sin venganza*)." In *Actor y técnica de representación del teatro clásico español*, edited by José María Díez Borque, Tamesis, 1989, 55–74.

Edwards, Gwynne. "Lope and Calderón: the Tragic Pattern of *El castigo sin venganza*." *Bulletin of the Comediantes* 33 (1981), no. 2: 107–20.

Fischer, Susan L. "(Re)staging the Tragic Gaze in Lope's *El Castigo sin venganza*: A Verbal (Mis)representation of a Visual Representation?" *Comedia Performance* 12 (2015), no. 1: 137–67.

Foakes, Reginald A. "Performance Theory and Textual Theory: A Retort Courteous." *Shakespeare* 2 (2006), no. 1: 47–58.

Friedman, Edward H. "*El castigo sin vengaza* and the Ironies of Rhetoric." In *A Companion to Lope de Vega*, edited by Alexander Samson and Jonathan Thacker, Tamesis, 2008, 215–25.

Gardner, Helen. "Shakespeare in the Directors' Theatre." In *In Defence of the Imagination*, edited by Helen Gardner, Harvard University Press, 1982, 55–82.

Helbo, André J., Dines Johansen, Patrice Pavis, and Anne Ubersfeld. *Approaching Theatre*. Indiana University Press, 1991.

Lodge, David. *Therapy*. Penguin, 1995.

May, T. E. "Lope de Vega's *El castigo sin venganza*: The Idolatry of the Duke of Ferrara." *Bulletin of Hispanic Studies* 37 (1960), no. 3: 154–82.

McKendrick, Melveena. "Language and Silence in *El castigo sin venganza*." *Bulletin of the Comediantes* 35 (1983): 79–95.

Mujica, Bárbara. "Lope de Vega's *El castigo sin venganza*: What do Viewers Know and How They Know It?" *Comedia Performance* 12 (2015), no. 1: 50–78.

Shakespeare, William. *The Taming of the Shrew*. In *The Norton Shakespeare*, edited by Stephen Greenblatt, Walter Cohen, Jean E. Howard, and Katharine Eisaman Maus, Norton, 1997, 142–201.

Vega Carpio, Lope de. *El castigo sin venganza*. Edited by Cyril A. Jones. Oxford: Pergamon Press, 1966.

———. *Fuenteovejuna*. Edited by Donald McGrady, Barcelona: Crítica, 1993.

Wilson, Edward M. "'Quando Lope quiere, quiere.'" In *Spanish and English Literature in the 16th and 17th Centuries: Studies in Discretion, Illusion and Mutability*, edited by Edward M. Wilson, Cambridge University Press, 1980, 155–83. Originally published in *Cuadernos Hispanoamericanos* 54 (1963): 265–98.

Part III

Women in Literature and Culture

Poets, Readers, Holy Subjects

EMILY C. FRANCOMANO

"Entre las Otras Sois Vos"
The *Cancionero de Herberay* and Women's Cultural Production

THE DEARTH OF KNOWN female writers in the *cancioneros* would seem to make these manuscript and printed anthologies infertile ground for studying the cultural production of women. While several *motes* [epigrams] and *invenciones* [emblems] glossed by poets are attributed to "una dama" and to several named women, whole poems attributed to named women authors are few and far between.[1] Women are, presumably, the inspiration for many of the *cancionero* poems about love, and, as such, are transformed into literary devices used by male writers, who create images of transgressive and ideal women for their own projects of self-fashioning within the institution of the court.[2] Women writers, however, "are markedly absent" in the *cancioneros*, as Jane Whetnall observes ("Isabel González" 60). Indeed, historical women are perhaps never more absent than when presented as the objects of men's poetic virtuosity.

This essay explores the traces of women's cultural production in the *cancionero* tradition through an analysis of the *Cancionero de Herberay des Essarts* (*CH*) (BL Ms. Add. 33.382; Dutton Index LB2), where women appear as writers, characters, patrons, and interpellated readers. In a sense, I follow Whetnall's call to recover lost voices from a wide-ranging silence in the folios of manuscript *cancioneros*, an approach further developed by Ana Gómez-Bravo in her work *Textual Agency* on the importance of bringing a historicized view of authorship to *cancionero* studies in order to better understand women's participation in the cooperative and social nature of *cancionero* literary creation.

Scholarship on *cancionero* poetry tends to follow the text-author paradigm, often in the interests of identifying and analyzing a single author's oeuvre out of manuscript context. Studies on the few women poets in the *cancioneros* have maintained this emphasis. They have also focused on Florencia Pinar, the most prolific of the few named women. A historicized expansion of the notion of authorship, however, offers new perspectives on women's participation in *cancionero* poetics, which includes the collaboration of writers, patrons, audiences, and whoever else has left a mark in the text or on the physical book-object.[3] Moreover, I concur with Michel García's assertion that the *cancioneros* should themselves be considered "literary objects in their own right" (49). Consequently, in addition to historicizing authorship, I take a material hermeneutic approach, viewing the material book and its texts as symbiotically connected, although in the space of this short essay, I will not address the *CH* in its complex entirety.

The *CH*, so called because in the early sixteenth century it belonged to Nicolas de Herberay, the translator of *Amadis de Gaula* and other Spanish works into French, is a manuscript that was compiled circa 1467, with close ties to the court of Navarre and particularly to princess and future queen Leonor of Navarre, heir of Juan II of Aragon and Blanca of Navarre. Leonor served as regent for a quarter of a century, and very briefly during the twenty-four days between her father's death and her own, as Queen Regnant of Navarre in 1469.[4] The *CH* is an extraordinary book that contains 203 poems and seven humanistic prose works by authors from the courts of Castile, Aragon, and Navarre. Many of its contents are anonymous and also unique to the manuscript. Despite the varied contents and geographic origins of the writers represented in the *CH*, as Carlos Conde Solares observes, codicological evidence indicates that it was designed as a coherent anthology, possibly copied from an earlier iteration of the design (3).

Because the configuration of the *CH* is likely the result of copying from another source or sources, speaking of its original manuscript matrix is highly speculative. The contents, however, do appear to have been organized (and then perhaps reorganized) loosely by theme and/or author. The first section contains the prose *Declamación de Lucrecia* (an adaptation of Coluccio Salutati's *Declamationes Lucretiae*), Juan Rodríguez del Padrón's *Epístola de la Madreselva a Mauseol*, the *Letra que fue embiada por çitas a Alexandre*, the Marqués de Santillana's *Lamentaçión de Spanya*, Pere Torrellas's *Razonamiento en defensa de las damas* and *Complaynta sobre la muerte de Inés de Cleves*, and lastly a *Leyes de amor* (2r–24r).[5] A series of poems celebrating Leonor's beauty, dignity, prudence, and other regal virtues—the section that will most concern me here—begins on folio 24r and seems to conclude on 36r. However, a final poem in her honor appears on 194v. Other coherent groupings of poems are included throughout, including Hugo Urríes's poems on conjugal love, works by Juan de Mena, Villalpando, and Torrellas's *Maldezir de mugeres*.[6] Many of the contents of the *CH* are presented anonymously under the rubric "otra" [another poem] or "canción" [song or lyric], among them "Cuyado nuevo venido," a poem attributed to Florencia Pinar in one later manuscript, the *Cancionero de Rennert*.[7] It seems quite possible that an earlier manuscript of poems dedicated to Leonor was expanded to become part of the *CH* as it has come down to us.

As the list of contents demonstrates, the *CH* was a key contributor to the *querella de las mujeres* [debate on women], and as such, as Carlos Conde Solares concludes (111), it is of particular interest for the study of the works of Pere Torrellas. Above and beyond the compilation's interest for scholars of the *querella* texts and authors, the *CH* is concerned not only with discourses about and for women but also with depictions of women's cultural production. Not only does the *CH* contain verses attributed to Vayona, one of the five named women writers in the *cancionero* corpus, but it also contains many representations of women's voices, from the legendary eloquence of the suicidally chaste Roman matron Lucretia and the Amazon warrior Penthesilea's *planctus*, to anonymous verses written from a female perspective, such as "Malmaridada" (28v) and "Siempre m'aveis querido" (32v) [You have always loved me].

In the words of Harold Love, early modern authorship is often best understood as a "repertoire of practices ... and functions" that combine to locate texts "within time, place, a culture, a genre, an institution" (32), rather than a straightforward relationship between writer and text. Noting that distinct author functions, or *authemes*, are often distributed among different individuals involved with the creation of a work, Love proposes a typology to identify the "varieties of individual agency" expressed by the single term *authorship* (50). While I am well aware of the potential pitfalls that opening up the notion of authorship might pose in the history of women's writing, where the identification of historical individual women writers and the attribution of specific works to them are of central importance, shifting critical perspective away from the text-author paradigm in order to attend to the varieties of agency expressed in the *CH* helps to make visible the extensive participation of women as patrons, poets, interlocutors, and unnamed *damas* who inspire and create verses.

The *CH*'s celebration of Leonor begins with a *pregunta* and *respuesta* [question and answer] between two courtier-poets, Diego de Sevilla and Vayona (24r–24v). This sort of back and forth is a frequent dynamic genre in *cancioneros*. *Cancionero* poetry is also often occasional, and written records bear the traces of improvisation, of verses delivered orally in response to some theme or question. Games of rhetorical one-upmanship abound. Humor, double-entendres, and *agudeza* [wit] are the chief stylistic ideals of much amatory *cancionero* lyric. Not surprisingly, *cancionero* poetics often elevate style over substance and wit over sincerity. A true poet, Juan Alfonso de Baena explains, must be "noble fidalgo e cortés . . . e que tenga miel e açucar e sal e donaire en su razonar, e otrosí que sea amador, e que siempre se precie e se finja de ser enamordado" (50) [a noble gentleman and courtly . . . and should have honey, sugar, salt, and clever finesse in his verbal expression, and moreover he should be a lover, and always imagine himself in love and playact being in love]. The pose of the courtly lover may have been something of a game, but as Julian Weiss argues, it was a consequential game "that constructed and institutionalized a particular set of values based on class and, particularly, gender," a world created by poets that was "populated by fictions of aristocratic masculine power" ("'Qué demandamos de las mugeres'" 242–43). The *CH* demonstrates how fictions of aristocratic feminine power could also be constructed within the *cancionero* world.

Diego de Sevilla, apparently observing Princess Leonor, poses a question to Vayona:

Pregunta de Diego de Sevilla
Dezitme Señora, si dios vos dé vida,
pues la discreçión con vos sienpre mora.
La viril infanta de todas Señora,
¿para qué se nos muestra en son de dormida?
Si es por estar tan bien basteçida
de noble mesura, sosiego en oyr,
la cara serena con poco reyr,
acto es de dama por çierto entendida.
    (CH 24r; ID 2147)[8]

[Diego de Sevilla's question. Tell me, I beg you, my Lady, you, who are the very soul of discretion. Why does our virile princess, who is above all others, seem to be sleeping? If it is because she is so well endowed with noble equanimity and listens so calmly, her face serene and serious, it is the mark of a lady who is truly intelligent.]

Diego's question demands a response that is equally piquant, as he is, in effect, inviting Vayona to join him in a joke that takes the princess as its target. Vayona responds, matching Diego's meter and redeploying his words:

> Respuesta que fizo Vayona
> Si mirades más vezes, Diego y hermano,
> aquesta Señora tanto excelente,
> fallares que su real continente
> es muy más divino que no humano.
> Su rostro y sosiego con tanta mesura,
> su mirar tan honesto de sabia entendida,
> todos aquestos con gran fermosura
> la tienen velada y no adormida.
> (CH 24v; ID 2148; R2147)

[Vayona's response. If you look again, Diego my friend, at our most excellent Lady, you will see that her regal countenance is far more divine than human. Her face and most serene discretion, the great virtue of her gaze, shows her learned intelligence; all these traits, along with her great beauty, keep her veiled, but not asleep.]

These verses introduce the section in the *CH* fêting Leonor as a play of gazes in heterosocial dialogue. The triangular dynamic staged in the exchange neatly represents the participatory poetics of social authorship found in the *CH*. Diego de Sevilla asks, or perhaps demands, Vayona to join him in looking at and interpreting the affect of the *viril infanta* [virile princess], who, he seems to joke, is not terribly interested in the entertainments he has to offer. Both Sevilla and Vayona convert the object of their gazes into text, but theirs is an ekphrasis of adjectives, a vivid depiction that can only be understood in the moment, as both look upon the princess. The scenario constructed in the exchange suggests two courtiers whispering between themselves during an entertainment. The *pregunta* and its *respuesta* are catalogued as separate, if related, poems in the Dutton index, as ID 2147 and ID 2148; R2147. Nevertheless, their mutual dependence is clear; *pregunta* and *respuesta* are two equal parts of a socially authored whole.

The courtier's stylized complaint for not getting the recognition expected from his most important literary observer certainly suggests some anxiety that he will not get the regal attention he seeks. The lady's *respuesta* reassures him that he has the princess's attention, while it also gently reprimands him for even supposing that the princess may be sleeping through an event in her honor. Moreover, the masculine presence in the triangle of courtly wordplay represents something of an incursion into the princess's retinue, which would have been, by and large, a gynocentric social space where relationships of service and clientage between women were fostered (see Pelaz Flores).

The exchange also serves as the lead-in to Diego de Sevilla's eight-stanza "Loores a la muy exçelente Señora infanta" [Verses praising the most excellent princess, our Lady], which extends his textual gaze upon the princess. The rubric of the "Loores" also requests the princess's attention: "Plega a su Alteza mirarlas" [(the poet) entreats her highness to read them]. The fifth poem in the series, the *desfecho* [finale], addresses Leonor in the guise of a lovesick *galán* [gallant] dying for the princess to look kindly upon him:

> Pues mi pena veys,
> miratme sin sany
> o no me mireys.
> A mí que soy vuestro
> continuo amador,
> penado d'amor
> mas que no demuestro
> quiero qu'os mostres
> alegre sin sanya,
> o no me mires.
>   (CH 26v; ID 2152)

[Since you can see my pain, either look upon me without ire, or do not look at me at all. As your constant lover, who cannot seem happy because he is suffering from love, I want to see you happy and without ire, or for you not to look at me at all.]

The "Loores" and "Pues mi pena veys" epitomize the blend of amorous veneration and complaint—one poetic mode just as formulaic as the other—that characterizes the following poems, many of which also revolve around gazes; the poetic voices look at their beloved object in admiration and beg to be looked upon by her, even though to be the object of her gaze is to feel the pain of "lindos ojos" [lovely eyes] that "matan con su mirada" [kill with a look]. The many "otras" that follow Diego de Sevilla's poems to the princess address unnamed *señoras*, but they lend themselves to readings that seamlessly associate Leonor with the idealized beloved ladies they describe.

Courtly love in the *cancioneros* and elsewhere takes feudal metaphors and turns them into erotic ones. The "otras," in which the dying lover beseeches his beautiful *amiga* for her favors in this most political of song cycles, re-allegorize feudal terms, circling them back around to their literal meanings. The *cancionero* sexual favor begged of an apotheosized *señora* easily translates into the royal favor sought from the princess. Moreover, and as is clear in the *CH*'s anthology of poems to the princess, speaking wittily about love is a way to express political solidarity, submission, and dependence—relationships just as important to the women in the princess's household as to male courtiers.

In terms of social, or coterie, authorship, Leonor is a, and perhaps *the*, historical "precursory author" of the anthology of poems in her honor in the *CH*, a figure whose influence "makes a substantial contribution to the shape and substance of the work" (Love 40). As patron, reader, and subject of the poems in her honor, her presence—historical and material—served to "shape the meaning and significance" of the texts in the *CH*, and to bring the *cancionero* into being (Hirschfeld 613). Leonor as a lyrically constructed character is also materially present in the folios of the compendium. She is the "Infanta muy singular" [most singular princess], "Condessa de grand stado" [countess of high standing], and "gentil dama generosa" [generous gentle lady] addressed directly by the poems; and, by extension, she is the unnamed "vos" [you], the all-powerful beloved interpellated in the anthology's songs of lovesickness and love-driven servitude.

Many of the "otras" that follow Diego de Sevilla and Vayona's shared poetic gaze upon Leonor also concern the *mirada* [gaze] of the lover upon the beloved, for example, "Tanto vos miro sin par" (27r; ID2153) [I gaze upon you (who are) without equal], "Mis ojos por qué mirastes?" (27v; ID2154) [My eyes, why did you look?]. and "Ojos tristes que llorareys" (29v; ID2157) [Sorrowful eyes that cry]. The majority of these verses speak from a masculine perspective. One poem however, is written from a feminine perspective and pokes fun at a would-be lover's lack of command over courtly amatory discourse:

> Siempre m'aveys querido;
> maldita sea si os olvido.
> Mi Señor no arreys de nada
> vos a mi tener pagada
> y segunt vuestra embaxada
> avreys mi cuerpo garrido.
> (32v; ID2165)

[You have always loved me; I'd be dammed if I forget you. My lord, you will do nothing to please me, and yet, according to your message (to me), you will have my lovely body.]

"Siempre m'aveys querido" is in fact the first half of a dialogue, to which a male poetic voice responds:

Pues que te puedes llamar
la que más que todas vale
este es tu nombre no cale
no te fagas de rogar.
   (32v; ID2166)

[Since you can call yourself she who is worth more than all others, this is your name, look no further, do not play hard to get.][9]

Scholars have endeavored to prove that Diego de Sevilla wrote many of the poems immediately following his *loores* [verses of praise] to Leonor, and that Hugo Urriés authored twelve more of the poems in the sequence of unattributed verses.[10] The evidence for attribution to Diego de Sevilla, according to Conde Solares, resides in the meter, the rhyme schemes, the vocabulary, and the recurring theme of eyes and gazes (23). Nevertheless, another possibility is that the exchange about gazes between Diego de Sevilla and Vayona set a pattern for the sequence of poems that follow. In a poetic modality so conventional, filled with *glosas*, responses, borrowed lines, and set phrases, in addition to the rather limited range of vocabulary used in *cancionero* poems, affixing the name of a single historical poet to a given work is challenging.

The poems to and about Leonor were likely commissioned to mark an important occasion, possibly the princess's accession to the position of Princess Regnant in 1455, or the event of one of her many children's strategic marriages. Such celebrations were frequently commemorated by a *certamen* in which members of her court could vie to produce and perform the best poems, which in turn were memorialized in books. Leonor, perhaps more than other monarchs whose courts and court poetry were also memorialized and celebrated in the *cancioneros*, needed just such symbolic support of her sovereignty. Her promotion to lieutenant queen and heir to the throne in 1455 was something of a "radical move," as Elena Woodacre (112) explains. Leonor was the third and youngest child of Juan II of Navarre and Aragon, who promoted her over the claims of her brother Carlos of Viana and her sister Blanca, who both died in suspicious circumstances. Leonor has been implicated, when not accused outright, by medieval and modern historiographers in causing her siblings' convenient deaths in 1461 and 1464. A series of poems in praise of her, whether sincere or merely sycophantic, would have served as a testament to the court's approval of the princess.

The "otra" later attributed to Florencia Pinar, which appears in another series anonymous poems, concerns the desperate pain of love:

> Cuydado nuevo venido
> me da de nueva manera
> pena la más verdadera
> que jamás he padeçido.
> Yo ardo sin ser quemado
> en vivas llamas d'amores
> peno sin aver dolores
> muero sin ser visitado
> de quien con poder complido
> me tiene so su bandera.
> Es mi pena verdadera
> secreto fuego ençendido.
>   (92r; ID 0450)

[New cares pain me in new ways with the truest pain I have ever suffered. I am afire without burning in the hot flames of love, I suffer without affliction, I die without seeing the one who, with overwhelming power, has recruited me to their cause. Truly my pain is a blazing secret fire.]

It is easy to imagine the anonymous poems written from female perspectives as having been composed or performed by female members of the court. However, the poem later attributed to Florencia Pinar grammatically genders the speaker as male. In defense of the attribution to Pinar, Miguel Ángel Pérez Priego notes that "nuestra autora nunca exhibe gramaticalmente su condición femenina" [our author never grammatically displays her femininity] (92). What is perhaps more important is the fact that, decades after the *CH*'s composition, a poem so clearly written in a male voice was attributed to a female poet.

In a groundbreaking article, Barbara Weissberger reviews critical approaches to the small corpus of poems ascribed to Florencia Pinar, asserting that there is no reason to read female *cancionero* poets as any more sincere in their expressions of love than male poets, nor is there reason to suppose that women writers would have been any less adept at imitating and deploying the same poetic conventions found in verses written by men. Pinar, Weissberger argues, may have been writing "as a man for men" in order to construct her own poetic and courtly identity "in order to gain status and power," just as the male poets did (39). Further, as Gómez-Bravo asserts of the Trastámaran courts of the day, "El entorno de las mujeres adscritas a la cámara de la reina o de las infantas formaría un lugar ideal para el estudio y la práctica poética" ("'A huma senhora que lhe disse'" 63) [The circle of women belonging to the queen's or princesses' chambers would create an ideal environment for the cultivation and practice of poetry]. The "social fictions" intrinsic to playing the role of a courtly lover were not always played "straight," as Victoria Burrus argues, observing that "skilled and playful poets were wont to subvert the role of the impassioned noble lover" (133). Burrus's characterization refers to male poets pushing the limits of courtly conventions, but I believe that skillful and playful women poets, much like Florencia Pinar, were also able to play the role of the lover whose object of reverence and objectification was female. In the case of the *CH*'s poems to Leonor, the revered object was a woman who wielded considerable political and economic power.

The fictional role of the courtly lover allows for cross-gender casting. If we can picture a male hand writing as the *Malmaridada*, Lucretia, or Penthesilea in the *CH* and, like the compiler of the *Cancionero de Rennert*, imagine that Pinar wrote "ardo sin ser quemado," then why not consider the possibility that other female poets also took on masculine personae when they joined in the games of *cancionero* poetic play? The sequence of poems in honor of Leonor clearly work as a tool of regal image projection to exalt the Princess Regent. Along with the seven prose works in the first section of the *CH*, the sequence may have been meant to serve as proof of the culture and learnedness of her court, and the manuscript that preserved the text as hard evidence of her power and cultural capital.

In the final stanza of his infamous *Maldezir de mugeres*, Pere Torrellas assures his *dama* that "entre las otras sois vos" [you are among the others], while all the previous stanzas, numbering eleven in the *CH*, are addressed to those ill-advised lovers who court women (190r; ID0043). I would like to suggest that some of the *CH*'s anonymous poems may well be the work of other women in the court of Navarre who adeptly took up the conventions of *cancionero* poetics. Virginia Woolf's theory that "Anon, who wrote so many poems without signing them, was often a woman" is apt for the *CH*, where we may find not only images of women but also women's writing among the poems introduced through the rubric of "otras" (38). Reading a compilation like the *CH*—or sections of it—as a socially authored anthology suggests that Florencia Pinar, Vayona, and the three other named women poets of the *cancionero* tradition are not female anomalies among scores of male poets, but rather five voices among many, if unnamed, *otras* who participated in the courtly networks of poetic production.

Multiple social practices and codicological processes combined in the making of the *CH*. As a whole, the anthology offers many perspectives on the intersections of gender, gendered role-playing, politics, and poetics in the *cancionero* tradition. The *CH* presents women writers, constructs female sovereignty, and combines the conventional use of "ladies" as poetic devices with its concerted overture to historical women readers. When read as the product of social authorship, the *Cancionero de Herberay* is also a book *by* women, one that can give us a better understanding of women's agency in the composition and symbolic uses of poetry, and also indicates that women were able to play the *cancionero*'s games of love and politics and play them well.

Notes

This essay originated as a panel presentation at the Biennial Conference of GEMELA (Grupo de estudios de la mujer española y latinoamericana) in San Juan, Puerto Rico, September 30, 2016.

1. The named women poets in the *cancionero* tradition are: Mayor Arias, María Sarmiento, Vayona, Juana of Portugal, Isabel González, and Florencia Pinar.

2. Much enlightening work has been done on *cancionero* poetry as a key masculine social practice in the fifteenth century. See, for example, the work of Victoria Burrus, Michel García, Julian Weiss, and Barbara Weissberger, and Ana Gómez-Bravo's *Textual Agency*.

3. Margaret Ezell coined the term "social authors" to describe seventeenth- and eighteenth-century writers who "existed on the margins of the commercial literary domain" and whose work was often produced and circulated in manuscript. Such margins could be spaces for female authorship (4). Brian Richardson writes of coteries of writers who preferred manuscript circulation to print because it circumscribed readership, creating intimacy within the coterie, and at times shielding authors from censure. For Ezell and for Richardson, whose work focuses on seventeenth- and eighteenth-century English and sixteenth-century Italian contexts, respectively, social manuscript circulation contrasts with "public" print culture. In the mid-fifteenth century, of course, print circulation of Trastámaran court poetry was not yet an option, but the coterie dynamics described by both authors predates the distinction of print from manuscript culture.

4. It is interesting to note that the Kingdom of Navarre had the largest group of

female sovereigns in any one European realm during the Middle Ages, as Elena Woodacre demonstrates in her study of the five queens of Navarre to rule in their own right between 1274 and 1512.

5. On romance translations of the *Declamationes Lucretiae* and the version in the *CH*, see María Morrás.

6. Conde Solares provides a complete listing of the *CH*'s contents.

7. "Cuydado nuevo venido" is also credited to Pedro de Quiñones and to Juan Rodríguez del Padrón in other *cancioneros*. Whetnall asserts that "Cuydado nuevo venido" cannot be by Florencia Pinar because it first appeared in the *Cancionero de Gallardo*, which was copied circa 1454, two decades before Pinar is thought to have been active ("Isabel González" 59).

8. I have based this text and others on the transcriptions in *An Electronic Corpus of 15th Century Castilian Cancionero Manuscripts*, available at http://cancionerovirtual.liv.ac.uk; translations are my own. Translating *cancionero* poetry into English is, needless to say, quite a challenge. I believe that the only translations that could even approach conveying their full meanings and poetics are creative and free interpretations. Here, however, in the interests of academic reading, I have endeavored to render each poem literally, embedding some explanatory syntax.

9. The *Electronic Corpus of 15th Century Castilian Cancionero Manuscripts* lists the two parts of the dialogue as separate poems, as does Charles Aubrun's edition (44), but they appear under a single rubric in the manuscript.

10. On Diego de Sevilla, see Conde Solares (73–75). On Urriés, see Whetnall's article "Unmasking the Devout Lover." Charles Aubrun, in his edition, attributed all of the anonymous poems as well as the *CH*'s compilation to Urriés (xliii).

References

Aubrun, Charles. *Le Chansonnier espagnol d'Herberay des Essarts*. Edited by Charles Aubrun, Bordeaux: Féret et Fils, 1951.
Baena, Juan Alfonso de. "Prologus Baenenssis." In *Poesía Cancioneril Castellana*, edited by E. Michael Gerli, Madrid: Akal, 1994, 47–50.
Burrus, Victoria. "Role Playing in the Amatory Poetry of the *Cancioneros*." In *Poetry at Court in Trastamaran Spain: From the* Cancionero de Baena *to the* Cancionero General, edited by E. Michael Gerli and Julian Weiss, Tempe, AZ: Medieval and Renaissance Texts and Studies, 1998, 111–33.
Conde Solares, Carlos. *El* Cancionero de Herberay *y la corte literaria del Reino de Navarra*. Newcastle upon Tyne: Arts and Humanities Research Council, 2009.
An Electronic Corpus of 15th Century Castilian Cancionero Manuscripts. Edited by Dorothy S. Severin, et al., cancionerovirtual.liv.ac.uk.
Ezell, Margaret. *Social Authorship and the Advent of Print*. Johns Hopkins University Press, 1991.
García, Michel. "In Praise of the *Cancionero*, Considerations on the Social Meaning of the Castilian *Cancioneros*." In *Poetry at Court in Trastamaran Spain: From the* Can-

cionero de Baena to the Cancionero General, edited by E. Michael Gerli and Julian Weiss, Tempe, AZ: Medieval and Renaissance Texts and Studies, 1998, 47–56.

Gómez-Bravo, Ana. "'A huma senhora que lhe disse': Sobre la naturaleza social de la autoría y la noción de texto en el *Cancioneiro geral de Resende* y la lírica cancioneril ibérica." *La corónica* 32 (2003), no.1: 43–64.

———. *Textual Agency: Writing Culture and Social Networks in Fifteenth-Century Spain*. University of Toronto Press, 2013.

Hirschfeld, Heather. "Early Modern Collaboration and Theories of Authorship." *PMLA* 116 (2001), no. 3: 609–22.

Love, Harold. *Attributing Authorship: An Introduction*. Cambridge University Press, 2002.

Morrás, María. "Coluccio Salutati en España: La versión romance de las *Declamationes Lucretiae*." *La corónica* 39 (2010), no. 1: 209–47.

Pelaz Flores, Diana. "Tejiendo redes, estrechando lazos. Amistad femenina, proteccion y promocion social en la Casa de la Reina de Castilla (1406–54)." In *Reginae Iberiae : el poder regio femenino en los reinos medievales peninsulares*, edited by Miguel García-Fernández and Silvia Cernadas Martínez, Santiago de Compostela, Spain: Universidade de Santiago de Compostela, Servizo de Publicacións e Intercambio Científico, 2015, 227–300.

Pérez Priego, Miguel Ángel, ed. *Poesía femenina en los cancioneros*. Madrid: Castalia, 1989.

Richardson, Brian. *Manuscript Culture in Renaissance Italy*. Cambridge University Press, 2009.

Weiss, Julian. "Álvaro de Luna, Juan de Mena, and the Power of Courtly Love." *Modern Language Notes* 106 (1991), no. 2: 241–56.

———. *The Poet's Art: Literary Theory in Castile c. 1400–60*. Oxford: The Society for Medieval Languages and Literature, 1990.

———. "'Qué demandamos de las mugeres': Forming the Debate about Women in Late Medieval and Early Modern Spain (with A Baroque Response)." In *Gender in Debate from the Early Middle Ages to the Renaissance*, edited by Thelma S. Fenster and Clare A. Lees, Palgrave, 2002, 237–74.

Weissberger, Barbara. "The Critics and Florencia Pinar: The Problem with Assigning Feminism to a Medieval Court Poet." In *Recovering Spain's Feminist Tradition*, edited by Lisa Vollendorf, The Modern Language Association of America, 2001, 31–47.

Whetnall, Jane. "Isabel González of the *Cancionero de Baena* and Other Lost Voices." *La corónica* 21 (1992–1993), no. 1: 59–82.

———. "Unmasking the Devout Lover: Hugo Urriés in the *Cancionero de Herberay*." *Bulletin of Hispanic Studies* 74 (1997): 275–98.

Woodacre, Elena. *The Queens Regnant of Navarre: Succession, Politics, and Partnership, 1274–1512*. Palgrave, 2013.

Woolf, Virginia. *A Room of One's Own and Three Guineas*, second revised edition. Oxford University Press, 2015.

Sense(s) and Sensibility in Two Sonnets of Catalina Clara Rodríguez de Guzmán

> What syllable are you seeking,
> Vocalissimus,
> In the distances of sleep?
> Speak it.
>
> —Wallace Stevens, "To the Roaring Wind"

> There is a fifth dimension beyond that which is known to [us] ... a dimension as vast as space and as timeless as infinity ... a dimension not only of sight and sound but of mind.... It is the middle ground between light and shadow, between science and superstition, and it lies between the pit of [our] fears and the summit of [our] knowledge ... a land of both shadow and substance, of things and ideas.... This is the dimension of imagination.
>
> —Rod Serling, voiceover introduction to *The Twilight Zone*

IN THE DIMENSION of imagination, poetry can emerge as a twilight zone where the signposts are of a varied sort, for in its essence, poetry speaks to our senses in its pervasive way of foregrounding the human experiences of hearing, touch, and sight. Poetry is also, in the words of Wallace Stevens, "the act of finding / what will suffice" (254), a search for those qualities that will imbue a poem with sense as meaning and as full a sensorial expression as possible, especially of sound. Robert Frost writes: "Now it is possible to have sense without the sound of sense ... and the sound of sense without sense.... The best place to get the abstract sound of sense is from voices behind a door that cuts off the words" (664). On the surface, at least, Frost employs the word "sense" in its meaning of "understanding" or "knowledge," but "sense" also implies knowledge as sensory, as "feeling" conveyed frequently in poetry through how we capture it auditorily.

Yet other voices would seem to complicate the function of sound in poetry:

"La poesía es silencio. Este no sólo se opone a la palabra, sino que la afirma y la sostiene, la apoya y la activa" [Poetry is silence. This quality is in opposition to the spoken word at the same time that it affirms it and sustains it, supports it and activates it] (Egido 93). This insightful remark by Aurora Egido appears to be paradoxical. How can a poem be silence at the same time that it is the voiced affirmation—voiced sound, as Aristotle would have it—of the poet and of sense? One way of attempting to respond to this vexing question is to focus on poetry created out of the condition of absence; the poet directs the composition to one who cannot respond to, or ease the emotional burden of, the writer (or speaker). As Egido has suggested, poetry arises from the silences of introspection and meditation. She brings to bear Fernando de Herrera's lines from Sonnet XIX, "Del fiero Marte el canto numeroso":

El silencio, el semblante descontento;
y el confuso gemido es muestra abierta
de mi penoso y luengo desvarío
   (v. 9)

[The silence, the unhappy expression, and the unintelligble moan form a clear sign of my long and painful delirium.]

Herrera, in a common employment of the outstanding sibilant, expresses his silence as "silencio," "semblante," "descontento," "confuso," "es," "muestra," and the like.

To Egido's engagement of Herrera I would add San Juan de la Cruz, whose mystical poetry, drinking from the well of the same Garcilasian fonts as Herrera's verses, underlines sound's significance for many Spanish poets of the sixteenth and seventeenth centuries. San Juan de la Cruz incorporates sibilants to serve as meditative indicators of the soul already purged of its Earth-bound sentience: "Salí sin ser notada / estando ya mi casa sosegada" (vv. 4–5) [I left without being seen, my house calm and in order]. The silence of which Egido speaks, then, is at once metaphorical and metaphysical, often reflective of internal anguish, turmoil, or yearning, and constituent of the quality of sound, a *sine qua non* condition of poetic language. The manner of presentation, the imagery of a poem, reflects its time, while the sounds of poetry as an utterance of human speech open it to universal understanding unbound by time and project to the reader's present. Lyric poetry serves, in Susan Stewart's words, as "a record of a first-person speaker across and through historical and cultural contexts" (41).

The poet I address in this essay is Catalina Clara Ramírez de Guzmán, a seventeenth-century Spanish poet from Llerena (Extremadura) with a significant corpus of poetic work, a novel titled *El extremeño* [The Extremaduran], and possibly a *comedia* (no copies of these last two works have been discovered).[1] Ramírez de Guzmán's poetry has received sporadic but growing attention, particularly over the past fifteen years; it rightly has found its way into anthologies, such as Bárbara Mujica's *Women Writers of Early Modern Spain: Sophia's Daughters*, as well as into an increasing number of individual studies, some of which appear in Julián Olivares's fundamental *Studies on Women's Poetry of the Golden Age: Tras el espejo la musa escribe*.

The most recent compendium of her writing is *Obra poética*, edited with a lengthy introduction and study by Aránzazu Borrachero Mendíbil and Karl McLaughlin. McLaughlin's doctoral dissertation "Defragmenting the Portrait" also contributes to the poet's recent reception. These two scholars provide readers with the most complete selection of Ramírez de Guzmán's known poetry, building on and revising the first important collection by Joaquín de Entrambasaguas Peña, which has often been reedited. Borrachero Mendíbil and McLaughlin lament the sparse biographical information available about the writer, particularly the lack of memoirs and correspondence that could shed light on her act of writing, on her direct, non-poetic communication with friends, family, and/or readers.

As with many writers whom we hold in particular regard, we attempt to tease out life's secrets through their literary "self-portraits" or other artfully disguised treatments of the self. María Salgado speaks to Ramírez de Guzmán's ability to employ the "typical" style as practiced, for example, by Cervantes, and to holding on to conventions of female literary portraiture while subverting it through an ironic individualization (57).[2] Yet even where we hope to find, especially with women writers of the early modern period, telltale markers of individuality and challenges to the primary discursive practices, it is crucial to keep in mind, as Lisa Vollendorf and Grady Wray (107) have argued, that readers contemporary to the writing of the "portraits" may have seen the female authors as working within the dominant discourse, however slippery it may have been, even if, as Adrienne Martín offers, Ramírez de Guzmán's audience was primarily female. Martín holds that much of her writing is "a genial poetics of everyday life as experienced by women" (221–22n13). Although I do not take up the portrait poem except as a point of departure, the two compositions that are the focus of this essay reveal the writer's inner self and are more than a "genial poetics"; rather, they show that this poet was capable of producing intricate sonnets that should raise her profile significantly and that deserve to be read—and taught—more widely today.

The edges and borders between dominant and non-dominant discourses are the territory of many women writers. In two poems of heartfelt distress arising from the absence of beloved companions in her life, Ramírez de Guzmán inhabits this space as a poet of the senses. Her work, naturally like that of many of her contemporaries, savors the sound of language as a medium that serves to touch the listener—emotionally and physically—enhancing the verses' overall effect. "Cuando quiero deciros lo que siento" (XCVI, 313) [When I try to tell you what I feel] and "Acertar a decir mi sentimiento" (XVII, 181–82) [To give true voice to my feelings] confront the implicit silence of absent individuals, a dear friend in the one, a brother in the other (according to the epigraphs that accompany each poem), and the concomitant panoply of the senses evinced by the poet's piercing loneliness. Because these poems to date have received only limited commentary and are not widely known, I include the complete texts at the outset of each discussion:

XCVI

    Cuando quiero deciros lo que siento,
siento que he de callaros lo que quiero,
que no explican amor tan verdadero
las voces que se forman de un aliento.
    Si de dulces memorias me alimento,
que enfermo[3] del remedio considero,
y con un accidente vivo y muero,
siendo el dolor alivio del tormento.
    ¿Qué importa que me mate vuestra ausencia
si en el morir por vos hallo la vida
y vivo de la muerte a la violencia,
    pues el remedio sólo está en la herida?
Mas si no he de gozar vuestra asistencia,
la piedad de que vivo es mi homicida.[4]

    [When I try to tell you what I feel,
I sense that I must silence what I desire
for the sounds that tumble forth
cannot account for as true a love as mine.

> If I nourish myself with sweet memories
> I believe they succumb to the remedy itself,
> and I live and die hanging by a thread,
> my torment's relief found only in pain.
> What does it matter if your absence kills me
> if in dying for you I find life
> and I live from death to violence (I live for the violence of death)[5]
> for the remedy is found in the wound alone?
> But if I cannot take pleasure in your presence
> the devotion that grants me life me is my executioner.]

"Cuando quiero deciros lo que siento" suggests that silence in absence may be the only solution to the poetic voice's plight, yet the immateriality of memory cedes to the very material image of (metaphorical) food: "Si de dulces memorias me alimento" (v. 5). The poet's act of ingesting memory as both further pain and relief from it enables us to read into these poems a yearning for physicality sought by the voice(s) within them. Ingestion is a motif that was employed not infrequently by many writers of the day, often in reference to women who eat clay.[6] The inclusion of this specific imagery yields a full sensorial picture. In Aristotle's *De anima* and *De sensu*, and as elaborated by Daniel Heller-Roazen in *The Inner Touch*, all the senses in some way participate in touch—which ingesting and tasting are forms of—so its potential becomes imbued in all sensory perception and expression, even sound as expressed in the alliterative d's and m's. We can recall San Juan de la Cruz's use of "hería" [wounded or burned] in his "Noche oscura del alma" [Dark night of the soul] (v. 34), a passionate burning prepared for earlier in the poem by his use of "ardía" [was burning] (v. 15) that comes through as a touch keenly felt despite the physical absence of the other, standing in paradoxical opposition to and in line with the sibilants, "todos mis sentidos suspendía" [held all of my senses in suspense] (v. 35).

Women poets of this time, as Julián Olivares and Elizabeth Boyce neatly summarize (92), confronted the masculine discourse so evident in courtly literature and later in Garcilasian influences, as these established a codified language in both rhetorical devices and imagery. Not surprisingly, interpretive difficulties arise when we speak of these writers, as we face the daunting task of disentangling the rhetoric of clever challenge to the dominant mode from the discourse of acquiescence.[7] Ramírez de Guzmán partakes of both. Considered this way, "Cuando quiero deciros lo que siento" could very well be the poet's gaze at her reflection, questioning who she is, where she is, and straining against the prevailing winds both to feel and to hear. In her verses, Petrarchan imagery is not straightforward, and this poem engages the language of courtly love with its "dulces memorias" [sweet memories], a tasty sonorous treat. Voicing and hearing are of little emotional support, as the first quatrain makes clear. Speech and silence were commonplace poetic imagery in the period and Ramírez de Guzmán struggles to find an appropriate register to express loneliness, all the while working within established parameters. The struggle to modify and mold her voiced signature literally leaves her breathless.

Three elements are at play, or even at war, here: the chiasmus of "quiero"/"siento" and "siento"/"quiero"; the internal autorhyme; and the e-o assonance in the quatrains. These work together to produce mutual privileging as well as echoes—soon to be reinforced in the "aliento"/"alimento" rhyme that links the two quatrains in this nicely crafted sonnet—that reverberate and therefore jar the speaker, who begins to confront the ache emanating from an absence, now of the friend's voice. The sonnet both reinforces the sudden and painful discovery of Garcilaso de la Vega's "dulces prendas" [sweet tokens]—objects painfully evocative of and associated with a former love—as Amanda Powell has indicated (71), and signals the painfulness of separation from the other's voice and touch. "Memorias" may provide "alimento" but they are also like "palabras y plumas" [words and feathers], easily carried away by the wind: the sustenance they afford is tantalizing but the poet and her voice remain bereft of full sensory knowledge. One phrase helpful in speaking of sensory experience, from a 1717 preacher's manual, reads: "materias no tocadas no dan satisfacciones cumplidas" [untouched matters do not provide complete satisfaction (knowledge)] (Domingo López f. 135). The delightful play between literal and secular meaning, as well as between metaphorical and religious implications, becomes an apt accompaniment to Ramírez de Guzmán's poetry and its ambiguities. Complicating the friend's absent voice is his or her missing physical presence, starved as the poetic voice is for the emotional bond and complete sensorial connection. Ramírez de Guzmán unquestionably touches upon the materiality of friendship and the dolorous sense of absence when the friend's presence dissolves into memory. So the ironic "touching" occurs in the frustrated attempt to ingest, to physically hold on to the sweet memories.

The poem's first word, "Quiero," is of course an expression of desire, whereas "siento" makes felt the hearing and feeling completely fulfilled only in close physical proximity. Philosopher Richard Kearney lays out the following in his introduction to a "carnal hermeneutics": "We live in the flesh and we sense in all of its meaning: sensation, understanding and direction, our orientation in space and time" (100). The tensions of the poem's quatrains produce the life/death, *vivo/muero* paradox from v. 7 onward. The sonnet glances toward Francisco de Quevedo in the "os" repetition of vv. 1–2 ("Si quien ha de veros ha de pintaros," no. 345) [If he who is to paint you is to see you]. That repetition renders an echo of sight in the service of male voyeurism.[8] Ramírez de Guzmán, along with her female contemporaries, anticipates Sor Juana in an elaboration of inherited conceits that take on new life.[9] Quevedo's reliance on sight, the sense atop the hierarchy, allows him to gaze down on the woman he wishes to "paint," whereas Ramírez appropriates the "os" in order to describe female sensorial experience along a continuum of the senses and move away from the dominance of sight through direct mention of and indirect allusion to other senses. The sonnet's partaking of erotic mystical discourse, which Santa Teresa expressed in "muero porque no muero" [I die because I do not die]—embodied yet body-less—reveals the frustration occasioned by the friend's absence. The want of verbs indicative of sight is telling. The lyric "I" moves from a voice that cannot be heard to keener frustrations—"herida" [wound or burning], "asistencia" [presence]—that suggest the realm of touch, a synesthetic quality in its creation of haptic knowledge.

The sonnet "Acertar a decir" [To give true voice] shares similarities with the other poem in that it conveys an almost mystical quality:

XVII

    Acertar a decir mi sentimiento
fuera desaire de mi pena grave,
que en el silencio solamente cabe
la significación de mi tormento.
    De esperanzas de veros me alimento,
que es manjar en la ausencia el más süave,
y mudamente mi silencio sabe
decir callando lo que amando siento.
    Y aunque paso esta pena por amaros,
no puedo arrepentirme de quereros,
que no déjame el gusto de adoraros
    por ahorrar la pena de no veros;
que el alma que no tiene ya que daros
gusta de tener ansias que ofreceros.[10]

[To give true voice to my feelings
would be an insult to my deep heartache,
for only silence can accommodate
the meaning of my torment.

The hope of seeing you is my only sustenance,
the sweetest delicacy in your absence,
and my mute silence is able
to speak wordlessly what I feel in my loving soul.
　　And though I withstand this sorrow out of love for you
I cannot repent for loving you
for what never abandons me is the pleasure of adoring you
　　to save myself from the sorrow of not seeing you;
as my soul, with nothing left to bestow on you,
is contented to have yearning to offer you.]

This composition is charged with soothing sibilants reflective of meditational poetry, and denotes movement through the twisting, meandering *s* sound, a physical journey through enforced solitude and absence. The sound both quiets and unsettles us as it presents calm as well as the ominous, disquieting effect of longing. To give voice to the desolation the speaker feels at her brother's absence, to make herself heard, she presents an almost insurmountable challenge. The sentiment cannot be voiced (the telltale first verse of each sonnet prepares the reader well); it must live in silence, but the task before the poet is the enigma of how to express silence in a verbal construct, the challenge Egido has presented. When the poetic voice says "en el silencio solamente cabe / la significación de mi tormento" (v. 7–8), she adds weight and mass to the silence. Striving to secure a sensorial foothold against the potent winds of her emotional turmoil, Ramírez de Guzmán returns anew to taste. The metaphorical food, a "manjar . . . el más süave" (v. 6), allows hope to become concrete or materialized to the extent that when we hear "mudamente mi silencio sabe / decir callando lo que amando siento" (v. 7–8), "saber" takes on its double role of tasting and knowing, knowledge produced through the senses. In the poem before us, the external shifts to the interior as Ramírez de Guzmán swallows her grief, now more tactile than any literal food could be. Life returns to her as the closing verses read: "que el alma que no tiene ya que daros / gusta de tener ansias que ofreceros" (v. 13–14). The pain of absence is both imagined and real, while it also renders to the speaker the ultimate sensation of being alive despite remaining anchored in loneliness.

　　Another structural element connects the two sonnets: their tercets. In "Cuando quiero deciros," "death" by absence is an unremitting cruelty, unrelieved and emphasized by the rhyme progression in the tercets, from "vida" to "herida" to "homicida." The breath that had given voice to voice, to expressions of desire, quickly devolves into a "lower" sensory realm of implicit physicality commonly associated with the female (Classen 70) against the present doleful situation ("la piedad de que vivo es mi homicida," v. 14).[11] A curious reinforcement of touching physicality occurs between "voces" (v. 4) and "herida" (v. 12). One definition of "voz," from the *Diccionario de autoridades*, reads: "Por extensión se llama el sonido, que forman algunas cosas inanimadas heridas del viento, ù hiriendo en él" [Likewise (voice) also means the sound that some inanimate objects create when struck by the wind, or striking the wind]. A "voice" is created when an object comes into contact with the wind, the crucial element of this being physical contact. Similarly, the movement among the three rhyming words in a poem of absence configures a different sort of time removed from the more prosaic past-present-future, because the timelessness of the poem exists in its own continuum of memory, longing, desire, silence, anxiety, frustration, and hope. "Acertar a decir" (v. 1) communicates less the pleasure/pain dichotomy than filial love (she is speaking to her brother).

The sonnet moves toward a sonorous conclusion with the crescendo, perceived by Gwyn Fox (139), of "amaros," "quereros," and "adoraros," continued by "veros," "daros," and "ofreceros"; the first three "metaphysical" verbs do not rely solely on presence for their impact and are synonymous in their fundamental affect though with modulation in intensity (*Dicc. Aut.*), while the last three carry implicitly the sensation and possibility of touch. The alternating "-eros"/"-aros" rhyme offers a sonorous similarity anchored by the "os" in order to draw in the other as a necessary complement to the lyric voice. Poetry about absence, as well as poetry about loss, seeks to recuperate the missing substance, the one of whom the poem speaks. The rhyming words bring together subject and object, silence and sound. Rhyme as sensation, as Allen Grossman notes, "articulates silence as sound (the meaning of words and sentences)" (362). Egido's ostensible paradox described at the outset—silence as being in opposition to the word yet supporting and sustaining it—resolves itself at the moment that we recognize how sensation becomes poetically staged.

The search for a voice, such as that which Ramírez de Guzmán puts forth in these compositions, is more than speechlessness, as voice carries with it the ability to know oneself, to speak one's name. Susan Stewart recalls that Io, as Ovid recounts in the *Metamorphoses*, was turned into a heifer and became "'terrified by her own voice.'" Similarly, Hecuba, in her rage at Polymestor for having killed her son Polydorus, gouges out his eyes and chases after the Thracians who attacked her

> with spears and stones, but she,
> Snarling and Growling, chased the stones and bit them,

Opened her mouth for words, but what came out
Was barking.
(Ovid 13: 567–69)

Stewart (61) holds that the inability to speak is joined to both the loss of human form, the form of the self, and to the proper name (Hecuba's tomb, in the *Metamorphoses*, carries the inscription "Cynossema, The Bitch's Tomb" [Ovid 13: 570]). Absence is a call into a voided presence. The lyric, the sonnet, goes out to the absent one, from whom there is no response. The speaker expects the silence and proceeds to forge the indispensible path to express a life-sized lament more fully than would be otherwise possible. The lack of presence might suggest a lack of the sensory, but the pain expressed in the poems arises from that inner touch, effecting another, sensorial transformation of a speaker whose words may be full of import and poetic transcendence, yet frequently depend on a third-party listener. A symbiotic relationship through sound is implicit, "a sense of knowing what another does not or cannot speak about" (Gross 28). The poet can never respond in the way that the implied reader, the recipient of the poem, is able to. Ramírez de Guzmán's poems become even more powerful statements of love and loss when imbued with the panoply of not just emotion but also sensoriality, presenting a body that is aching from absence. These two poems both conjure presence and present the difficulties of finding voice and a concomitant register. Even the poem cannot bring the person to his or her fullest measure; we are both tied to and left with sense impressions that substitute for the form, for the flesh and blood.

A poem is a bridge to another moment (Stewart 34)—Garcilaso's "verme morir entre memorias tristes" [to see me die among sad memories]—and a poem of absence becomes a *memento* (*mori*), as that which Garcilaso embedded in the silent "memori" within his voiced silence. That founding poet's "prendas," evoked in Ramírez de Guzmán's "dulces memorias" in "Cuando quiero deciros," cannot speak or respond, yet they do shout. They break the silence but cannot lessen the pain evinced by memory; in "Acertar a decir," they are converted into reminders of tension or "ansias." Reading a lyric poem offers us the "ecstatic desolation" (Grossman 30) of a double absence, as if the lyric voice must fill the void doubly, work doubly hard to express sense and the senses to make up for the missing physical object. To evoke absence, Catalina Clara Ramírez de Guzmán describes the effect of that absence on—and in—her poetic voice, how it leaves her senseless, even as she clamors and clambers to find expression for it. The lack of her friend or her brother teaches her that words and their sounds—voices behind a door—are all that are left to her to give her lost loved ones the form and presence (Grossman 37) she so avidly pursues.

Notes

I would like to thank Bárbara Mujica who, through her book *Women Writers of Early Modern Spain: Sophia's Daughters*, first brought Catalina Clara Ramírez de Guzmán to my attention.

   1. For the reference to the novel, see Julián Olivares and Elizabeth Boyce, *Tras el espejo la musa escribe: Lírica femenina de los Siglos de Oro*, 53–54. The first of the two poems, a *romance* by Ramírez de Guzmán, is a barbed reply to the Sevillan writer Fernando de la Torre Farfán, to whom she had sent a *comedia* manuscript for his advice; to date, his probably negative and condescending comments (judging from Ramírez de Guzmán's poem) have not been located. The second poem is Torre Farfán's equally pointed *romance*. For the text of the two poems along with a brief study and notes, see María José Osuna Cabezas and Immaculada Osuna Rodríguez's article "Catalina Clara Ramírez de Guzmán y Fernando de la Torre Farfán: Dos romance cruzados a cuenta de una comedia desconocida de la escritora."

   2. Salgado refers to "Un retrato me has pedido" [You have asked me for a portrait] (Ramírez de Guzmán, *Obra poética*, no. XLIX, 237–43). The poem's first verse allusion to Lope's "Un soneto me manda hacer Violante" [Violante commands me to write a sonnet] trades on the famous sonnet by "teaching" the reader, as well as the recipient ("un hermano suyo") [her brother], how a literary portrait is carried out, while subverting the standard comparisons and calling into question the genre itself. For additional commentary, see Ramírez de Guzmán, *Obra poética*, 75–83, and Amanda Powell, "'¡Oh qué diversas estamos," 69. A second portrait poem, a sonnet (no. LXX, 274) discussed as well by Borrachero Mendíbil ("Catalina Clara Ramírez de Guzmán") and McLaughlin (*"Defragmenting the Portrait"* 121–27), leads one to wonder somewhat dreamily if Sor Juana Inés de la Cruz could have read it.

   3. If "enfermo" modifies the speaker, then a logical reading suggests it should be "enferma." Entrambasaguas Peña, Borrachero Mendíbil, and McLaughlin indicate "enfermo," but the only solution is to consult the manuscript (Ms. 3884, f.241 in the Biblioteca Nacional Española), as it is not available online.

   4. The Roman numerals and page numbers refer to the order in the edition of Borrachero Mendíbil and McLaughlin, and McLaughlin's dissertation, some of which follows Entrambasaguas Peña's numbering in his 1929 limited collection. All other references to Ramírez de Guzmán's poems are to the Borrachero and McLaughlin edition via poem and page numbers. The two editors briefly discuss this first sonnet (88–90) as a love poem with potential lesbian overtones. They also provide a brief survey of critical commentary on the poet's work (56ff.).

   5. All translations are my own unless otherwise noted. I would like to thank Catherine Larson and Gwyn Campbell for helpful suggestions on translating both sonnets. V. 11 is not clear so I offer two possible interpretations.

6. Ramírez offers her own take on geophagy in her satirical piece about "una mujer tan amiga de barro que se desayunaba con él" [a woman so fond of clay that she ate it for breakfast] (*Obra poética*, no. VI, 163). Maríaluz López-Terrada discusses the practice among other representations of illness in the *comedia*; she also offers a bibliography on the subject.

7. In an essay in preparation, I discuss the two poems indicated in note 2 above specifically as an examination of the poet's manipulation of the discourse to her advantage.

8. Writing at the end of the nineteenth century, Arturo Gazul believed that Ramírez de Guzmán had familiarity with Quevedo's writings, and he referred to her laudable satiric verses (qtd. in Ramírez de Guzmán, *Obra poética*, 66). Powell's and Adrienne Martín's work on the satiric and burlesque in Ramírez de Guzmán's poetry entice us to look more fully at her clever appropriation of Quevedo's style.

9. See "Rosa divina que en gentil cultura" and "Detente, sombra de mi bien esquivo," though one could adduce many others where Sor Juana responds to her male predecessors by turning their language against them and in the process realigning poetic discourse (Juana Inés de la Cruz 257, 113).

10. Borrachero Mendíbil ("Catalina Clara Ramírez de Guzmán") and McLaughlin ("Defragmenting the Portrait" 87–88) assert that this poem deals with the insufficiency of language.

11. Sensual attributes according to gender occupied many early modern European writers, but few women dedicated themselves to elaborating on these differences. Of note is Lucrezia Marinella (1571–1653), whose *La nobiltà et l'eccellenza delle donne* (1600) is at the center of arguments concerning distinct attributes, sensorial and otherwise, between women and men. For an overview of Marinella's work (her name also appears as "Marinelli"), see Prudence Allen and Filippo Salvatore's "Lucrezia Marinelli and Woman's Identity in Late Italian Renaissance"; and Stephen Kolsky provides a closer look at the *Nobiltà* in its context as a refutation of Guiseppe Passi's mysoginist *I donneschi diffetti* (1599) in his "Moderata Fonte, Lucrezia Marinella, Guiseppe Passi: An Early Seventeenth-Century Feminist Controversy."

References

Allen, Prudence, and Filippo Salvatore. "Lucrezia Marinelli and Woman's Identity in Late Italian Renaissance." *Renaissance and Reformation* 28 (1992), no. 4: 5–39.

Aristotle. *On the Soul [De Anima]* and *Sense and Sensibilia [De Sensu]*, 2 vols. Edited by Jonathan Barnes, Princeton University Press, 1984, I: 641–92; 693–713.

Borrachero Mendíbil, Aránzazu. "El autorretrato en la poesía de Catalina Clara Ramírez de Guzmán." In *Studies on Women's Poetry of the Golden Age. Tras el espejo la musa escribe*, edited by Julián Olivares, Tamesis, 2009, 81–99.

Classen, Constance. "The Witch's Senses: Sensory Ideologies and Transgressive Femininities from the Renaissance to Modernity." In *Empire of the Senses: The Sensual Culture Reader*, edited by David Howes, Berg, 2005, 70–84.

Diccionario de Autoridades. 1726, web.frl.es/DA.html.

Domingo López, Fray. *Talentos del Superior. Symbolos en los cincos sentidos corporales.* Granada: Imprenta de la Santísima Trinidad, 1717.
Egido, Aurora. "La poética del silencio en el siglo de oro. Su pervivencia." *Bulletin Hispanique* 88 (1986), nos. 1–2: 93–120.
Fox, Gwyn. *Subtle Subversions: Reading Golden Age Sonnets by Iberian Women.* Catholic University Press of America, 2008.
Frost, Robert. *Collected Poems, Prose & Plays.* Library of America, 1995.
Gross, Kenneth. "The Survival of Strange Sounds: Forms of Life in Lyric Poetry." *Yale Review* 103 (2015), no. 2: 27–46.
Grossman, Allen, with Mark Halliday. *The Sighted Singer: Two Works on Poetry for Readers and Writers.* Johns Hopkins University Press, 1992.
Heller-Roazen, Daniel. *The Inner Touch: Archaeology of a Sensation.* Zone, 2009.
Herrera, Fernando de. *Sonetos.* Edited by Ramón García González, Cervantes Virtual, www.cervantesvirtual.com/obra-visor/sonetos-14/html/.
Juan de la Cruz, San. "Noche oscura del alma." In *Poesía lírica del Siglo de Oro*, edited by Elias Rivers, Madrid: Cátedra, 2005, 176–78.
Juana Inés de la Cruz, Sor. In *Poesía lírica*, 3rd ed. Edited by José Carlos González Boixo, Madrid: Cátedra, 1997.
Kearney, Richard. "What is Carnal Hermeneutics?" *New Literary History* 46 (2015), no. 1: 99–124.
Kolsky, Stephen. "Moderata Fonte, Lucrezia Marinella, Guiseppe Passi: An Early Seventeenth-Century Feminist Controversy." *Modern Language Review* 96 (2001), no. 4: 973–89.
López-Terrada, Maríaluz. "'Sallow-faced Girl, Either it's Love or You've Been Eating Clay': The Representation of Illness in Golden Age Theater." In *Medical Cultures of the Early Modern Spanish Empire*, edited by John Slater, Maríaluz López-Terrada, and José Pardo-Tomás, Ashgate, 2014, 167–87.
Marinella, Lucrezia. *The Nobility and Excellence of Women, and the Defects and Vices of Men.* Edited and translated by Anne Dunhill, University of Chicago Press, 1999.
Martín, Adrienne. *An Erotic Philology of Golden Age Spain.* Vanderbilt University Press, 2008.
McLaughlin, Karl. *"Defragmenting the Portrait": Catalina Clara Ramírez de Guzmán, Extremadura's no conocida señora of the Golden Age.* PhD diss., University of Bradford, 2010.
Mujica, Bárbara. *Women Writers of Early Modern Spain: Sophia's Daughters.* Yale University Press, 2004.
Olivares, Julián, ed. *Studies on Women's Poetry of the Golden Age: Tras el espejo la musa escribe.* Tamesis, 2009.
Olivares, Julián and Elizabeth S. Boyce, eds. *Tras el espejo la musa escribe: Lírica femenina de los Siglos de Oro.* Madrid: Siglo Veintiuno, 1993.
Osuna Cabezas, María José, and Inmaculada Osuna Rodríguez. "Catalina Clara Ramírez de Guzmán y Fernando de la Torre Farfán: Dos romance cruzados a cuenta de una comedia desconocida de la escritora." In *Aurea Poesis. Estudios para Begoña López*

Bueno, edited by Luis Gómez Canseco, Juan Montero, and Pedro Ruiz Pérez, Servicio de Publicaciones de la Universidad de Córdoba, 2014, 393–410.

Ovid. *Metamorphoses*. Translated by Rolfe Humphries, Indiana University Press, 1955.

Powell, Amanda. "'¡Oh qué diversas estamos, / dulce prenda, vos y yo!' Multiple Voicings in Love Poems to Women by Marcia Belisarda, Catalina Clara Ramírez de Guzmán, and Sor Violante del Cielo." In *Studies on Women's Poetry of the Golden Age: Tras el espejo la musa escribe*, edited by Julián Olivares, Tamesis, 2009, 51–80.

Quevedo, Francisco de. *Obras completas, I. Poesía original*. Edited by José Manuel Blecua, Barcelona: Planeta, 1963.

Ramírez de Guzmán, Catalina Clara. *Obra poética*. Edited by Aránzazu Borrachero Mendíbil and Karl McLaughlin, Mérida, Spain: Editora Regional de Extremadura, 2010.

———. *Poesías*. Edited by Joaquín de Entrambasaguas Peña, Mérida, Spain: Antonio Arqueros, 1929.

Salgado, María. "En torno al 'Segundo autorretrato' de Ana María Fagundo y el 'Retrato de la autora' de Catalina Clara Ramírez de Guzmán." *Hispania* 85 (2002), no. 1: 54–66.

Stevens, Wallace. "Of Modern Poetry." In *The Collected Poems of Wallace Stevens*, corrected edition, 2nd ed. Edited by John S. Serio and Chris Beyers, Vintage, 2015.

Stewart, Susan. *Poetry and the Fate of the Senses*. University of Chicago Press, 2004.

Vollendorf, Lisa, and Grady C. Wray. "Gender in the Atlantic World: Women's Writing in Iberia and Latin America." In *Theorising the Ibero-American Atlantic*, edited by Harald E. Braun and Lisa Vollendorf, Brill, 2013, 99–116.

GILLIAN T. W. AHLGREN

Women's Vision, Women's Truth
Teresa of Ávila's Defense of Women's Access to God

SINCE 1990, a whirlwind of historical and literary critical scholarship has helped contextualize the origins of Teresa of Ávila's *Interior Castle* (1577). Written in direct response to the Inquisitional sequestration of *The Book of Her Life*, Teresa began the *Interior Castle* just a year after an Inquisitional investigation into the authenticity of her relationship with God, an investigation that cast further doubt, for some, on the legitimacy of her reform of the Carmelite Order. By 1575, Teresa was experiencing a broad and bewildering array of challenges, carefully documented by scholars like Bárbara Mujica in *Teresa de Ávila: Lettered Woman*, Alison Weber, and Carole Slade, triggered by her more public presence as a writer and reformer. Whether it was Teresa herself and her claims to intimacy with God that had now been made more public through her *Life* (which circulated only in a few manuscript copies), or whether it was the expansion of her Discalced Carmelite foundations (which subsequently threatened the prestige of the non-reformed Carmelite monasteries), success bred some significant resistance. In analyzing Teresa's careful strategies in her multiple roles as prioress, administrator, legislator, disciplinarian, counselor, and even politician and diplomat, many scholars have noticed Teresa's admirable skill and persistent vulnerabilities as a woman operating in a patriarchal milieu.

Deeply dedicated not only to the success of the Carmelite reform but also to the depth of women's spiritual growth and the flourishing of women's collaborative life with God (and the apostolic works that emerged from this partnership), Teresa sought to create convent spaces where women would be free from the scorn they seemed to face, in print and in public, as they sought to claim their baptismal vocation to live fully in the body of Christ. And the more successful she was, the more widespread and complicated were the challenges to her authority and therefore the more numerous and complex were the strategies Teresa had to employ in order to continue her work of reform.[1] In this essay, I will highlight the uniqueness of Teresa's defense of women's direct access to God in an environment increasingly inclined to deprive women of spiritual, theological, and religious authority. I will focus on the sixth dwelling places of Teresa's *Interior Castle*, which I will argue is her contribution and corrective to the burgeoning literature on the discernment of spirits, and her attempt to protect women's spiritual integrity, the authenticity of their experience of God, and the theological reflections and insights that emerged from such experience, no matter the prevailing ecclesiastical or socio-political climate.

To state the thesis in another way: although by 1577, Teresa had engaged in a variety of actions to insulate women from scorn, accusation, and shame in their quest for deepening spiritual perfection—including establishing a network of spiritual and sacramental support from sympathetic priests and spiritual directors—she knew that it was important to provide internal, female-authored textual support as another facet of her advocacy for the flourishing of women's spirituality (and, by extension, the health and well-being of the entire people of God). Mujica outlines Teresa's initial strategies in this way:

> Having suffered at the hands of inept confessors who mortified her with allegations that her visions came from the devil, Teresa insisted that her nuns be guided by competent men. Throughout her books she reiterates the importance of compassionate, learned confessors who respect women's spiritual integrity. She believed nuns should be able to choose their confessors and even allowed them to select priests from outside the order or to change confessors if they were dissatisfied. When confessors became abusive in her convents, Teresa appealed not only to God but also to temporal authorities. She replaced the malicious Calced Carmelite confessors of Incarnation Convent in Ávila with two benevolent Discalced friars, Juan de la Cruz and Germán de San Matías. When the infuriated Calced kidnapped and imprisoned these two, Teresa complained directly to King Philip II. ("Was Teresa of Avila a Feminist?" 79)

But by the time of the travesty of Juan de la Cruz's imprisonment, Teresa knew better than to expect just outcomes from human systems, even systems that should be guided by divine inspiration and light. Teresa had, by then, experienced the inner machinations of Inquisitional interrogation and seen the capacity of her contemporaries to impute malicious motivations and engage slander with impunity, including accusations, among other things, of using the Discalced convents as a front for operating houses of prostitution.

A review of the context from 1575–1576 will help us to recognize the counsels in the sixth dwelling places of Teresa's *Interior Castle* as a strong protection for women, not only "against incompetent spiritual directors" ("Was Teresa of Avila a Feminist?" 79) but also as a validation of women's worth, their dignity, and the goodness of their desire to be of service to God as instruments and models of how genuine partnership with God takes form in human life. What I suggest we notice is the careful counsel that Teresa provides her sisters, so that they will be neither deceived nor discounted by their male contemporaries, who often considered women unable to recognize God's presence in their own lives and easily deceived by the devil masquerading as an angel of light. Having experienced far more personally the possibility of both Inquisitional censure during the resurgence of prosecutorial activity against *alumbrados* [the "falsely illumined"] in the 1570s and external resistance to reform movements, Teresa's experiences in Seville in 1575–1576 also made her more keenly aware of the need for all of the Discalced, particularly prioresses, to recognize signs of spiritual authenticity. The material on discernment of spirits in the sixth dwelling places represents one of the profound differences of the *Interior Castle* from *The Book of Her Life*; in addition to demonstrating Teresa's own spiritual maturity, the former is suggestive of a greater command of the pastoral theology necessary for authentic spiritual administration and leadership. Both Teresa and María de San José Salazar, the astute and educated prioress of the Discalced convent in Seville, learned over the course of hardships and persecutions how easily external religious authorities could disrupt the order and well-being of a religious community and even threaten the existence of the reformed convents.[2]

Moving into the province of Andalucía to found a convent in Seville, Teresa entered a territory full of minefields that necessitated a careful and strategic defense of her life's work. As the drama of Seville heightened, Teresa found herself in a six-month quagmire of political struggle that threatened her personally, threatened her beloved brother Lorenzo, and even threatened the success of her reform movement. "Things are dreadful here," she confided to her sister Juana, catching her up on the occasion of the arrival of their brothers at the port of Seville from the Americas in August 1575 (*Obras completas* 1362), and they only proceeded to get worse in early 1576 once an Inquisitorial investigation of Teresa and Isabel de San Jerónimo began. Combined with the disarming withdrawal of Prior General Juan Bautista Rubeo's support, Teresa found herself absorbed in a continual struggle to assert her legitimacy as the spiritual architect of a reform movement under attack on multiple fronts.

As the dust of 1575 settled, into the early months of 1576, the Inquisitional tribunal of Seville declined to press charges against Teresa, a considerable victory, even as her confessor Domingo Báñez's report to the Inquisitional Tribunal of Valladolid on the orthodoxy of *The Book of Her Life* led to her first book's sequestration. Teresa herself was ordered to stop founding Discalced convents and to retire from Seville to a convent in Castile. She did not receive this news directly from Rubeo but rather from the Andalusian Provincial Angel de Salazar, through the Calced Prior Miguel de Ulloa, and her lengthy letter to Rubeo reflects Teresa's personal disappointment in him:

> I have learned of the order which came from the Chapter-General, requiring me to remain in one convent. Fray Angel, the Father Provincial, had it sent to Father Ulloa, with the injunction to notify me of it. He thought I should be deeply hurt by it, as these Fathers intended when they passed it, so he had been keeping it from me. It must have been rather more than a month ago that I got him to give it to me: I had learned of it from elsewhere.
>
> I will certainly not hide from Your Reverence that, so far as I understand my own mind, it would have been a great kindness, and a satisfaction to me, if you yourself had conveyed this order to me in a letter. I should have taken it that you were sorry for the severe trials that I have suffered in making these foundations—I who am unfit for much suffering—and that, as a reward for enduring them, you were ordering me to rest. For even taking into the account the way the order has come, this possibility of getting some quietness has given me the greatest happiness. (*The Letters of Saint Teresa*, Letter 91, I:224)[3]

Perhaps the order to retire to a convent in Castile did come as something of a relief, even providing a respite and a place to retrench. As Mujica ("Was Teresa of Avila a Feminist?" 69–70) notes, Teresa's reference to reform as a form of war, while something of a constant, became a strong theme in her correspondence after 1575. If, in fact, "Mental prayer was the ammunition with which the Discalced Carmelites would fight the multiple menaces they faced" (70), then the decision to write the *Interior Castle* to replace the missing *Life* was a major campaign strategy. And the sixth dwelling places would provide a way for Teresa to immortalize the spiritual counsels that she hoped might protect her sisters from the treatment that she and other collaborators, like María de San José, were receiving.

The story of the genesis of the *Interior Castle* is well known. On the other side of the troubles in Seville, Teresa and the Discalced provincial for Andalucía, Jerónimo Gracián, were meeting in Toledo and speaking of prayer, and Teresa lamented the absence of the *Book of Her Life*. Gracián recounts: "She said to me, 'Oh, how well that point is written in the book of my life, which the Inquisition has!' And I said to her: 'Well, since we can't recover it, write down what you remember, and other things, and write another book" (*Anotaciones al P. Ribera*, cited in Ahlgren, *Teresa of Avila*, 61; see also Ahlgren, *A Reader's Companion*, 6–7). In fact, the *Interior Castle* is a very different book from the *Life*. Not only does it represent a different literary genre and a full fifteen years of spiritual maturation, but also Teresa deals head on in it with the obstacles that women with spiritual ambitions faced.

Concern about this was not new for Teresa. As early as 1565, with the draft of the first version of her *Way of Perfection*, she was articulating and lamenting to God the unequal treatment of women. In passages that did not survive Inquisitional censure, she wrote, for example:

> Isn't it enough, Lord, that the world keeps us silenced and incapable of doing anything of value for You in public and we don't dare speak of truths we bewail in secret, but You won't hear our rightful petition? I don't believe it of such a good and just lord; You are a just judge, not like the world's judges, who, since they are sons of Adam, and are, in short, all men, there is no female virtue they don't view as suspect. (Translation mine; *Obras completas*; see Ahlgren, *Teresa of Avila*, 88)[4]

In many passages of the *Way of Perfection*, Teresa provided her nuns with strategies and even arguments that they could use to explain and defend their vocation to mental prayer if they met with resistance or hostility.[5] Thus, Teresa was quite aware, even prior to having significant contact with the Inquisition, of the inhospitable climate for women's spiritual and theological expression. By the time she wrote the *Interior Castle*, she was not only defending women's right to pray, but also highlighting the "incomparable and magnificent beauty" of the soul, the "precious things" that can be found in it, and God's own delight in us as we turn to God and allow God to show us our own "magnificent capacity" as persons created in God's own image and likeness (Teresa, *The Interior Castle*, 35–36). In a context of patriarchal deprecation and abuse, this opening salvo announces an entirely different orientation and trajectory. Recovery of the soul's great dignity becomes both a spiritual task requiring great commitment from us but also a graced, energizing remedy to the grief of sin and injustice.

In the *Interior Castle*, Teresa identifies seven stages of growth in a transformative process that leads the soul to union with God—a union that is in no way static and is best known as "the unitive life," an active partnership with God that manifests in creative, life-giving activity. Teresa teaches that we are created to be collaborators with God in the work of making the world a fitting, just, and loving place for all who inhabit it. This begins with the work of inner transformation, some of which we can (and must) accomplish, as we rid ourselves of sinful, self-defeating practices that deny or even impede God's loving intent for us and for our fragile world. This also involves allowing God to transform us, opening ourselves to and availing ourselves of God's indwelling presence, preferring that presence to any other thing and nurturing that presence in us and in our encounters with others. As early as the fourth dwelling places, the midpoint of the journey, we begin to experience an inner expansion that Teresa describes as "spiritual delights," which God produces in us "with the greatest peace and quiet and sweetness in the very interior part of ourselves" (*The Interior Castle* 74), a moment of divine encounter that "swells and expands our whole interior being producing ineffable blessings" (75). And to convey the experience of the fifth dwelling places, Teresa uses the metaphor of a caterpillar, cocoon, and butterfly, to express the concurrence of metamorphosis, resting in God, and the soul's first experiences of participating in the empowering energy of God. The union that the soul experiences here is "above all earthly joys, above all delights, above all consolations and still more than that . . . I once said that the difference is like that between feeling something with the rough outer covering of the body or in the marrow of the bones" (88).[6] Teresa writes elsewhere: "God so places Godself in the interior of the soul that when it returns to itself it can in no way doubt that it was in God and God was in it. This truth remains with it so firmly that even though years go by without God granting it that favor again, the soul can neither forget nor doubt that it was in God and God was in it" (89).

By the sixth dwelling places, the space of the *Interior Castle* that most concerns us, the effective presence and action of God in the soul are so profound that the soul's identity is slowly "undone" as a unitive partnership works its way into our very being. The depth of this transformation—the soul's "undoing" into a being-with-God—involves a number of steps, many of which try the soul's patience. The first chapter of the sixth dwelling places describes a series of exterior trials that can cause a person serious doubt. The catalog of these trials replicates much of what Teresa herself suffered at the hands of others: gossip, suspicion, shunning, and ostracism ("Those she considers her friends turn away from her, and they are the ones who take the largest and most painful bite at her, 'That soul has gone astray and is clearly mistaken; these are things of the devil; she will turn out like this person or that other that went astray . . . ; she has deceived her confessors . . .'" [*The Interior Castle* 109]). Even more troublesome were the difficulties brought on by inexperienced confessors who misread and misjudged the person, provoking terrible scruples of conscience and doubt of both self and God:

> Let us begin with the torment one meets with from a confessor who is so discreet and has so little experience that there is nothing he is sure of: He fears everything and finds in everything something to doubt because he sees these unusual experiences. He becomes especially doubtful if he notices some imperfection in a soul that has them, for it seems to such confessors that the ones to whom God grants these favors must be angels—but that is impossible as long as they are in this body. Everything is immediately condemned as from the devil or melancholy. . . . But the poor soul that walks with fear and goes to its confessor as to its judge, and is condemned by him cannot help but be deeply tormented and disturbed. (111–12)[7]

The more that the person, especially one who is beginning along the path of contemplative prayer and has deep inner experiences for which she has few words, tries to communicate with her confessor about these inner dynamics, the more she feels that "she is incapable of explaining things to her confessors" and therefore is deceiving them, even though she goes to them with every possible good intention. Teresa calls these intense scruples "keen and unbearable," even a form of hell (*The Interior Castle* 112). Coupled with an awareness of our shortcomings, our "nothingness," and our misery, which is seemingly exacerbated after each encounter with the perfection of God, the purifying space of the sixth dwelling places is a challenging one, requiring patience, discretion, and genuine pastoral companionship. "In sum," she says, "there is no remedy in this tempest but to wait for the mercy of God" (113). But in the meantime, engaging in external works of love and charity can make that wait a bit more bearable (114).

The soul's deepening interiority is now accompanied by forms of direct communication from God, outlined in chapters two through six of the sixth dwelling places. These forms of communication are subtle, even as they are intense, arresting, and transforming. Teresa speaks of them as

> impulses so delicate and refined, for they proceed from very deep within the interior part of the soul, that I don't know any comparison that will fit. They are far different from all that we can acquire of ourselves here below and even from the spiritual delights that were mentioned. For often when a person is distracted and forgetful of God, His Majesty will awaken it. His action is as quick as a falling comet. And as with a thunderclap, even though no sound is heard, the soul understands very clearly that it was called by God. (*The Interior Castle* 115–16)[8]

In a very real sense, Teresa is trying to describe the variety of ways that humans begin to integrate the action of God into their being. She uses analogies of cosmic forces, like the comet and bolts of thunder, to communicate their power and otherness. To experience such things intimately is disconcerting, awe-inspiring, humbling, and empowering. If we said that chapters two through six represent a catalog of paramystical phenomona designed to serve as a diagnostic for both the one experiencing these communications and for the one who serves as spiritual companion or mentor, then we would not be wrong. But we would also not be capturing all of what Teresa is accomplishing in this section of the *Interior Castle*.

Far from being a cold manual of symptoms that might be used to judge a person for their treatment or condemn them for falsifying religious experience, as many contemporary manuals for discernment of spirits were, Teresa treats the internal communications that the soul receives from God as sacred, intimate, real, and authentic. Above all else, they are loving impulses, meant to draw us into a mystery that brings us home—"delicate and refined," she says. Even when such experiences are new to us and therefore quite foreign, the soul still has an intuitive sense of both their transforming power and their precious value. She affirms: "This action of love is so powerful that the soul dissolves with desire, and yet it doesn't know what to ask for since clearly it thinks that its God is with it" (*The Interior Castle* 116).

In her descriptions, Teresa seems to capture well both the isolation and self-doubt she herself felt when she had neither confessor nor companion to help her identify the mystical phenomena that she was experiencing. It was precisely for this reason that she was moved to establish communities for women seeking the depth of contemplative prayer and the necessary communal solidarity for such a demanding process. While any human being would likely struggle for language to express mystical experiences and seek reassurance, it could not have helped any to have been a woman and been met with assumptions about a woman's moral and spiritual inferiority. Particularly when there were physical elements to prayer—that is, when prayer was deeply embodied and took over the person—the assumption was either that the devil was at work or the human being was faking an inner intensity of prayer in order to impress others.

But Teresa presents a compelling alternative. In chapters four through six of the sixth dwelling places, for example, when she discusses embodied prayer, she expresses deep concern over contemporary suspicions about mental prayer, visions, and raptures. For Teresa it was coherent and logical to expect that when one experiences the immensity of God in one's being, such a thing is overwhelming. Calmly and cogently, she explains the various ways that we might experience deepening encounters with and communications from God, cataloging them and their effects on us. For example, as she explains, in a state of rapture the soul is deprived of consciousness and receives revelations either in the form of imaginary or intellectual visions. Breath leaves the body, the senses cannot operate, and at times the body can become as cold as death.[9] For her male contemporaries, for example Hernando del Castillo, a Dominican who served as a theological consultant to the Inquisition, the physical elements that accompanied mental prayer were a clear sign that phenomena like visions and levitation were induced by the person herself. In an opinion rendered in about 1575, Castillo wrote: "Therefore these feelings which appear with such violence and torment people, leaving them as if they were dead is a sign that they come from the flesh, and there they end."[10]

For Teresa, however, there is a deep, internal reality that such descriptions of the *external* effects of God's communication could not capture. Puzzling her way through the dilemma of expressing these ineffable but very real experiences, Teresa writes: "I was thinking now that it's as though from this fire enkindled in the brazier that is my God a spark leapt forth and so struck the soul that the flaming fire was felt by it. And since the spark was not enough to set the soul on fire, and the fire is so delightful, the soul is left with that pain; but the spark merely by touching the soul produces that effect" (*The Interior Castle*

116).¹¹ It is almost as if Teresa is conveying an internalized experience of the encounter between Moses and the burning bush. The divine origins of such a fiery, transforming love are known and communicated in a piercing mystery that bewilders and captivates, leaving no room for doubt. She continues:

> Here there is no reason to wonder whether the experience is brought on naturally or caused by melancholy, or whether it is some trick by the devil or some illusion. It is something that leaves clear understanding of how this activity comes from the place where the Lord, who is unchanging, dwells. The activity is not like that found in other feelings of devotion, where the great absorption in delight can make us doubtful. Here all the senses and faculties remain free of any absorption, wondering what this could be, without hindering anything or being able, in my opinion, to increase or take away that delightful pain.
>
> Anyone to whom our Lord may have granted this favor—for if He has, that fact will be recognized on reading this—should thank Him very much. Such a person doesn't have to fear deception. Let his great fear be that he might prove ungrateful for so generous a favor, and let him strive to better his entire life, and to serve, and he will see the results and how he receives more and more. (116)¹²

We should note that Teresa never encourages people to seek out such experiences. In fact, she repeatedly counsels both those who receive them and those prioresses or confessors who will be in a position to assess the veracity of those experiences simply to ignore the spiritual gifts that God may grant, considering them irrelevant to a person's spiritual growth. For Teresa, the important thing is always the quality and depth of our relationship with God and with others; that is the measure of our spiritual progress. As she puts it, the Christian life is about how we express love—love of God and love of neighbor—and growing in love should be our constant focus.¹³

Nonetheless, Teresa is aware of the frequency of embodied experiences of God in convent life, and for that reason she determines it necessary to give detailed descriptions of them and careful counsel about how to respond. About locutions, for example, she writes:

> If I can manage to do so, I shall give, with the help of the Lord, the signs as to when they [locutions] come from different sources [from God or from the devil or from one's own imagination] and when they are dangerous; for there are many souls among prayerful people who

> hear them. My desire, Sisters, is that you realize you are doing the right thing if you refuse to give credence to them, even when they are destined just for you (such as some consolation, or advice about your faults), no matter who tells you about them, or if they are an illusion, for it doesn't matter where they come from. One thing I advise you: do not think, even if the locutions are from God, that you are better because of them, for He spoke frequently with the Pharisees. (*The Interior Castle* 120)[14]

Teresa then outlines signs to recognize the authenticity of words given to a person in the interior. The surest sign, she writes, is "the power and authority they bear, for locutions from God effect what they say." And to explain this better, she gives the example of a person in tribulation and disturbance who receives the words "Do not be distressed" and then "is left calm and free from all distress, with great light," even though it would have seemed to her that no one could have removed her from distress (120–21). True locutions also leave the person with a sense of great quiet, peaceful recollection, and deep desire to praise and serve God (121). Further, the words "remain in the memory for a very long time, and some are never forgotten," as if engraved in the heart or soul (*The Interior Castle* 121; Proverbs 7:3; Deuteronomy 11:18).

Given the moral and spiritual improvements that such experiences impart, Teresa concludes: "Wherefore, the experience, obviously, is not from the devil; it would be impossible for the imagination or the devil to represent things that leave so much virtue, peace, calm, and improvement in the soul" (*The Interior Castle* 137). These improvements are conveyed in the comportment of the person, who now "goes about with such tender love [that] any occasion that enkindles this fire more makes the soul fly aloft."[15]

Although Teresa describes these phenomena in a way that might suggest to readers that people who experience them are hardly human anymore, she quickly attends to the ongoing embodiment of the mystical life. For her, the many internal, transformative demonstrations of God's active love actually distill into a more companionate relationship with the human Jesus, who models a kind of loving companionship that we can imitate and share with others. Chapters seven through nine of the sixth dwelling places reflect Teresa's insistent dedication to intimacy with the incarnate God.

> It will also seem to you that anyone who enjoys such lofty things will no longer meditate on the mysteries of the most sacred humanity of our Lord Jesus Christ. Such a person would now be engaged entirely

in loving. This is a matter I wrote about at length elsewhere. They have contradicted me about it and said that I don't understand . . . and that when souls have already passed beyond the beginning stages it is better for them to deal with things concerning the divinity and flee from corporeal things. Nonetheless, they will not make me admit that such a road is a good one. . . . To be always withdrawn from corporeal things and enkindled in love is the trait of angelic spirits, not of those who live in mortal bodies. It's necessary that we speak to, think about, and become the companions of those who, having had a mortal body, accomplished such great feats for God. How much more is it necessary not to withdraw through one's own efforts from all our good and help, which is the most sacred humanity of our Lord Jesus Christ. (*The Interior Castle* 145)[16]

For the rest of this section of the *Interior Castle*, Teresa focuses on how the soul gradually moves from the individual, piercing moments of God's love to a "continual companionship" with God, in Christ, that "bears with it a particular knowledge of God," as well as "a most tender love for His Majesty, . . . and to a great purity of conscience because the presence at its side makes the soul pay attention to everything." She continues, noting: "For even though we already know that God is present in all we do, our nature is such that we neglect to think of this. Here the truth cannot be forgotten, for the Lord awakens the soul to His presence beside it. And even the favors that were mentioned became much more common since the soul goes about almost continually with an actual love for the One who it sees and understands is at its side" (152–53).[17]

In this way, Teresa completely normalizes a partnered relationship with God that bears fruit in our daily lives. The reassuring familiarity of Teresa's narrative voice as she takes readers through this process ends up echoing and replicating the familiarity of God, whose desire to share life with us, in all of its human and picayune details, never fails to astonish and humble her. Indeed, the remaining material in the sixth dwelling places of the *Interior Castle* is replete with pastoral counsel, a kind of counsel that perhaps only Teresa could provide, to all (but especially to women) who seek the empowering companionship of the incarnate God, despite the fears, prejudices, and skepticism of so many of their male counterparts.

Although I do not think that Teresa intended for her message about God's constant invitation to the mystical life to be read only by women, I do think that it could not possibly have been heard the same way by male and female readers. In a climate of intense suspicion of interiority, where theological discourse was limited to men, who also controlled all major mechanisms to monitor religious authority, Teresa's rich expressions of God's generosity toward all, and her particular recourse to Christ as a friend to, and advocate for, women opened up possibilities for women's exploration of divine power as it incarnated itself in their embodied, prayerful, and prophetic presence. Keenly aware of the challenges women faced, as they nurtured and articulated experiences of God's transformative power in their lives and world, Teresa in her *Interior Castle* provided the tools for women to participate as full partners and collaborators in the apostolic witness of Christianity. Teresa was able to learn from and use her own struggles to support and cultivate the spiritual and intellectual lives of women, especially those who sought partnership with God in a religious context in which it would have preferred that they kept silent. Teresa's extraordinary chronicle of the mystical life contained in her *Interior Castle* demonstrates her decisive impact on the Christian mystical tradition, the history of Christian theology, and the trajectory of women's spirituality.

Notes

1. For example, in working with the hybrid text of the *Book of the Foundations*, which Teresa wrote in fits and starts between 1573 and 1582, Helen Reed has shown that the book is "a didactic and purposeful memoir, meant to teach how future convents might function successfully ... [Teresa's] natural inclination to accept limits to human knowledge and rely on experience and faith in God, enables her to undermine the authority of the educated ecclesiastics that might disagree with her plans" (226).

2. María de San José's Eighth and Ninth Recreations in her 1585 *Book for the Hour of Recreation* recount in detail these struggles. María herself was deposed as prioress and deprived of a voice and a vote in convent deliberations, and the impact of the situation in Andalusia threatened the whole of the reform. See Salazar, 100–64, esp. 156–58.

3. "Yo supe la Acta que viene del capítulo general para que yo no salga de una casa. Habíala enviado aquí el padre provincial fray Angel al padre Ulloa con un mandamiento que me notificase. El pensó me diera mucha pena (como el intento de estos padres ha sido dármela en procurar esto) y así se lo tenía guardado. Debe haber poco más de un mes que yo procuré me lo diesen, porque lo supe por otra parte.

Yo digo a vuestra señoría cierto que, a cuanto puedo entender de mí, que me fuera gran regalo y contento si vuestra señoría por una carta me lo mandara y viera yo que era doliéndose de los grandes trabajos que para mí, que soy para padecer poco, en esas fundaciones he pasado, y que por premio me mandaba vuestra señoría a descansar. Porque aun entendiendo por la vía que viene, me ha dado harto consuelo poder estar en mi sosiego" (Teresa, *Obras completas*, 1388). For an analysis of the variety of rhetorical strategies contained in this rather extraordinary letter, see Mujica, *Teresa de Ávila: Lettered Woman*, 75–79.

4. "No basta, Señor, que nos tiene el mundo acorraladas e incapaces para que no hagamos cosa que valga nada por Vos en público ni osemos hablar algunas verdades que lloramos en secreto, sino que no nos habíais de oir petición tan justa? No lo creo yo, Señor, de vuestra bondad y justicia, que sois justo juez, y no como los jueces del mundo, que como son hijos de Adán y, en fin, todos varones, no hay virtud de mujer que no tengan por sospechosa" (Teresa, *Obras completas*, 545).

5. For more of Teresa's early defense of women's right to prayer in the *Way of Perfection*, see Ahlgren, *Teresa of Avila and the Politics of Sanctity*, 87–91.

6. "Es sobre todos los gozos de la tierra y sobre todos los deleites y sobre todos los contentos y más, que no tiene que ver adonde se engendran estos contentos o los de la tierra, que es muy diferente su sentir, como lo tendréis experimentado. Dije yo una vez, que es como si fuesen en esta grosería del cuerpo o en los tuétanos, y atiné bien, que no sé cómo lo decir mejor" (Teresa, *Obras completas*, 891).

7. "Comencemos por el tormento que da topar con un confesor tan cuerdo y poco experimentado que no hay cosa que tenga por segura: todo lo teme, en todo pone duda, como ve cosas no ordinarias; en especial, si en el alma que las tiene ve alguna imperfección—que les parece han de ser ángeles a quien Dios hiciere estas Mercedes, y es imposible mientras estuvieren en este cuerpo—, luego es todo condenado a demonio o melancolía.... Mas la pobre alma que anda con el mismo temor, y va al confesor como a juez, y ése la condena, no puede dejar de recibir tan gran tormento y turbación" (Teresa, *Obras completas*, 914).

8. "impulsos tan delicados y sutiles que proceden de lo muy interior del alma, que no sé comparación que poner que cuadre. Va bien diferente de todo lo que acá podemos procurar y aun de los gustos que quedan dichos, que muchas veces, estando la misma persona descuidada y sin tener la memoria en Dios, su Majestad la despierta a manera de una cometa que pasa de presto o un relámpago-trueno aunque ni se ve luz ni se oye ruido; mas entiende muy bien el alma que fue llamada de Dios" (Teresa, *Obras completas*, 918).

9. See, e.g.: "In desiring to carry off this soul, God sometimes takes away the breath so that, even though the other senses sometimes last a little longer, a person cannot speak at all; although at other times everything is taken away at once, and the hands and the body grow cold so that the person doesn't seems to have any life; nor sometimes is it known whether he is breathing. This situation lasts but a short while, I mean in its intensity; for when this extreme suspension lets up a little, it seems that the body returns to itself somewhat and is nourished so as to die again and give more life to the soul" (Teresa, *The Interior Castle*, 131).

10. See Archivo Histórico Nacional, Inquisición, leg. 4443, no. 24, fol. 16r. According to Alvaro Huerga, Hernando de Castillo wrote this *calificación* between 1573 and 1575 (340). Luis Sala Balust attributes this same *calificación* to Alonso de la Fuente (517).

11. "Estaba pensando ahora si sería que en este fuego del brasero encendido que es mi Dios, saltaba alguna centella y daba en el alma de manera que se dejaba sentir aquel encendido fuego, y, como no era aún bastante para quemarla y él es tan deleitoso, queda con aquella pena, y, al tocar, hace aquella operación" (Teresa, *Obras completas*, 919).

12. "Aquí no hay que pensar si es cosa movida del mismo natural, ni causada de melancholía, ni tampoco engaño del demonio, ni si es antojo; porque es cosa que se deja muy bien entender ser este movimiento de adonde está el Señor, que es inmutable; y las operaciones no son como de otras devociones que el mucho embebecimiento del gusto nos puede hacer dudar. Aquí están todos los sentidos y potencias sin ningún embebecimiento mirando qué podrá ser, sin estorbar nada, ni poder acrecentar aquella pena deleitosa, ni quitarla. A mi parecer, a quien nuestro Señor hiciere esta merced—que, si se la ha hecho, en leyendo esto, lo entenderá—déle muy muchas gracias, que no tiene que temer si es engaño; tema mucho se ha de ser ingrato a tan gran merced, y procure esforzarse a servir y a mejorar en todo su vida, y verá en lo que para, y cómo recibe más y más" (Teresa, *Obras completas*, 919–20). In subsequent paragraphs, Teresa gives extensive reasons to demonstrate the veracity and certainty of the divine origins of this experience. See Teresa, *The Interior Castle*, 117–18; *Obras completas*, 920.

13. See, e.g., Teresa, *The Interior Castle*, 76–77, 97–98, 119–20, 121–22.

14. "Diré, si acertare, con el favor del Señor, las señales que hay en estas diferencias y cuándo serán estas hablas peligrosas; porque hay muchas almas que las entienden entre gente de oración y querría, hermanas, que no penséis hacéis mal en no las dar crédito ni tampoco en dársele cuando son solamente para vosotras mismas, de regalo o aviso de faltas vuestras, dígalas quien las dijere, o sea antojo, que poco va en ello. De una cosa os aviso: que no penséis, aunque sean de Dios, seréis por eso mejores, que harto habló a los fariseos" (Teresa, *Obras completas*, 922).

15. The person's tender susceptibility to this action of God's love is not something that can be kept entirely to herself. Teresa writes: "In this dwelling place the raptures are very common and there is no means to avoid them even though they may take place in public. Hence, persecutions and criticism. Even though the soul may want to be free from fears, others do not allow this freedom. For there are many persons who cause these fears, especially confessors. And even though on the one hand the soul seems to feel very secure in its interior part, especially when it is alone with God, on the other hand it goes about in deep distress because it fears the devil may in some way beguile it into offending the One whom it loves so much. Little does it suffer over criticism, unless the confessor himself distresses it, as if it could do more. . . . [But] it is intensely afflicted upon seeing that it cannot free itself from unknowingly committing many venial sins. God gives these souls the strongest desire not to displease Him in anything, however small, and the desire to avoid if possible every imperfection. For this reason alone, if for no other, the soul wants to flee people, and it has great envy of those who have lived in deserts" (*The Interior Castle* 138–39). Teresa reflects further on the radical purity of the conscience of a person who is this deeply attuned to the movements of God in the next chapter, likening theirs to the sufferings of the earliest companions of Jesus who, she says, probably often suffered from feeling that they had fallen far short of what they would have wanted to do for Christ: "I think such a realization was a great martyrdom for Saint Peter and the Magdalene. Since their love for God had grown so deep and they had received so many favors and come to know the grandeur and majesty of God, the

remembrance of their misery would have been difficult to suffer, and they would have suffered it with tender sentiments" (144–45).

16. "También os parecerá que quien goza de cosas tan altas no tendrá meditación en los misterios de la sacratísima Humanidad de nuestro Señor Jesucristo, porque se ejercitará ya toda en amor. Esto es una cosa que escribí largo en otra parte y, aunque me han contradecido en ella y dicho que no lo entiendo—porque son caminos por donde lleva nuestro Señor y que, cuando ya han pasado de los principios, es mejor tratar en cosas de la Divinidad y huir de las corpóreas—, a mí no me harán confesar que es buen camino. . . . [A]partados de todo lo corpóreo, para espíritus angélicos es estar siempre abrasados en amor, que no para los que vivimos en cuerpo mortal, que es menester trate y piense y se acompañen de los que, teniéndole, hicieron tan grandes hazañas por Dios; cuánto más apartarse de industria de todo nuestro bien y remedio que es la sacratísima Humanidad de nuestro Señor Jesucristo" (Teresa, *Obras completas*, 947).

17. "Esta [merced] trae consigo un particular conocimiento de Dios, y de esta compañía tan continua nace un amor ternísimo con su Majestad y unos deseos aún mayores que los que quedan dichos de entregarse toda a su servicio y una limpieza de conciencia grande, porque hace advertir a todo la presencia que trae cabe sí; porque, aunque ya sabemos que lo está Dios a todo lo que hacemos, es nuestro natural que se descuida en pensarlo; lo que no se puede descuidar acá, que la despierta el Señor que está cabe ella. Y aun para las mercedes que quedan dichas, como anda el alma casi continuo con un actual amor al que ve o entiende estar cabe sí, son muy más ordinarias" (Teresa, *Obras completas*, 954).

References

Ahlgren, Gillian T. W. *Entering Teresa of Avila's Interior Castle: A Reader's Companion.* Paulist Press, 2005.
———. *Teresa of Avila and the Politics of Sanctity.* Cornell University Press, 1996.
Huerga, Alvaro. *Historia de los alumbrados: Los alumbrados de Extremadura (1570–1582).* Fundación Universitaria Española, 1978.
Mujica, Bárbara. *Teresa de Ávila: Lettered Woman.* Vanderbilt University Press, 2009.
———. "Was Teresa of Avila a Feminist?" In *Approaches to Teaching Teresa of Avila and the Spanish Mystics*, edited by Alison Weber, Modern Language Association of America, 2009, 74–82.
Reed, Helen H. "Teaching Teresa's *Libro de las fundaciones (The Book of Foundations)*." In *Approaches to Teaching Teresa of Avila and the Spanish Mystics*, edited by Alison Weber, Modern Language Association of America, 2009, 225–31.
Sala Balust, Luis. "En torno al grupo de alumbrados de Llerena." In *Corrientes espirituales en la España del Siglo XVI*, Barcelona: Juan Flors, 1963, 509–23.
Salazar, María de San José. *Book for the Hour of Recreation.* 1585. Edited by Alison Weber and translated by Amanda Powell, University of Chicago Press, 2002.

Slade, Carole. *St. Teresa of Ávila: Author of a Heroic Life*. University of California Press, 1995.
Teresa de Jesús (de Ávila). *The Interior Castle*. 1577. Translated by Kieran Kavanaugh and Otilio Rodriguez, Paulist Press, 1979.
———. *The Letters of Saint Teresa*, 2 vols. Translated by E. Allison Peers, Burns and Oates, 1951.
———. *Obras completas*. Edited by Alberto Barrientos, et al., Madrid: Editorial de Espiritualidad, 1984.
Weber, Alison, ed. *Approaches to Teaching Teresa of Avila and the Spanish Mystics*. Modern Language Association of America, 2009.

SHARON D. VOROS

Teresa of Ávila and Jeanne Guyon Read the *Song of Songs*

IN HER BOOK *Teresa de Avila: Lettered Woman*, Bárbara Mujica cites Teresa's meditations on the Song of Songs as evidence that she understood the importance of social relationships (61). If a peasant girl (the soul) marries a king, then her children also have royal blood (Kavanaugh and Rodríguez 240). Here, Teresa illustrates her notion of the union of God with the soul and also shows her understanding of this foundational mystical text. Over a century later, Jeanne Guyon, in her commentary on the *Cantique des Cantiques de Salomon* [Song of Songs by Solomon], also sought to explain this mystical union with the image of a drop of water in a wine cask (209).[1] The object of this study is to examine ways in which Teresa and Jeanne both developed reading strategies that show not only their understanding of perhaps one of the most controversial of biblical texts, but also their attempts to connect with potential readers. Wolfgang Iser defines the "implied reader" as a concept in which textual structure anticipates "the presence of a recipient without necessarily defining him" (34) and locates these connecting points between author and reader within the text itself. While Teresa meant for her commentary to be read within convent walls, Jeanne sought to address the public at large.

It is perhaps not surprising that women reading sacred scripture and writing about that experience were rare in early modern Europe. Even today, scholars such as Alison Weber wonder if women were up to the task, such as when she compares women mystics to John of the Cross, whose academic training allowed him to excel as a writer ("Could Women Write Mystical

Poetry?" 185). Such commentaries, however, are problematic for all writers if we consider that Fray Luis de León was brought up on charges by the Inquisition, in part for his translations of this very text, the Song of Songs ("Could Women Write Mystical Poetry?" 187). Teresa not only read Scripture, but she also instituted time for reflection and study on it (Weber, Introduction to *Book*, 10). However, Gillian Ahlgren shows that Teresa had a great deal of difficulty in establishing her "theological agenda" (85), for women as accepted authorities on spiritual matters remained problematic for her. Although she was ordered to burn her commentaries on the Song of Songs, since the topic was deemed unsuitable for women, copies of them had been made. Jerónimo Gracián later published them in manuscript in Belgium in 1611 (Kavanaugh and Rodríguez 211–12). Teresa read sacred texts as preparation for prayer and discussed her experience of reading the Latin of the Song of Songs and grappling with its meaning, inspired by the weekly recitation of the Office of our Lady (Kavanaugh and Rodríguez 217). Carole Slade points out that Teresa's commentary on the Song of Songs represents the most "extended application of her feminist hermeneutic" (49), and dates the work as having been written between 1566 and 1571.

Just what happened when Teresa's Carmelite Reform moves across the Pyrenees offers another perspective on women as readers of Scripture. Jeanne-Marie Bouvier de la Mothe Guyon (1648–1717), not always recognized as one of her followers, also emphasized reading Scripture and the theology of interiority, yet her publications and her relationship with Bishop Fénelon brought her under scrutiny and resulted in eight years in prison, including in the Bastille.[2] She was accused of being a follower of the Quietist Miguel de Molinos, although her commentaries on the Song of Songs were published in Lyon in 1687.[3] Bernard McGinn argues that both Teresa and John of the Cross were "devoted to the prayer of quiet, and that Quietism was more an invention of its opponents" (23). In her defense, Jeanne argued that her practice of the interior way adhered to Church doctrine, and she cited Saint Teresa in her prison memoirs (Guyon, *Bastille Witness*, 78). I have found no evidence of her having read Teresa's commentaries on the Song of Songs directly, although she could have read John of the Cross's *Cántico espiritual* [Spiritual Canticle] in French translation by Cyprien de la Nativité de la Vierge, who also translated Teresa's works.[4]

Parallels with Teresa are particularly strong, however, for both women wrote spiritual autobiographies and treatises on prayer. Teresa was accused of having inappropriate relationships with her confessors (Mujica, "Paul the Enchanter," 32), as was Guyon (James, *"Pure Love,"* 15). Further, both women were influenced by Franciscans, Teresa by Francisco de Osuna and Jeanne by Archange Enguerrand, who advised her on prayer, which led to her Teresian experience of her heart being pierced by an arrow (Melchior-Bonnet 89). Affective theology came under attack both in Teresa's time and later in France. As Sophie Houdard argues in *Les invasions mystiques* [Mystic Invasions], Teresa's reform caused concerns to arise in France over Illuminism (47). Teresa's way of reading and Jeanne's almost line-by-line commentary of the entire Canticle show a personal approach, not strictly biblical exegeses, but emphasis on the soul Bride as lover of God with the powerful imagery of the epithalamium that takes on a structuring function, especially through the image of the mystical kiss, with the textual and spiritual center of the heart as a dwelling place for God. Enguerrand says, "Le Coeur purifié et vidé de l'amour propre est dans son fond le lieu de l'union de Dieu" [The Heart purified and emptied of self-love is in its core the place for union with God] (qtd. in Derville 184). As María Mercedes Carrión points out, references to the kiss caused Teresa's confessor to condemn the entire book ("Este amor y este temor la llevan a explicar en las *Meditaciones sobre los Cantares* temas tan cercanos a la experiencia corporal como lo son el beso y la boca de Dios" [263]) [This love and this fear cause her to explain themes in the Meditations on the Song of Songs so close to corporal experience as are the kiss and the mouth of God]. Since Teresa's commentary on the Song of Songs appears first chronologically, I will begin with her *Meditaciones* and then consider Jeanne's commentary, written almost a hundred years later. Both commentaries show indications regarding the importance of a soul and its spiritual center in search of the Divine, along with a concern for ways in which readers interpret or misinterpret Scripture.

Teresa justifies her reading of the Song of Songs because it not only brings great consolation to its readers, but also teaches the soul how to speak to God. Thus, her emphasis on the Bride's request in its first line—"bésame con los besos de tu boca" [kiss me with the kisses of your mouth]—sets in motion the spiritual journey. The Biblioteca de Autores Cristianos edition follows Gracián's divisions of her commentary into seven chapters, although she only comments on the first three chapters of the Canticle (Efren de la Madre de Dios and Steggink 321). Teresa's justification for her reading of the Song of Songs suggests that Osuna may have been an inspiration for her, for he spoke of consolation in reading as a value for spiritual life, despite those who seem to denounce it, including Miguel de Molinos (142). Osuna also included references to the Canticle as well as to the peaceful kiss on the mouth (281). For him, the phrase "My beloved to me and I to my beloved" epitomized the purpose of prayer to all who experience it (350). He understood recollection as the narrow gate the soul passes through to be alone with God and "interior consolation" (244).

For Teresa, experience is essential to understanding the Song of Songs, and she uses digressions to connect with her readers. An example is the experience she discusses of another sister: "Y sé de alguna que estuvo hartos años con muchos temores, y no huvo cosa que la haya asegurado sino que fue el Señor servido oyese algunas cosas de los Cánticos y en ellas entendió ir bien guiado su alma" (Teresa, *Meditaciones*, 323) [I know someone who for a number of years had many fears, and nothing gave her asssurance, but the Lord was pleased that she heard some words from the *Song of Songs* and through them she understood that her soul was being well guided] (Kavanaugh and Rodríguez 218). The soul in love with her Spouse, "el alma enamorada de su Esposo" (*Meditaciones*, 323), becomes "given over" to Him (Kavanaugh and Rodríguez 218). Here, a connection with Jeanne Guyon becomes apparent, for Guyon's reading of the Canticle as an allegory for interiority stresses the notion of annihilation, the progressive emptying of the soul to receive God that Claude Morali calls "la perte de soi" or the loss of self (48–58). On this great love, Teresa cautions her readers not to be frightened, but to derive consolation from the mysteries in these sacred words that even learned men or *letrados* puzzle over (*Meditaciones* 324), for some consolation emerges in the reading process. Thus, her own reading experience extends to all readers, not only to her daughters, "hijas mías" (323), but also to Christians, "cristianos" (335), more generally. We are to be consoled and find delight in these words and works: "nos consolamos y deleitamos en sus palabras y obras" (*Meditaciones* 324; Kavanaugh and Rodríguez 219), for women are not to be left out of enjoying the riches of the Lord, "las riquezas del Señor" (*Meditaciones* 324). While Guyon intended her works to be read by the general public, Teresa's writing for the benefit of her sisters eventually extended to the entire Christian community.

In her first chapter, Teresa provides another engaging digression on the misinterpretation of "los grandes misterios que este lenguaje encierra en sí" (*Meditaciones* 323) [the great mysteries this language ... contains within itself] (Kavanaugh and Rodríguez 219). This was during a sermon she herself heard: "... me acuerdo oír a un religioso un sermón harto admirable, ... declarando de estos regales que la Esposa tratava con Dios. Y huvo tanta risa y fue tan mal tomado lo que dijo, porque hablava de amor ... que yo estava espantada" (*Meditaciones* 323) [I recall hearing a priest who was a religious preach a very admirable sermon, ... an explanation of those loving delights with which the bride communed with God. And there was so much laughter, and what he said was so poorly taken, that I was shocked. He was speaking about love] (Kavanaugh and Rodríguez 217–18). From the experience of a priest who lost control of his sermon, she understands that the congregation's laughter occurs because they do not practice love of God. She further cautions that those who do not understand love will easily read the Canticle but will derive no benefit from the experience: "porque estas palabras y otras semejantes que están en los Cantares, dícelas el amor; y como no le tienen, bien pueden leer los Cantares cada día, y no se ejercitar en ellas" (*Meditaciones* 325) [for these words and other similar ones in the *Song of Songs* are said by love. Since such persons have no love, they can easily read the *Song of Songs* every day and not themselves become involved with the words] (Kavanaugh and Rodríguez 221). Thus one can read the Canticle every day, but that is not enough to progress spiritually, since such progress depends on faith, "fe viva" (*Meditaciones* 325). Again, we have a connection to the reader and the reading process enhanced by faith.

In chapter two, she returns to the kiss, for not all kisses lead to spiritual progress. She discusses the false peace conveyed by Judas's kiss (Kavanaugh and Rodríguez 227; *Meditaciones* 328). This section includes a series of imperative verbs: "acordaos," "despertad," "creed" (*Meditaciones* 328) [remember, wake up, believe], another way of engaging the reader. Praise leads to self-love and arrogance, not humility. Thus, Teresa gives advice to her sisters on ways to read the Song of Songs, not just in the praising of the soul and its efforts but in obeying God's will, a topic she continues in chapter three with "juntarse con la voluntad de Dios" [to join with God's will] (332). There is no division between God the Bridegroom and the soul his Bride (332), an issue that Jeanne takes up as well with the metaphor of the drop of water in a wine cask (Guyon, *Commentaire*, 209). Teresa also brings up the frailty of sinners and tells her readers not to be discouraged about weaknesses, since Jesus himself suffered on the Cross but did not complain (*Meditaciones* 334). In this world, she continues, we are never lacking sorrows (333), although in reading the Canticle, we can find consolation in the Bride who has attained peace. The soul unites with God in this mortal life, as the words of the Song of Songs convey, for God teaches the soul through Scripture what to say. Teresa returns to her request, the invitational poem,[5] and changes the third-person verb to the second person: "beséis con beso de vuestra boca" (334) [You kiss me with the kiss of Your mouth], while she continues in chapter four with the commentary of her most daring image: "son mejores tus pechos y más sabrosos que el vino" (334) [your breasts are better and sweeter than wine].

Not all editions of the Song of Songs include this maternal image for the masculine breast.[6] This image conveys the notion of the next stage of prayer, however: "... en esta oración de que hablo, que llamo yo de quietud, por el sosiego que hace en todas las potencias" (*Meditaciones* 334) [In this prayer of which I speak, that I call "quiet" because of the calm cause in all the faculties] (Kavanaugh and Rodríguez 242). Teresa introduces her own corporeal metaphor of "los tuétanos" (*Meditaciones* 334) [bone marrow]. She mentions the phrase: "Mejores son tus pechos que el vino" [Your breasts are sweeter than wine] at least four times, for she returns it as a kind of refrain for the interior way, the perfume for which reaches the very marrow of one's bones (334). Both the interior and the exterior of the person are comforted, as if a sweet ointment has been poured into one's bones. She relates this experience to maternal love as a comparison, another of her strategies to address readers, for the soul does not know what to compare this experience of prayer to, except to that of a mother and her child: "No sabe a qué lo comparar, sino al regalo de la madre que ama mucho al hijo y le cría y le regala" (335) [It doesn't know what to compare His graces to unless to the great love a mother has for her child in nourishing and caressing it] (Kavanaugh and Rodríguez 245).

In his extensive commentary on the Song of Songs, Carmelite scholar Roland Murphy prefers "your love" as a more pleasing comparison for wine than to "your breast," a translation more in keeping, as he states, with "the favorite term used by the woman for the man" (125). The *Biblia Sacra Vulgata's Canticum Canticorum* says, "Oculetur me osculo oris sui / quia meliora sunt ubera tua vino" (997), the source of Teresa's image, as it is for Jeanne, who appears to follow Louis-Isaac Lemaître de Sacy's seventeenth-century translation: "Qu'il me donne un baiser de sa bouche; car vos mamelles sont meilleures que le vin" (799) [May he kiss me with his mouth for your breasts are better than wine]. However, Denys Turner points out that this is Jerome's mistranslation from Hebrew, since *dodeka* (love) could be misread as *dadeka* (breasts) (204n2). Thus, both women follow the Vulgate and discover sacred meaning in a mistranslation.

Teresa continues with the image of breasts: "le parece que se queda suspendida en aquellos divinos brazos y arrimada a aquel sagrado costado y aquellos pechos divinos" (*Meditaciones* 335) [it seems to the soul it is left suspended in those divine arms, leaning on that sacred side and those divine breasts] (Kavanaugh and Rodríguez 244). The soul does not understand how she grows: "como un niño no entiende cómo crece ni sabe cómo mama ... ansí ... el alma no sabe cómo ni por dónde—ni lo puede entender—le vino aquel bien tan grande" (*Meditaciones* 335) [An infant doesn't understand how it grows nor does it know how it gets its milk.... Likewise, here the soul is completely ignorant. It knows neither how nor from where that great blessing came to it.]

(Kavanaugh and Rodríguez 244). In chapter five, she begins with "boca divina" [divine mouth] and "pechos celestiales" [heavenly breasts] to make sure that her readers understand that the corporeal image refers to the Divine. The soul now sits in the shade that she compares to the words of the angel to Mary: "la virtud del muy alto os hará sombra" (*Meditaciones* 336) [the power of the most high will overshadow you] (Kavanaugh and Rodríguez 248). References to Mary also connect to readers, for here Teresa mentions the "Oficio que rezamos de nuestra Señora cada semana" (*Meditaciones* 339) [the Office of Our Lady, which we recite each week] (Kavanaugh and Rodríguez 253). Thus, she relates the experience of her sisters in their weekly prayers to her commentary on the Song of Songs that has come to be a foundational text for Spanish mystics. The tree of God's love, the apple tree, she relates to Martha and Mary in chapter seven in reference to both the active and the interior life of the soul: "sin ningún interés propio" (*Meditaciones* 341) [without self-interest]. This disinterestedness in the love of God became associated with Quietism (James, "*Pure Love*," 107). The notion of the soul disinterested in God's love, however, can be found in Teresa's commentary. These disinterested souls look only to please God: "solo miran al servir y contentar al Señor" (*Meditaciones* 341) [They look only at serving and pleasing the Lord] (Kavanaugh and Rodríguez 258). She includes the Samaritan woman at the well as an example of Jesus's relationship to women who are believed, for although she is a humble woman, she nonetheless was given credit for speaking with Jesus himself (*Meditaciones* 341).

The question of belief in God's gifts ends with notions of "consuelo" [consolation] and again "divinos pechos" [divine breasts] (*Meditaciones* 342). Teresa apparently did not intend to comment on the remaining sections of the Song of Songs, for she says: "no lo quiero decir aquí ni alargarme más en esto, pues mi intento fue ... daros a entender cómo podéis regalaros cuando oyerdes algunas palabras de los Cánticos" (342) [I do not want to mention the matter here or enlarge upon this any more ... for my intention was simply to explain how your can find confort when you hear some words from the *Song of Songs*] (Kavanaugh and Rodríguez 260)]. The maternal image of divine milk and breasts carries through until the end in what Slade has called a hermeneutics of feminism (49). It is this kind of imagery of breasts and nurturing that Jacques Bénigne Bossuet considered most offensive in his denunciation of Jeanne Guyon's scandalous metaphors, "métaphores scandaleuses" (Melchior-Bonnet 155), although in reading Teresa, we can see that Jeanne did not invent maternal imagery for sacred purposes, as we can also see from Caroline Bynum's research into medieval sources (see *Jesus as Mother*).

Apophatic theology and scriptural exegesis are two areas of common ground for Teresa and Jeanne Guyon (Mujica, "Beyond Image," 741; James, "Pure Love," 117). Patricia Ward states, in her book on Madame Guyon, that "Reading the Scriptures for Madame Guyon became a way of affirming her experience" (63). This experience was for all souls who engage in the interior way for which Scripture is an extended allegory (62). While Guyon comments on the entire *Sainte Bible*, only her commentary on the Song of Songs was published in her lifetime. Bossuet called her "une femme qui est capable de tromper les âmes" (1107) [a woman who is capable of deceiving souls] because her notion of plenitude, being filled with the Holy Spirit, came under attack; the notion of plenitude is also embedded in her commentary. While Teresa uses digressions regarding personal experiences, not always her own, Guyon uses a different approach in connecting with her readers. She approaches the Canticle with academic categorizations, imagery, and warnings to readers. In her introduction, Guyon notes textual obscurities, for this is "un Livre des plus obscures de la Sainte Écriture" [one of the most obscure books of Holy Scripture][7] and only those who experience the "onction divine" [divine anointing] can understand this song between Bridegroom and Bride (*Commentaire* 193), something like Teresa's priest who loses control of his sermon on love, understood by his flock literally as a sermon on sex. Only the annihilated souls raised by God understand such divine mysteries: "qui par l'anéantissement d'eux mêmes et par leurs élévation en Dieu seront capables de comprendre ce chant royal de l'Epoux céleste et de son Amante" (193) [who by annihilation of themselves and by their elevation in God will be capable of understanding this royal canticle of the heavenly Spouse and his Lover]. The Canticle itself is a mirror of the interior experience, "l'expérience interieur" (193). Guyon provides a list of key bodily images, "ce Cantique de baisers, d'embrassements, de joues, de mamelles, de jambes, et de cuisses, de lit de mariage" (200) [this Canticle of kisses, embracing, cheeks, breasts, legs, thighs, the marriage bed], all of which recall Jesus's lowering of himself to make humanity understand the union of the Divine and pure souls: "la Divinité et son union avec les âmes pures" (200). She outlines ways in which to read these corporeal images that seem to be so often misunderstood: "Nous ne devons donc chercher dans ces figures corporelles que ce qu'il y a d'intérieur, et il faut ici parler des corps, comme si l'on était hors du corps même" (200) [We should only look for what there is inside in these corporeal figures, and one must speak of bodies as if one were outside the body itself]. Speak of the body, then, as if one were outside the body.

Guyon understands that Jewish tradition, Origen, and Saint Jerome limited the reading of the Song of Songs: "aux personnes avancées en âge et d'une grande maturité d'esprit. Ce chaste et secret commerce de l'Epoux et de l'Epouse n'est pas pour ceux qui sont encore enfoncés dans la boue de leurs pechés" (*Commentaire* 199) [to persons advanced in age and of great maturity of spirit. This chaste and secret relation between Husband and Wife is not for those who are still immersed in the mud of their sins]. While there is meaning for those at any stage in their spiritual journey (200), Guyon warns that this text is for "perfected ones" in silence and interior repose, the soul disengaged from itself and magnified by God in perfect abandon (200). She calls for "un coeur souple" [a supple heart] for one to understand the Canticle and the love the Bridegroom expresses to his Bride (201). So, as Teresa does, Guyon advises readers as to how they are to read and understand this sacred text. While Guyon comments on the entire Canticle, I will limit my comments to her understanding of its central images, such as the mystical kiss (Howe 303) and divine breasts. Claude Morali argues that Guyon's originality in her reading of the Song of Songs is her emphasis on spiritual annihilation as necessary for union with the Divine, the loss of self or "perte de soi" (48–58).

As with Teresa, Jeanne Guyon was inspired to pursue the interior way by a Franciscan whom she met personally, Archange Enguerrand. She may have even found out about Teresa's writing through him, for he cited Teresa's *Le chemin de perfection* [The Way of Perfection] in a letter dated 1665, three years before he met Guyon in her hometown of Montargis in 1668 (qtd. in Derville 182). In her title, she says that her commentary is: "interpreté selon le sens mystique et la vraie représentation des états intérieurs" (*Commentaire* 205) [Interpreted According to the Mystical Path and the True Representation of the Interior Life] (James, *Song of Songs*, 95). She relates the kiss to the spiritual marriage, but then distinguishes between two types of union, "l'union des puissances" [union of powers] and "l'union essentielle" [essential union] (*Commentaire* 205). The union of powers is superficial and temporary, like touching, and it involves the powers of the soul, understanding, memory, and will. The essential union, symbolized by the mouth of God, is permanent, and involves the union of essence to essence; God takes the soul for his Bride and unites with her. Guyon calls this the apostolic state, during which the soul is not just a Bride, but also fecund, another maternal image here: "The mouth of God unites to the soul, making the soul fruitful through God's own fertility" (James, *Song of Songs*, 99). Such union is possible in this life, although she recognizes that some persons say that it can only happen in the afterlife. Guyon says that in this life one possesses without seeing, while in the afterlife, one sees what one possesses (*Commentaire* 207). As with Teresa, the experience demands belief in that experience, just as the Samaritan woman was believed. The union with Jesus Christ comes first as a temporary one and begins the life of illumination, "la vie illuminative" (208). Guyon's first comparison indicates that a marriage must be consummated before any benefits appear: "les fruits et les productions du mariage ne se font qu'après qu'il a été consommé" (208) [As in marriage, the fruits and products . . . come only after its consummation] (James, *Song of Songs*, 99). Further, she states that the enjoyment of God is permanent and durable (*Commentaire* 208).

The interior way explains the mystical marriage, along with image of water, the river that begins in the sea, but is different from it outside of its place of origin; when it finds its way back to the sea, it becomes indistinguishable from it (*Commentaire* 208): "ou bien, c'est comme une eau versée dans une autre eau, qui peut être tellement mêlée avec elle, qu'on n'y peut remarquer aucune distinction" (209) [or rather, it is like one water poured into another that can be so mixed with it that one cannot distinguish between the two]. Another image that Guyon adds to the discussion is the drop of water that loses its consistency in a cup of wine when she speaks of the union of powers, a union one experiences without being transformed (209). This also describes her understanding of annihilation of the soul that can still be separated from God. So river and sea symbolize the union of essence and the drop of wine in water symbolizes the union of powers, after which the soul may become separated from God, a spiritual state during which the soul cries out: "Let him kiss me with the kisses of his mouth" (210).

Guyon also understands the second part of this verse as referring to divine breasts (*Commentaire* 210).[8] She begins her commentary with an exclamation to God: "Les mamelles, ô Dieu, dont vous nourrissez les âmes commençantes, sont si douces et si agréables" (210) [Your breasts, O God, with which you nourish novice souls are so sweet and agreeable]. This divine nourishment makes children stronger and men more robust. This beginning of the Canticle, she says, really should be the ending, for it alludes to the perfect union of the Bride and Bridegroom. She sees the reference to divine breasts as symbolizing spiritual infancy (210). Guyon recreates the words of the Bride in this Song of Invitation (Gray 371): "Tirez-moi, dit-elle, dans le plus intime de mon fond" (*Commentaire* 211) [Draw me after you, she says, into the interior chambers of my soul] (James, *Song of Songs*, 103). At this point in the soul's progress, Guyon says that the perfume referenced in the Song symbolizes the prayer of recollection, similar to Teresa's prayer of quiet: "Cet excellent parfum opère l'Oraison de recueillement" (*Commentaire* 212) [This excellent perfume gives rise to the Prayer of Recollection] (James, *Song of Songs*, 103).

While Guyon attempts to align her commentary with conventional theological exegeses, including different types of union of God and the soul, she connects with Teresa on the use of maternal imagery, and the powers of consolation of divine breasts, again a hermeneutics of femininity, as Carole Slade has suggested (49). However, Guyon avoids the notion of consolation, for the Bride prefers the sweetness of divine milk to the wine of the pleasures of this world (*Commentaire* 213). The annihilated soul foregoes consolation and prefers God: "Ici elle préfère son Dieu à ses consolations spirituelles et aux douceurs de la grâce qu'elle éprouvait en suçant le lait de ses mamelles" (213) [Here the soul prefers her God to spiritual consolations and sweetnesses of grace that she experiences in drinking the milk of His breasts]. The soul then seeks to lose herself in her God: "se perdre en son Dieu" (213). Teresa also speaks of this state as indifference to the pleasures of the world (*Meditaciones* 341). Guyon concludes with the Bridegroom's instructions to the Bride to teach other souls about the interior life and what they should do to please Him.

Thus, both women provide a profound commentary on this foundational mystical text on divine love. There are no personal stories woven into Guyon's explanations in her zeal to explain ways in which the language of the Song of Songs relates to the interior way as allegory. Teresa's personal stories point out differences in interpretations of the text. However, modern translations have removed what is perhaps one of the Canticle's most compelling images, the breasts of God and divine nurturing milk, which Teresa returns to in her concluding statements: "Esténse cabe aquellos divinos pechos, que el Señor terná cuidado, cuando estén ya con fuerzas, de sacarlas a más porque no harían el provecho que piensan, antes se la dañarían a sí" (*Meditaciones* 342) [Let them remain close to those divine breasts, for the Lord will take care, when they are strong, to bring them further. Otherwise, they would not do the good they think; rather they would harm themselves] (Kavanaugh and Rodríguez 260). The feminine thus touches the divine in both commentaries, for Teresa provides a hermeneutics of femininity and humility while Guyon gives readers a hermeneutics of annihilation.

Another connection between Guyon and Teresa, and also a connection to readers, is the reference to Scripture. Both women speak of suffering as part of the mystical experience, an issue that all human beings must eventually deal with. However, both women cite the same reference to Saint Paul in Romans 8:18: "existimo enim quod non sunt condignae passions huius temporis ad futuram gloriam / quae revelabitur in nobis" (Vulgate 1994) [I consider that the troubles of this time do not compare with the glory that will be revealed to us]. Teresa says: "San Pablo dice que no 'son dignos todos los trabajos del mundo de la Gloria que esperamos'" (*Meditaciones* 335) [Saint Paul says *all the trials of the world are not worthy to be compared with the glory which we await*] (Kavanaugh and Rodríguez 245). The idea that trials are not worth anything if they are not endured for God also appears in Guyon's commentary on chapter three of the Canticle, for the soul is searching for the Beloved in the first trial: "C'est pourquoi saint Paul disait que les peines, même les plus grandes de cette vie, n'ont nulle proportion avec la gloire qui sera découverte en nous" (*Commentaire* 242) [This is why Saint Paul said that sorrows, even the greatest ones in this life, do not compare with the glory that will be discovered in us]. Thus, both women use a familiar passage from Paul to connect with their readers on the difficulties of the mystical journey, the images for which abound in the Canticle. Guyon had French translations available to her, while Teresa relied on the Vulgate for this reference. In any event, they include the passage in their commentary perhaps because it is familiar to readers with its contrast between trials and glory.

To conclude, Wolfgang Iser's notion of reader response includes indications in the structure of a text that both engage the "implied" reader while illustrating ways in which the author is a reader. The dialogic structure of the Canticle itself, with its direct address in the second person, suggests implied readers. Erik Gray argues that the Canticle as an "invitation poem" precisely because of its "dialogic framework" (371). Gray also notes, as do Teresa and Guyon, that this is a matter of seeking not just pleasure in the search for the Divine Lover but also self-sacrifice (371). Both women writers use Scripture to point this out, most notably the passage by Saint Paul cited in both texts here on trials of this life versus glory in the next. References to Scripture familiar to potential readers is only one of the discursive strategies here. Teresa uses digressions on personal experiences, either her own or those of other sisters. Guyon, despite her emphasis on direct experience with the Divine, does not go into her own experiences in her commentary, though she cites the significance of experience, probably because she has commented on such matters extensively in her autobiography, her *Vie* of 1720. In all, she maintains her focus on the Canticle itself with some academic categorizations such as those of the different kinds of union. Both women, however, bring in their own imagery, such as the bone marrow in Teresa's commentary and the drop of water in the wine cask in Guyon's. Both women also follow the Vulgate with its provocative maternal imagery for Jesus, with the mystical kiss and his breasts being sweeter than wine. The corporeal imagery of the Canticle text itself is in essence an invitation to the reader through references to the human body familiar to everyone (Carrión 263). Both women express caution regarding the interpretation of this imagery. Teresa tells the story of the priest who lost control of his sermon on the Canticle and caused his congregation to react with laughter. Guyon explains that corporeal imagery is allegorical in nature for it describes the body while being outside the body. Thus, both women are very aware of reader interpretations of the Song of Songs and address these issues directly. With their expertise as writers and readers, Teresa de Ávila and Jeanne Guyon leave an enduring legacy of allegorical interpretation in search of the Divine.

Notes

1. Quotations in English for Jeanne Guyon's *Cantique des Cantiques de Salomon* are from the translation by Nancy Carol James in *The Song of Songs: The Complete Madame Guyon*. Quotations in French are from the 1992 edition by Claude Morali. Other translations are mine.

2. See my translation of Guyon's prison autobiography *Bastille Witness*. Guyon met Bishop Fénelon in 1688 and was a strong influence on him (Melchior-Bonnet 87–106).

3. Guyon's commentaries on *La Sainte Bible* were published in 1717 from notes she made and sent to the Protestant minister Pierre Poiret. See Chevalier, 93–107.

4. For a study on French translations of Spanish mystics and Cyprien de la Nativité de la Vierge, see Daniel Hanna's "Translating Teresa." I would like to express my gratitude to the librarians at Whitefriars Hall Order of Carmelites in Washington, DC, especially Father Patrick McMahon, who kindly allowed me to consult Cyprien's 1652 translation of John of the Cross's *Cántico espiritual*.

5. See Gray, 370–85.

6. See Caroline Bynum for a detailed analysis of maternal images for Jesus that have prevailed since medieval times. She cites the Song of Songs as the source of maternal images in the works of Bernard de Clairvaux (117).

7. Translations to the Préface to Guyon's *Commentaire*, 193–201, are mine.

8. Fray Luis de León does not follow the Vulgate here but prefers to translate from the Hebrew with the term used today, "love" or *amor*, not *pechos* or "breasts" (Nahson 84).

References

Ahlgren, Gillian T. W. *Teresa of Ávila and the Politics of Sanctity*. Cornell University Press, 1996.

Biblia Sacra Vulgata. Edited by Robertus Weber, Stuttgart: Deutche Bibelgesellschaft, 1994.

Bossuet, Jacques Bénigne. *Oeuvres*. Edited by L'Abbé Velat and Yvonne Champailler, Paris: Bibliothèque de la Pléiade, 1961.

Bynum, Caroline Walker. *Jesus as Mother: Studies in the Spirituality of the High Middle Ages.* University of California Press, 1982.

Carrión, María Mercedes. *Aquitectura y cuerpo en la figura autorial de Teresa de Jesús.* Barcelona: Editorial Anthropos, 1994.

Chevalier, Marjolaine. *Pierre Poiret (1646–1719): du protestantisme à la mystique.* Geneva: Labor et Fides, 1994.

Derville, André. "Un Récollet Français méconnu: Archange Enguerrand." *Archivum Franciscanum Historicum* 90 (1997): 177–203.

Efren de la Madre de Dios, O.C.D., and Otger Steggink, O. Carm. Introduction to *Meditaciones sobre los Cantares.* Madrid: Biblioteca de Autores Cristianos, 1962, 321.

Gray, Erik. "Come Be My Love: The Song of Songs, *Paradise Lost*, and the Tradition of the Invitation Poem." *PMLA* 128 (2013): 370–85.

Guyon, Jeanne Bouvier de la Motte. *Bastille Witness: The Prison Autobiography of Madame Guyon (1648–1717).* Introduction by Nancy Carol James. Translated by Sharon D. Voros, University Press of America, 2012.

———. *Commentaire au Cantique des Cantiques. Les Torrents et Commentaire au Cantique des Cantiques de Salomon.* 1688. Edited by Claude Morali, Grenoble: Jérôme Millon, 1992, 193–305.

———. *La vie de Madame Guyon écrite par elle meme.* 1720. Edited by Benjamin Sahler, introduction by Jean Tourniac, Paris: Dervy-Livres, 1983.

Hanna, Daniel J. "Translating Teresa: *Muero porque no muero* in 17th-Century France." *1611 Revista de Historia de la Traducción* 8 (2014), www.traduccionliteraria.org/1611/art/hanna.htm.

Houdard, Sophie. *Les invasions mystiques. Spiritualité, heterodoxies et censures au début de l'époque moderne.* Paris: Les Belles Lettres, 2008.

Howe, Elizabeth. "The Mystical Kiss and the Canticle of Canticles: Three Interpretations." *The American Benedictine Review* 33 (1982): 302–11.

Iser, Wolfgang. *The Art of Reading: A Theory of Aesthetic Response.* Johns Hopkins University Press, 1978.

James, Nancy Carol. *The Conflict Over the Heresy of "Pure Love" in Seventeenth-Century France: The Tumult over the Mysticism of Madame Guyon.* The Edwin Mellen Press, 2008.

———, trans. *The Song of Songs: The Complete Madame Guyon.* Paraclete Press, 2001, 95–192.

John of the Cross. *Les oeuvres spirituelles du B. Père Jean de la Croix, premier Carme Deschaussé de la reforme de Nostre Dame du Mont-Carmel & Coadjuteur de la Sainte Mère Thérèse de Jésus.* Translated by Cyprien de la Nativité de la Vierge, Paris: Chez la Veuve Pierre Chevalier, 1652.

Kavanaugh, Kevin, O.D.C and Otilio Rodríguez, O.C.D., trans. Introduction to *Meditations on the Song of Songs,* Vol. 2, ICS Publications, 1980, 215–60, 297–314.

Lemaître de Sacy, Louis-Isaac. *La Bible.* Edited by Phillipe Sellier, Paris: Éditions Robert Laffont, 1990.

McGinn, Bernard. "Miguel de Molinos and the *Spiritual Guide*: A Theological Reappraisal. Introduction. Part Two." In *The Spiritual Guide by Miguel de Molinos*, Paulist Press, 2010, 21–39.

Melchior-Bonnet, Sabine. *Fénelon*. Saint-Amand Montrond, France: Perrin, 2008.

Molinos, Miguel de. *The Spiritual Guide*. Edited and translated by Robert P. Baird, Paulist Press, 2010.

Morali, Claude. "Jeanne Guyon ou la pensée nue." Introduction to *Les torrents et Commentaire au Cantique des Cantiques de Salomon*, Geneva: Jérôme Millon, 1992, 7–68.

Mujica, Bárbara. "Beyond Image: The Apophatic-Kataphatic Dialectic in Teresa de Ávila." *Hispania* 84 (2001): 741–48.

———. "Paul the Enchanter. Saint Teresa's Vow of Obedience to Gracián." In *The Heirs of St. Teresa of Ávila*, edited by Christopher Wilson, ICS Publications, 2006, 21–44.

———. *Teresa of Ávila: Lettered Woman*. Vanderbilt University Press, 2009.

Murphy, Roland E. O. Carm. *A Commentary of The Song of Songs*. Edited by S. Dean McBride, Jr., Fortress Press, 1990.

Nahson, David. *Amor sensual por el cielo. La Exposición del Cantar de los Cantares de Fray Luis de Léon*. Iberoamericana/Vervuert, 2006.

Osuna, Francisco de. *The Third Spiritual Alphabet*. Translated by Mary E. Giles, Paulist Press, 1981.

Slade, Carole. *St. Teresa of Ávila: Author of a Heroic Life*. University of California Press, 1995.

Teresa de Ávila. *Meditaciones sobre los Cantares*. In *Obras completas de Santa Teresa*, edited by Efren de la Madre de Dios, O.C.D. and Otger Steggink. O. Carm., Madrid: Biblioteca de Autores Cristianos, 1962, 322–43.

———. *Meditations on the Song of Songs*. In *The Collected Works of Teresa of Ávila*, Vol. 2, translated by Kieran Kavanuagh, O.C.D. and Otilio Rodríguez, O.C.D., ICS Publications, 1980, 207–60.

Turner, Denys. *Eros and Allegory: Medieval Exegesis of the Song of Songs*. Kalamazoo, MI: Cistercian Publications, 1995.

Ward, Patricia A. *Experimental Theology in America: Madame Guyon, Fénelon and Their Readers*. Baylor University Press, 2009.

Weber, Alison. "Could Women Write Mystical Poetry? The Literary Daughters of Juan de la Cruz." In *Studies on Women's Poetry of the Golden Age. Tras el espejo la musa escribe*, edited by Julián Olivares, Tamesis, 2009, 185–201.

———. Introduction to the *Book for the Hour of Recreation*, by María de San José Salazar, translated by Amanda Powell, The University of Chicago Press, 2002, 1–26.

Part IV

Teresa of Ávila Refashioned on the Stage and on the Page

SHERRY VELASCO

Vision, Vulnerability, and the Provocative "Higas" in Lope de Vega's *Santa Teresa de Jesús*

SCHOLARLY ATTENTION to the ways in which Teresa de Jesús's icon was carefully cultivated and promoted soon after her death in 1582 until her canonization in 1622 has increasingly been focused on the role of visual images in establishing the Carmelite nun as an icon of holiness. Critics such as Bárbara Mujica ("Performing Sanctity"), Margit Thofner, Christopher C. Wilson, Cordula van Wyhe, and María José Pinilla Martín ("La ilustración" and *Iconografía de Santa Teresa de Jesús*), among others, have studied the ways in which Teresa's early supporters wanted her iconographic image to "look like a saint" and thereby counter detractors such as Dominican preacher Alonso de la Fuente, who insisted that Teresa's visions were delusions created by the devil (Weber 160; Mujica, "Performing Sanctity," 185). Aware that the main hurdle to sainthood would be Teresa's status as a woman, when her protégée Ana de Jesús selected episodes from Teresa's life to be featured in the prints of the prestigious engravers Cornelis Galle and Adriaen Collaert (see Pinilla Martín, "Teresa de Jesús"), which were published in 1613, she sought to depict her friend as humble yet "unwomanly" in her ability to achieve great success in the predominantly male milieu of theology and monastic reform (Thofner 62). As her first biographer Francisco Ribera asserted in 1590, Teresa had a strong and virile spirit that allowed her to overcome the limitations of most women (420).

The religious iconography that would establish Teresa's experiences as saintly not only included paintings and print engravings but also visually impactful performances on stage. Theatergoers could see moving images depicting scenes from Teresa's life in two hagiographic plays during the period when Teresa's supporters were preparing her case for beatification and canonization that were attributed to Lope de Vega (*La bienaventurada Madre Santa Teresa de Jesús*, written between 1590–1604, and *Vida y muerte de Santa Teresa de Jesús*, written between 1620–1630), as well as in post-canonization plays such as Juan Bautista Diamante's *Santa Teresa de Jesús* (published in 1671) and José de Cañizares's *A cual mejor, confesada y confesor, San Juan de la Cruz y Santa Teresa de Jesús* (published in 1747).[1] In fact, when composing *comedias de santos* or other religious dramas, playwrights frequently made references to portraits, paintings, and prints to create the orthodox "look" for a particular scene (which could determine set design, props, wardrobe, staging, gestures, actions, poses, and so forth) expressed succinctly as "como se pintan" [like they are painted] (Bastianutti 713; Mayberry 18–20).[2] As a result, hagiographic plays such as Lope's *Santa Teresa de Jesús* portray scenes resembling a series of *tableaux vivants* or "pictures formed by live people," as Mujica has described Lope's theatrical vision of Teresa's life.[3] Indeed, the two extant plays devoted to Teresa de Jesús that are attributed to Lope de Vega highlight some of the more recognizable scenes from Teresa's life—episodes that include, for example, the transverberation and the miraculous deeds she performed such as reviving her dead nephew.

When considering the relationship between pictorial representations of Teresa's religious authority and the vivid images portrayed on stage, one troublesome episode deserves further exploration, in large part because Lope forces his audience to ponder visually a scene that by all accounts would have been unsettling for many spectators. I refer here to the fig-hand gesture, which was formed by making a fist and inserting the thumb between the index and middle fingers; considering the disturbing nature of the controversial topic, Lope's dramatization creates a completely singular visual portrait of a familiar episode recorded multiple times in Teresa's writing, yet one that was and continues to be absent from Teresian iconography. As early modern theologians and more recent scholars have noted, the *higas* scandal involving the "fig-hand gesture" recounted by Teresa in chapter 29 of her autobiography (and again referenced in the *Moradas* [6:9] as well as in chapter 8 of the *Fundaciones*) was considered especially offensive for informed readers. During this traumatic moment in Teresa's religious life (which she related shortly before recounting the iconic transverberation episode), one confessor had concluded that the best way to fight her recurring visions of Christ—determined by the priest to be delusions from the devil—was for her to make the sign of the Cross and give the fig-hand gesture of contempt ("dar higas").

Knowing how insulting this gesture was, Teresa was traumatized by doing to Christ what could be compared today to "giving someone the finger." In chapter 29 of her autobiography, Teresa explains: "Como las visions fueron creciendo, uno de ellos que antes me ayudaba . . . comenzó a decir que claro era demonio. Mándanme que, . . . siempre me santiguase cuando alguna visión viese, y diese higas, . . . A mí me era esto grande pena; porque como yo no podia creer sino que era Dios, era cosa terrible para mí" (*Obras completas* 348–49). [Since the visions were increasing, one from the group who previously helped me . . . began to say that it was clearly the devil. He ordered that . . . I should always bless myself when I saw one and make the gesture of scorn called the fig; . . . Following this advice was very painful to me. Since I couldn't believe but that the vision was from God, it was a terrible thing for me to have to do what I was commanded] (*The Book of Her Life* 196).

Demonstrating how significant this impertinent gesture was, Teresa reiterates her resistance to having to give the sign: "Dábame este dar higas grandísima pena . . . era un género de penitencia grande para mí; y, por no andar tanto santiguándome, tomaba una cruz en la mano. Esto hacía casi siempre; las higas no tan cotino, porque sentía mucho" (*Libro de la vida* 349) [Making the fig at this vision of the Lord caused me the greatest of pain. . . . it was a kind of severe penance for me. So that I would not be forever making the sign of the cross, I held a cross in my hand. I did this almost all the time; I didn't make the fig so continually, because it grieved me deeply to do so] (*The Book of Her Life* 196, with modifications). While this incident took place in Ávila between 1560–1561, the fact that Teresa continued to write about it for nearly two decades (in the *Fundaciones* and in the *Moradas*) is significant for understanding the impact that this conflictive mandate had on her.

As Teresa was deeply disturbed by having to give the *higa* gesture to what she knew to be an authentic vision of Christ, she found a way to both obey her confessor and lessen the insult by begging for forgiveness while carrying out the offensive order: "Suplicábale me perdonase, pues yo lo hacía por obedecer a el que tenía en su lugar, y que no me culpase, pues eran los ministros que Él tenía puestos en su Ilesia" (*Libro de la vida* 349) [I . . . begged Him to pardon me since I was doing it in order to obey the one who stood in His place, and not to blame me, since they were the ministers that He had placed in His Church] (*The Book of Her Life* 196). As she reassigns blame to her misguided confessor, Christ himself reassures her that the command she had been given was a form of tyranny, yet that she was right to obey (*Libro de la vida* 349). Other confessors, however, strongly disagreed with the *higas* mandate. As reported by Teresa in her *Fundaciones*, Fray Domingo Báñez told her that she was acting wrongly in giving the fig gesture to a vision of Christ and that "ninguna persona hiciese esto" (*Obras completas* 703) [no one should ever do this] (*Complete Works* 41). Not surprisingly, San Juan de Ávila wrote in a letter to Teresa in 1568 that he was horrified and greatly pained when he read about the fig drama in an early draft of her autobiography (Álvarez 754). Her first biographer followed suit by drawing attention to Teresa's emotional torment over the mandate: "This was terrible for her ... she felt it was horrific" (Ribera 142–43). Even when Teresa's defenders were more tempered in their critique of the confessor's judgment, they inevitably repeated the offensive mandate and consequently kept the scandalous image fresh in the minds of their readers. Father Pedro Ibáñez, for example, affirmed that "after mature and joint deliberation (for a great many of them had been discussing the matter), they had decided that she was being afflicted and deceived by the devil" before reminding his readers "que le diese muchas higas" [she must make a great many gestures of contempt"] (327).

Given the obscene nature of the sign Teresa was told to make, it is not surprising that priests reading her account would be horrified. The *higa*, in fact, was an obscene phallic figure that dated back to antiquity. Early modern lexicographer Sebastián de Covarrubias Horozco states as much in his definition of the *higa* gesture, which was a symbol of the ancient god Priapus whose primary attribute was a hyperbolic erect phallus:

> Es una manera de menosprecio que hacemos cerrando el puño y mostrando el dedo pulgar por entre el dedo índice y el medio; es disfrazada pulla. La higa antigua era tan solamente una semejanza del miembro viril, estendiendo el dedo medio y encogiendo el índice y el auricular. . . . [Y] también porque en quanto a la figura es supersticiosa, derivada de la gentilidad, que estava persuadida tener fuerça contra la fascinación la efigie priapeya, que como tenemos dicho era la higa. (689)

> [It is a way of showing contempt by closing the fist and showing the thumb between the first and middle finger. It is an obscene expression in disguise. The ancient fig gesture was an imitation of the male member by extending the middle finger while pulling back the index finger and third finger. . . . And with regard to the figure, it is superstitious,

derived from the pagans, who were convinced that the effigy of Priapus (which, as we already mentioned, was the fig-hand) had power against the evil eye.]

Not all of Teresa's contemporaries were cognizant of the phallic origins of the gesture, and those who did know its history seemed keen to silence or prohibit its popular usage. Juan Eusebio Nieremberg, a natural scientist and theologian who took the evil eye seriously, devoting eighteen chapters to the topic in his work on the secrets of the natural world, was emphatic in his 1633 treatise *Curiosa y oculta filosofía* about his condemnation of the superstitious and idolatrous use of the *higa*: "[L]a higa que traen los niños, es indigno que le usen los Christianos; y no dudo sino que si se supiese su principio, se dejara totalmente. Es su origen tan de supersticiosos, e idolatras y por otra parte tan sucio y abominable, que ni aun pensarla puede un pecho religioso" (43v). [The fig-hand worn by children is improper for any Christian to use. No doubt that if they knew its origin, they would stop using it immediately. Its origin is not only superstitious and idolatrous but so lewd and abhorrent that a religious person can't even think about.]

With such reactions of disgust for the familiar sign, one wonders why Lope chose to showcase the performance of the *higas* episode on stage, thereby creating a unique *tableau vivant* of a potential saint making an insulting phallic gesture at the figure of Christ. Despite possibly disrespecting the sensibilities of certain spectators, Lope took full advantage of his and his audience's knowledge of both popular and learned notions of the *higa* and its relationship to pervasive fears of the evil eye. In fact, Lope also referenced the *higa* and the evil eye for varying purposes in other plays, including *La Dorotea, La prisión sin culpa, El caballero de Olmedo, La hermosa fea, La mal casada, La bella malmariada, El acero de Madrid, Las flores de don Juan*, and *Con su pan se lo coma*, to name a few.[4] In his play celebrating Teresa's sanctity, however, he went beyond mere allusion to the gesture when, following his textual sources, he required the protagonist to dramatize the obscene gesture before wielding the symbol in the form of an apotropaic amulet/prop.

As a keen observer of the human condition, Lope knew that the fig-hand gesture was not just an aggressive sign of contempt but was also linked to primal fears about vulnerability to illness and misfortune attributed to the evil eye. Indeed, both Teresa and Lope de Vega wrote at a time when physicians, theologians, writers, poets, and the general public were engaged in anxious discussions about "fascination," or what was commonly called the "evil eye" ("mal de ojo," "fascinación," or "aojar"). Dating back to classical antiquity, the evil eye was understood by some to be an infectious disease in which certain poisonous vapors issued from the eyes of one person, contaminated the air and absorbed into the body of another person, causing illness, injury, or death. The provocative debate that emerged during the early modern period sought to determine whether the evil eye was merely a superstitious belief, the result of demonic intervention, or a life-threatening illness that required medical diagnosis, treatment, and prevention. In popular practice, however, people sought their own defensive measures. These actions commonly involved the use of apotropaic or protective amulets such as the *higa* (especially when it was made from efficacious materials like jet, coral, or crystal) or the display of the denigrating hand gesture of *dar higas*. Given the persistent fear of the evil eye among all groups of people, from kings to commoners, it is not surprising that Teresa, her confessors, and Lope de Vega would engage issues associated with the menacing phenomenon.

Both popular practices regarding, and theoretical discussions of, the evil eye consistently linked it to ideas that are key to understanding Lope de Vega's specific interest in this episode. Among those individuals considered most likely to infect others by means of the evil eye were women, particularly older women, given that their blood was assumed to be toxic, even lethal. Therefore, the belief in the venomous nature of women's bodies during menstruation and after menopause surely motivated the playwright to transform these ideas and practices to defend Teresa from misogynist fears that women's physiology (toxic blood and infectious vision) could produce serious harm. The often repeated warnings regarding the health risk that menstruating and post-menopausal women posed to the vulnerable implied that older women were even more dangerous primarily because, unlike younger women who only menstruate during limited days, post-menopausal women always carry the venomous toxins left over from the residue of menstrual blood in their veins. Theologian Martín de Castañega, for example, outlines many of these topics in his explanation of the mechanics of the evil eye:

> The most subtle impurities of the body come out through the eyes like rays, and the more subtle they are the more they penetrate and are most infectious. This is how a menstruating woman can stain a new and clean mirror with the rays that come from her eyes, ... Some have this infection and poison more than others, especially old women who no longer menstruate, because they then purge more impurities through the eyes. (cited in Darst 309–10)

As Fernando Salmón and Montserrat Cabré explain, "in the cultural frame where the disease was located, fascination was thought to be produced by a harmful power that women naturally possessed: . . . the potential or actual venomousness of women's bodies, based on the noxiousness of the menses" (61). That Teresa was approaching her late forties when she was forced to engage with a popular yet controversial practice linked to the evil eye surely increased the polemic nature of the *higa* episode in light of current medical beliefs about the physiology of women her age.

While non-procreating women were considered to be agents of visual toxicity, children were believed to be the group most vulnerable to the life-threatening phenomenon of the evil eye, regardless of the child's gender or his/her family's socio-economic status. As a result, children were often at the center of discussions about the evil eye, primarily because of high infant mortality rates and the human need to understand random or sudden misfortune as the unexplained illness or death of the young. The reason most commonly cited for the frequency of infection among young children was their open pores and delicate blood (Covarrubias Horozco 183; Sanz Hermida 51). Not surprisingly, the medical community took seriously the belief that children were considered at high risk for disease, injury, and death as the result of visual contagion. Physicians writing on pregnancy, childbirth, and infant health frequently included material on the evil eye. Francisco Pérez Cascales, in his 1611 treatise on children's diseases (*Liber de affectionibus puerorum . . . Altera vero de Fascinatione*) closed his study with a chapter questioning whether a natural form of fascination exists by which older women can harm infants or children (Sanz Hermida 337–44). Physician Francisco Nuñez, writing on childbirth and children's diseases in 1638 (*Libro del parto humano . . . y a las enfermedades de los niños*), also included one chapter on the evil eye and its cure in his work; while Juan Alonso y de los Ruizes y Fontecha, in his 1606 treatise on pregnancy and childbirth (*Diez previlegios para mugeres preñadas*), devoted the final and longest chapter to the evil eye. That 105-page chapter comprises nearly twenty-five percent of his treatise, thereby providing one indication of the importance given to the topic of the evil eye for those "healthcare" workers and others interested in how fascination impacts pregnant or nursing women and their infants. Juan Alonso y de los Ruizes y Fontecha explained that the most immediate concern is how to avert the infected gaze, which can be done by adorning a newborn with distracting figures made of jet or coral, materials believed to possess natural qualities capable of eliminating infectious vapors (177–78). These striking amulets divert the harmful gaze away from the baby, thus preventing the infected vapors from making a straight trajectory to the newborn. It is in this context of superstitious popular practices and learned discussions linking the evil eye, disease, demonology, misogyny, and vulnerability that Lope confronts, counters, and capitalizes on the beliefs that women are producers of a toxic gaze, that children are the vulnerable victims of dangerous women's infected vision, and that the devil takes advantage of these weaknesses to deceive and harm.

Lope achieves his goal of proving Teresa's holy vision in a sequence of scenes surrounding the *higa* drama (a total of 180 verses) that appears near the midpoint of Act Two. The devil's role in convincing Mariano that Teresa's visions of Christ were in fact the devil in disguise (which leads the deceived priest to command her to employ the *higas y cruces* response) plays on the theory that the evil eye could also result from "maleficio del demonio" [witchcraft caused by the devil] as defined by both theologians and physicians.[5] Writing his play between 1590 and 1604, however (when his source material would have been limited to Teresa's writings published in 1588, Ribera's 1590 biography, and perhaps oral histories), Lope replaced the adult Christ in Teresa's and her biographer's texts with a Christ child (*Niño Jesús*). The child provides one of the most compelling indications of the opportunities inherent in the controversial *higa* and its long-standing link to vision and vulnerability. Lope's "intention" to play on the emotions of the audience through the participation of a child actor is made clear by Teresa's first response to the young figure: "Dulce voz, el pecho ablanda" (Vega Carpio 203) [A sweet voice that melts the heart]. As Maria Grazia Profeti observes in her study of Lope's use of children on the stage that the unprotected or victimized child provides an opportunity to "move the audience" and inspire compassion and tenderness (68). In fact, during the same period that Lope was drafting *Santa Teresa de Jesús*, he was also writing plays for Baltasar de Pinedo, which often required child actors (he wrote some nineteen *comedias* for Pinedo between 1599 and 1606, after the latter broke away from the company of the playwright's old friend Gaspar de Porras) (Wilder 23–24). It was Porras's company, however, that performed Lope's Santa Teresa *comedia* in 1606 in Salamanca, while eight years later Juan de Morales Medrano's company performed the same play as part of Teresa's beatification celebrations in 1614.[6]

Expectedly, the actress playing the part of Teresa carries the scene with more lines than the child actor playing the young Jesus (who has twenty-two verses), but their complex dialogue creates a dynamic tension that requires a combination of commanding authority and emotional vulnerability from both actors. Teresa starts with timidity, as she reluctantly obeys the demon-inspired mandate of her confessor ("Higas y cruces prevengo" [Vega Carpio 204] [I give figs and crosses]); and when the Christ child asks her "¿por qué me huyes?" [Why do you run from me?], the nun explains her impious behavior:

> Por obedecer, Señor;
> perdonadme si os ofendo;
> y si peco obedeciendo
> culpad a mi confesor . . .
> Pues tomad higas y cruces
>   (1383–86, 1390; Vega Carpio 204)

> [To obey, Lord. Forgive me if I offend you and if I sin by obeying then blame my confessor. . . . So take these figs and crosses.]

While there are no explicit stage directions to indicate whether the *higas y cruces* are acted out with gestures, objects, or a combination thereof, the audience is reassured that the cross is not the problem. Whether motioning with her hand or displaying an actual crucifix, Teresa does not hesitate to brandish the sacred symbol (evident in her own writings on the Lopean stage and depicted in the 1613 print engravings of Galle and Collaert).

At the same time, as I have already noted, the *higa* gesture is always provocative and Lope responds to the risk of shocking (and potentially alienating) his audience by rewriting Teresa's traumatic experience into one of poignant piety. To do so, he must transform the *higa* from obscene gesture to protective amulet. Lope begins by defining the *higa* insult as proof of Teresa's willingness to remain obedient:

> *Niño:* ¿qué me das?
> *Teresa:* Cruces con higas
> como el confesor ordena.
> *Niño:* Obedece enhorabuena;
> obedeciendo me obligas.
> *Teresa:* Higas y cruces mandó
> que mis manos hoy os den.
>   (Vega Carpio 204)

> [*Child:* What are you giving me?
> *Teresa:* Crosses with figs as my confessor commands.

Child: I congratulate you on obeying, as you are obliged to obey.
Teresa: He commanded the figs and crosses that my hands give you today].

Once Teresa's fears begin to dissolve with the Christ child's validation, she can focus on the *cruces*, celebrating them as a treasured gift that she can offer the Christ child as a remembrance of his triumph:

> dos mil cruces os dare,
> ... Gozoso podéis mirarlas;
> que vuestra armas son éstas.
>   (Vega Carpio 204)

[I will give you two thousand crosses ... You can look at them with pleasure as these are your weapons.]

After the Christ child's confirmation of her good intentions, Lope then returns to the *higa* sign of contempt and converts it into a loving and protective amulet, as Teresa's celebratory speech demonstrates:

> De las higas, me temía
> cómo podéroslas dar;
> pero ya no hay que dudar,
> *que os vienen bien este día.*
> Tomad mil higas, mi Esposo;
> *que en nadie mi dulce amor*
> *las puede emplear mejor*
> *que en un Niño tan hermoso.* ...
> que daros, Niño, deseo
> tantas higas como cruces.
> *Mis ojos no os hagan mal;*
> tomad, aunque es *indecencia;*
> que en ser higas de obediencia,
> *valen más que de cristal.*
> *Bello Infante soberano,*
> higas y cruces os doy,
> porque tengáis desde hoy
> *estos dijes de mi mano*
> Guardaldos, mi Niño bello;
> ved que no pasa de raya

que *un Niño por dijes traiga*
cruces e higas al cuello.
(Vega Carpio 204, emphasis mine)

[As for the fig, I was fearful about how to give it to you but there is no doubt that it serves you well today. May you have a thousand figs today, my Spouse. Nobody, my sweet love, could employ them better than such a beautiful child. . . . I wish to give you, Child, as many figs as crosses. May my eyes not cause you any harm, so take these, although it is indecent, since they are figs of obedience they are worth more than crystal. Beautiful Infant Sovereign, figs and crosses I offer you so that you will have from this day on, these amulets from my hands. Keep them my beautiful Child, and see that it is not inappropriate for a child to wear crosses and figs as amulets around his neck.]

For Antonio F. Cao, this scene transforms the "grotesque" gesture into a "sublime" object through a "desplazamiento semántico" (Vega Carpio 302) [semantic displacement], since Lope plays on the phonological similarity between "*higas* de obediencia" and "*hijas* de obediencia" (301) [figs/daughters of obediencia]. This shift, however, goes beyond mere semantics. Through Teresa's confident transformation from fearful and apologetic (albeit potentially blasphemous) aggressor to loving and protective defender, Lope engages a combination of scientific, theological, artistic, and popular debates about the evil eye as they relate to women, children, and a pernicious—at times lethal—gaze to show how Teresa is part of a holy solution to problems that face all people.

Despite warnings against the popular apotropaic amulets, people from all stations of life continued to adorn babies and young children with objects, figures, and materials believed to ward off evil forces and purify contaminated air that could affect children. Portraits, artifacts, inventories, and dramatic works provide significant evidence for understanding how deeply rooted the belief in amulets as protective gear was for early modern royals as well as ordinary citizens. Many of the portraits of royal toddlers—such as Juan Pantoja de la Cruz's 1602 painting of Princess Ana de Austria, Santiago Morán's 1610 portrait of Princess Margarita Francisca, Bartolomé González y Serrano's 1613 portrait of Prince Alfonso el Caro and Princess Ana Margarita, and Velázquez's 1659 portrait of the two-year-old heir to the throne Felipe Próspero—feature various amulets believed to protect the vulnerable children from illness, misfortune, and the ever-threatening evil eye. The sickly Prince Felipe, for example, is depicted wearing a sash (*banda de hombros*) with a fig-hand amulet hanging from the shoulder and a pomander or perfume sphere (*poma de olor* or *per-*

fumero) positioned over his chest. Around his waist, the young prince wore a charm belt (*ceñidor* or *dijero*) from which hung another fig-hand, another pomander, and a small bell. Juan Pantoja de la Cruz's early seventeenth-century portraits of the princess Ana de Austria also feature *higas* made from jet and coral, as well as a coral branch, a crystal heart reliquary, a *campanilla* or little bell, and a perfume sphere. Less than a decade later, Santiago Morán's portrait of Princess Margarita Francisca likewise displayed common protective amulets, including a small bell, a badger's foot (*garra de tejón*), a chestnut, a spheric *perfumero*, a reliquary medallion, and a ring pull (*arandela*).[7]

While Lope did not have pictorial images of Teresa's *higa* incident from which to shape his own moving image, he undoubtedly had in mind the portraits of royal children sporting the fig amulet.[8] It is not by chance that, in the play, Teresa refers to the Christ child as the "Bello Infante soberano," who, like the future heirs to the throne, is adorned and protected by her offering of

> higas de obediencia,
> valen más de cristal ... dijes traiga
> cruces e higas al cuello.
>   (Vega Carpio 204)

[since they are figs of obedience they are worth more than crystal ... to wear crosses and figs as amulets around your neck.]

The reference to the fig amulet made of crystal is undoubtedly intended to mitigate any suspicions of superstitious practices, as the material was believed to be efficacious and therefore safe from both medical and theological scrutiny (see Covarrubias Horozco 183).

Along similar lines, Teresa's insistence on the beauty of the Christ child ("Niño tan hermoso ... Bello Infante ... mi Niño bello") and his potential need for the apotropaic fig amulet points to widespread beliefs that individuals considered to be beautiful were thought to attract the attention and praise of onlookers, thereby inviting visual infection. Theologian and demonologist Martín del Río offers an explanation for why children and those considered beautiful become targets for contagion:

> It now remains to be seen whence comes the common idea that fascination springs from a person's eyesight because of someone is being praised.... [P]erhaps it happens because men and women usually take more notice of children who are somewhat plumper than usual, have a healthier sheen to their faces, and are prettier than normal. People

praise such children.... So when, as often happens, these children (who have hitherto given every appearance of being in the best of health) happen to fall into some great misfortune of life, the common people do not understand the reason for such a sudden change and, because they do not understand, suspect some evil–doing and throw the blame for it upon the eyes and words of those who look at the children and praise them. Every day plump, pretty little children attract such looks and praises, and since it is easy to find some wrinkled, misshapen old woman among their admirers, and since this kind of person is physically offensive, morose, and hateful, the harm is attributed to her rather than to anyone else. [cited in Sanz Hermida 330–31]

That Lope could anticipate the public's ability to link the *higa*, the evil eye, and the potentially harmful gaze of women is most evident in Teresa's defensive affirmation "Mis ojos no os hagan mal" (Vega Carpio 204) [May my eyes not hurt you]. Diffusing the cultural pattern of blaming the noxious gaze of older women for sudden illness, accidents, or the death of children, the playwright shields the nun by presenting her as the maternal protector of a holy yet vulnerable sovereign.

The strategy of depicting susceptible children in need of protection and saving could be guaranteed to elicit the public's sympathy, so the same approach is developed further in Act Three when Teresa is called upon to bring her dead nephew Gonzalo back to life. While the cause of his death is not disclosed (consistent with Ribera's 1590 biography, yet contrary to Diego de Yepes's 1606 biography, Galle and Collaert's 1613 engravings, and even Lope's later *Vida y muerte*, which all attribute the tragedy to a wall that collapsed during the construction of her convent), the child's mother Doña Juana is inconsolable as she carries his limp body to her sister Teresa. This heartbreaking scene again allows Lope to play on spectators' fears of the vulnerable nature of children and the often unexpected and unexplained conditions that can befall them: "Don Juan: De verte llorar me aflijo. Doña Juana: No hay llanto que no me cuadre, ... lloraré como leona" (Vega Carpio 217) [Don Juan: It pains me to see you cry. Doña Juana: Sobbing is all I can do ... I will wail like a lioness].

Teresa's miraculous prayer on behalf of her nephew proves successful in restoring his life, yet it is another miracle that Teresa performs prior to resuscitating her nephew that most effectively separates the holy nun from the cultural beliefs about women's toxic blood and harmful gaze. Earlier in Act Three, Teresa cuts her finger and must use a handkerchief to stop the bleeding. Her brother-in-law Valle (Juan de Ovalle, the father of the nephew who would soon need the triumphant resuscitation) fortuitously retains a fragment of the blood-stained fabric as a relic, which he places inside his vest. When a competing and vengeful suitor shoots Valle, Teresa's holy blood on the cloth is credited with miraculously stopping the bullet from harming the targeted victim:

> Sólo de la ropilla me ha pasado;
> porque a la sangre de este medio paño,
> perdigones y bala han respetado.
> (Vega Carpio 214)

[It only penetrated my clothing because the gun and bullet respected the blood on this piece of fabric.]

The lifesaving power of Teresa's blood is highlighted throughout the post-miracle conversation, describing the bullet as thirsty for blood but coming up empty, as the blood-stained cloth becomes a wall as well as the canvas on which the miracle was painted (Vega Carpio 215–16).

Although this miraculous incident is Lope's invention and not drawn from Teresa's writings, it was likely inspired by the numerous accounts of healing miracles involving fragments of the garments and bed-clothing that were stained with Teresa's blood upon her death. Appropriately, some of these hematic miracles involved children, as Ribera testifies: "They had a 2-year-old child who was so far gone that there was no hope that he would live.... [T]hey put a piece of cloth with her blood on his head and later the child came to life" (661). Along similar lines, given the prominence of Teresa's hands and fingers as implicated in the *higa* gesture, it is significant that her hands and fingers were highlighted in narratives about the miraculous bodily relics, as Ribera recounts: "She said it felt like her bones were breaking and that her heart was being ripped out . . . so they brought the Mother's hand and put it on her and as soon as it touched her she was cured, as if she had never been afflicted" (657). Lope follows this example by emphasizing her hands and fingers during the *higa* episode ("higas y cruces mandó / que mis manos hoy os den," "porque tengáis desde hoy / estos dijes de mi mano" [Vega Carpio 204]), and later during the first miracle in Act Three ("me corté un dedo . . . mucha es la sangre" (Vega Carpio 214) [I cut my finger and there is much blood]. Surely the playwright was keen to protect Teresa from misogynist beliefs about women's infectious blood (whose toxins were released through the eyes) by demonstrating that her blood, hands, fingers, and eyes were sacred and capable of saving, not destroying, lives.

As a father who had suffered the deaths of four of his children during the years he was drafting *Santa Teresa de Jesús,* Lope surely understood the anxiety of parents worried about the well-being of their offspring.[9] Nonetheless, the playwright may also have been inspired to transform the adult Jesus from the written sources into a child, based on his personal knowledge of Teresa's own devotion to images of the Christ child. In fact, Teresa's well-documented attachment to religious iconography seemed to include a special devotion to the Christ child, as evidenced by the print of the young Jesus she kept inside in her breviary and the numerous statues of the *Niño Jesús* installed in the Carmelite communities in San José de Avila, Valladolid, Toledo, Segovia, Medina el Campo, and Villanueva de la Jara (see Álvarez 840–41; Wilson, "Teresa vs. the Iconoclasts," 48–49, 118).

While those close to the nun would have known of her fondness for the holy child figure (although Ana de Jesús did not include this devotion in her selection of materials to be featured in the twenty-five-print series by Galle and Collaert), pictorial representations of Teresa with the Christ child did not appear until *after* Lope had written his play, which makes one wonder whether the artists may have been influenced by Lope's play instead of the playwright having relyied on iconographic motifs. According to Bastianutti, Lope typically specified "como le pintan" in his stage directions when pictorial materials were available (718). The fact that Lope did not invoke this guiding reference in *Santa Teresa* may reflect the nascent stage of Teresian iconography at the time he was drafting his hagiographic *comedia.* Moreover, by greatly reducing the age of Christ in his rendition of the *higas y cruces* episode, Lope was the first to visually depict the conclusion to the *higas y cruces* event (in which Christ returned to Teresa a cross bejeweled with precious stones) with the image of a child Jesus bestowing upon the nun the adorned cross. It is Lope's version, then, that appeared later on canvas in the anonymous *Santa Teresa recibe una cruz de oro y piedras preciosas* in Salamanca in 1608, just two years after Gaspar de Porras's company performed Lope's play in the same location.[10] Conversely, by the time Lope's play was performed by Juan de Morales Medrano's company during Teresa's beatification celebrations in 1614, the widely circulated prints by Galle and Collaert published one year earlier would have been familiar to many spectators and may have influenced their expectations, as well as the staging and performative choices of the directors and actors. Galle and Collaert's twenty-five-print series naturally avoids the specificity of the *higas* gesture, yet includes an engraving of Teresa positioned between Saint Paul and Saint Peter, reminiscent of how they appear in written accounts of the fig-hand debacle as well as in Lope's play, where they physically block

Teresa from escaping when she tries to flee from having to give the Christ child the *higa* gesture.

A different engraving in the Galle and Collaert series, however, may have more to do with Teresa's multifaceted experience with the fig-hand incident and her subsequent narrative strategies (as well as Lope's interpretation of the *higas y cruces* scene) than meets the eye. In this engraving, Teresa is depicted in a commanding stance as she wields a sizable cross to expel a group of demons. Similarly, in a lengthy discourse in chapter 25 of her *Vida* (to which she refers again later when she recounts the fig-hand episode in chapter 29), Teresa uses the fig-hand image as a verbal expression of repudiation while characterizing the ecclesiastics as blind, child-like, and fixated on demons:

> Cuando él ve escurecido el entendimiento, ayuda lindamente a que *se quiebren los ojos*; porque si a uno ve ya *ciego* en poner su descanso en cosas vanas, y tan vanas que parecen las de este mundo cosa de *juego de niño*, ya él ve que éste es *niño*, pues trata como tal ... y *una higa para todos los demonios*, que ellos me temerán a mí. No entiendo estos miedos: ¡demonio, demonio!, adonde podemos decir: ¡Dios, Dios!, y hacerle temblar.... Es sin duda que tengo ya más miedo a los que tan grande le tienen al demonio que a él mesmo; porque él no me puede hacer nada, y estotros, en especial si son confesores, inquietan mucho, y he pasado algunos años de tan gran trabajo, que ahora me espanto cómo lo he podido sufrir. (*Libro de la vida* 318–19, emphasis mine)

> [When he (the devil) sees the intellect darkened, he subtly helps to *blind the eyes*. For if he sees people already blind by the fact that they place their trust in vain things ... like *children's games* ... he concludes that they are then *children*, treats them as such ... *and a fig for all the devils*, because they shall fear me. I don't understand these fears, "The devil! The devil," when we can say "God! God".... Without doubt, I fear those who have such great fear of the devil more than I do the devil himself. (*The Book of Her Life* 171, emphasis mine)]

Both Teresa and Lope agree that demons are ultimately behind the confessors' doubts and subsequent fig-hand mandate. In Lope's play, it is the devil who whispers in Mariano's ear "dile que huya esas visiones" [tell her to chase away those visions], which the priest then repeats to Teresa ("Pues yo soy de parecer que huyas esas tentaciones" [Well its my opinion that you should chase away those temptations]) before commanding her to give the figs and crosses (Vega Carpio 203). When Teresa complies with the command she has been given, to whom, then, is she giving the fig-hand? Does Lope understand that the fig fiasco is really about the devil's ability to blind confessors and infect their perception of her visions? If so, then the *higa* as a symbol of rebellious obedience is not directed at the Christ child but at the child-like confessors. In the end, the real toxic gaze is that of the confessors who have succumbed to demonic intervention, proving that Teresa does *look like a saint*.

Notes

1. See Ignacio Elizalde, "Teresa de Jesús, protagonist de la dramática Española del siglo XVII," and Nicolás Marin, "Teresa de Jesús en el teatro barroco" for analysis of all four plays. For a chronology of Lope's play, see Morley and Bruerton, 499, and Haley.
2. All translations are mine unless otherwise noted.
3. See Mujica, *A New Anthology of Early Modern Spanish Theater: Play and Playtext*, 174. See also Bastianutti, 714, and Mujica ("Performing Sanctity" 191; *Play and Playtext* 671).
4. See Caro Baroja (265–76) and Sanz Hermida (372–80), for more on early modern plays that reference the *higa* and the evil eye.
5. See Jacobo Sanz Hermida's *Cuatro tratados medicos renacentistas sobre el mal de ojo* for a partial anthology of medical and theological texts addressing the evil eye.
6. See José Romera Castillo for a discussion of various performances of Teresa's life during the beatification celebrations in "Compendio literario en honor de Santa Teresa. Notas de Historia literaria sobre justas poéticas y representaciones teatrales."
7. Examples of these kinds of amulet belts have survived and are on display in Spain at museums such as the National Museum of Anthropology (Madrid), the Museo Sorolla (Madrid), and the Casa Museo Lope de Vega (Madrid). See Herradón Figueroa ("Higa" 94–97); Timón Tiemblo; Bandrés Oto (91, 369–74); and Baroja (9, 20, and "láminas" 1–4 and 22).
8. Mujica (citing Antonio Feros Carrasco) reminds us that "Lope de Vega and other authors adapted to the stage the same images of power that painters used in their royal portraits" ("Performing Sanctity" 198).
9. For details of Lope's private and professional life, see Rennert.
10. A variation of the painting with the Christ child offering Teresa the ornamented cross also appeared from the same workshop a year later, in 1609. See Pinilla Martín, *Iconografía*, 112–14, 218–19, 419, 555, 731–32.

References

Alonso y de los Ruizes y Fontecha, Juan. *Diez previlegios para mugeres preñadas*. Alcalá de Henares, Spain: Luis Martínez Grande, 1606.

Álvarez, Tomás, ed. *Diccionario de Santa Teresa de Jesús*. Burgos, Spain: Monte Carmelo, 2001.
Bandrés Oto, Maribel. *La moda en la pintura: Velázquez: usos y costumbres del siglo XVII*. Navarra: EUNSA, 2002.
Baroja, Carmen. *Catálogo de amuletos del Museo del Pueblo español*. Madrid: Museo del Pueblo Español, 1945.
Bastianutti, Diego L. "La inspiración pictórica en el teatro hagiográfico de Lope de Vega." In *Lope de Vega y los orígenes del teatro español*, edited by Manuel Criado de Val, Madrid: EDI, 1981, 711–18.
Cao, Antonio F. "La santidad y su refracción irónica: su expresión dramática y liguistica en la *Comedia de la Bienaventurada Madre Santa Teresa de Jesús*, de Lope de Vega." In *Santa Teresa y la literatura mística hispánica*, edited by Manuel Criado de Val, Madrid: EDI, 1984, 297–302.
Caro Baroja, Julio. *Algunos mitos españoles y otros ensayos*. Madrid: Editora Nacional, 1944.
Covarrubias Horozco, Sebastián de. *Tesoro de la lengua castellana o española*. Edited by Ignacio Arellano and Rafael Zafra, Iberoamericana, 2006.
Darst, David H. "Witchcraft in Spain: The Testimony of Martín de Castañega's Treatise on Superstition and Witchcraft (1529)." In *Proceedings of the American Philosophical Society* 123 (1979): 298–322.
Del Río, Martín. "De la fascinación." In *Cuatro tratados medicos renacentistas sobre el mal de ojo*, edited by Jacobo Sanz Hermida, 322–31. Salamanca: Junta de Castilla y León, 2001.
Elizalde, Ignacio. "Teresa de Jesús, protagonist de la dramática Española del siglo XVII." *Letras de Deusto* 12 (1982): 173–98.
Galle, Cornelis, and Adriaen Collaert. *Estampas de la vida de la santa madre Teresa de Jesús: grabadas por los famosos artistas*. Edited by María José Pinilla Martín. Madrid: Espiritualidad, 2012.
Haley, George. "Lope de Vega y el repertorio de Gaspar de Porras en 1604 y 1606." In *Homenaje a William L. Fichter. Estudios sobre el teatro antiguo hispánico y otros ensayos*, edited by A. D. Kossoff and J. Amor y Vázquez, Madrid: Castalia, 1971, 257–68.
Ibáñez, Pedro. "Appendix. Documents Illustrative of the Life, Works and Virtues of Saint Teresa." In *The Complete Works of St Teresa of Jesus*, Vol. 3, translated and edited by E. Allison Peers, Sheed and Ward, 1950, 313–33.
Herradón Figueroa, María Antonia. "Higa." In *Catálogo de la exposición Castillo interior Teresa de Jesús y el siglo XVI*, edited by José Ignacio Piera Delgado, Ávila: Catedral de Ávila, 1995, 94–97.
———. "Higa." In *La joyería española de Felipe II a Alfonso XIII en los museos estatales*, edited by Letizia Arbeteta, Madrid: Nerea, 1998, 88–92.
Marin, Nicolás. "Teresa de Jesús en el teatro barroco." In *Actas del Congreso Internacional Teresiano*, edited by Teófanes Egido Martínez, Victor García de la Concha, and Olegario González de Cardenal, Universidad de Salamanca, 1992, 699–719.
Mayberry, Nancy K., ed. "Introducción." *La fundadora de la Santa Concepción. Comedia*

en dos partes. Blas Fernández de Mesa, edited by Nancy K. Mayberry, 1–33, Peter Lang, 1996.
Morley, S. Griswold, and Courtney Bruerton, ed. *Cronología de las comedias de Lope de Vega*. Madrid: Gredos, 1968.
Mujica, Bárbara, ed. *A New Anthology of Early Modern Spanish Theater: Play and Playtext*. Yale University Press, 2004.
———. "Performing Sanctity: Lope's Use of Teresian Iconography in *Santa Teresa de Jesús*." In *A Companion to Lope de Vega*, edited by Alexander Samson and Jonathan Thacker, Tamesis, 2008, 183–98.
Nieremberg, Juan Eusebio, ed. *Curiosa y oculta filosofía*. Alcalá, Spain: María Fernandez, 1649.
Pinilla Martín, María José. "Estampas de la vida de la santa madre Teresa de Jesús": In *Iconografía teresiana. Estampas de la vida de la santa madre Teresa de Jesús: grabadas por los famosos artistas Cornelio Galle y Adrian Collaert, impresas en Amberes en 1613*, by Cornelis Galle and Adriaen Collaert, Madrid: Espiritualidad, 2012, 3–15.
———. *Iconografía de Santa Teresa de Jesús*. PhD diss., Universidad de Valladolid, 2014.
———. "La ilustración de los escritos teresianos: grabados de las primeras ediciones." *Boletín del Seminario de Estudios de Arte y Arqueología* 74 (2008): 185–202.
Profeti, Maria Grazia. "Los niños de Lope: entre encargo y pathos." In *En torno al Teatro del Siglo de Oro*, edited by H. Castellón Alcalá, A. de la Granja López, and A. Agulló, Almería, Spain: Instituto de Estudios Almerienses, 1991, 65–85.
Rennert, Hugo Albert. *The Life of Lope de Vega (1562–1635)*. Campion, 1904.
Ribera, Francisco de. *La vida de la Madre Teresa de Jesús. Fundadora de las Descalzas y Descalzos Carmelitas*. Madrid: Edibesa, 2004.
Romera Castillo, José. "Compendio literario en honor de Santa Teresa. Notas de Historia literaria sobre justas poéticas y representaciones teatrales." In *Teresa de Jesús. Studi Storico–letterari*, Rome: Teresianum, 1983, 193–227.
Salmón, Fernando, and Montserrat Cabré. "Fascinating Women: The Evil Eye in Medical Scholasticism." In *Medicine from the Black Death to the French Disease*, edited by Roger French, Jon Arrizabalaga, Andrew Cunningham, and Luis García-Ballester, Ashgate, 1998, 53–84.
Sanz Hermida, Jacobo. *Cuatro tratados medicos renacentistas sobre el mal de ojo*. Salamanca: Junta de Castilla y León, 2001.
Teresa de Jesús (de Ávila). *The Book of Her Life*. Translated by Kieran Kavanaugh and Otilio Rodríguez, introduction by Jodi Bilinkoff, Hackett, 2008.
———. *The Complete Works of St Teresa of Jesus*, Vol. 3. Translated and edited by E. Allison Peers, Sheed and Ward, 1950.
———. *Libro de la vida*. Edited by Dámasco Chicharro, Madrid: Cátedra, 1987.
———. *Obras completas*. Translated and edited by Efren de la Madre de Dios and Otger Steggink, Madrid: Biblioteca de Autores Cristianos, 2006.
Thofner, Margit. "How to Look Like a (Female) Saint: The Early Iconography of St Teresa of Avila." In *Female Monasticism in Early Modern Europe: An Interdisciplinary View*, edited by Cordula van Wyhe, Ashgate, 2008, 59–78.

Timón Tiemblo, María Pía. "La infancia en época de El Quijote: males y elementos protectors," www.museocasanataldecervantes.org/wp-content/uploads/2013/12/infanciaenlaepocadelquijote.pdf.

Van Wyhe, Cordula. "The *Idea Vitae Teresianae* (1687): The Teresian Mystic Life and its Visual Representation in the Low Countries." In *Female Monasticism in Early Modern Europe: An Interdisciplinary View*, edited by Cordula van Wyhe, Ashgate, 2008, 173–207.

Vega Carpio, Lope de (attributed). *Santa Teresa de Jesús: Monja Descalza de Nuestra Señora del Carmen*. In *A New Anthology of Early Modern Spanish Theater: Play and Playtext*, edited by Bárbara Mujica, Yale University Press, 2014, 179–225.

Weber, Alison. *Teresa of Avila and the Rhetoric of Femininity*. Princeton University Press, 1990.

Wilder, Thornton. "Lope, Pinedo, Some Child-Actors, and a Lion." *Romance Philology* 7 (1953): 19–25.

Wilson, Christopher C. "Teresa of Ávila vs. the Iconoclasts: Convent Art in Support of a Church in Crisis." In *Imagery, Spirituality, and Ideology in Baroque Spain and Latin America*, edited by Jeremy Roe and Marta Bustillo, Cambridge Scholars, 2010, 45–57.

———. "Where's Teresa? The Construction of Teresa of Ávila in the Visual Arts." In *Approaches to Teaching Teresa of Ávila and the Spanish Mystics*, edited by Alison Weber, Modern Language Association, 2009, 190–201.

Yepes, Diego de. *Vida, virtudes y milagros de la Bienaventurada Virgen Teresa de Jesús*. Zaragoza, Spain: Ángelo Tavano, 1606.

SUSAN L. FISCHER

Teresa of Ávila, Spiritual Warrior Secularized
Going for the Subjective in Bárbara Mujica's Biographical Fiction

POSTMODERNISM HAS led to the rise of a new type of biography, one that acknowledges, vis-à-vis its form as fiction, that accurate representation of the biographical subject is no longer possible. Linda Hutcheon theorized biographical fiction as a postmodern genre as far back as 1989, observing that "the certainty of direct reference of the historical novel or even the nonfictional novel is gone" (4). This idea was interpreted in the following way (by Bruce Duffy) in a roundtable conversation moderated by Michael Lackey on biographical fiction, a genre that is said to have come into being mainly in the twentieth century: "[Hutcheon is] talking about fiction that is highly aware of talking about pastness; we are always being written, rewritten, erased, reformatted, and retold, edited. Her argument is . . . that these kinds of novels aren't about the past, but about the problematization of historical knowledge" (Lackey, Parini, Duffy, Olsen 170). The biographical novel, in other words, has superseded the classical historical novel in response to contemporary theories of consciousness that have had a major effect on the way we apprehend and approach history. According to Lackey, traditional historical novelists arguably have a "positivist" approach to history: they "picture the external factors that objectively shape and determine consciousness and thereby make historical collisions possible" ("Rise of the Biographical Novel" 33). For biographical novelists, on the other hand, "there is a surreal dimension to consciousness, so that they shift the focus from the objective external world to the subjective internal world in order to picture the forces that have given birth to major historical collisions" ("Rise of the Biographical Novel" 33).

Jay Parini, regarded as one of the leading innovators in the genre of biographical fiction, puts the postmodern view of history simply but forcefully: "The relationship between fact and fiction is vexed" (299). Key here is how the poststructuralist shift toward subjectivity affects a novelist or biographer. The term fiction, we will recall, derives from the Latin *fictio*, which translates as "shaping," and, according to Parini, "suggests a process of selection and arrangement.... It takes a certain frame of reference, a shaping point of view, and, yes, an ideology, to make a fruitful selectivity" (301–2). This kind of selectivity is perforce subjective; Parini elaborates: "the relation among the facts assumes not only a narrative of events or repetition of facts but an imaginative revision and rearrangement—a mosaic that is, in effect, an interpretation" (303). He goes on to speak of the "vexed" relationship between fact and fiction, truth and authenticity:

> Novels are about lives, after all: about pieces of lives or whole lives. Traditionally, these lives have been made up, with half-believable disclosures at the outset that read, "The characters in this novel are entirely fictitious and any relation to persons living or dead is entirely accidental." I would prefer that novelists of the future write: "Everything in the following pages is authentic, which is to say it is as true as I could make it. Take it or leave it." (306–7)

Lackey, for his part, states: "What we get in a biographical novel is a person's life" ("Biofiction" 5). In other words:

> biographical novelists differ from biographers because, while authors of traditional and fictional biographies seek to represent the life (or a dimension of a life) of an actual historical figure as clearly and accurately as possible, biographical novelists forgo the desire to get the biographical subject's life "right" and, rather, use the biographical subject in order to project their own vision of life and the world. ("Biofiction" 5)

The point is to use history and biography in order to tell a story, to construct a narrative. The process has been likened to the one deployed by reputed classical writers: "It is not to correct history or write an addendum to the historical or biographical record," but to appropriate historical material in ways that Shakespeare or Homer felt entitled to do. The writer's "respect and use of historical facts are really based on [a] need for plausibility" rather than on a "particular concern for historical record as such" (Banks 205).

Going for the Subjective in Biographical Fiction

This brief foray into the modus operandi of biographical fiction as a postmodern genre serves as ground against which to approach Bárbara Mujica's novel, *Sister Teresa: The Woman Who Became Saint Teresa of Ávila*, which Coco Blignaut of the Actor's Studio (Los Angeles) adapted for the stage in 2013 as *God's Gypsy*. Driving Mujica's method is the notion that historical novels "indulge in the great game of narrating the past afresh and of diverging from the official version of the past offered by historians into the realm of invented reality" (Kehlmann). Mujica avers that for Daniel Kehlmann (author of the biographical novel *Measuring the World*, whose subjects are mathematician and astronomer Carl Friedrich Gauss and geographer and naturalist Alexander von Humboldt), "historical fiction does not really exist because writers must always filter history through their own *Weltanschauung*" ("Going for the Subjective" 89); they are limited by their own subjectivity. Moreover, even if authors of biographical fiction have access to their subject's diaries and letters, for example, they are inevitably constrained by the "subject's self-representation" ("Going for the Subjective" 88). One way to deal with the issue of multiple subjectivities, according to Mujica, is "to accentuate the subjective element that is unavoidable in all historical writing by inventing an unabashedly opinionated narrative voice." This technique provides "an angle or point of view that is clearly not the protagonist's and allows the author to interpret his or her material with no pretense to objectivity" ("Going for the Subjective" 89). The challenge facing all writers of historical fiction, including biographical fiction, is "to find the right balance between historical accuracy and readability" ("Going for the Subjective" 96), often "[sacrificing] (callously!) historical completeness (but not historical accuracy) for effective narrative" ("Going for the Subjective" 92).

In writing the biographical novel that is *Sister Teresa* (as opposed to a hagiography or a romance), Mujica drew on her academic study of the subject's correspondence, *Teresa de Ávila: Lettered Woman*, insofar as such epistolary material disclosed personality traits, emotions, and concerns that would have perforce been masked in treatises to be read by censors of The Tribunal of the Holy Office of the Inquisition. From Teresa's correspondence, it became clear to Mujica that the person who got to be Saint Teresa of Ávila "was a strong-willed, temperamental woman, who was deeply spiritual, yet practical and shrewd. She was warm and loving, but she could be manipulative and imperious" ("Going for the Subjective" 92). If she was "a mystic, a visionary, and an ecstatic," she could also be "a vain, bossy, impatient woman" ("Going for the Subjective" 93), as evidenced in her writings. Mujica's idea was "to humanize the saint without defiling her, yet build into the plot the adventure, romance, sexual tension, and mystery a novel requires" ("Going for the Subjective" 93).

Therefore, in the refashioning of her character through the genre of biographical fiction, questions such as these surfaced: "What would it be like... to be close to a person who went into trances and saw visions? ... To know someone who spoke to God and became impatient with you because you couldn't? Someone who struggled with prayer while you were struggling to put bread on the table? Someone who made a fetish of self-deprivation when all you wanted was a good meal?" ("Going for the Subjective" 93). To this end, the author invented an unreliable narrator attached to the material world, the character Pancracia, who enters the convent with Teresa as Sister Angélica and offers a self-conscious response to the main character's actions and reactions, showing an awareness of the fallibility of her memory (e.g., "Days, seasons, years and decades melt into one another, forming one amorphous blob" [Mujica, *Sister Teresa*, 154]). Angélica is, as Mujica explains, "close enough to Teresa to observe and narrate her life story, yet distant enough to provide a personal commentary that, at times, conflicts radically with Teresa's own perceptions" ("Going for the Subjective" 93). The differences between protagonist and narrator are apparent: if Teresa is "rich and beautiful," then Angélica is "poor and plain," but "smart and perceptive" ("Going for the Subjective" 93). When Teresa begins to have visions and professes to speak with God, Angélica struggles with how to react, often losing patience because flights of mysticism are so foreign to her. Though she loves Teresa as a mentor, friend, and sister, she is skeptical about all of Teresa's ecstasies, locutions, and mortifications. She also evinces a carnal appetite based on stories of seduction and deceit found in Carmelite chronicles, thereby contributing sexual tension essential to a latter-day novel about nuns.

The character of Teresa's fictional companion allows the author to examine the ambiguities in the story of the protagonist and fill in the gaps of the official record, arguably challenging aspects of received history. The opposing perspectives of Teresa and Angélica point up the subjectivity of both the fictional voice and the historical—"official"—voice of the Church and the Carmelite Order: "the alterity of the unreliable narrator diffuses the authority of the official narrative, reminding us that Teresa, like the chroniclers of the Church and of her order, represents a particular point of view" ("Going for the Subjective," 94). Our purpose here is to examine the ways in which Mujica invents and executes the technique of the unreliable narrator in a biographical novel that showcases the early modern "warrior" woman as subject.

When Does *Sister Teresa* Begin?

David Lodge states provocatively that the question, "[w]hen does a novel begin?" is almost as difficult to answer as the question, "when does the human embryo become a person?" (4). As Lodge implies, it is deceptively simple to observe that the beginning of a novel is a "threshold" that, in separating the "real" world we live in from the one the novelist has imagined, must "draw us in" (5). Three beginnings are arguably discernible with respect to the biographical novel at hand. Mujica cleverly draws us in—in Cervantine fashion—by framing the work, on the very first page, *as though* it were the English translation of a Spanish manuscript discovered in France: "I found this manuscript in Dijon, in a tiny antiquarian's shop on the Rue Sainte Anne, near the old Carmelite convent. It was a pile of yellowed, crumbling papers tied with a ribbon, colorless and frayed from age" (*Sister Teresa* 5). This technique enables Mujica as surrogate author/translator to ponder questions of transmission style (e.g., translation into modern English; addition of chapter titles, paragraphs, modern punctuation), to indicate the verifiability of most of the information in this *"testimonio personal"* or kind of "spiritual chronicle" (*Sister Teresa* 5), and to confirm the historical existence of many of the people mentioned therein—three exceptions being the pseudo-narrator/nun, Angélica del Sagrado Corazón (née Pancracia Soto y Fuentes), her lover, Fray Braulio Estévez y Pontenegro, and Teresa's cousin and unrequited suitor, Javier Sánchez Colón. The explanation conveyed in Mujica's opening page, "About the Translation," offers a befitting intertextual reference-with-a-twist to the proverbial Cervantine play with the identity of *Don Quixote*'s author, in which he becomes the "padrastro" [stepfather] of a work translated by a "morisco" from a manuscript found in a Toldean marketplace.

The manuscript's Prologue likewise lures us in, beginning thus: "We'd just escaped from Seville and were heading north through the mountains" (Mujica, *Teresa of Ávila*, 7). We are connected *in medias res* to the year 1576, when Teresa de Jesús and Sister Angélica have been interrogated by the Inquisition. We are immersed directly in their life and times as nun and companion stop—fictitiously—at a convent in San Miguel de Pinares, where the foundress knows the prioress Paula from her initial stay with the Augustinian sisters. The prologue is, at the same time, a retrospective testimony to a trilogy of threads running throughout the story: first, the interrogation and persecution of *conversos* accused of heresy, and the horrific burning of a woman changed with having "spurious visions" (Mujica, *Teresa of Ávila*, 8); second, Teresa's strong, stubborn, forthright, and often irreverent character painted in broad but accurate brushstrokes, when Angélica observes, for example, that she did not tolerate resting in herself or in others (*Teresa of Ávila* 12), and when Teresa asserts—"unflinchingly"—according to the narrator: "Priests are like manure.... You have to spread them around for them to do any good. Put too many together and they begin to stink" (*Teresa of Ávila* 13); and third, Teresa's otherworldly visions, as filtered through Angélica's memory, when she fixed her eyes in ecstasy and was "motionless" and "radiant" as the Lord's image "seemed to quiver with an awareness of her presence" (*Teresa of Ávila* 17).

The manuscript thus sets the stage for the young "Belle of Ávila" to emerge in what the translator later denominated Chapter 1, "October Roses." Angélica recreates a memorable moment in which she sees Teresa's shoulders shaking with emotion, which could effectively have been the opening for a cloak-and-dagger play by Lope de Vega or Calderón de la Barca, down to details and norms of period dress:

> A girl, lithe and quick, had darted out from an alley. She wore a dark-colored dress, burgundy or russet, trimmed in lace and partially concealed by a cape.... A male figure appeared from behind the chandler's shop, his cape flapping loosely on his shoulders.... Aside from his white gloves and the stiff, fluted ruff at his throat, he was dressed all in black.... Teresa flew to him.... He took her hand and they vanished into a passageway. (Mujica, *Sister Teresa*, 22)

If there was no doubt as to the authenticity of the girl, then the male figure emerged as much from Mujica's subjective consciousness as from Teresa's own admission, at the end of Chapter 2 of her autobiography *Libro de la Vida* [The Book of Her Life], that she originally entered the convent because of a "friendship with one of [her] cousins [which] was in view of a possible marriage" (*Teresa of Ávila* 128). Teresa does not say more about that friendship, except to avow that her confessor told her that she was "doing nothing against God." Mujica opts to respect the Carmelite nun's ambiguity on that score by having rumors about the young Teresa's sexual transgressions circulate in Angélica's subjective memory. The moral precepts inculcated in her from the pulpit, as well as from her mother and aunt's chatter as they sat embroidering, spinning, or sewing in the *estrado* or "ladies' haven" of the house—"Suspicion alone was enough to justify a bloodbath" (Mujica, *Sister Teresa*, 25)—smack of those of avenging husbands in Calderón's honor plots, anachronism notwithstanding. In fact as well as in fiction, then, the Spanish laws of honor provided the motive for the departure, in 1531, of Teresa Sánchez de Cepeda y Ahumada to the Augustinian convent Nuestra Señora de la Gracia as a *doncella de piso*, a boarder to be educated.

Mujica's novelistic discourse, bolstered by vibrant dialogue and action-packed scenes, is not only infused with the stuff of (Golden Age Spanish) drama, but it also reflects and refracts other socio-cultural norms of the period. It evokes, for example, the misogynist voice of Juan Luis Vives in his conduct manual, *De institutione feminae Christinanae* (1523/1538), when Angélica brings forth the following introjection from childhood: "Women were weak...and that's what made them easy prey for Satan" (Mujica, *Sister Teresa*, 25). Vives's censure is also felt through Angélica's recollection of her mother's criticism of Teresa's supposed use of cosmetics and lavender water (*Sister Teresa* 33). Significant, too, in conjuring up the terror of the times is Angélica's detailed recreation of the verified background story of Teresa's father, Alonso de Cepeda Sánchez. After having been forced as a child to put on a *sambenitillo* (or knee-length yellow cloak decorated with black crosses), parade by every church in Toledo, and be stoned in support of the Catholic Church, this *converso* merchant not only purchased a patent of nobility to prove his Old Christian ancestry and lack of "tainted blood," but he also cleansed his lineage by taking two wives who were Old Christians (*Sister Teresa* 27–28).

Though Lodge finds the question, "when does a novel begin?" difficult to answer, he deems no less problematic the question, "when does the *beginning* of a novel end?" (4, emphasis added). The beginning of Mujica's novel, with its socio-cultural and historical exposition and its creative and subjective adjustments, purportedly ends at the close of the so-called first chapter, as Teresa's carriage rolls toward the convent on the outskirts of Ávila and Angélica associates the fragrance of October roses with her friend, mentor, and spiritual guide. We, as readers, have crossed the threshold and been drawn in.

Subjectivity Unveiled: Angélica's Voice

The Spanish virtue of *arrogancia* or "pride, character, sense of self" (Mujica, *Sister Teresa*, 39) shone in Angélica's vision of Teresa as a young woman who caused endless "fatalities" (*Sister Teresa* 23), and it is no less apparent in her own character as she evokes her friend's calling to love and serve the Lord and remarks on the social position of women in sixteenth-century Spain. While Teresa spent her days studying and attending to her religious duties, eschewing thoughts of marriage because she purportedly feared the possibility of dying in childbirth—her mother had died giving birth to her sister Juana (*Sister Teresa* 45)—Angélica passed the time dreaming of marriage, even fantasizing above her station about her unrequited cousin/suitor, Don Javier. The idea of marriage became a reality, however, once the narrator left the convent with Teresa and was hit on the head (figuratively and literally) with the constraints of an angry mother's will. At nearly fourteen, Angélica was to be married to one Basilio, a young apprentice cartwright whom her aunt had chosen for her, given that Teresa's father, a man with "*converso* blood"—who had turned suddenly "kind" in her mother's eyes—had provided the dowry (*Sister Teresa* 63). Angélica learned quickly, after her mother's "underhanded" if not hypocritical acceptance of Don Alonso's dowry money, that a woman of humble lineage who could cook, sew, spin, and, above all, read "immoral and dangerous" romance tales of "caballeros and their women humping by the river" (*Sister Teresa* 75) would not necessarily be considered "valuable merchandise" (*Sister Teresa* 69) in matrimony. (The educated and self-assured Teresa had seen to it that, during their stay in the Augustinian convent, her companion had learned to read.) "Today a fit young man doesn't have to settle for a book-reading whore for a wife," Angélica recalls Basilio's father bellowing (*Sister Teresa* 75). That this prototypic misogynist was hypocritically aware of the content of the "dirty books" (*Sister Teresa* 75) he claimed to scorn conjures up, for this reader/critic, the way in which those who burn Don Quijote's books of chivalry have read (and enjoyed) what they profess to censure (Chapter 6).

A woman who did not marry had little choice but to enter a convent. Because she always got her way, Teresa arranged for Angélica to stay with her as a boarder in the Carmelite convent of Encarnación, where she had just taken her vows. The wedding ceremony and profession are well-documented by the narrator (Mujica, *Sister Teresa*, 64–70), not just from the viewpoint of verified details (including the girdle as a sign of chastity; the discarding of hair out of love for the Lord Jesus Christ; the donning of a white veil as a symbol of widowhood, and then a black veil as a sign of contempt for the world; not to mention the ensuing ritual feast of lamb stew and kid, *olla podrida*, and *comida blanca*). Don Alonso's human reaction, not simply as a *converso* but finally as a man of Jewish blood, is also envisioned: he looked as though he were "witnessing his own daughter's crucifixion" (*Sister Teresa* 66), notes Angélica, who was beginning to sense the cross borne by Spaniards of Jewish ancestry in the aftermath of forced conversions, expulsion, and accusations of heresy. Later, she would come face to face with "contaminated" Spanish Judaizers who either practiced "heretical rites," or guarded "heirlooms" from their families' Jewish past (*Sister Teresa* 108). She discovered, hidden in a linen chest in the house of Teresa's older half-sister María de Cepeda de Guzmán, a spice holder with strange letters and a platter with a "six-pointed star" in the center and symbolic inscriptions on the back, "squared-off characters with little foot-like tips" (*Sister Teresa* 107), which she would subsequently learn when Inquisitors produced such an object was for the commemoration of the Exodus. She knew that, if anyone found out about such secret objects, they would all be subject to investigation by the Inquisition.

Angélica's reasons for taking the habit as a black-veiled nun (as opposed to a tertiary, lower order, white-veiled nun) in the convent of Encarnación, following the death of her mother and aunt, stand in sharp contrast to what had motivated Teresa to profess. Serving Jesus never entered her mind, she confesses (Mujica, *Sister Teresa*, 85). Rather, she loved the convent because it gave her the chance to study, to read books about the history of her order, though not forbidden books of chivalry like her revered *Amadís de Gaula*. She liked socializing with priests, gentleman, musicians, and even courtesans in the convent parlor, and gossiping with friends and admirers from behind the grille, not to mention naughtily fanning the flames of true love in "uniting Amadís with Oriana" (*Sister Teresa* 92). That is, she played the go-between for a (fictional) novice, Rosa, who considered herself "married" to her admirer because they had exchanged vows; that incident had occurred, the narrator carefully observes, before the Council of Trent forced a couple to marry by making their vows in public (*Sister Teresa* 89). Nevertheless, the arrangement ended in disaster, Angélica reports, because Rosa's escape from the convent became a public scandal; her father considered himself dishonored and therefore drew his sword and murdered his daughter (*Sister Teresa* 119), as though he were a Calderonian character (re)acting in an honor drama. The horrific predictions Angélica had heard while sewing in her aunt's *estrado* rang tragically true. The convent, in sum, was a social organization unto itself, consisting of nuns, boarders, servants, orphans, and lay sisters who lived there without professing. That it was far from being a monolithic world was manifested in the recorded reaction of the (fictional) nurse and pharmacist at Encarnación to Teresa's fasting and flagellating herself, mortifications recommended by her confessor that were ruining her already fragile health. "I'll mortify him, that bastard" (*Sister Teresa* 93), said Sister Josefa, who eventually became prioress.

Convent Life Humanized: Rapture, Rape, and Revelation

"I think it best to search for God in our hearts, for it is written: 'I found much wisdom in myself, and I profited from it'" (Mujica, *Sister Teresa,* 103). Thus read a skeptical Angélica from *The Third Spiritual Alphabet* by Francisco Osuna, a book bequeathed to Teresa by her uncle, Pedro de Cepeda, which changed her idea of prayer. Teresa provided Angélica with a close exegesis that would guide her own spiritual path. Osuna believed in a simpler form of Christianity in which one sought God within oneself, within one's own soul. He espoused mental prayer, which required absolute awareness and attention; later, one learned to transcend words and images by clearing the mind completely and losing the self in darkness. Then, if God willed it, in that quintessential darkness, one reached the light — "a state of illumination or insight in which you *know* God.... You're one with God" (*Sister Teresa* 102, 104). That was perhaps the first time, Angélica reflects, that she ever saw her "pigheaded" friend (an attribute Teresa ascribed to herself) "in ecstasy" (*Sister Teresa* 110, 104).

But to desire *"an intimate, personal relationship with God"* without the rituals of the Holy Mother Church was to be imbued with ideas from the devil (Mujica, *Sister Teresa,* 123). So Angélica was told when she confessed all too ingenuously with Father Tomé, a (fictional) visionary-fearing, Dominican interrogator. Recalling her aunt's descriptions of *autos-da-fe,* of Jews parading down the streets in *sambenitos,* the young nun began to grasp why *conversos,* even those who sincerely loved Christ, felt more comfortable praying mentally than in church with those who had mistreated them, and why they wanted a personal relationship with God (*Sister Teresa* 124). She remembers not realizing then how dangerous such unorthodox prayer practices were, how the Council of Trent — called by Paulo III to address the accusations that had led to the Lutheran uprising — could get Teresa into trouble with the Inquisitors. She evokes the work of such men, supposedly performed on behalf of the Church, with razor-sharp irony:

> They ask questions. When they don't get the answers they want, they take measures. They can be very persuasive. They have ingenious instruments, these clever men.... They have machines for squeezing the fingers till the bones splinter.... They have boiling pitch to pour down your throat and molten rods to probe between your legs.... Their imaginations are boundless. We've all heard about these machines.... It's a way of encouraging good behavior. But, course, this is for our own

good.... They're serving the cause of Christ by protecting us from the Devil. (*Sister Teresa* 149)

If, through *The Third Spiritual Alphabet*, Osuna brought Teresa into an intimate, personal relationship with God, then Mujica, by virtue of Angélica's subjective narrative retrospectively inscribed, provides a humanizing and confidential connection not only with the woman who became Saint Teresa but also with convent life. We are privy to Angélica's private thoughts once Teresa returned from her bout with illness and seeming death, from having been in Heaven and seen Hell. Experiencing her rather as a "pest" (Mujica, *Sister Teresa*, 136), the seamstress-sister criticizes her friend's "sanctimonious exhibitionism" (*Sister Teresa* 138) in crawling to chapel, (true) paralysis notwithstanding, to show her gratitude to God; and accuses her of being a "phony," constantly "flitting around pretending to be a *santa*," and a "fraud" for professing to be forgiving when she was actually furious after the disabled novice Cándida had slid down her chest until Cándida's lips touched her breast (*Sister Teresa* 142–43). (Later, the ever-understanding Sister Josefa calmly states that Cándida's subsequent love for an astonished Angélica "happens," even if it is an "aberration" [*Sister Teresa* 192]). Was Teresa speaking from the heart, or continuing her act, when she called herself a "vile creature" (*Sister Teresa* 143), incapable of praying but just going through the motions? Angélica recalls feeling "pity" (*Sister Teresa* 153) when Teresa spoke of seeing Him with her "spiritual senses" (*Sister Teresa* 147) and then the devil in the form of a huge toad (*Sister Teresa* 152)—"spurious visions" as the priests called them (*Sister Teresa* 151), suspect when articulated not only by sibyls and mystics but also by *conversos*, who at times faked ecstasies to prove their authenticity as Catholics.

As Teresa struggled with her divine passion in the form of visions and locutions, Angélica admits to having been a victim of her own passion, more "evil" than godly (Mujica, *Sister Teresa*, 171). This began when she queried of her (fictional) Carmelite confessor, Father Braulio, as to whether mental prayer was a sin, all while the priest smiled warmly, caressed her hand, spoke of the purity of her heart, and brushed his hard sex against her shoulder (*Sister Teresa* 162). With the hindsight of a woman in her fifties, Angélica censures the ongoing depravity within the Church (for example, priests with a number of mistresses and bastard children [*Sister Teresa* 163]), and also reveals how she, as a lonely and longing pious woman of twenty-two who had entered the convent because she had nowhere else to go, fell into the trap of such hypocritical posturing. For almost eight years, she met Braulio for "confession" twice a week: an extended period of sinning, fornication, and lies. Angélica's epiphany, her understanding that whatever she had done God would forgive provided that she repented wholeheartedly and changed her ways, coincided with Teresa's "conversion," as the narrator puts it. Finally, Teresa has experienced "the awe-inspiring presence of God's grace and self-revelation" (Mujica, *Sister Teresa*, 173), thereby freeing herself from being tortured by two (historical) individuals: Francisco de Salcedo, a cousin by marriage who eventually became a priest but, according to Angélica, was "nauseating" for his "exemplary humility" (*Sister Teresa* 167); and the theologian Father Gaspar Daza, who believed that her visions came from the devil, not because of her method of praying, but because she was a "weak, vain female," one of those "hysterical" women who thought they were in direct contact with God (*Sister Teresa* 169).

The details of Braulio's rape of Angélica, as she endeavored to end their affair, are recounted with such graphic precision and dramatic intensity — encompassing physical and verbal abuse, blackmail (against Teresa for being a Jew and praying like one), female powerlessness, nightmares, fear, rage, self-disgust — that everything seems to be happening in the historical present (in fact, the scene became a dominant, if not sensational, through line in Coco Blignaut's play adaptation of the novel for a twenty-first-century audience). No less potent is Sister Josefa's merciful and human understanding of Angélica's confession of carnality, however sinful it was to "confess" to a woman because only a priest could administer the sacraments. Teresa is also caring and discreet, if not pragmatic: "Confessors. They have so many ways to hurt you" (Mujica, *Sister Teresa*, 183), she declares. These two sisters show sympathetic awareness and tolerance, while a Jesuit priest recommends mortifications in order for the victim to regain her capacity for concentration (*Sister Teresa* 190). The "warrior" Sister Josefa in fact engineers Braulio's forced departure to the North where Catholics are being killed. By intertwining the narratives of Angélica and Teresa and deviating from chronological order, moving rapidly back and forth over the course of the action, Mujica offers an earthy if human picture of the sisterhood as scrutinized from within. She also exposes for commentary an abusive, early modern circumstance that, regrettably, is not all that unfamiliar in (post)modern society.

Ecstasy Secularized: Warrior Women to Work

Teresa "had slumped down on the ground and was gently writhing as though ... she were making love to an invisible lover to whom she had completed surrendered .... Her face was turned upward, her trembling lips slightly parted as if awaiting a kiss .... She was panting heavily now, as if trying to catch her breath. Finally her body went limp, and she was silent" (Mujica, *Sister Teresa*, 200). Angélica's highly sensual and non-spiritual reaction to how Teresa had "yielded" to whatever she had seen—angel or devil—is hardly out of character, given that she herself knew all about surrendering to sensual desire. Whether the nun's convulsions meant that she was having a seizure or hallucination, dreaming, going into a trance, or levitating mattered little; such instances of "esoteric beliefs," "mystical outbreaks," or "ecstasies" (*Sister Teresa* 201), in the parlance of the Council of Trent, were suspect in that they might be the work of the devil. That they could attract notice of the authorities and endanger the life of the convent was what the detractors amongst her sisters cared about. Angélica evokes her own skeptical stance of 1558: "What was she? God's creature? An angel? A fraud? or just a befuddled woman?" (*Sister Teresa* 209). For Teresa, her visions were pure "non-sense" (*Sister Teresa* 213), something beyond one's ability to make sense of, understand, or control.

Angélica cites from Teresa's memoir, of which she (fortuitously) had made a copy, to provide a firsthand account of the painful experience of the nun's having seen an angel that plunged a dart repeatedly into her heart, reaching deep within her; when he withdrew it, he "left [her] all on fire with great love of God" (Mujica, *Sister Teresa*, 218). Angélica's down-to-earth commentary—"All I see are baskets of cloth to be cut into albs.... Or containers of charcoal to be ground into powder for diarrhea" (*Sister Teresa* 219)—wryly secularizes Teresa's otherworldly visions, revealing the chasm between the two sisters' experiences, ethereal on the one hand, and material on the other. Angélica remembers regarding Teresa first as a "madwoman" and only secondly as a "saint" (*Sister Teresa* 223), and herself as the woman behind the woman in the mad enterprise of founding a convent in Ávila, where women could live in silence and poverty and devote themselves to God, and where nuns would be discalced Carmelites, barefoot as an indication of their disconnection from material comforts.

Underlying Teresa's initiative to create a "real community of women" (Mujica, *Sister Teresa*, 227) was a warrior attitude, a woman's adherence to her God-given right to make her own decisions and to define her own identity. Clearly, she was a woman who battled the status quo, defended causes, challenged authority, and broke barriers. If men could be priests and soldiers, women could be active too, by which she meant that they should display those characteristics often associated with men: perseverance, clear-sightedness, determination, and valor. The "dynamic beehive" that she intended to create, where sisters could pray and learn, would be her way of combating not only the apathy and futile ritualism besetting the faith but also the skepticism advanced by the Lutherans: "*Her nuns would be fighters.* She didn't see prayer as passivity, but as a form of assertiveness. She would save the heretics by praying for them. Her brothers were battling pagans in the New World, and she would battle the church's foes in the old. Men could be priests and soldiers, but women could be active, too" (*Sister Teresa* 227, emphasis added).

In becoming Teresa's right-hand woman in establishing convents and reforming the Carmelite order, Angélica displayed the warrior spirit that the virtue of *arrogancia* (Mujica, *Sister Teresa,* 39) implies, proudly asserting: "She couldn't have done it without me. My name may not go down in history, but Teresa de Ahumada would never had succeeded if it hadn't been for me" (*Sister Teresa* 234). Mujica, in playing with Angélica's subjectivity and rearranging the chain of temporality, may be reminding us that, as Lodge posits, the point of using an unreliable narrator who is part of the story is "to reveal in an interesting way the gap between appearance and reality, and to show how human beings distort or conceal the latter" (155). That, in this biographical novel, form and content mirror one another is brought home when we read comments like this one: "Everyone in Ávila from the count to the cobbler's apprentice had an opinion on Teresa's project" (*Sister Teresa* 241). To get the "facts" straight, as Angélica implies, is no less a daunting task in a *testimonio personal* than it is in an "historical" account.

The rest of the narration, in taking us on Teresa's politically astute and historically verifiable warrior path, underscores *en passant* the *human* qualities that enabled the Carmelite entrepreneur to succeed, monetary and ministerial hurdles notwithstanding. The story is not, as the narrator quips with reference to her own illicit reading addiction, a chivalric romance, where the hero "slays the dragon and everything just falls into place" (Mujica, *Sister Teresa,* 254). To the rebuke that she could not just go from one priest to another until she heard what she wanted to hear, but had to obey God through her superiors, Teresa counters: "I will ... when I find a superior who understands what God wants me to do" (*Sister Teresa* 240). That is her clever strategy: if one priest does not stand by her, then she turns to another who will; she can simultaneously follow and break the rules. She takes the same attitude when, upon setting the rules for her first cloistered convent, she insists that, if obedience is the most sacred of their vows, then rules do not exist for their own sake: "What's the point of being a slave to rules if your rigor makes you cruel, rather than sensitive to the needs of your sisters?" (*Sister Teresa* 270). She would even say that the "spirit" of the rule counted more than the rule itself: after prohibiting kissing amongst sisters, she kisses Angélica on the cheek, reasoning that between "real sisters" it is all right (*Sister Teresa* 277).

Angélica bases her own—earthbound—view of sainthood on that kind of mindset: being a saint is not just about being good but also about being shrewd, about getting things done. She gets what she wants because, like a seasoned actor or politician, she adapts her style to her audience. She knows, for example, how to maneuver God's will to accord with material deficits. To the challenge posed by the charitable if enraged widow, Doña Guiomar de Ulloa, that God should provide the money for a project if that is His will, Teresa responds (with excruciating calm) that He has, and that the money is in her mother's purse (Mujica, *Sister Teresa*, 255–56). That is why, Angélica notes with characteristic irony, one sister was "the leader of the reform," and the other was just "the leader of the sewing brigade" (*Sister Teresa* 250). The tinny-sounding bell of the Carmel of San José de Ávila added its "clink-clink" (*Sister Teresa* 257) to those of all the churches and convents that clanged in unison on August 14, 1562. Surrogate author/translator Mujica, though her pseudo-narrator Angélica, is true to the marked polarities and complexities of Teresa's warrior character.

Onward, Carmelite General

As Teresa embarked on the founding of discalced convents from Toledo to Burgos via Seville, she came into contact with an assemblage of people, including: Isabel de Santo Domingo, Ana Mendoza de la Cerda (Princess of Éboli), María de Salazar (María de San José), Juan de la Cruz, Jerónimo Gracian (Fray Jerónimo de la Madre de Dios), Ana de San Bartolomé, Juan Bautista Rubeo, Felipe Sega, and Jerónimo Tostado. Though, in the novel, these encounters are filtered through the unreliable narrative voice of Angélica, the information provided is historically verifiable. No less accurate are the novel's myriad descriptions of daily life in early modern Spain, from "farthingales to chamber pots, from marriage rituals to eating customs" (Mujica, *Sister Teresa*, 372). Since, finally, *Sister Teresa* is a work of biographical fiction, we shall allow history and habit to remain in the background and focus selectively on the ways in which Angélica's personal commentary may clash with the factual data she records about the reform, at times calling into question received viewpoints.

If Teresa's detractors thought that she was moving around Spain "like a gypsy," a "restless vagabond" (Mujica, *Sister Teresa*, 281), even assuming the role of a priest in offering spiritual direction to men and women, then Angélica shared some of their irritation. Teresa was a "hypocrite" (*Sister Teresa* 277): though she had given the nuns a cloister where they could retreat from the world and get close to God, she herself went off "playing politics, raising money, and cozying up to the powerful" (*Sister Teresa* 281), not to mention displaying sinful gluttony in houses of nobility ("Oh, Lord, when there's food in front of me, I just can't leave it alone" [*Sister Teresa* 288], the foundress confessed). By 1569, Teresa had become a "larger-than-life holy woman, a great mystic and reformer" (*Sister Teresa* 303). Being Teresa's friend, Angélica thinks with characteristic *arrogancia*, made her important too (so important, in fact, that she had her fingers almost broken when interrogated by the Seville Inquisition, while Teresa was treated gently). Despite her high standing, Teresa had to quash growing rivalries and hostilities within the order, which the narrator perceives with her keen seamstress's eye that allows her to notice not just where embroidery and sewing thread belong in a well-ordered workroom (*Sister Teresa* 296), but also the subtle details of human relationships.

Teresa was immediately taken with the enticing sermons and relaxed spiritual guidance of Jerónimo Gracián, whom she met in Beas in 1575, so much so that she made a vow of obedience to him in spiritual (but not administrative) matters. Angélica disliked the friar from the first; she saw him as a young "operator," "glib and smart and seductive" (Mujica, *Sister Teresa*, 313–14). María de San José, of whom Teresa had begun to speak as a possible heir to her title of foundress, also fell under Gracián's spell. When he arrived at the Seville convent that he had hounded Teresa to found against regulations, as patents had only been issued for carrying out her reform in Castile, Angélica records that the two women faced him like the infants offered up to Solomon by their mothers: one would live and one would die. After gazing from one to the other, he greeted Teresa as "Mother!" and María de San José bowed her head in a sign of submission: "Teresa raised chin her almost imperceptibly, and a look crossed her face . . . the look of haughty defiance. She had won" (*Sister Teresa* 320). Though she was the foundress, she needed Gracián, not only to help with the male branch of the order, but also because he made her feel like a "heroine" with his veneration and deference. María could not be allowed to threaten her position. Thus spake Angélica of the power struggle between the "general in God's army" and an "aide-de-camp" (*Sister Teresa* 320).

Gracián's poor judgment caused Teresa (and Angélica) to be hauled before the Seville Inquisition, reported by a new postulant whom the friar had supported. Angélica's account of the methods of torture jibes with Inquisition documents (especially with respect to "heretic" *conversos* who were interrogated, tortured, and burned), and it also contains a gripping element of surprise, which was both convincing and unexpected. The (fictional) Javier Sánchez de Colón, Teresa's unrequited, *converso* cousin, was ordained as a

Dominican priest soon after she had taken her vows. Earlier Angélica had noted, almost in passing, that Melchor Cano, the (historical) priest with whom Javier had studied, was among the most radical, conservative, and anti-Jewish theologians, and that the Dominicans were at the helm of the Inquisition (Mujica, *Sister Teresa*, 96). Later, while she was being interrogated by the Seville Inquisition, the narrator recognized the identity of the secretary—the brutal Javier turned Inquisitor of Valladolid—and imagined that he had come to exact reprisals for Teresa's having rejected him some forty years before. After her ordeal, Angélica found Teresa talking with Javier as if nothing were happening in the Inquisitorial chambers close by. Javier had intervened on his cousin's behalf, protecting her first in Valladolid by enabling her memoir, *Life*, to be absolved quickly by the Inquisition (*Sister Teresa* 313), and then in Seville. Had he turned "traitor" toward his own people (*Sister Teresa* 96), as Angélica had surmised, or had he perhaps become a priest and an Inquisitor to save his people, as the outcome seemed to imply? In her fashioning of Javier, then, Mujica provides a narrative twist that is not necessarily predictable since, in her subjective analysis, Angélica is slow to connect all the threads. Enough information is supplied to make the revelation convincing when it comes, but not so much that it is easily anticipated.

After the Seville interrogation, something inside Teresa broke; that was, the narrator recalls knowing instinctively, the "beginning of the end" (Mujica, *Sister Teresa*, 333). The foundress simply shut her eyes and seemed not to hear Angélica's scolding for placing so much faith in Gracián and carrying the reform to Seville, thereby riling the calced friars (*Sister Teresa* 334). Nevertheless, even after being betrayed by him (he had exhibited a letter in which the foundress's secret plans to put San José de Ávila under his authority were revealed), Teresa wrote letters on his behalf to King Felipe II and to María de San José in Seville. Gracián's discalced brothers had betrayed him, and his life was in danger. Angélica's imputation to keep Teresa from asking María to risk her life to shield him—"Are you mad? Jerónimo has ruined everything" (*Sister Teresa* 341)—fell on deaf ears. For the narrator, the answer was clear: Teresa's life's work seemed to be falling apart, and he was her "beloved" Gracián.

Ending

In the same way that Teresa was winding down physically, if not spiritually, so Mujica was winding down her novel, though not without providing unexpected but plausible and convincing twists and turns. If Teresa still had the fortitude of a soldier, then the continual warring between the calced and the discalced, the political maneuvering, and the devious ways of certain prelates were enervating her. She used the fall in which she broke her arm to offer up pain for the safety of Juan de la Cruz, whom she had recruited for the discalced Carmelites, but who had been seized and imprisoned by calced friars—as Angélica put it, "Just like her, ... trying to turn bitter herbs into relish" (Mujica, *Sister Teresa*, 345). Eventually, her *frailcito* [little friar] escaped his tormentors, not just by fleeing from prison, but also by composing in his head a poem, "En una noche oscura" [One dark night], which was eventually written down. By reproducing it in its entirety, Angélica gives an extra-textual sense of validity to her account. And finally, the papal nuncio gave the discalced their independence: Felipe II formally approved the separation of the Carmelites into two orders. They could write "discalced" with a capital D, follow their own rules, and pray in their own way (*Sister Teresa* 351). Teresa marked the polarity of the situation in her inimitable way: because they had gone into Seville illegally, causing the calced to attack the reform, they were granted independence, but not without her having dispatched countless letters behind the scenes and fought against many insuperable forces.

Though Teresa was a larger-than-life holy woman, the great mystic and reformer, she was old: her mouth was "opening and closing like a fish's" (Mujica, *Sister Teresa*, 354), Angélica notes. Nevertheless, she still adhered to her—questionable—apparitions: after summoning Juan de la Cruz to accompany her to Granada to take the reform there, she reneged, for God had told that her next foundation would be in Burgos. Angélica's reading of the turnabout was racked by doubt. Most learned men did not believe in apparitions and locutions experienced by women, and even Juan, a profoundly spiritual friar, must have had qualms (*Sister Teresa* 356). Teresa was tenacious until the end: "Who [sic] should I listen to, you or God?" she snapped to Angélica, as she pushed on to Burgos (*Sister Teresa* 356). Then she went to Alba de Tormes to make peace, not just with feuding sisters, but also with herself and God. Her journey came to an end on October 4, 1582. Angélica lyrically marks the moment by citing the foundress's poem, "Vivo sin vivir en mí" [I live without really living]. She will remember Teresa as "a woman of dazzling beauty, a woman in a brown habit and a black veil dancing, twirling, leaping joyously in the air while she bangs a tambourine and sings (slightly off key), 'Caminemos para el cielo / monjas del Carmelo'" (*Sister Teresa* 365).

Lodge posits distinguishing between "the end of a novel's story—the resolution or the deliberate non-resolution of the narrative questions it has raised in the minds of its readers—and the last page or two of the text, which often act as a kind of epilogue or postscript, a gentle deceleration of the discourse as it draws to a halt" (224). Mujica's sense of an ending is infused, on the one hand, with the poetry of Juan de la Cruz and Teresa de Jesús, and with authentic letters penned by the latter; and, on the other hand, with a climactic if fictitious missive to Angélica from the absent Braulio, and with an Epilogue.

Exiled to the North, Braulio had sent a letter detailing how the Duke of Alba had established the Inquisition in the Low Countries, which was being presided over by Javier Sánchez Colón (another way in which the reappearance of Teresa's cousin at the Seville Inquisition is anticipated) (Mujica, *Sister Teresa*, 282–85). In a second letter, Braulio told of how he had made his way to Germany, renounced the Roman Church, and become a Lutheran because, he reasoned, "*Luther understood what I've long known: that the desire of man for woman is so strong that it cannot be denied*" (*Sister Teresa* 342). Through Braulio's decision to follow Luther, take a wife, and anticipate naming a daughter Pancracia after Angélica—avowing that God would punish those who embrace a purer faith, and lamenting that Angélica was still in the clutches of the reformists—Mujica virtually kills off the rapist-priest by exposing his hypocrisy in violating religion as he had violated women. Angélica's wry response about it says it all: "He's as good as dead. He's a Lutheran" (*Sister Teresa* 343). Loose ends are therefore linked up, and sixteenth-century behavior is shown to be not all that unrelated to twenty-first-century concerns.

Angélica's Epilogue provides a final effect of *peripeteia* or reversal. She had preserved her testimony twenty years earlier by sewing it into her bedding and thus burying it in straw, but at the age of eighty-six, she writes that she has been informed that the Inquisitors are coming for her. On October 30, 1606, she queries what to do with those incriminating pages, insofar as they are not just a death sentence for her but also potentially harmful for Teresa in terms of her beatification procedures. One would have to know what in the pages could be told, and what had to be concealed. Whether Angélica buried them in the garden we do not know; fortunately for her readers, they made their way to the antiquarian's shop in Dijon, near the old Carmelite convent, so that surrogate author Bárbara Mujica could find them, translate them for a twenty-first-century reading public, and reveal how a novel is patently a *Gestalt:* "a perpetual pattern or structure possessing qualities as a whole that cannot be described merely as a sum of its parts" (Lodge 230).

References

Banks, Russell. "The Truth Contract in the Biographical Novel." In *Biographical Fiction: A Reader*, edited by Michael Lackey, 203–16, Bloomsbury Press, 2017. Originally published in Michael Lackey, ed., *Truthful Fictions: Conversations with American Biographical Novelists.* Bloomsbury Press, 2014, 43–56.

Hutcheon, Linda. "Historiographic Metafiction Parody and the Intertextuality of History." In *Intertextuality and Contemporary American Fiction,* edited by Patrick O'Donnell and Robert Con Davis, Johns Hopkins University Press, 1989, 3–32.

Kehlmann, Daniel. "Out of This World." *Guardian,* April 21, 2007, www.theguardian.com/books/2007/apr/21/featuresreviews.guardianreview30.

Lackey, Michael. "Locating and Defining the Bio in Biofiction." *a/b: Auto/Biography Studies* 31 (2016), no. 1: 3–10.

———. "The Rise of the Biographical Novel and the Fall of the Historical Novel." *a/b: Auto/Biography Studies* 31 (2016), no. 1: 33–58.

Lackey, Michael, Jay Parini, Bruce Duffy, and Lance Olsen. "The Uses of History in the Biographical Novel." In *Biographical Fiction: A Reader,* edited by Michael Lackey, Bloomsbury Press, 2017, 167–85. Also published in Michael Lackey, ed., *Conversations with Jay Parini.* University Press of Mississippi, 2014, 125–48.

Lodge, David. 2011. *The Art of Fiction.* Vintage, 1992.

Mujica, Bárbara. "Going for the Subjective: One Way to Write Biographical Fiction." In *Biographical Fiction: A Reader,* edited by Michael Lackey, Bloomsbury Press, 2017, 88–97. Originally published in *a/b: Auto/Biography Studies* 31, no. 1 (2015): 11–20.

———. *Sister Teresa: The Woman Who Became Saint Teresa of Ávila.* Overlook, 2007. Spanish edition, *Hermana Teresa.* Santiago, Chile: Cuarto Propio, 2018.

———. *Teresa of Ávila: Lettered Woman.* Vanderbilt University Press, 2009.

Parini, Jay. "Fact or Fiction: Writing Biographies Versus Writing Novels." In *Biographical Fiction: A Reader,* edited by Michael Lackey, Bloomsbury Press, 2017, 299–312. Originally published in Jay Parini, *Some Necessary Angels: Essays on Writing and Politics.* Columbia University Press, 1997, 241–56.

Teresa de Jesus (de Ávila). *Libro de la Vida.* Edited by Damaso Chicharro, Madrid: Cátedra, 1993.

ALISON WEBER

Revisionism, Prolepsis, and Anachronism
Two Contemporary Spanish Novels about Teresa of Ávila

BETWEEN 2011 AND 2015, five novels about Teresa of Ávila were published in Spanish. This should come as no surprise, since 2015 was the five-hundredth anniversary of the birth of the Carmelite saint. Undoubtedly, publishers counted on exhibitions, conferences, and media coverage to supply an audience of readers eager to learn more about a sixteenth-century mystic and reformer.[1] But why would these readers choose to satisfy their curiosity by reading novels rather than (or in addition to) histories or biographies about Teresa? What are the particular satisfactions that historical fiction offers readers? And how do writers of historical fiction attempt to satisfy the seemingly contradictory expectations for historical accuracy and novelistic invention?

We might start with an astute observation by Stephen Greenblatt, who in a review of Hilary Mantel's prize-winning historical novel *Wolf Hall* wrote, "[The historical novel] offers the dream of full access, access to what went on behind closed doors, off the record, in private, when no one was listening or recording" (Greenblatt n.p.).[2] The two novels considered in this essay indeed offer the pleasures of revealing what went on "behind closed doors." They also might be called revisionist historical fiction: their narratives not only fill in the gaps of the historical record but also challenge received history. They draw us in, saying, in effect, "This is what official history *failed* to see."

Teresa of Ávila is in many ways ideally suited for this kind of revisionist history. Even before her canonization in 1622, she was a controversial figure, hailed by some as a living saint and disparaged by others as a presumptuous gadabout. Since her elevation to the altars, her reputation has been deployed for a wide range of ideological purposes (see Rowe; Alabrús and García Cárcel). For the intellectuals of the Generation of '98, she was the embodiment of *casticismo* [national purity], while in Francoist Spain, she was celebrated as the "santa de la raza" [the saint of the Spanish race] and declared the patron saint of the Falangist party's Sección Femenina [Female Section] (see Di Febo; Casero). The myth of Teresa as "la santa de la raza" has been the target of demystification for several decades now, beginning with the discovery of her Jewish lineage in 1947, followed by essays by Francisco Márquez Villanueva, Américo Castro, and others, who explored the possible influences of her outsider status as the descendant of Spanish Jews.[3] Fictional revisionism can be said to have begun in the last quarter of the twentieth century, when a generation of writers brought up on pious biographies of the Carmelite saint began to reimagine a different kind of heroine—one who was less pious, more feminist, and more heroically embattled than the emblem of Francoist femininity.[4] The re-figuring of Teresa continues today and perhaps reflects the larger movement of revisionism related to the Civil War and Franco's dictatorship, officially recognized and promoted by the Ley de Memoria Histórica [Historical Memory Act] of 2007.

This essay explores several revisionist tropes in two recent novels about the Carmelite founder: *Malas palabras* [Swear Words] by Cristina Morales and *Un corazón tan recio* [A Strong Heart] by Alicia Dujovne Ortiz. Like the late-twentieth-century Teresian narratives, but to a greater extent, these novels puncture hagiographic stereotypes, revealing Teresa to be heir to all the human foibles—erotic passions, pride, jealousy, envy, and doubt. I call this the "flawed saint" trope. The second trope, which sometimes undermines the first, refers to the way that Teresa is portrayed as a modern woman with enlightened attitudes toward gender, race, class, and institutional authority. Inculpation/exculpation alludes to an inversion or modification of customary moral judgments regarding figures close to Teresa such as her family, patrons, confessors, and monastic daughters. Finally, the novels develop a "secret trauma" trope; that is, they attempt to trace Teresa's mystical experiences to traumatic experiences from her childhood or adolescence. In the course of examining these tropes, I will point out occasional anachronisms, although I am fully aware that, if fiction in general requires the willing suspension of disbelief, then the historical novel presumes a particular relaxation of historical meticulousness. Modifying Philippe Lejeune's notion of an autobiographical pact, we might posit a historical novel pact, that is, a way of reading that assumes an implicit contract between authors and readers, in which the authors commit themselves not to historical exactitude but rather to an elastic recreation of historical events and personalities, and readers agree to "go along" with this elasticity. My larger purpose in an essay dedicated to Bárbara Mujica, a Teresian scholar who is also a historical novelist, is to explore the paradoxical pleasures of this genre, one that promises the gratification of learning something that "really happened" along with the creative freedom of imagining what might have happened.

The more tightly executed of the two novels discussed here, in my opinion, is Cristina Morales's *Malas palabras*. Born in Granada in 1985, Morales is the author of a 2013 prize-winning novel, *Los combatientes* [The Combatants], and a 2008 collection of stories, *La merienda de las niñas* [The Girls' Snack].[5] In *Malas palabras*, Morales imagines an alternative version of *Libro de la vida* [The Book of Her Life]—a secret autobiography that Teresa wrote in addition to the official text she produced in 1562 at the behest of her confessor García de Toledo. In a strikingly original use of the inculpation trope, Morales portrays Toledo not as the intimate, sympathetic reader of *Libro de la Vida*. This Toledo is instead an ambitious cleric who is more interested in hitching his wagon to the rising star of a living saint than in helping Teresa achieve her desires to found a reformed convent: "Maldita la fama, padre, y maldita la hora en que vuestra paternidad vio en mí una atracción de la eclesiástica feria" (Morales 140) [Cursed be my fame, father, and cursed be the hour in which your grace saw in me an attraction in the church fair]. Teresa knows that Toledo's command to describe her divine favors—visions, locutions, and ecstasies—is an invitation that comes with strings attached: she must write to please learned men and Inquisitors, confessing her vainglorious and wretched youth and assuring her readers that she is not a rebellious religious reformer but an obedient daughter of the Church. This she understands, but at the same time, she declares that she will write another story, a secret autobiography she has no intention of sharing with Toledo, "porque una se cansa de que no la entiendan, una se cansa de que quieran quemarla" (Morales 14) [because you get tired of not being understood; you get tired of knowing they want to burn you].

Morales's next revisionist target is Teresa's father, Alonso de Cepeda. Readers of Teresa's *Libro de la vida* (published in *Obras completas*; composed 1562–1565) will remember her description of her father as a loving, pious, chaste, and charitable *hidalgo*: "Era mi padre hombre de mucha caridad con los pobres y piedad con los enfermos, y aun con los criados; tanta, que jamás se pudo acabar con él tuviese esclavos.... Era de gran verdad. Jamás nadie le vio jurar ni murmurar. Muy honesto en gran manera" (*Obras completas* 9–10) [My father was a man very charitable with the poor and compassionate toward the sick, and even toward servants. So great was his compassion that nobody was ever able to convince him to accept slaves.... He was very honest. No one ever saw him swear or engage in fault-finding. He was an upright man (1:54)].[6] Morales shatters this benevolent portrait. In *Malas palabras*, Don Alonso is a benighted hypocrite who forces his wife to engage in sexual relations even when she is ill: "A mi madre la mató mi padre, poco a poco y sin darse cuenta, igual que infecta la cantera de mercurio los pulmones de los condenados. Desde los catorce años que tenía cuando se casó, noche tras noche, cada vez que mi padre la cubría en el lecho, le quitaba un poco de vida" (17) [My father killed my mother, little by little, without realizing it, just as the mercury quarry infects the lungs of the condemned prisoners. From the time she married at the age of fourteen, night after night, every time my father got on top of her, he took from her a little bit of her life]. Morales replaces the bookish *hidalgo* with an insecure *converso* who reprimands his wife for teaching their daughter to read.

Morales's disturbing portrait of Alonso is crucial to her deployment of the proleptic feminism trope: this fictional Teresa is a ferocious censor of men's sexual predation, and Alonso is the principal vector of this criticism. Why, she asks, did her father have sexual relations with her mother while she was still convalescing from the difficult birth of her ninth child? "Yo os lo diré: someterla es lo que quiere. Recordarle hasta el último momento que ella es suya, es suya en la salud y en la enfermedad, es suya su hacienda y son suyos sus hijos" (95) [I will tell you why. What he wants to do is subject her. To remind her until the last moment that she is his, she is his in health and sickness; her wealth is his; her children are his]. Teresa's mother, Beatriz de Ahumada, a shadowy figure in *Libro de la vida*, remembered for her modest dress and penchant for reading books of chivalry behind her husband's back, is conversely the object of an exculpation trope. She, not Alonso, is the book-lover who encourages her daughter to read, but she has made a bad bargain in marrying an insecure, honor obsessed *converso*: "Lista Beatriz, que supiste hacer valer tu sangre limpia ante el judío para que te dejara libros y habitación propia. Pobre Beatriz que con sangre tan limpia dejaste sábanas tan sucias" (95) [Clever Beatriz. You knew how to take advantage of your clean blood so that the Jew would let you have books and a room of your own. Poor Beatriz. With your clean blood you left such dirty sheets].

Yet another target of inculpation is Doña Luisa de la Cerda, Teresa's powerful benefactor and the patron of the second convent Teresa founded.

Morales's Doña Luisa is so insufferably vain and blind to the injustices of patriarchy that she provokes Teresa's outrage: "[Q]ue es así como quieren [los hombres] vernos: aderezadas para servirles de aderezo, es decir, para darles gusto, darles hijos, darles hacienda y darles linaje, que es lo único para lo que nos estiman" (31) [This is how men want to see us: adorned to be their adornments, that is, to give them pleasure, give them children, give them wealth and lineage, which is the only reason why they value us]. Yet Teresa also comes to feel compassion for Doña Luisa, whom she follows as the noblewoman steals away at night to lie in her dead husband's sarcophagus. The historical Teresa does indeed criticize aristocratic values, albeit discreetly. In chapter 34 of *Libro de la Vida*, Teresa describes the foolish tyranny of aristocratic protocol in Doña Luisa's palace; her criticism of the Princess of Éboli's erratic behavior following the death of her husband in chapter 17 of *Libro de las fundaciones* (*Obras completas*; composed 1574–1576) is a masterpiece of understatement. Also in chapter 20 of this convent chronicle, Teresa gives a horrifying account of the way some aristocrats attempted to rid themselves of their "excess" female progeny—essentially leaving them alone to starve to death. But as I have argued in another study, Teresa was grateful to her female patrons and tried to redirect their pious impulses in ways that were compatible with the ideals of her reform (Weber, "Saint Teresa's Problematic Patrons"). Morales has clearly grasped, but also amplified, the Carmelite's combination of pity and disdain for aristocratic women who have interiorized the misogyny of their class.

Teresa's ambiguous account of the scandal that led her father to send her away, at the age of sixteen, to the convent school of Santa María de Gracia in Ávila has confounded generations of historians. Alluding to the unsupervised time she shared with her cousins, Teresa writes in chapter 2 of *Libro de la vida*, "De los cuales [peligros de pecado] me libró Dios de manera que se parece bien procuraba contra mi voluntad que del todo no me perdiese, aunque no pudo ser tan secreto que no hubiese harta quiebra de mi honra y sospecha en mi padre" (*Obras completas* 16) [God saved me from occasions of sin in such a way that it seems he was striving against my will so that I would not be completely lost, although what happened could not be kept so secret that my honor and my father's wasn't endangered a lot (my translation)].[7] At the end of this chapter, she adds with tantalizing imprecision, "Una cosa tenía, que parece me podía ser alguna disculpa, si no tuviera tantas culpas; y es que era el trato con quien por vía de casamiento me parecía podía acabar en bien; e informada de con quien me confesaba y de otras personas, en muchas cosas me decían no iba contra Dios" (18) [One thing, it seems, that could have amounted to some excuse for me, should I not have had so many faults, was that the friendship with one of my cousins was in view of a possible marriage; and having inquired of my confessor and other persons about many things, I was told (regarding many things that) I was doing nothing against God (1:60–61)]. Is Teresa confessing to erotic peccadillos or to something more consequential? Historians of marriage have shown that, before the reforms of the Council of Trent were widely implemented, so-called clandestine marriages based on the exchange of words of consent (*verba de presenti*) were considered fully valid (see Sperling). It is therefore conceivable that Teresa and one of her cousins were permitted time alone together under the presumption that they would soon be married, whether by *verba de presenti* or after the publication of bans. The precise nature of the relationship that threatened Teresa's honor is something historians can never know with certainty, but this is precisely the kind of aporia that lends itself to the novelistic invention of a secret history.

In Morales's narrative, Teresa gradually reveals her enduring, though ambivalent, love for her cousin Diego de Cepeda, who was her childhood companion in games of "martyr." Teresa's memories of these games are evoked as she learns of Doña Luisa's sexual history. Orphaned at a young age, Luisa, the heir of the second duke of Medinaceli, was sent to live in the ducal palace of her cousin Doña Catalina de Mendoza. There, according to Morales's narrative, the fourteen-year-old Luisa was raped by her cousin's husband, the forty-four-year-old Diego Hurtado de Mendoza. Luisa's passive acceptance of this abuse, imagined in horrifying detail, infuriates Teresa: "Pero la doña no ha dicho fuerza, ni forzaron, ni violación. Ha dicho que don Diego 'la hubo doncella'" (Morales 130) [But Lady Luisa did not say "forced" or "coerced" or "raped." She said Don Diego had his way with her when she was a maiden]. This euphemistic language leads Teresa to reflect on the increasingly sadomasochistic games she played in her own childhood with Diego. The juxtaposition of the two seduction narratives shows Morales's skill in weaving together what went on "behind closed doors" while leaving certain doors closed. Doña Luisa de la Cerda (d. 1596) did indeed have a premarital liaison with Diego Hurtado de Mendoza, the Prince of Mélito, and from this union a daughter, Isabel, was born. Morales fills the gap in the historical record by baldly affirming Doña Luisa's lack of consent, but leaves open the question of Teresa's consent in her relationship with her cousin.[8] In this way, she subtly satisfies the reader's desire to know a secret history and recognizes the limits of recovering motives that remain hidden even to the characters themselves.

Historical studies show that the Convent of the Incarnation in Ávila where Teresa made her profession was a large convent housing approximately 180 women, where some nuns lived in comfortable suites with servants or slaves while others suffered extreme poverty. Nuns living under the mitigated Carmelite rule were not required to observe enclosure, and indeed, poverty obliged many to spend long periods with their families or patrons or receive visitors who might offer them alms. In *Libro de la vida,* Teresa confesses that these visits, although not sinful, were a distraction and an impediment to a life of mental prayer. Once again, Morales's fiction fills in the gaps: she imagines that the permissive atmosphere at the Incarnation allowed Teresa to continue her love affair with Diego de Cepeda, until she broke it off to spend time with her books.[9] But Morales is interested in more than the sexual permissiveness of the Incarnation. Her imagined convent is a dumping ground for unprofitable daughters. When Diego's daughter, María Ocampo, becomes a nun at the Incarnation, Teresa longs to tell her, "Que os metió tu padre a ti y a tu hermana porque le cuesta más manteneros en La Puebla de Montalbán . . . que en un convento. . . . Porque sois hembras y no rentáis" (Morales 152) [You should know your father put you and your sister here because it's more expensive to keep you in La Puebla de Montalbán . . . than in a convent . . . because you are females and don't turn a profit].[10] Furthermore, the Incarnation is rife with corruption; while many of its inhabitants suffer from cold and hunger, the prioress and her extended family live well from interest on the convent's loans. Morales's accusations are not implausible. Family economic strategies strongly influenced (when they did not impose) the choice of a religious vocation (Schutte). Clan rivalry was the bane of many monastic orders and many nuns continued to be deeply involved in managing family finances (Lehfeldt). Morales's sensitivity to the theme of institutional corruption is understandable as it resonates with life in early twenty-first-century Spain, when stories of politicians—on the Right and the Left—who unethically enrich themselves and their families are almost daily newspaper fare.

Morales further develops the trope of Teresa as proleptic feminist, but with a fiercely anti-clerical emphasis. In the letter that the fictional Teresa writes but will never send to García de Toledo, she protests: "[A] la vez que la Iglesia nos abraza, digo, a otras las quema por llevar una vulgata en el rebozo. . . . Antes prefieren vernos con dos dedos más de escote y percutiendo el abanico que arrebujadas en una capa y con la mirada en el cielo" (Morales 84) [At the same time the Church embraces us, it burns others for carrying a Vulgate in their shawls. . . . They would rather see us with two inches more cleavage, fluttering our fans, than wrapped in a cape with our gaze on heaven]. Although the suggestion that the Inquisition burned women for reading the Vulgate is an extravagant falsehood,[11] the frustration Morales's heroine expresses is corroborated by numerous remarks dispersed throughout the writings of the historical Teresa, in which she laments the ecclesiastical misogyny that severely limited women's ability to read Scripture, engage in religious teaching, and be of greater service to a Church in crisis.[12]

At the end of the novel, Teresa imagines a community of solidarity, equality, and freedom from ambition or materialism:

> En San José no habrá repique de campana llamando a capítulo para votar un endeudamiento, porque nunca nos endeudaremos; ni para votar quién será ropera, porque cada una se coserá su hábito; ni para votar los turnos de limpieza, pues en la tabla del barrer la priora será la primera.... En el libro de elecciones del convento de San José de Ávila podrá leerse que tal día a tal hora, siendo priora Fulana y supriora Mengana, el capítulo de hermanas decidió que al día siguiente haría sol y buen tiempo. (Morales 175)

> [In San José there will be no ringing of the bell calling us to chapter to vote on our debts, because we will never go into debt. Nor will we have to vote on who will be the wardrobe mistress, because each one will sew her own habit. Nor will we have to vote on whose turn it is to do the cleaning, because the prioress will be the first to take up the broom.... In the book of elections for the Convent of San José de Ávila one may read that on such and such a day and such an hour, when So-and-So was prioress and So-and-So was sub-prioress, the chapter of sisters decided that the following day would be sunny and fair.]

This closing vision is consonant with the kind of harmonious egalitarianism that Teresa envisioned for Discalced nuns. As she prescribed in the Constitutions for the Reform (composed circa 1567): "La tabla del barrer se comience desde la madre priora, para que en todo dé buen ejemplo.... Nunca jamás la priora ni ninguna de las hermanas pueda llamarse 'don'" (*Obras completas* 1278, 1282) [The Mother prioress should be the first on the list for sweeping so that she might give good example to all.... Never should the prioress or any of the Sisters use the title Doña (3:326, 329)]. In sum, Morales attributes Teresa's feminism to her smoldering anger over men's sexual predation, economic exploitation, and intellectual domination over women. This Teresa is not so much a Church reformer and mystic as a feminist utopian longing for a refuge from the world of men.[13]

The first-person narrator of Alicia Dujovne Ortiz's *Un corazón tan recio*

[*A Strong Heart*], like Morales's Teresa, suffers from a secret trauma: the discovery that she is the granddaughter of a *marrano*, a crypto-Jew:[14]

> Siete viernes seguidos se los pasó caminando mi abuelo Sánchez con su tropa llorosa, de una iglesia a la otra, ... rezando por lo que no deseaba rezar, trastabillando un poco pero tragándose las lágrimas mientras la gente se reía llamándolo "judío", y le arrojaba piedras, podredumbres, manchando el paño vil que lo cubría, sin advertir que una nena contemplaría el espectáculo, años después, no con los ojos del cuerpo pero mismo ardiendo de rabia. (10)

> [For seven Fridays in a row my grandfather Sánchez processed from one church to another with his weeping troop, ... praying for what he did not want to pray, stumbling a little but swallowing his tears while the people laughed, calling him "Jew", throwing stones and rotting refuse at him, staining the vile cloth that covered him, without being aware that a little girl would contemplate the spectacle, years later, not with corporeal eyes but burning with rage nonetheless.]

The pious young Teresa, realizing she is the daughter of a *converso* father and an Old Christian mother, asks, "¿He venido al mundo partida en dos, como el hilo del almíbar más dulce?" (Dujovne Ortiz 30) [Have I come into the world split in two, like the sweetest thread of sugar syrup?]. Her mixed heritage is never far from her thoughts. A childhood game of building hermitages elicits the following meditations: "Atardeceres desollados. Yo escucho, miro, doy el pasito atrás, espigo, y me lo voy guardando todo en un sótano mío donde todas las cosas—el abuelo, la honra, el martirio, la ermita, el agua, las hormigas, las hojas—van quedando" (39) [Flayed afternoons. I listen, look, take a little step backwards, I scrutinize and keep all impressions in my own cellar where all things—grandfather, honor, martyrdom, the hermitage, the water, the ants, the leaves—remain]. Cosmetics, pretty dresses, and pointed shoes are ways to quiet the dueling voices of the old Jewish servant and the Virgin of Charity: "[N]i la vieja ni la Virgen y ni siquiera los demás contertulios me encontrarán allí donde me escondo, entre jubones ajustados y faldas anchas" (44) [Not the old lady nor the Virgin nor the other guests will find me there where I hide among the tight bodices and wide skirts]. Of her first year in the Convent of the Incarnation, Teresa writes: "Como colgarme un cartel al cuello donde pueda leerse:'convento,'novicia.' Ser nieta de converso es carecer del cartel que corresponde. Ahora lo tengo" (67) [It is like hanging a sign around your neck that reads: 'convent,' 'novice.' To be the granddaughter of a *converso* is to lack a similar sign. Now I have one]. In brief, Teresa's love of nature, her adolescent flirtations, religious vocation, career as a monastic reformer, and mystical experiences are all figured as manifestations of a self divided between Jewish and Christian identities.

The flawed sanctity of Dujovne Ortiz's protagonist derives not so much from Teresa's feminist outrage—the tone that predominates in Morales's narrative—as from a pragmatism that at times bleeds into cynicism. Dujovne Ortiz's Teresa is critical of her confessors (as was the historical Teresa) but she is not contemptuous. She welcomes the command to write the story of her life: "A qué negarlo, soy escritora.... Pero esto no lo digo ni ante Pedro Ibáñez ni ante nadie, más bien me contoneo pudorosa como si me pesara cumplir, fingiendo no hacerlo sino por obediencia" (Dujovne Ortiz 149) [Why deny it? I'm a writer.... But I don't say this to Pedro Ibáñez (her confessor) or anyone; rather I wiggle shyly as if I regretted having to obey, pretending that I would not write except from obedience]. Thus, Teresa slyly admits to playing the fool and writing like a woman, misspelling words and feigning incompetence. Similarly, she finds inspiration in the stories of the "pícaros" (159) [rogues] of the Hebrew Bible (Abraham, Jacob, and Thamar) for the deceptions she engages in to establish her convents. But her pragmatism gives way to self-conscious cynicism when she accepts money from her brother Lorenzo, money she knows is stained with the blood of Indians: "Milagro turbador, ¿será que para Dios no hay oro sucio?" (167) [Disturbing miracle. Does this mean that for God there is no dirty gold?]. Teresa is her own harshest critic.

If Morales subordinates Teresa's religious sentiments to her resistance to patriarchy, then Dujovne Ortiz takes Teresa's faith seriously, hypothesizing for her protagonist a *marrano* split identity vacillating between faith and doubt. When Teresa finds a hidden copy of the *Zohar: The Book of Splendors*, she marvels at the similarity between this Jewish mystical treatise and Francisco de Osuna's *Third Spiritual Alphabet*. Then weeping, she castigates herself: "Traidora. Judas. El *Libro de los Esplendores*, guardado antes en un sótano y ahora bajo mi cama, me condena sin remedio" (Dujovne Ortiz 88) [Traitor. Judas. *The Book of Splendors*, once kept in a cellar and now under my bed, condemns me forever]. In Dujovne Ortiz's novel, the origin of the mysterious ailment that leaves Teresa mute and paralyzed is not an adolescent love affair but guilt over denying her Jewish blood. She sees in her illness the fulfillment of the malediction of Psalms 37: "If I forget thee, O Jerusalem, let my right hand forget her cunning. If I do not remember thee, let my tongue cleave to the roof of my mouth" (KJV).

The resolution to Teresa's religious crisis (and the turning point in the novel) arrives when Teresa, praying before a statue of Christ at the column, recognizes the figure of her grandfather being led through the streets of Toledo in an *auto de fé:* "Estupefacta quedo, ¿un viejo judío maltratado contará tanto como Jesús? Al responderme por la afirmativa, la unión de mis pedazos queda sellada" (Dujovne Ortiz 109) [I am stupefied. Is an old, mistreated Jew worth as much as Jesus? When I answer in the affirmative, the pieces of my soul come together]. The coming together of pity for Christ and for the victims of cruelty in general becomes the stimulus for Teresa's subsequent religious life. Her determination to found convents in poverty is figured as a Judeo-Christian *imitatio Christi.*

For Dujovne Ortiz, as for Morales, Teresa's proleptic modernity is manifested in her awareness of and opposition to women's economic and sexual exploitation. Like Morales's protagonist, this Teresa reproaches her father for subjecting her mother to dangerous yearly pregnancies (and is especially devoted to Saint Joseph because, unlike her father, he left his wife "in peace"). She is also appalled by the aristocrats who marry off their daughters at a young age to solidify their economic interests. Startlingly frank letters from her brother Rodrigo recounting the atrocities he has participated in as a conquistador in Paraguay further reinforce her awareness of women's subjugation. She imagines reproaching her brother: "¿Cuántos años habrán tenido las jovencitas a las que de seguro hiciste hijos que aún pasan sus días en la selva, Ahumaditas salvajes, Cepeditas desnudos y con plumas? ¿Catorce, como nuestra madre, Beatriz? ¿Doce, como la pobre doña Casilda, . . . la que huyó de su viejo marido, para peor su tío . . . ?" (Dujovne Ortiz 216) [How old were those girls you surely made children with, who still spend their days in the jungle, savage little Ahumadas, little naked Cepedas with feathers? Fourteen, like our mother Beatriz? Twelve, like poor Doña Casilda . . . the one who ran away from her old husband—what's worse, her uncle . . . ?][15] As expiation for her brother's sins, Teresa dreams of establishing convents for Guaraní, Quecha, and Araucana girls, thus saving them from further male predation.

This *marrano* Teresa is also proleptically tolerant, and in fact, she ponders a kind of religious universalism. Is there an afterlife for conquistadors like her brother Rodrigo who, syphilitic and unrepentant, may die in the jungles of Paraguay? Coming upon a peasants' Bacchanalian fiesta, she muses, "¿Y si a todos un solo viento o espíritu nos menease, pero cada uno se moviera según su ser? ¿Y las fiestas de los labriegos y las nuestras, bien mirado, fueran la misma?" (Dujovne Ortiz 232) [What if only one wind or spirit moves us, but each one moved according to his being? What if the peasants' fiestas and our own, all things considered, were the same?]. Dujovne Ortiz, it would appear, is drawing upon a school of Jewish history that posits a kind of *marrano* religiosity that embraces syncretism, universalism, and skepticism (see Wachtel; Yovel). This Teresa's double bloodlines—and her consciousness of the blood spilt by her conquistador brothers—have opened her mind to alternative faiths and cosmologies that coexist with her Christocentric spirituality.

If Morales's novel is the *Libro de la Vida* that Teresa wanted to write but could not, then the second half of Dujovne Ortiz's novel reads like an uncensored version of *Libro de las fundaciones* [Book of Foundations], the convent history Teresa would have written if she had not been afraid that the work might fall into the hands of her enemies or offend her capricious patrons. Dujovne Ortiz magnifies the exasperation that is discreetly controlled in Teresa's writings. Her aristocratic patrons are not simply vain; they are spiritually impoverished. When, for example, the noble Bernardino de Mendoza dies suddenly, without absolution, his family offers to finance a convent. Teresa remarks sarcastically: "La cosa urge. Hay que apurarse a fundar el convento de Valladolid para que el desdichado perdulario salga del Purgatorio" (Dujovne Ortiz 240) [The situation is urgent. We must hurry to found the convent in Valladolid to get the unfortunate ne'er-do-well out of Purgatory]. She is similarly disdainful of the hermitess Catalina de Cardona (described with exquisite ambiguity in chapter 29 of *Libro de las fundaciones* [composed 1580–1582]): "[S]e ha llenado de oro y de joyas pero vive en una cueva comiendo raíces" (*Obras completas* 269) [She has stored up with gold and jewels but she lives in a cave eating roots . . .]. King Philip II is simultaneously dismissed as a credulous fool: "Don Felipe la ha recibido reverencioso porque todo lo más parecido a la muerte le cae bien" (269) [Don Felipe has reverently received her because he likes whatever most resembles death]. Juan de la Cruz comes across as critical and cold; Teresa wonders why he says not a word about the suffering Christ. (Interestingly, this portrait coincides somewhat with a recent historical reassessment of the friar [Bilinkoff, "First Friar"].) Dujovne Ortiz's vision of a *Marrano*-Christian Teresa pushes the limits of the historical novel pact. At least for this reader, her inculpation tropes, suggestively anchored in Teresa's writings (including her voluminous correspondence), are more satisfactory.

As argued earlier, Dujovne Ortiz traces Teresa's spiritual anguish to the discovery of her Jewish heritage and not to sexual trauma. This does not mean that she ignores the question of Teresa's relations with men. On the contrary, her protagonist is a woman who longs for spiritual companionship with men. There is a moving, brief portrait of Martín Gutiérrez, the Jesuit who helped Teresa build the Salamanca foundation.[16] When he dies at the hands of Huguenots in France, Teresa, acknowledging that her love for the Jesuit has a human side, refuses to rejoice in his martyrdom. But the love of her life is Jerónimo Gracián (Teresa's junior by thirty years), the confessor who (many modern historians would agree) led Teresa to make several disastrous decisions that plunged the Discalced Carmelites into a five-year war with the Calced [Mitigated] branch of their order.[17] Writing as an old woman at the end of her life, Dujovne Ortiz's Teresa is mercilessly self-aware as she describes her infatuation upon meeting the young Carmelite friar: "En realidad ya sé que es un hombre mediano: ninguna lumbrera, ningún espiritual. O no lo sé todavía pero sé que lo sabré enseguida. Y sin embargo lo amo.... Felicidad embobada pero felicidad al fin" (283, 285) [In truth I already know that he is an ordinary man: not a genius, not a mystic. Or I don't know it yet but I know that I will soon know. And yet I love him.... It's a foolish happiness, but happiness after all].

As the novel draws to a conclusion, Teresa's disappointments and feelings of betrayal accumulate, and the narration becomes increasingly condensed, fragmented, and tentative. Teresa struggles to describe one last ecstasy: "Dicen que los judíos no pronuncian su nombre. Los comprendo, cuando estoy en brazos de eso que me acuna me olvido de nombrarlo. Ya no sé si es alguien o si es algo, si es lugar o aliento o alimento" (Dujovne Ortiz 322) [They say the Jews do not pronounce his name. I understand. When I am in the arms of that which cradles me, I forget to name it. I no longer know if it is someone or something, if it is a place, a breath, or nourishment]. We realize that what we have been reading are the recollections of a woman who is approaching the hour of her death.

These are not radically innovative novels. Although they glancingly explore the vagaries of memory, they do not excavate the boundaries between fact and fiction. They are not purposefully counter-historical.[18] Instead, they work within a conventional reader-writer pact for historical novels, embroidering upon what is known with the insights of the present, foregrounding Teresa as a proleptic heroine—a critic of patriarchy and class privilege—and, in Dujovne Ortiz's novel, a convert to religious universalism. We might bear in mind the definition of prolepsis as rhetorical trope: "the representation or assumption of a future act or development *as if* presently existing or accomplished" (Merriam-Webster, emphasis added). The reader must renounce the conviction of "surely was" for "as if" to enjoy the promise of the historical novel: that it offers not only prescience but moral clarity, however illusory.

We must also bear in mind that the historical novel is inherently anachronistic. No writer, no matter how learned and meticulous, can recreate flawlessly the language, emotions, and intellectual assumptions, or the material conditions of a bygone era. The best she can hope for is to create a plausibly accurate historical moment and count on the readers' willingness to accept the illusion of historicity and restrain their most punctilious impulses. To be sure, in these novels there are anachronisms that push these limits,[19] but for the most part, both novelists fulfill their side of this reader-writer pact. Did the historical Teresa hate her father and blame him for her mother's early death? Probably not. But Morales's depiction of Doña Beatriz's bloody sheets is a vivid emblem for the dangers of early modern marriage and childbirth. Did Teresa really hide a copy of the *Zohar* under her bed? I doubt it. But Dujovne Ortiz's premise keeps alive the controversies over the extent of Teresa's knowledge of her family's Jewish past and reminds us that religious identity can be extraordinarily labile. The portrayal of Teresa, disheartened and exhausted in her final days, is compelling, poignant, and historically plausible. Though they read Teresa through the lens of contemporary concerns and value judgments, Morales and Dujovne Ortiz are nevertheless good readers of the Carmelite founder: they tease out what she may have wanted to reveal—if she had had the freedom to do so—and what she may have revealed in spite of herself. As Bárbara Mujica demonstrated in her own historical novel, *Sister Teresa*, whether we read as historians, literary scholars, or curious laymen and women, the questions these texts raise offer aesthetic and intellectual pleasures.

Notes

1. The novels I will not be able to discuss here due to considerations of space are *Y de repente, Teresa* [And Suddenly, Teresa] by Jesús Sánchez Adalid, *El Castillo de Diamante* [The Diamond Castle] by Juan Manuel de Prada, and *Sus ojos en mí* [His Eyes on Me] by Fernando Delgado.
2. Mantel won the Mann Booker prize for *Wolf Hall* in 2009. The sequel, *Bring Up the Bodies*, was awarded the prize in 2012.
3. For a concise review of the controversies that followed the discovery of Teresa's *converso* heritage, see Teófanes Egido's essay "La biografía teresiana y nuevas claves de comprensión histórica."
4. In her excellent essay on novelistic treatments of Teresa written in Spain from the 1970s to the end of the 1990s, Isabelle Touton concludes: "Las novelas populares de finales del milenio se centran casi exclusivamente en esa identidad de mujer libre que forja su propio destino, quizás a expensas de todo lo que hizo la desmesura de la Santa y de toda dimensión espiritual" (1109) [The popular novels of the end of millennium focus almost exclusively on the identity of a free woman who forges her own destiny, perhaps

at the expense of all the saint's excesses and her spiritual dimension]. All translations are my own, except for translations from the original works of Teresa of Ávila. See note 6 below.

5. *Los combatientes* won the INJUVE prize in 2012. *La merienda de las niñas* was a finalist for the X Premio Booket de Relato Corto.

6. Citations from the works of Teresa of Ávila (Teresa de Jesús) are to the edition of Tomás Álvarez. The English translations, unless otherwise noted, are from the three-volume edition of Kieran Kavanaugh and Otilio Rodríguez.

7. I have tried to preserve Teresa's convoluted syntax here. "Harta quiebra" means literally a "significant rupture."

8. On the historical Luisa de la Cerda and her long friendship with Teresa, see María Pilar Manero Sorolla's "On the Margins of the Mendozas."

9. Although the notion that nuns frequently had lovers has long been a popular trope in film and novels, and although there are several documented cases of such relations, historians surmise that contact between nuns and lay suitors ("galanes" or "devotos de monjas") was generally limited to flirtation (see Lorenzo Pinar).

10. Diego's daughter María Bautista (Ocampo) (1543–1603) did indeed become a Discalced Carmelite. She was a trusted collaborator in the Discalced Reform (see Álvarez). In Morales's novel, Diego, Teresa's former lover, begs her to take this daughter off his hands since he cannot afford to pay a matrimonial dowry.

11. Morales seems to have confused the Vulgate—the Latin version of the Bible translated mainly by Saint Jerome in the fourth century—with vernacular translations of the Bible. The latter were placed on the Inquisition's Index of Prohibited Books of 1559, but reading a prohibited book was not a capital offense.

12. On Teresa's frustration over limits to women's apostolic role, see especially Jodi Bilinkoff's "Teresa of Ávila." Bárbara Mujica defends the historical legitimacy of calling Teresa a feminist in "Was Teresa of Ávila a Feminist?"

13. For a study of Teresa's monastic reforms in the context of her ecclesial feminism, see Alison Weber's "Spiritual Administration."

14. Dujovne Ortiz, a prolific novelist, biographer, and journalist, was born in Buenos Aires in 1939 and now lives in Paris. She is the recipient of awards from the John Simon Guggenheim Memorial Foundation and from the French Ministry of Foreign Relations.

15. Dujovne Ortiz here alludes to Casilda de Padilla, who ran away to a Discalced Convent to avoid a forced marriage to her uncle. Teresa tells the story of Casilda in chapter 11 of *Book of Foundations*. See Weber, *Teresa of Ávila*, 48–50.

16. He is the probable addressee of Teresa's *Relación* #15 (*Spiritual Testimony* #12), in which she describes the transpiercing of her soul. The translation by Kavanaugh and Rodríguez in volume one of *The Collected Works* follows a different numbering system for this work than that used by Álvarez in his 1998 edition of Teresa's works. Gutiérrez was killed by Huguenots in 1573 (Álvarez 923–24).

17. For a sensitive historical study of Teresa's relationship with Gracián, see Mujica's "Paul, the 'Enchanter.'"

18. Examples of the subgenre of the counter-historical novel include Gabriel García Márquez's *El general en su laberinto* (1989) [The General in His Labyrinth] and Reinaldo Arenas's *El mundo alucinante* (1966) [The Amazing World]. The widely acclaimed novel by Colson Whitehead, *The Underground Railroad* (2016), is another example of a novel that deliberately falsifies historical events and chronology.

19. As observed in note 11 above, Morales confuses the Vulgate with vernacular translations of the Bible and exaggerates the reach of the Inquisition. Dujovne Ortiz's anachronistic liberties are not only historical (no one has been able to trace the direct influence of Jewish or Arabic mysticism on Teresa) but also linguistic: one character, a servant, speaks in Judeo-Spanish (Ladino), a dialect developed by post-expulsion Jews in the Mediterranean.

References

Alabrús, Rosa María, and Ricardo García Cárcel. *Teresa de Jesús: La construcción de la santidad femenina*. Madrid: Cátedra, 2015.

Álvarez, Tomás. *Diccionario de Santa Teresa: doctrina e historia*. Burgos, Spain: Monte Carmelo, 2006.

Bilinkoff, Jodi. "First Friar, Problematic Founder: John of the Cross and His Earliest Biographies." In *Reforming Reformation*, edited by Thomas F. Mayer, Ashgate, 2012, 103–18.

———. "Teresa of Ávila: Woman with a Mission." In *A Linking of Heaven and Earth: Essays in Honor of Carlos M. N. Eire*, edited by Emily Michelson, Scott Taylor, and Mary Noll Venables, Ashgate, 2012, 101–11.

Casero, Estrella. *La España que bailó con Franco. Coros y danzas de la Sección Femenina*. Madrid: Nuevas Estructuras, 2000.

Castro, Américo. *Teresa la santa y otros ensayos*. Madrid: Alfaguara, 1972.

De Prada, Juan Manuel. *El Castillo de Diamante*. Madrid: Espasa Calpe, 2015.

Delgado, Fernando. *Sus ojos en mí*. Barcelona: Planeta, 2015.

Di Febo, Giuliana. *La Santa de la raza. Teresa de Ávila: un culto barroco en la España franquista (1947–1962)*. Barcelona: Icaria, 1988.

Dujovne Ortiz, Alicia. *Un corazón tan recio*. Buenos Aires: Alfaguara, 2011.

Egido, Teófanes. "La biografía teresiana y nuevas claves de comprensión histórica." In *La recepción de los místicos. Teresa de Jesús y Juan de la Cruz*, edited by Salvador Ros, Universidad Pontificia de Salamanca, 1997, 388–94.

Greenblatt, Stephen. "How It Must Have Been." Review of *Wolf Hall* by Hilary Mantel. *New York Review of Books*, November 5, 2009, www.nybooks.com/articles/2009/11/05/how-it-must-have-been/.

Lehfeldt, Elizabeth. "Convents as Litigants: Dowry and Inheritance Disputes in Early-Modern Spain." *Journal of Social History* 33 (2000): 645–64.

Lejeune, Philippe. *Le Pact autobiographique*. Seuil, 1975.

Lorenzo Pinar, Francisco Javier. *Beatas y mancebas*. Zamora, Spain: Semuret, 1995.

Manero Sorolla, María Pilar. "On the Margins of the Mendozas: Luisa de la Cerda and María de San José (Salazar)." In *Power and Gender in Renaissance Spain: Eight Women of the Mendoza Family, 1450–1650*, edited by Helen Nader, University of Illinois Press, 2004, 113–31.

Márquez Villanueva, Francisco. "Santa Teresa y el linaje." In *Espiritualidad y literatura en el siglo XVI*. Madrid: Alfaguara, 1968, 141–205.

Morales, Cristina. *Malas palabras*. Barcelona: Lumen, 2015.

Mujica, Bárbara. "Paul, the 'Enchanter': Saint Teresa's Letters to Jerónimo Gracián." In *The Heirs of St. Teresa of Avila: Defenders and Disseminators of the Founding Mother's Legacy*, edited by Christopher Wilson, Washington, D.C.: Institute of Carmelite Studies, 2006, 21–44.

———. *Sister Teresa: The Woman Who Became Saint Teresa of Ávila*. Overlook, 2007.

———. "Was Teresa of Ávila a Feminist?" In *Approaches to Teaching Teresa of Ávila and the Spanish Mystics*, edited by Alison Weber, Modern Language Association of America, 2009, 74–82.

Rowe, Erin Katherine. *Saint and Nation: Santiago, Teresa of Avila, and Plural Identities in Early Modern Spain*. Pennsylvania State University Press, 2011.

Sánchez Adalid, Jesús. *Y de repente, Teresa*. Barcelona: Ediciones B, 2014.

Schutte, Anne Jacobson. *By Force and Fear: Taking and Breaking Monastic Vows in Early Modern Europe*. Cornell University Press, 2011.

Sperling, Jutta. "Marriage at the Time of the Council of Trent (1560–70): Clandestine Marriage, Kinship Prohibitions, and Dowry Exchange in European Comparison." *Journal of Early Modern History* 8 (2004): 67–108.

Teresa de Jesús. *The Collected Works of St. Teresa of Avila*. 3 vols. Translated by Kieran Kavanaugh and Otilio Rodriguez, Washington, D.C., Institute of Carmelite Studies, 1976–1985.

———. *Obras completas de Santa Teresa*. Edited by Tomás Álvarez. Burgos, Spain: Monte Carmelo, 1998.

Touton, Isabelle. "Santa Teresa en algunas novelas contemporáneas españolas." In *Homenaje a Henri Guerreiro: La hagiografía entre historia y literatura en la España de la Edad Media y del Siglo de Oro*, edited by Marc Vitse, Iberoamericana, 2005, 1097–1111.

Wachtel, Nathan. "Marrano Religiosity in Hispanic America in the Seventeenth Century." In *The Jews and the Expansion of Europe to the West, 1450 to 1800*, edited by Paolo Bernardini and Norman Fiering, Berghahn Books, 2001, 149–71.

Weber, Alison. "Saint Teresa's Problematic Patrons." *Journal of Medieval and Early Modern Studies* 29 (1999): 357–79.

———. "Spiritual Administration: Gender and Discernment in the Carmelite Reform." *Sixteenth Century Journal* (2000) 31: 127–50.

———. *Teresa of Ávila and the Rhetoric of Femininity*. Princeton University Press, 1990.

Yovel, Yirmiyahu. *The Other Within. The Marranos: Split Identity and Emerging Modernity*. Princeton University Press, 2009.

Part V

Epilogue

Call to Battle

MARJORIE AGOSÍN

Bárbara, la alquimista de palabras

Desde la temprana infancia
Amabas las palabras.
Aprendiste como una alquimista intrépida a hilvanarlas,
Las sabías escoger
Y de pronto fuiste llenando las páginas
De tu mundo en ellas.

Niña precoz y traviesa,
Bárbara imaginaria y lúcida,
Has amado desde siempre los cuentos y las historias,
Las grandes y pequeñas hazañas.
Tu vocación fue de contar al mundo
Historias y proezas.
Arriesgaste tu alma
Para salir al encuentro de la verdad.
Tu vocación fue de armar libros,
Tejerlos, bordarlos, hilarlos.
Y así con tu mirada generosa,
Con tu mirada sabia y jamás juzgadora,
Seguiste la pasión de entender y contar.
Escribiste sobre la belleza y el dolor,

Sobre las soledades y la plenitud.
Armaste historias, cuentos, novelas, ensayos,
Dirigiste un teatro vivo,
Como quien necesita escribir para entender al mundo,
Como quien necesita escribir para cambiar el mundo contando.

Elegiste a las mujeres desobedientes y lúcidas en su valentía:
Santa Teresa, la hacedora de conventos, de casas portables,
Santa Teresa, la que sabía conversar con Dios.
También pensaste en Frida la pintora,
Frida la intrépida,
Frida, la que pintaba el dolor . . .
También te acercaste a otras historias:
A un bombero llamado Gottlieb en el lejano Chile,
O a un pintor llamado Velázquez,
Y su historia fue contada por otra mujer audaz.
Tienes el don de entenderlos, de descubrirlos
Porque eres sabia en tus palabras,
Respetuosa al oír a los otros.
Y llenas las páginas con la visión de una mujer
Que escribe porque ama.

Bárbara,
Hermana Bárbara,
Hacedora y soñadora,
Niña traviesa,
Mujer de un alma clarividente,
Eres una estrella
Agradecida por el don concedido,
Maestra y madre,
Directora de comedias,
Doctora en literatura,
Compañera de los soldados que regresan,
Alumbradora de los que no vuelven.
Eres una luz espléndida en los caminos tortuosos
De tantas almas,
Un faro encendido,
Como una casa iluminada y abierta.

Te celebramos mientras tú eres la que nos enseñas a celebrar,
Bárbara simple y compleja,
Extraordinaria Bárbara,
Abundante en la alegría y la imaginación.
Gracias por tus ofrendas asombrosas.

Bárbara, the Alchemist of Words

In your early childhood
You fell in love with words.
Like an intrepid alchemist,
You learned how to blend them together,
You knew how to choose just the right ones,
And soon you were filling pages with them,
Narrating your world.

You were a precocious and gifted girl,
You were Bárbara the eloquent
With the most vivid of imaginations.
You have always loved stories and tales,
And relating feats both large and small.
Your calling was to tell the world
Of legends and exploits.
You risked your soul
In pursuit of the truth.
Your passion was creating books,
Weaving them, stitching them, embroidering them.
And so, with your generous gaze,
With your wise and never judgmental gaze,

BÁRBARA, THE ALCHEMIST OF WORDS

You followed your passion to understand and narrate.
You wrote about beauty and pain,
About solitude and plenitude.
You created stories, tales, novels, essays,
You directed live theater,
Like someone who needs to write to understand the world,
Like someone who needs to write to change the world with words.

You chose brave women who were disobedient and magnificent:
Santa Teresa, the maker of convents and portable houses,
Santa Teresa, who knew how to speak with God.
You also pondered Frida, the painter,
Frida, the intrepid,
Frida, who knew how to paint pain . . .
You recounted other stories as well:
A fireman named Gottlieb in far-away Chile,
Or a painter named Velázquez,
Whose story was told by another courageous woman.
You have the gift of understanding them, divining them,
Because you are wise with your words,
And respectful while listening to others.
You fill pages with the vision of a woman
Who writes because she loves.

Bárbara,
Sister Bárbara,
Creator and dreamer,
Clever girl,
Woman with a clairvoyant soul,
You are a star,
Grateful for the gift you have been given,
You are a teacher and a mother,
A director of plays,
A doctor of literature,
A champion of soldiers who return home from war
And a beacon of remembrance for those who do not.
You are a resplendent light in the torturous journeys
Of so many souls,

A guiding light,
Like a bright and open house.

We celebrate you while you are the one who teaches us to celebrate,
Simple and complex Bárbara,
Extraordinary Bárbara,
Abounding in happiness and imagination.
Thank you for your wonderful gifts.

Contributors

Frederick A. de Armas is Andrew W. Mellon Distinguished Service Professor in Romance Languages and Comparative Literature at the University of Chicago, where he has also served as Chair of the Department and Director of Graduate Studies. He has served as President of the Cervantes Society of America and is now President of AISO (Asociación Internacional Siglo de Oro). He has been awarded several NEH Fellowships and has directed several NEH Seminars. De Armas focuses on the literature of early modern Spain, often from a comparative perspective. His books reflect an interest in the role of women in the literature of the period, starting with *The Invisible Mistress: Aspects of Feminism and Fantasy in the Golden Age* (Siglo de Oro 1976) and continuing with *The Return of Astraea: An Astral-Imperial Myth in Calderón* (Kentucky 1986, 2015). His more recent book and collections include: *Ovid in the Age of Cervantes* (Toronto 2010); *Don Quixote among the Saracens: Clashes of Civilizations and Literary Genres* (Toronto 2011), which was recognized with honorable mention for the PROSE Award in Literature; and the co-edited collection *Objects of Culture in the Literature of Imperial Spain* (Toronto 2013).

Susan L. Fischer is Professor of Spanish and Comparative Literature *Emerita* at Bucknell University and a Visiting Scholar at Harvard University. She is author of *Reading Performance: Spanish Golden Age Theatre and Shakespeare on the Modern Stage* (Tamesis 2009). She has published scores of studies on Calderón, Lope, Tirso, and Shakespeare, focusing primarily on modern stagings in Spain, England, and France. She has also treated the double-crossing of the Mexican nun, Sor Juana Inés de la Cruz, to the boards of the Royal Shakespeare Company in productions of her play, *Los empeños de una casa* [House of Desires] (2004), and of Helen Edmundson's biographical play, *The Heresy of Love* (2012), which deals with Sor Juana's trials of faith and the enduring power of a female consciousness. Fischer has also written on Catherine of Aragon as revisited in Tudor history, and on the transnational stage, in productions in Spain and England (2015); and worked on the warrior queen, Isabella of Castile, as seen in history and in early modern drama. In addition, she is the editor of, and co-contributor to, two volumes: *Comedias del siglo de oro and Shakespeare* (Bucknell 1989); and *Self-Conscious Art: A Tribute to John W. Kronik* (Bucknell 1996). Finally, she is editor-in-chief of the psychology journal *Gestalt Review*, published by the Pennsylvania State University Press.

Marjorie Agosín is the Luella Lamer Slaner Professor of Latin American Studies at Wellesley College and an award winning poet and human rights activist. She has authored nearly forty books in diverse genres, from poetry to short stories, essays and memoirs, on human rights, social justice, and the consequences of war. Her works deal with the dirty wars in Chile and Argentina, the Holocaust, and human rights violations on the Mexican-U.S. border. Among her books are *Ashes of Revolt* (White Pine 1996) and the edited anthologies *A Map of Hope: Women's Writing on Human Rights* (Rutgers 1999) and *Writing Toward Hope: The Literature of Human Rights in Latin America* (Yale 2006). Her most recent poetry collection is *Las Islas Blancas / The White Islands* (Swan Isle 2015), a collection of poems about the extermination of Sephardic communities during the Nazi Occupation.

Gillian T. W. Ahlgren is Professor of Theology at Xavier University (Cincinnati, Ohio), where she teaches courses in the history of Christianity and Christian spirituality. She is the author of six books, including *Teresa of Avila and the Politics of Sanctity* (Cornell 1996), *Entering Teresa of Avila's Interior Castle: A Reader's Companion* (Paulist 2005), *Enkindling Love: The Legacy of Teresa of Avila and John of the Cross* (Fortress 2016), and most recently *The Tenderness of God: Reclaiming Our Humanity* (Fortress 2017). She is the Founding Director of Xavier's Institute for Spirituality and Social Justice, lectures widely, and facilitates retreats.

Isaac Benabu holds the Lipsky Chair in Drama at The Hebrew University of Jerusalem, and teaches in the departments of Theatre Studies and English. His areas of research include the Spanish Golden Age *comedia*, including a focus on problematic female characters in the plays of Calderón de la Barca and Tirso de Molina; early modern European theater; reading Shakespeare for the stage; and female protagonists in the theatre of Federico García Lorca. He has published two books: *On the Boards and in the Press* (Reichenberger 1991) and *Reading for the Stage: Calderón and his Contemporaries* (Tamesis 2003). Benabu has been a visiting professor at a number of universities in the U.K., Europe, and North and South America. He is a theater director and has directed internationally. He was the initiator and former director of *Thespis*: the Jerusalem International Festival of Theatre.

Emilie L. Bergmann is Professor of Spanish at the University of California, Berkeley, with fields of specialization in early modern Spain and Spanish America, focusing on gender, the maternal, and queer sexualities; and on relationships among poetics, visual perception, and sound studies. She is co-editor with Stacey Schlau of *The Routledge Research Companion to the Works of Sor Juana Inés de la Cruz* (2017). She is also co-editor with Paul Julian Smith of *¿Entiendes? Queer Readings, Hispanic Writings* (Duke 1995); with Stacey Schlau of *Approaches to Teaching the Works of Sor Juana Inés de la Cruz* (MLA 2007); and with Richard Herr of *Mirrors and Echoes: Women's Writing in Twentieth-Century Spain* (California 2007). Topics of recent publications include optics and sonorities in Sor Juana; Cervantes and the poetics of madness; and cross-dressing, gender transgression, and violence in early modern Spanish theater. She has also published articles on twentieth-century women writers in Castilian and Catalan, including Carmen Martín-Gaite, Mercè Rodoreda, and Montserrat Roig.

Emily C. Francomano is Professor in the Department of Spanish and Portuguese at Georgetown University, where she also serves as a core faculty member of the programs in Comparative Literature and Medieval Studies. Her research revolves around two areas that often intersect: processes of adaptation and *translatio*—material, visual, and linguistic—and gender studies in medieval and Early Modern literatures. This research agenda is accompanied by her own work as a translator of fifteenth-century Castilian texts into English for twenty-first century readers. She is the author of *Wisdom and Her Lovers in Medieval and Early Modern Hispanic Literature* (Palgrave 2008) and *The Prison of Love: Romance, Translation, and the Book in the Sixteenth Century* (2018), as well as a recent bilingual edition, translation, and study, *Three Spanish Querelle Texts*: Grisel and Mirabella, The Slander against Women, and The Defense of Women against Slanderers (CRRS/ITER 2013). Recent articles include "Taking the Gold out of Egypt: Prostitution and the Economy of Salvation" and "The Greeks and the Romans: Translation and *Translatio* in the *Libro de buen amor*."

Edward H. Friedman is Gertrude Conaway Vanderbilt Professor of Spanish, Professor of Comparative Literature, and director of the Robert Penn Warren Center for the Humanities at Vanderbilt University. He studied at the University of Virginia and Johns Hopkins University, and he has taught at Vanderbilt since 2000. His primary field of research is early modern Spanish literature, with emphasis on the picaresque, Cervantes, and the *comedia*. He is the author of *The Antiheroine's Voice* (Missouri 1987) and essays on María de Zayas, Ana Caro, Sor Juana Inés de la Cruz, and the role of women in narrative and drama. His creative works include adaptations of Cervantes's *El laberinto de amor* and Juan Ruiz de Alarcón's *Mudarse por mejorarse*.

Charles Victor Ganelin is Professor Emeritus of Spanish at Miami University (Oxford, OH). He has published a critical edition of Andrés de Claramonte's *La infelice Dorotea* (Tamesis 1988); a co-edited collection of essays, with Howard Mancing, *The Golden Age Comedia: Text, Theory and Performance* (Purdue 1994); and a monograph, *Rewriting Theatre: The Nineteenth-Century Theatre and the Refundición* (Bucknell 1994). Much of his work has focused on the *comedia* and Spanish theatre, though more recently his publications have dealt with aspects of the body and the senses in Cervantes (the *Quijote* and the *Novelas ejemplares*). Of late, he has begun to work on the distinct voices of women poets of Spain's early modern period. One essay, currently in preparation, treats a poem by Catalina Clara Ramírez de Guzmán that offers insight into a practiced satirical vein in her poetry and her still undiscovered *comedia*. This project explores the sensorial aspects of selected poems by Ramírez de Guzmán and seeks to determine if women writers adopted a register distinct from that of their male counterparts.

Susan Paun de García is Professor Emerita of Spanish at Denison University. She has written articles on María de Zayas, on the seventeenth-century *Comedia*, and the post-baroque *comedia* of the early eighteenth century, particularly the work of José de Cañizares, of whose Don Juan de Espina plays she has published critical editions. With Donald R. Larson, she co-edited *The Comedia in English* (Tamesis 2008), and with Harley Erdman, she co-edited *Remaking the Comedia* (Tamesis 2015). She is President of the Association for Hispanic Classical Theater, serves as a member of the editorial advisory board of the journal *Comedia Performance*, and oversees the Association's committee for the *comedia* in English.

Elizabeth Cruz Petersen holds a Postdoctoral Fellow position at the Center for Body, Mind, and Culture at Florida Atlantic University, and an adjunct faculty position in the Department of Languages, Linguistics, and Comparative Literature. She also serves as assistant editor for the *Journal of Somaesthetics*. Her book, *Women's Somatic Training in Early Modern Spanish Theater* (Routledge 2016), explores somatic practices of seventeenth-century Spanish women actors preparing for their roles. Her other publications include articles on early modern Spanish theater and translation, as well as theater reviews, in the peer-reviewed journal *Comedia Performance*, and an essay, "A Mindful Audience: Embodied Spectatorship in Early Modern Madrid." Cruz Petersen's scholarly work extends from seventeenth-century Spanish Peninsular and Colonial studies to contemporary Latino/Chicano Performance studies.

Teresa Scott Soufas is Professor Emerita of early modern Spanish at Temple University. Her scholarly interests have led her to author numerous articles and read many conference papers on the drama, prose, and poetry of sixteenth- and seventeenth-century Spain. She has published three books: *Melancholy and the Secular Mind in Spanish Golden Age Literature* (Missouri 1990), *Dramas of Distinction: Plays by Golden Age Women* (Kentucky 1997), and *Women's Acts: Plays by Women Dramatists of Spain's Golden Age* (Kentucky 1997), the latter a work she edited that contains eight plays by five female authors. She has dedicated much of her research to women writers and women characters and to the theatrical practice in Spain in this period of depicting women dressed as men to obtain a resolution to a serious problem, often an honor dilemma.

Sherry Velasco is Professor of Early Modern Spanish literature and culture in the Department of Spanish and Portuguese at the University of Southern California and Professor of Gender Studies. She is currently the chair of the Department of French and Italian and the interim chair of the Department of Spanish and Portuguese. Velasco is the author of four books: *Lesbians in Early Modern Spain* (Vanderbilt 2011), *Male Delivery: Reproduction, Effeminacy, and Pregnant Men in Early Modern Spain* (Vanderbilt 2006), *The Lieutenant Nun: Transgenderism, Lesbian Desire, and Catalina de Erauso* (Texas 2000), and *Demons, Nausea, and Resistance in the Autobiography of Isabel de Jesús 1611–1682* (New Mexico 1996). She has also published articles and book chapters on early modern Spanish prose, theater, and women's narrative with special emphasis on gender studies, queer theory, and visual cultural studies.

Sharon D. Voros, Professor Emerita of Spanish and French and former chair of the Languages and Cultures Department at the United States Naval Academy, Annapolis, MD, is the author of *Petrarch and Garcilaso: A Linguistic Approach to Style* (under the name Ghertman) (Tamesis 1975), editor with Barbara Mujica of *Looking at the Comedia in the Year of the Quincentennial* (UPA 1993), and editor with Ricardo Saéz of *Aquel breve sueño: Dreams on the Early Modern Spanish Stage* (University of the South 1995). Her articles include studies on women writers, Lope de Vega, Tirso de Molina, and Pedro Calderón, such as "Calderón's Writing Women and Women Writers: The Subversion of the *Exempla*," "Leonor's Library: the Last Will and Testament of Leonor de la Cueva y Silva," and "Tried and True: Leonor de la Cueva's Tirso Connection," which includes *Le favori* by Madame de Villedieu. She published a translation from the French, *Bastille Witness: The Prison Autobiography of Madame Guyon, 1648 -1717* (UPA 2011). Her translation of Leonor de la Cueva's *La firmeza en la ausencia* as *Tried and True* was performed at Oklahoma City University under the direction of David Pasto.

Alison Weber is Professor Emerita of Spanish at the University of Virginia. Her main areas of research are women and religion in early modern Europe and convent literature in Spain. The author of numerous book chapters and articles, she has also written *Teresa de Avila and the Rhetoric of Femininity* (Princeton 1990), and edited *For the Hour of Recreation* by María de San José (translated by Amanda Powell and published in The Other Voice Series of the University of Chicago Press in 2002). In addition, she has edited *Approaches to Teaching Teresa of Avila and the Spanish Mystics* (MLA 2009) and *Devout Laywomen in the Early Modern World* (Routledge 2016). Selected articles and book chapters include: "Gender and Mysticism," in *The Cambridge Companion to Christian Mysticism*, ed. Amy Hollywood and Patricia Beckman (Cambridge 2012); "'Golden Age' or 'Early Modern': What's in a Name?" in *Publications of the Modern Language Association of America*, and "Teresa di Jesu e i rapporti con i confessori," in *Storia della direzione spirituale, III, L'età moderna,* edited by Gabriella Zarri (Morcelliana 2008).

Index

Ahumada, Beatriz de, fictional treatment of, 264, 274
Amazon, 58
Apollo, 55
Arellano, Ignacio, 56
Astraea, 55, 56, 60
authorship, 160, 161, 165, 166; precursory, 165; social, 163, 169, 169n3; women and, 150–60, 161, 163, 165, 168–69

Baena, Juan Alfonso de, 162
Báñez, Domingo, 224
beatas, 13, 21
biographical novel/fiction: Michael Lackey, 241–42; Bárbara Mujica, 243–45; narrative twists, unpredictible and plausible, 257; Jay Parini, 242
Boccaccio, Giovanni, *Famous Women*, 51
Borrachero Mendíbil, Aránzau, 174, 182nn2–4, 183n10
Bossuet, Jacques-Bénigne, 209, 210, 215

Calderón de la Barca, Pedro, 246; *La Gran Cenobia*, 50–65; *La Vida es sueño*, 50, 54
Cancionero poetry, 159, 162, 165–66, 168
cancioneros, 160, 168; *Cancionero de Herberay des Essarts*, 159–61, 165, 168–69; and manuscript matrices, 160
Cardona, Catalina, fictional treatment of, 272
Caro, Ana, 34, 35, 37
Castañega, Martín de, 226

Castro, Francisca de, 119, 128, 132, 134, 135, 136n2, 137nn9–10, 138n16
Casaubon, Isaac, 52
Cenobia, 50–65
Cepeda, Alonso de, fictional treatment of, 263–64
Cepeda, Diego de, fictional treatment of, 266, 267
Cerda, Luisa de la, fictional treatment of, 264–66
Cervantes, Miguel de, 33, 36–47; *La Casa de los celos*, 43, 44; *Don Quijote*, 248; *La Entretenida*, 43; *La Gran sultana*, 41, 42; *La Laberinto de amor*, 43; *La Numancia*, 36, 37, 38, 39, 40, 46; *Pedro de Urdemalas*, 44, 45, 46, 47
childhood, of girls, 19
children: actors, 228; child-like, 236; Christ child, 228, 229–30, 231, 232, 237; evil eye, 227–28, 231, 232–33, 234, 235; fig-hand, 225, 228, 229–30, 231, 232, 234, 236, 237; Lope as father of, 235; Teresa's devotion to, 235
Claudius (Roman emperor), 51
claustration, 12
conduct manuals, 4–6
convents, 11–12; in Americas, 12, 14; convent writing, 11; music, 13; painting 14; theater, 13
conversos, 12
Corpus Christi Festival, 106, 109
Costa, Gustavo, 50–51

293

Covarrubias Horozco, Sebastián de, 224, 227, 232
Council of Trent, 249, 250, 253
courtly love, 159, 162, 164–65, 167–68, 169
Curtius, Robert Ernst, 50
Cyprien de la Nativité de la Vierge, 204, 215, 216

Deguy, Michel, 50, 51
Del Río, Martín, 232
Diego de Sevilla, 162–64, 165–66, 170n10
Dujovne Ortiz, Alicia, 268–74

education, of girls and women, 4–5, 9–10
Egido, Aurora, 173, 179, 180
Enguerrand, Archange, 205, 211, 216
Euripides, 59

Felipe V, 119, 124, 136n1
Fénelon, Bishop, 204, 217
fortitudo, 57

Galle, Cornelis, and Adriaen Collaert, 221, 229, 233, 235, 236
Garcilaso de la Vega, 173, 172, 177, 181
Gracián, Jerónimo, 204; fictional treatment of, 256–57, 273
Greenblatt, Stephen, 261
Guevara, Antonio de, *Familiar Epistles*, 51
Gutierrez, Martín, SJ, fictional treatment of, 272–73
Guyon, Jeanne, reader of *Song of Songs*, 210–12, 216

Heiple, Daniel L., 56
Herrera, Fernando de, 173
Historia Augusta, 52
Homer, 57, 58
honor, as dramatic convention, 8, 143, 148, 249
Hutcheon, Linda, 241

Inquisition, 4, 8, 13; fictional treatment of, 250–51
Ibáñez, Pedro, 224
Iser, Wolfgang, 203, 214, 216

James, Nancy Carol (translator), 211, 212, 215, 216; *Pure Love*, 204, 216
Jibaja, Petronila, 119, 123, 128, 129, 133–34, 135, 136nn2–3
Juan de la Cruz, 173, 176, 203, 204, 215, 216, 258; fictional treatment of, 258, 272
Juana Inés de la Cruz, 178, 182n2, 183n9
Jupiter, 57

Kearney, Richard, 177

Lemaître de Sacy, Louis-Isaac, 208, 216
León, Fray Luis de, 204, 215
Leonor (princess and queen regnant of Navarre), 160–61, 162–64, 165, 166–67, 168; as author-figure, 165
letters, women's, 13
Lodge, David, 245, 247, 258–59
Longinus, *On the Sublime*, 50–65
Lucretia, 160, 161, 168
Luna, Alvaro de, *Book of Virtuous and Famous Women*, 51

Mantel, Hilary (*Wolf Hall*), 269
marriage, 4, 5
McKendrick, Melveena, 53, 91–92, 112–13
McLaughlin, Karl, 174, 182nn2–4
medicine, in convents, 14; in homes, 14
Menéndez Pelayo, Marcelino, 53, 60
Molinos, Miguel de, 204, 205, 217
Montalbán, Juan Pérez de, *La Monja Alférez*, 89–100
Moors, Moorish influence, 6
Morales, Cristina, 263–68, 274
Morales Medrano, Juan de, 228, 233, 234, 235
mujer varonil, 15
music in theater, 124, 125–28, 130, 131, 133, 135, 136n1, 137n8, 137n10; Italian influence in theater and music (eighteenth century), 125, 127, 134, 137n8; opera, 124, 125–28, 129, 132–35, 136n1, 137n10, 138n16; zarzuela, 124–27, 131, 133, 134, 137n8

Narcissus, 55
Navas, María de, 119, 123, 129–30, 131, 132, 136nn2–4

Nieremberg, Juan Eusebio, *Curiosoa y oculta filosofía*, 225
novel, historical: and anachronism, 273–74; reader-writer pact, 262–63, 271, 273; tropes, 262
Nieremberg, Juan Eusebio, *Curiosoa y oculta filosofía*, 225

Olivares, Julián, 176
Orozco, Juana de, 119, 122, 123, 127, 128, 131–33, 136nn2–3, 137n10, 138n16
Osuna, Francisco, 205, 217, 250
Ovid, 181

Palmyra, kingdom of, 50, 52, 56, 60
Pascual, Sabina, 119, 123, 130, 131, 132–33, 134, 136nn2–3
Penthesilea, 161, 168
Petrarch, *Triumphs*, 51
Phaeton, 59
phantasia, 54
Pinar, Florencia, 160
Pliny the Elder, *Natural History*, 52
Porras, Gaspar de, theatre company, 228, 235
Pseudo-Longinus. See Longinus

querelle des femmes, 3
Quevedo, Francisco de, 178
Quintero, María Cristina, 54

Ribera, Francisco de, 221, 224, 228
Robles, Teresa de, 119, 120, 123, 129, 130–31, 135, 136nn3–4, 137n13
Robortello, Francesco, 51
Rodríguez, Rosa, 119, 128, 134–35, 139n10
Rodríguez de Padrón, Juan, 160, 170n7
Rojas Villandrando, Agustín de, 110–11

sapientia, 57
Sellers, Abednego, *The Antiquities of Palmyra*, 52
Seneca, 59
Stewart, Susan, 173, 180, 181

Teresa de Jesús (de Ávila): blood, 226, 234, 235, 258; Carmelite reform, 186–89; devotion to children, 235; discernment of spirits, 193–96; *Interior Castle*, 186, 190–98; image in Francoist Spain, 262; Jewish lineage, 262; poetry, 178; pictorial representations and hagiographic plays, 221–22, 235; prioress, 190–93, 195–95; reader of *Song of Songs*, 205–9, 217, 243, 252, 255; Spanish Inquisition, 189–90; theologian, 186–88, 193–98
—, fictional treatment of: Constitutions of Discalced Carmelites, 268; crypto-Judaism, 248–49, 267–73; erotic history, 266, 272–73; *Libro de las fundaciones*, 264, 265, 272; *Libro de la vida*, 246, 257, 263–64, 265, 266, 267; as proleptic feminist, 252–55, 267–68, 271; religious universalism, 271–73; Seville Inquisition, 256–57; *Sister Teresa* (Mujica), 243–59
theater, 16–18; actresses, 14–15, 114, 115, 119, 120, 122, 124, 125, 127–36; *autor/autora*, 15, 119, 120–21, 122–24, 128, 129–35, 136n3, 137n13; *autora autónoma*, 108, 116n3; *autora de comedias por su Majestad*, 108; *co-autora*, 108; *compañías de título o reales* and *compañías de la legua*, 108; convent in, 13–14; *mayordoma*, 114; *mujer vestida de hombre*, 106, 112, 113, 92–100; schools (acting companies), 106, 112, 114, 116
theatrical reading, 141; Casandra (*El Castigo sin venganza*), 141–53; character-grouping, 143; characterization, 141, 143, 145; mood, 143; motivation, 142, 149; pacing, 142; spatial, 141; stage-action, 142
Tiepolo, Giovanni Battista, *Queen Zenobia Addressing Her Soldiers*, 51
Toledo, García de, fictional treatment of, 263
Torrellas, Pere, 160, 161, 168; *Maldezir de mugeres*, 161, 168
Trojan War, 58

Urriés, Hugo, 161, 166

Valerian, Emperor, 51
Valle, Pietro della, 52
Vayona, 161–64, 165, 166, 169

Vega Carpio, Lope Félix de, 33, 34, 35, 37, 39, 40, 41, 44, 246; *El Castigo sin venganza*, 141–54; *La Doncella Teodor*, 51; *La Fe rompida*, 51; *Fuenteovejuna*, 140–41; *Lo fingido verdadero*, 109–10, 111
Vives, Juan Luis, *Instructions for the Christian Woman*, 4–6, 10, 51, 61, 113, 247

widows, 5
woman question. See *querelle des femmes*

women's physiology, toxic blood, 226, 233–34
Woolf, Virginia, 168

Yepes, Diego de, 233

Zayas, María de, 34, 35, 37
Zenobia, 50–65